The Social Fabric

THE SOCIAL FABRIC

American Life from the Civil War to the Present

THIRD EDITION

Editors

JOHN H. CARY   *Cleveland State University*

JULIUS WEINBERG   *Cleveland State University*

LITTLE, BROWN AND COMPANY   *Boston   Toronto*

Dedicated with love to

Alezah

and to Naimah, Roni and Yisrael, and Shirah

LIBRARY OF CONGRESS CATALOG CARD NO. 80-82178
ISBN 0-316-130745

9 8 7 6 5 4 3 2 1

ALP

Published simultaneously in Canada
by Little, Brown & Company (Canada) Limited

PRINTED IN THE UNITED STATES OF AMERICA

Preface

I know histhry isn't thrue Hinnessy, because it ain't like what I see ivry day
in Halsted Sthreet. If any wan comes along with a histhry iv Greece or Rome
that'll show me th' people fightin', gettin' dhrunk, makin' love, gettin' married, owin' the grocery man an' bein' without hard-coal, I'll believe they was
a Greece or Rome, but not befure.

The sentiment of Mr. Dooley, Finley Peter Dunne's comic Irish philosopher,
expresses the attitude of many people toward history. Young Americans,
especially, question the relevance of a history that deals only with politics,
diplomacy, governments, and famous leaders, and ignores the daily life of
average men and women. Two recent trends, however, are doing much to
remedy this neglect. One is increased popular interest in the forgotten mass
of men and women who tilled our fields, built our cities, and fought our
wars, but who achieved no particular fame and left very little record of
their lives and thought. The second development is the renewed concern
of historians with social history.

    This kind of history has more meaning for us, and touches our lives more
directly, than any other aspect of our past. In an age seeking "relevance"
nothing is more relevant than American social history. Each of us has direct
experience, or an intimate awareness, of being part of a family, of falling
in love and marrying, of poverty and pain, of suffering in war, of earning
a living, of social oppression and reform. By understanding the social life
of an earlier age, we can gain an understanding of ourselves and of others,
in whatever time or place they lived.

    This is an anthology of American social history for college history courses.
It began with our belief that college students would find more meaning
in the kind of history described by Mr. Dooley than in political, diplomatic,
or constitutional history. This and the companion volume of *The Social*

Fabric, which covers the period from the earliest settlement of America to the Civil War, touch upon marrying and making love, fighting and getting drunk, owing the grocer, and going without heat. Covering the time from the end of the Civil War to the present, this volume contains descriptions of the segregation of southern blacks during Reconstruction and the way of life of whites on the Middle Border at the turn of the century, labor's efforts to organize in the coal mines of Pennsylvania, the impact of Prohibition on both gangsters and respectable Americans, the Great Depression of the 1930s, and the counterculture of the 1960s.

No single book can treat every aspect of our history, but these volumes examine American life in much of its diversity. There are essays on women as well as men; on Indians and blacks as well as whites; and on the poor and the oppressed as well as the rich and the powerful. The sectional, class, racial, and religious differences among our heterogeneous people have created serious strains that at times threatened to tear the nation apart. But with all their diversity, the American people have also shared many common attitudes and traditions that provided a common social fabric to bind them together.

We have selected the readings from some of the most interesting writing on the American past. We have prefaced each reading with an introductory note, explaining the relation of the subject to broader developments in American history of the period. Each selection is also accompanied by an illustration, which provides a visual commentary on the topic under consideration. The study guide that follows the selection will help you review the special aspects of the reading, and may suggest issues for class discussion. The bibliographical note will help you find further material, should you wish to read more on the topic.

The third edition of volume II of *The Social Fabric* retains many of the best readings of the earlier editions, with seven new selections. A number of them replace — and, in the opinion of the editors, improve on — essays on the same topics included in the first two editions; others — on the mores of college youth and on bootlegging in the 1920s, and on the tragic shootings at Kent State — take up topics not previously covered.

The response of students and teachers in both four-year colleges and community colleges to this anthology has been most gratifying. A number of teachers who used the earlier editions of *The Social Fabric* in introductory courses have indicated that these volumes rank with the most successful supplementary materials they have ever used. Many of them contributed suggestions, as have a number of students, which have been incorporated in this new edition. We have appreciated the comments that students have made on the evaluation form that appears as the last page of each volume.

J.C.
J.W.

Contents

The Social Fabric

I POSTBELLUM AMERICA

The Civil War surpasses all other wars in our history for the tragedy and destructiveness it brought to the American people. Earlier wars had not touched most people's lives; they consisted largely of military encounters between relatively small numbers of soldiers or sailors. While later wars, the two world wars in particular, engaged the mass of the American people, they were fought away from the nation. Not so the Civil War. For four years, the plantations and the cities of the Confederacy served as a battlefield, and by the war's end the toll in lives exceeded the total number of Americans killed in World War I and World War II.

The various regions of the nation responded differently to the aftermath of the war. For Southerners, the principal tasks were threefold: to repair the material and the economic damage caused by the war, to adjust to the social and psychological trauma of their defeat, and, finally, to work out a mode of relating to the millions of slaves freed by the war. With few exceptions, white Southerners sought to establish a social system that would retain the privileges of white supremacy under a structure of law, federal and state, that declared the races to be equal. The white Southern search for ways to segregate the races is the topic of our first selection.

In contrast to the South, the North and the West came out of the war stronger in many ways than they had been at its beginning. The North's cities and farms were untouched, its currency and economy intact, and its political leadership and institutions unharmed. Northerners turned to building an enterprising way of life for themselves both in the city and on the farm. In the West, on the Great Plains in particular, a transformation of culture and economy took place. First the miner, then the cattleman and the farmer, came to the region. The coming of the white man to the West created a hardship for the Plains Indians, the subject of the second selection. The third essay provides us with a portrait of the cowboy, the last hero of the American West.

Southern blacks in the post-Civil War South soon learned that emancipation did not bring social equality.

1

JOEL WILLIAMSON

After Slavery

Few dreams in the history of the United States have been so cruelly unrealized as the hope that with the end of the Civil War and the destruction of the institution of slavery, black Americans would be accorded some measure of equality and opportunity in American life. With the end of the war in 1865, reform-minded Republicans, known as Radical Republicans, sought to make this dream a reality. Through their control of Congress they initiated Reconstruction, a program designed to restructure the social and political relations between whites and blacks in the defeated South. In 1865 and 1866, Congress funded the Freedmen's Bureau to feed, clothe, and protect the ex-slaves; civil rights legislation was passed in 1866 and reinforced by the Civil Rights Act of 1875, intended to outlaw varied forms of segregation; and three amendments were added to the Constitution. The Thirteenth Amendment (1865) outlawed slavery, the Fourteenth Amendment (1868) extended federal citizenship to blacks and made illegal many parts of the black codes, and the Fifteenth Amendment (1870) protected the black man's right to vote.

Despite this and other legislation, and despite the ascension to power of Reconstruction governments in the Southern states — state governments in which political power was shared by a combination of Southern scalawags, Northern carpetbaggers, and emancipated blacks — the Radical Republican effort to reconstruct the relations between the races in the South ended in failure. The first stage of that failure, what one historian has so aptly called "darkness at noon," came with the end of Reconstruction. Reconstruction was ended by the disputed election of Republican Rutherford B. Hayes over Democrat Samuel J. Tilden in 1876 and by the Compromise of 1877, in which the rights of black Americans were made secondary to the economic opportunities and social privileges of white Americans, both Democrats and Republicans. The second stage in the disfranchisement and segregation of American blacks came between the end of Reconstruction and the American entry into World War I in 1914. The caste system created in these decades paralleled, to a degree, the relations between the races in parts of southern Africa today.

The selection that follows tells us about the origins of the Southern caste system. In "The Separation of the Races," Joel Williamson finds that patterns of segregation came to South Carolina in the Reconstruction period. Williamson thus refutes a cardinal assumption made by C. Vann Woodward, the dean of Southern historians. Woodward contends that until the 1890s, Southern whites still held open options in their treatment of Southern blacks and that "Jim Crow," the disfranchisement and the segregation of blacks, was a product of decisions made by Southern whites *after* Reconstruction, closer to the turn of the century. Williamson's essay, taken from his study of the Reconstruction in South Carolina, demonstrates that in South Carolina, this was not so.

The physical separation of the races was the most revolutionary change in relations between whites and Negroes in South Carolina during Reconstruction.

Separation had, of course, marked the Negro in slavery; yet the very nature of slavery necessitated a constant, physical intimacy between the races. In the peculiar institution, the white man had constantly and closely to oversee the labor of the Negro, preserve order in domestic arrangements within the slave quarters, and minister to the physical, medical, and moral needs of his laborers. In brief, slavery enforced its own special brand of interracial associations; in a sense, it married the interests of white to black at birth and the union followed both to the grave. Slavery watched the great mass of Negroes in South Carolina, but those Negroes who lived outside of the slave system were not exempt from the scrutiny of the whites. Even in Charleston, the free Negro community was never large enough to establish its economic and racial independence. In the mid-nineteenth century, as the bonds of

From *After Slavery: The Negro in South Carolina during Reconstruction, 1861–1877* by Joel Williamson. Copyright © 1965 by The University of North Carolina Press. Reprinted by permission of the publisher.

slavery tightened, the whites were forced to bring free Negroes under ever more stringent controls and to subject their lives to the closest surveillance.

During the spring and summer of 1865, as the centripetal force of slavery melted rapidly away, each race clearly tended to disasssociate itself from the other. The trend was evident in every phase of human endeavor: agriculture, business, occupations, schools and churches, in every aspect of social intercourse and politics. As early as July of 1865, a Bostonian in Charleston reported that "the worst sign here . . . is the growth of a bitter and hostile spirit between blacks and whites — a gap opening between the races which, it would seem may at some time result seriously." Well before the end of Reconstruction, separation had crystallized into a comprehensive pattern which, in its essence, remained unaltered until the middle of the twentieth century.

There is no clear, concise answer to the question of why separation occurred. Certainly, it was not simply a response of Negroes to the prejudiced fiat of dominant whites; nor was it a totally rationalized reaction on the part of either race. Actually, articulate whites and Negroes seldom attempted to explain their behavior. Yet, the philosophies and attitudes each race adopted toward the other lend a certain rationality to separation, and, if we are always mindful that this analysis presumes a unity which they never expressed, can be applied to promote an understanding of the phenomenon.

For the native white community, separation was a means of avoiding or minimizing problems which, they felt, would inevitably arise from the inherent inferiority of the Negro, problems which the North, in eradicating slavery and disallowing the Black Code, would not allow them to control by overt political means. In this limited sense, segregation was a substitute for slavery.

Thus, first, total separation was essential to racial purity, and racial purity was necessary to the preservation of a superior civilization which the whites had labored so arduously to construct, and suffered a long and bloody war to defend. After the war, that civilization was embattled, but not necessarily lost. Unguarded association with an inferior caste would obviously endanger white culture. In this view, children were peculiarly susceptible to damage. "Don't imagine that I allow my children to be with negroes out of my presence," wrote the mistress of a lowcountry plantation in 1868, "on one occasion only have they been so with my knowledge." Even the Negro wet nurse, that quintessence of maternalism upon which the slave period paternalist so often turned his case, emerged as the incubus of Southern infancy. "We gave our infants to the black wenches to suckle," lamented an elderly white, "and thus poisoned the blood of our children, and made them *cowards* . . . the Character of the people of the state was ruined by slavery and it will take 500 years, if not longer, by the infusion of new blood to eradicate the hereditary vices imbibed with the blood (milk is blood) of black wet nurses." . . .

Separation also facilitated the subordination of the inferior race by constantly reminding the Negro that he lived in a world in which the white man was dominant, and in which the non-white was steadfastly denied access to the higher caste. Further, the impression of Negro inferiority would be constantly re-enforced by relegating the baser element, whenever possible, to the use of inferior facilities. The sheer totality of the display alone might well serve to convince members of the lower caste that such, indeed, was in the natural order of things.

Many whites had envisioned the early elimination of the freedman from the Southern scene, and many had eagerly anticipated this event. In time, however, it became evident to all that the Negro would be neither dissolved nor transported to Africa. In a sense, separation was a means of securing the quasi elimination of Negroes at home. It was, perhaps, a more satisfactory solution than their demise or emigration, since it might produce many of the benefits of their disappearance without losing an advantageous, indeed, a necessary supply of labor.

Finally, separation was a logical solution to the problem posed by the widespread conviction that the races were inherently incompatible outside of the master-slave relationship. If the white man could not exist in contentment in the proximity of Negroes, then partial satisfaction might be achieved by withdrawal from associations with members of the inferior caste. This spirit was evident among some of the wealthier whites who voluntarily dispensed entirely with the services of Negro domestics. Elderly William Heyward, in 1868 still second to none in the ranks of the rice aristocracy, stopped taking his meals at the Charleston Hotel because, as he said, he found "the negro waiter so defiant and so familiar in their attentions." "A part of the satisfaction is," he explained to a friend, "that I am perfectly independent of having negroes about me; if I cannot have them as they used to be, I have no desire to see them except in the field." Planters were often manifesting precisely the same sentiment when they deserted their land and turned to grain culture, or to the use of immigrant labor. Separation was also a way of avoiding interracial violence. B. O. Duncan and James L. Orr, both native white Republicans, argued against mixing in the public schools because they were convinced that minor irritations between children would generate major altercations between parents of different races. Conceived as a means of avoiding violence, separation, ironically, was subsequently enforced by the use of violence. . . .

Contrary to common belief, the separation of the races was not entirely the work of the whites. Suspicious, resentful, and sometimes hateful toward the whites, chafed by white attitudes of superiority, and irritated by individual contacts with supercilious whites, Negroes, too, sought relief in withdrawal from association with the other race. In many instances, the disassociation was complete — that is, many Negroes left the state. During the war, Corporal Simon Crum of the First South Carolina declared his intention of leaving South Carolina after the capitulation because, as he phrased it, "dese yer Secesh [secessionists] will neber be cibilized in my time." For those who could not or would not leave, alternative forms of withdrawal were possible. A major facet in the new pattern of agriculture was the removal of Negro labor from the immediate supervision of white men. As the Negro agriculturalist moved his labor away from the eye of the white man, so also did he move his family and his home. Plantation villages became increasingly rare as Negro landowners and renters either built new houses on their plots or, in a rather graphic symbolic display, laboriously dragged their cabins away from the "Negro street." Negroes in the trades and in domestic service followed similar trends. Furthermore, Negroes chose to withdraw from white-dominated churches, though they were often urged to stay, and they attended racially separated schools in spite of the legal fact that all schools were open to all races. Negroes also tended to withdraw from political association with members of the white community.

Finally, on those few occasions when Negroes entered into polite social situations with whites, Northern as well as Southern, they were often ill at ease. For instance, while driving along a road near Columbia, a planter and his wife met William, "a fine looking light mulatto" who had been their stableboy as a slave. William was driving a buggy and seated beside him was a young white woman, elegantly attired. The woman was a "Yankee school marm," probably one of the new teachers in Columbia's Negro school. As he passed his late master and mistress, the Negro averted his gaze and did not speak. The following day, he approached the planter and apologized for having been escort to a "white woman." He had met the teacher at a celebration, he explained, and she had insisted on his taking her to see the countryside.

During Reconstruction, the Negro's withdrawal was never a categorical rejection of the white man and his society. In the early days of freedom, it was primarily a reaction against slavery, an attempt to escape the unpleasant associations of his previous condition and the derogatory implications of human bondage. However, as the memory of slavery faded, a more persistent reason for withdrawal emerged. Essentially, it was the Negro's answer to discrimination. Almost invariably, attempts by individual Negroes to establish satisfactory relations across the race line were unsuccessful, and, all too often, the pain of the experience was greater than the reward for having stood for principle. During Reconstruction and afterward, only a few were willing to undergo such pain without the certainty of success. It was much easier, after all, simply to withdraw.

Withdrawal as a solution to the race problem was by no means satisfactory to the Negro leadership. Implicit in the behavior of Negro leaders during Reconstruction was a yearning for complete and unreserved acceptance for members of their race by the white community. However, overtly, and rather politically, they carefully distinguished between "social equality" and what might be appropriately termed "public equality." For themselves, they claimed only the latter. "Our race do not demand social equality," declared W. J. Whipper, a member from Beaufort, on the floor of the house of representatives in Columbia. . . .

What the Negro leadership did insist upon was public equality, that is, absolute civil and political parity with whites and full and free access to most public facilities. These latter included restaurants, bars, saloons, railway and street cars, shipboard accommodations, the theater, and other such places of public amusement. Once they gained political power, Negro leaders hastened to embody this attitude in legislation. Within a week after the first sitting of the Constitutional Convention of 1868, a Negro delegate introduced a resolution which was eventually included in the state's bill of rights: "Distinction on account of race or color, in any case whatever, shall be prohibited, and all classes of citizens shall enjoy equally all common, public, legal and political privileges." Similarly, one of the first bills passed by the Republican legislature prohibited licensed businesses from discriminating "between persons, on account of race, color, or previous condition, who shall make lawful application for the benefit of such business, calling or pursuit." Convicted violators were liable to a fine of not less than $1,000 or imprisonment for not less than a year. During the debate on the measure in the house, not a single Negro member spoke against the bill, and only five of the twenty-four votes registered against it were cast by Negroes, while fifty-three of the sixty-one votes which secured its passage were those of Negro legislators.

Negro Congressmen were no less ardent in championing the same cause in Washington, particularly in 1874, when a federal civil rights bill was up for consideration. ". . . is it pretended anywhere," asked Congressman R. B. Elliott, who had only recently been denied service in the restaurant of a railway station in North Carolina on his journey to the capital, "that the evils of which we complain, our exclusion from the public inn, from the saloon and the table of the steamboat, from the sleeping-coach on the railway, from the right of sepulture in the public burial-ground, are an exercise of the police power of the State? . . . Are the colored people to be assimilated to an unwholesome trade or to combustible materials, to be interdicted, to be shut up within prescribed limits?" Several days later, in the same place, Congressman R. H. Cain declared, "We do not want any discrimination to be made. I do not ask any legislation for the colored people of this country that is not applied to the white people of this country. All that we seek is equal laws, equal legislation, and equal rights throughout the length and breadth of this land."

It was upon this emotional, uneven ground that an essentially new color line was drawn. It was established in a kind of racial warfare, of assaults and withdrawals, of attacks and counterattacks. Nevertheless, well before the end of Reconstruction, both forces had been fully engaged and the line was unmistakably formed.

Even before the Radicals came into power in South Carolina in 1868, native whites had already defined a color line in government-supported institutions, on common carriers, in places of public accommodation and amusement, and, of course, in private social organizations. The degree of separation in each of these areas varied. In many instances, obviously, some compromise between expense and the desire for complete separation had to be made. Usually, the compromise involved the division of available facilities in some manner. If this was thought to be inconvenient, Negroes were totally excluded.

Typical was the treatment of Negro and white prisoners in the state penitentiary under the James L. Orr regime [1865–68; South Carolina]. Criminals of both races were confined in the same institution but were quartered in separate cells. Ironically, the racial concepts of white prison officials sometimes redounded to the benefit of Negro inmates. Minor violations of prison rules were punished every Sunday by the offenders being tied closely together, blindfolded, and forced to work their way over a series of obstacles in the prison yard. The chief guard explained that the white offenders were placed in the most difficult middle positions of the "blind gang" because "they have more intelligence than the colored ones and are better able to understand the rules of the institution."

It is paradoxical that the Negro leadership, once in office, pressed vigorously for an end to separation in privately-owned facilities open to the public but they allowed a very distinct separation to prevail in every major governmental facility. The most obvious instance was the schools, but the distinction also stretched into the furthermost reaches of gubernatorial activity. For example, a visitor to the state insane asylum in Columbia in 1874 found that "The Negro female inmates occupy a separate part of the same building" in which the white women were housed.

On the other side, within a month after they had gained the vote, Negroes in South Carolina opened a frontal attack against racial discrimination on common carriers. Typical was their assault on the Charleston Street Car Company. At the time of its inauguration, the facilities of the company consisted of double tracks running the length of the peninsula with a spur branching off near the mid-point. Horse-drawn cars, each manned by a driver and a conductor, ran along the tracks at regular intervals. The cars contained seats in a compartment, and front and rear platforms. Before the cars began to run in December, 1866, the question of the accommodation of Negro passengers was thoroughly canvassed. "Proper arrangements will in due time be made to allow persons of color to avail themselves of the benefits of the railway," the management assured the Negro community, but it had not then decided between providing "special cars" for the Negroes as was done in New Orleans, or "assigning to them a portion of the ordinary cars as is more usual in other cities." Negro leaders rejected both alternatives. As a Northerner wrote from Charleston in January, 1867, "Every scheme that could be devised that did not contemplate the promiscuous use of the cars by whites and negroes alike, was scouted by the Negro paper here; and the result is that negroes are now debarred the use of the cars altogether, unless they choose to ride upon the platform." . . .

After the Negro gained political power, the battle against discrimination became more intense and assumed a wider front. The so-called antidiscrimination bill, passed in the summer of 1868, on paper was a most formidable weapon. In essence, it imposed severe penalties upon the owners of public accommodations who were convicted of discrimination. Burden of proof of innocence lay on the accused, and state solicitors (public prosecutors) who failed to prosecute suspected violators were themselves threatened with heavy punishments.

The effect of the new legislation on common carriers was immediate. A Northern teacher returning to Beaufort in the fall of 1868, after a few months' absence in the North, observed a portion of the results:

> We took a small steamer from Charleston for Beaufort. Here we found a decided change since we went North. Then no colored person was allowed on the upper deck, now there were no restrictions — there could be none, for a law had been passed in favor of the negroes. They were everywhere, choosing the best staterooms and best seats at the table. Two prominent colored members of the State Legislature were on board with their families. There were also several well-known Southerners, still uncompromising rebels. It was a curious scene and full of significance. An interesting study to watch the exultant faces of the negroes, and the scowling faces of the rebels . . .

The same legislation applied to railway facilities; and, apparently, it was applied without a great amount of dissent. Adjustment was made easier, perhaps, by the acquisition of some of the railroad companies by Radical politicians within the state, or by Northern capitalists, and by the close understanding which usually prevailed between Republican officeholders and those Conservatives who managed to retain control of their railroads. While formal discrimination was not practiced by railway operators, unofficial racial separation did occur on a large scale. On all of the major lines first- and second-class cars were available. Most Negroes apparently deliberately chose to ride in the more economical second-class accommodations, and virtually all of the whites — particularly white women — took passage on the first-class cars. The separation thus achieved was so nearly complete that the first-class car was often referred to as the "ladies' car." It is highly relevant that the first Jim Crow legislation affecting railroads in South Carolina provided for the separation of the races only in the first-class cars, because, of course, this was the only place on the railroads where there was any possibility of a significant degree of mixing. . . .

In the winter of 1869–1870 and through the summer which followed, a concerted attempt was made by the Negro leadership to win the full acceptance of Negroes into all places of public amusement, eating, drinking, and sleeping. Special provisions for the accommodation of Negroes at public entertainments had been made in ante-bellum times, but physical separation of the races was invariably the rule. In December, 1868, Charles Minort, a mulatto restaurateur and lesser political figure, nearly provoked a riot in a Columbia theater by presuming to seat his wife and himself in the front row, a section traditionally reserved for tardy white ladies. Presumably, he should have chosen seats among the other Negroes present who "had taken their seats, as has always been the custom, in the rear." Minort yielded to the clamor of the whites in the audience, but, a year later, the Negroes of Charleston instituted judicial proceedings against the manager of the Academy of Music for refusing to mix the races in the boxes of the theater. The management barely succeeded in winning a postponement but was able to complete the season before the case came to trial.

In the spring of 1870, Negro leaders in Charleston launched an attack against discrimination in restaurants, bars, and saloons. On March 25, for instance, Louis Kenake, accused of violating the antidiscrimination act, was brought before Magistrate T. J. Mackey and put on a bond of one thousand dollars while awaiting trial. Other white restaurant keepers of Charleston united to oppose and test the validity of the act, but, in the week which followed, at least six additional charges were lodged against operators of such businesses. The assault was not confined to Charleston and demonstrations by Radical politicians were frequent during the campaign of 1870. In April, a Laurens woman wrote to her son in Missouri that "On Monday the yankees & some negroes went to Hayne Williams' and asked for drink, which 'Ward' refused them, that is, to drink at the gentlemans bar. They quietly marched him off to jail, & locked the doors, putting the keys in their pockets. The family are all at Spartanburg, we look for H. Williams to night, and I am afraid of a fuss, for he is a great bully." In the same month, during a Radical meeting in Lancaster, a Negro was refused service in a local bar with the comment that no "nigger" could buy a drink there. Lucius Wimbush, a Negro senator, hearing of the incident, went to the bar, ordered a drink, and was refused. He immediately had the barkeeper arrested and placed under bail. . . .

Negroes were also ambitious to open sleeping accommodations to their race. In the summer of 1868, as the first Negro legislators gathered in Columbia, native whites had been extremely apprehensive that they would attempt to occupy rooms in the city's hotels. Even *The Nation,* which had applauded the opening of common carriers to both races, declared that hotels were another and "delicate" matter, where separation was everywhere observed. The white community was vastly relieved to find that no such invasion was attempted, one upcountry newspaper having sent a special correspondent to

Columbia to ascertain the fact. Nevertheless, when Negro legislators debated the antidiscrimination bill early in the session, they made it very clear that hotels were included. William E. Johnson, the African Methodist Minister then representing Sumter County in the statehouse, noting that the management of Nickerson's Hotel was concerned lest Negroes apply for rooms, declared that if he found private accommodations filled he would want to know that this resort was open to him. George Lee, a Negro member from Berkeley, observed that a group of junketing legislators had recently failed to find lodging in Greenville and that this law was desired to prevent that sort of occurrence. "Equal and exact justice to all," he demanded, ". . . it is what we must have." Negroes were subsequently allowed to attend meetings in Columbia hotels, but it is apparent that none were ever given lodging.

Negroes also decried the fact that places of permanent rest occupied by whites, as well as those of a more temporary variety, were denied to their race. For instance, S. G. W. Dill, the native white Radical who was assassinated in Kershaw in the summer of 1868, and Nestor Peavy, his Negro guard who was killed in the same assault, were buried in racially separated cemeteries.

Thus, from 1868 until 1889, when the antidiscrimination law was repealed, Negroes in South Carolina could legally use all public facilities which were open to whites. However, in actual practice, they seldom chose to do so. "The naturally docile negro makes no effort at unnecessary self-assertion," a Northern visitor in Charleston explained in 1870, "unless under the immediate instigation of some dangerous *friends* belonging to the other race, who undertake to manage his destiny." This particular reporter was certainly prejudiced against the race; but four years later another Northern observer congratulated the Negroes of South Carolina on the "moderation and good sense" which they exhibited in their "intercourse with the whites." He concluded, "They seldom intrude themselves into places frequented by the whites, and considering that in South Carolina they have a voting majority of some thirty thousand and control the entire State Government, it is somewhat remarkable that they conduct themselves with so much propriety." Indeed, after 1870, even the Negro leadership hardly seemed inclined to press further their political and legal advantage to end separation. Of the numerous charges lodged under the antidiscrimination law, not a single conviction was ever recorded.

Even when Negroes pressed themselves in upon the prejudice of whites, the latter adjusted by total or partial withdrawal, so that a high degree of separation was always and everywhere maintained.

Some whites responded to the pressure by total withdrawal, that is, by leaving the state entirely. Of course, many of those who left South Carolina did so primarily for economic reasons, but many also departed from purely racial motives. A Winnsboro lawyer and pre-war fire-eater revealed the thinking of many emigrants when he asked William Porcher Miles, in April, 1867, how he could live in a land where "Every 'mulatto' is your Equal & every 'Nigger' is your Superior." Pronouncing the Negro majority "revolting," he advised Miles to go to England. ". . . I have no doubt you could succeed & at any rate w[oul]d not have as many Negro Clients & negro witnesses to offend y[ou]r nostrils as in these USA. I can't conceive of any ones remaining here who can possibly get away — Suppose, it were certain, wh[ich]. it is not, that no U S Congress will ever pass a Law requiring that your Daughter & mine shall either marry Negroes or die unmarried. Still the Negro is already superior to them politically & to their Fathers also, & must ever be so henceforth." . . .

After Negroes were firmly entrenched in official positions in government, native whites evinced a distinct tendency to refrain from associations which recognized the authority of Negro officers over white citizens. For instance, in the heavily Negro county of Abbeville, in 1870, a distressed guardian asked one of the magistrates, who happened to be a Democrat, to dispatch a constable to return an orphan girl stolen away from his house. "When you send for Laura," he begged, "please send a white man, as she is a white girl under my charge, and I would not like to subject her to the mortification of being brought back by a colored man. Besides that I would be censured by the community as they would know nothing of the circumstances of the case." . . .

Withdrawal was also the means by which native whites combatted attempts by Republican officials to end separation in institutions supported by the government. The withdrawal of native whites from the University and the State School for the Deaf and Blind at the prospect of Negro admissions are illustrations of white determination either to maintain separation or to dispense with the services afforded by related state institutions. If the Radicals had attempted to end separation in the common schools, it is virtually certain that the whites would have removed their children from these schools too. As one post-Redemption [post-Reconstruction] proponent of universal education argued, separation was essential to academic progress. Only by this means, he explained to Governor [Wade] Hampton, could it be achieved "without any danger of social equality — *and this is the great bug bear.*" Doubtless, it was the threat of withdrawal by the whites which dissuaded the Radical leadership from further attempts to end separation in institutions over which they had, by political means, absolute control.

Whites also refused to engage in normal civic activities in which the color line was not distinctly drawn. Thus, native whites chose not to join militia companies in which Negroes participated and were reported to be extremely apprehensive of being forced to undergo the "humiliation" of joining a mixed company. Too, whites were reluctant to sit with Negroes in the jury box. An elderly Spartanburg farmer verbalized his feelings on this point in the summer of 1869: "When I go to court & see negroes on the jury & on the stand for witnesses it makes me glad that I am so near the end of my race to sit on a jury with them I dont intend to do it we have a law that exempt a man at 65 & I take the advantage of it." This kind of withdrawal often reached odd extremes. In the spring of 1870, at the peak of the Negro leadership's drive for admission to privately owned public accommodations, the white Democrats of the Charleston Fire Department refused to decorate their engines and join in the annual parade because Negro fire companies were being allowed to march in the procession. . . .

Native whites also tended to withdraw from public places where the color line could not be firmly fixed and the Negro could easily assert his equality. "The whites have, to a great extent — greater than ever before — yielded the streets to the negroes," wrote a Columbian on Christmas Day, 1868. Similarly, in Charleston, in the late spring of 1866, a young aristocrat noted that the battery with its music and strollers had been yielded to the ladies and gentlemen of non-noble lineage on Saturdays, and by all whites to the Negroes on Sundays. On Saturdays, he declared, "the battery is quite full of gentlemen and ladies but it is not much patronized by the elite. . . . On Sunday afternoon the ethiops spread themselves on the Battery."

The same reaction was manifested by the whites wherever the Negro leadership succeeded by legal means in ending separation. For instance, when Negroes won admission to the street cars of Charleston, the whites simply withdrew. "On Sunday I counted five Cars successively near the Battery crowded [with] negroes, with but one white man, the Conductor," wrote a native white in May, 1867. "The ladies are practically excluded." When the Academy of Music was threatened with a discrimination suit in 1870, the white community replied with a counterthreat to withdraw its patronage and thus close the theater. Adjustment which fell short of complete separation remained unsatisfactory to whites. "Even the Theatre is an uncertain pleasure," complained a Charleston lady in 1873, "no matter how attractive the program, for you know that you may have a negro next to you." Probably many of her contemporaries found the exposure too damaging and stayed home.

The social lives of native whites were, of course, absolutely closed to Negroes. Access to the homes of the whites was gained by Negroes only when they clearly acquiesced in the superior-inferior relationship dictated by the owners, and even then entrance was often denied. "I told him I would never allow negroes to go in it while I owned it," wrote a Laurenville woman, incensed that a man who had bought her former home had rented it to Negroes. In spite of the fact that some Negro domestics lived in quarters behind the houses of their employers, whites were already rejecting Negroes as neighbors. A real estate agent in Aiken in 1871 responded to this sentiment when he refused offers from Negroes for city lots at triple prices because, as he explained to the owner, "purchasers among the whites will not settle among the Negroes, and I am afraid to sell to only a few of the latter." Negroes were also not permitted to join any of the numerous social organizations in which native whites participated. The Patrons of Husbandry (the Grange), waxing strong in the state in the early 1870's, was not only exclusively white in membership, but was accused of widening the racial gap by its attitudes and actions toward Negroes. Of course, such separation had been practiced before, but the exclusion of the Negro in freedom from the social organizations of the whites was not so much tradition as it was deliberate decision. . . .

Separation is, of course, a relative term. It was obviously not possible for Negroes and whites to withdraw entirely from association with each other. If intimate contact led to irritation and violence, it also led to warm personal friendships — often with the superior-inferior, paternal bias, but no less real for all of that. Cordiality could and did breach the barrier of race. Yet the fact remained that it was difficult to establish a human bond across the color chasm and, once established, the tie had to be assiduously maintained against the constant erosion induced by a thousand and one external forces of social pressure.

That there was sometimes tenderness between individuals of different races is abundantly evident. On the Elmore plantation near Columbia, in the fall of 1865, the young white master was nightly importuned by the Negro children to get out his fiddle and play. Frequently he did so, the dozen or so Negro boys and girls dancing around the fire, begging for more after the fiddler had exhausted himself in a two-hour concert. The concern of many late masters for their ex-slaves was matched by the interest of individual Negroes in the welfare of their recent owners. A freedman seeking relief for a white family from a Bureau officer explained his motivation: "I used to belong to one branch of that family, and so I takes an interest in 'em." Occasionally, ex-slaveowners retained the friendship and assistance of their erstwhile bondsmen when all others had deserted them. . . .

Sometimes, intimacy became miscegenation. The census reports are uncertain witnesses and contemporaries are typically mute on the point; but scattered references suggest that racial interbreeding was markedly less common after emancipation than before. "Miscegenation between white men and negro women diminished under the new order of things," a Bureau officer later wrote. "Emancipation broke up the close family contact in which slavery held the two races, and, moreover young gentlemen did not want mulatto children sworn to them at a cost of three hundred dollars apiece. In short, the new relations of the two stocks tended to separation rather than to fusion." A Northern traveler visiting the state in 1870 concurred: "From all I could see and learn, there are far fewer half-breed children born now than before the Rebellion. There seems, indeed, a chance that the production of original half-breeds may be almost done away with. . . ."

Legal, moral, and social pressures exercised by the white community upon its members, as well as the physical separation of the races suggest that these were valid observations. The Black Code pointedly declared that "Marriage between a white person and a person of color shall be illegal and void," and when the code was revised in 1866 this portion emphatically remained in force. Children born of Negro mothers and white fathers, so recently especially prized for their pecuniary value, became simply illegimate issue and a liability to the community. In addition, the laws of bastardy came to be applied against the fathers of mulatto children. Perhaps most important was the fact that, in the minds of the native whites, children of mixed blood personified the adulteration of the superior race and embodied in living form the failure of Southern civilization. Many whites, turned to soul-searching by their defeat, fixed upon miscegenation as their great sin. "It does seem strange that so lovely a climate, and country, with a people in every way superior to the Yankees, should be overrun and destroyed by them," wrote a rice aristocrat in 1868. "But I believe that God has ordered it all, and I am firmly of opinion with Ariel that it is the judgement of the Almighty because the human and brute blood have mingled to the degree it has in the slave states. Was it not so in the French and British Islands and see what has become of them."

Just as complete separation of the races was physically impossible, there was little possibility that miscegenation might entirely cease. One does not have to travel far into contemporary sources to discover instances in which white men had children by Negro women. In 1867, a lowcountry planter, accused of fathering the mulatto child of his Negro house servant, wrote plaintively to his mother: "This child was begotten during my absence in Charlotte & Charleston, from the middle of December until nearly the middle of January, & the Father of it was seen night after night in Emma's house, this I heard on my return, but as it was no concern of mine I did not give it a thought. She was *free*, the Mother of 5 Children & could have a dozen lovers if she liked. I had no control over her virtue." In 1874, a planter on the Cooper River in St. John's noted the existence of circumstances on his plantation which might have led to similar results. "Found a white man staying with one of the colored people on the place," ran the laconic note in his journal. "He being engaged in rebuilding Mayrents Bridge." Some of these liaisons were of prolonged duration. In 1870, Maria Middleton, a Negro woman, brought suit against a Pineville physician for failure to support her three children which he had allegedly fathered. Strangely, the defendant's lawyer did not deny the paternity, but sought dismissal on the plea that the plaintiff had no legal grounds for suit.

Once in power, the Radicals hastened to repeal the prohibition against interracial marriage. Thereafter, informal arrangements were sometimes legalized. In the spring of 1869, a reporter stated that three such marriages had occurred within the state — a Massachusetts man had married a Beaufort mulatto woman, and two white women had married Negro men. In 1872, the legislature explicitly recognized interracial unions by declaring that the "children of white fathers and negro mothers may inherit from the father if he did not marry another woman but continued to live with their mother."

There were a surprisingly large number of cases in which white women gave birth to children by Negro fathers. During his stay in Greenville, Bureau officer John De Forest heard of two such births and noted other instances in which white women were supported by Negro men. Such situations, he believed, were largely the result of the loss of husbands and fathers in the war and the destitution of the country generally. In 1866, in neighboring Pickens District, a case came into the courts in which Sally Calhoun, "a white woman of low birth," and a Negro man were brought to trial for the murder of their child. Ironically, the Negro was freed, though obviously implicated, and the woman was convicted and imprisoned. Apparently, some of these liaisons were far from casual as a Spartanburg farmer rather painfully suggested to his brother in Alabama: "My dear Brother as you have made several Enquiries of me and desiring me to answer them I will attempt and endeavor to do So to the best information that I have on the Various Subjects alluded to by you the first Interrogatory is Relative to John H. Lipscomb's daughter haveing Negro Children, I am forced to answer in the affirmative no doubt but she has had two; and no hopes of her Stopping. . . ."

By the end of Reconstruction, Negroes had won the legal right to enjoy, along with whites, accommodations in all public places. In reality, however, they seldom did so. On the opposite side of the racial frontier, the pattern of separation was fixed in the minds of the whites almost simultaneously with the emancipation of the Negro. By 1868, the physical color line had, for the most part, already crystallized. During the Republican regime, it was breached only in minor ways. Once the whites regained political power, there was little need to establish legally a separation which already existed in fact. Moreover, to have done so would have been contrary to federal civil rights legislation and would have given needless offense to influential elements in the North. Finally, retention of the act had a certain propaganda value for use against liberals in the North and against Republican politicians at home. Again and again, the dead letter of the law was held up as exhibit "A" in South Carolina's case that she was being fair to the Negro in the Hampton tradition [a reference to the relatively mild and paternalistic forms of racism practiced by upper-class whites, who, for many years, were led by governor, and later senator, Wade Hampton]. After the federal statute was vitiated in the courts, after racial liberalism had become all but extinct in the North, and as the Negro was totally disfranchised in South Carolina, the white community was ready and able to close the few gaps which did exist in the color line, and to codify a social order which custom had already decreed.

Ultimately, the physical separation of the races is the least important portion of the story. The real separation was not that duo-chromatic order that prevailed on streetcars and trains, or in restaurants, saloons, and cemeteries.

The real color line lived in the minds of individuals of each race, and it had achieved full growth even before freedom for the Negro was born. Physical separation merely symbolized and reinforced mental separation. It is true that vigorous assults by one side or the other forced the enemy to yield his forward trenches and to alter slightly the precise line of the color front. It is also true that material changes in post-Reconstruction Southern society pushed the trenches into areas which had not existed before. This often gave the illusion of basic change, of a breakthrough by the dominant whites in the war of races, whereas, actually, it merely represented the extension of the old attitudinal conflict onto new ground, only to bring with it the stalemate that marked the struggle elsewhere. Viewed in relation to the total geography of race relations, the frontier hardly changed; and the rigidity of the physical situation, set as it was like a mosaic in black and white, itself suggested the intransigence of spirit which lay behind it. Well before the end of Reconstruction, this mental pattern was fixed; the heartland of racial exclusiveness remained inviolate; and South Carolina had become, in reality, two communities — one white and the other Negro.

STUDY GUIDE

1. What motives, according to the author, led Southern whites to seek segregation from their ex-slaves? Does Williamson consider these motives to be entirely rational?

2. What were the basic demands of the black leadership?

3. List the various institutions of the South in which segregation took place, and explain how.

4. Williamson draws a distinction between separation by segregation and separation by withdrawal. When did Southern whites tend to practice one and when the other?

5. Intimacy between the races does not appear to have ceased after emancipation. What evidence does the author have for this, and how does he account for it?

6. Would you, on the basic of this selection, agree that segregation began in the immediate postwar years? If so, why; if not, why not?

BIBLIOGRAPHY

The Reconstruction experience is dealt with in a number of volumes. James G. Randall and David Donald, *The Civil War and Reconstruction* (Boston, 1969) is basic. More specialized are the following: Kenneth M. Stampp, *The*

Era of Reconstruction * (New York, 1965); John Hope Franklin, *Reconstruction: After the Civil War* * (Chicago, 1961); and Rembert W. Patrick, *The Reconstruction of the Nation* (New York, 1967). Studies of race relations in individual states will be found in Joel Williamson, *After Slavery: The Negro in South Carolina during Reconstruction, 1861–1877* * (Chapel Hill, N.C., 1965), from which the above selection was taken, Vernon C. Wharton, *The Negro in Mississippi* * (New York, 1965), Herman Belz, *Emancipation and Equal Rights* (New York, 1978), and in Howard Rabinowitz, *Race Relations in the Urban South* (New York, 1978). White resistance to black freedom and equality is dealt with in Allen W. Trelease's *White Terror; the Ku Klux Klan Conspiracy and Southern Reconstruction* (New York, 1971), and in Michael Perman's *Reunion without Compromise: The South and Reconstruction, 1865–1868* (New Rochelle, N.Y., 1973). The institutionalization of white racism before the turn of the century is traced in the following: C. Vann Woodward, *The Strange Career of Jim Crow* * (New York, 1974); Hortense Powdermaker, *After Freedom: A Cultural Study in the Deep South* * (New York, 1930); John Dollard, *Caste and Class in a Southern Town* * (Garden City, N.Y., 1937); and Allison Davis, Burleigh B. Gardner, and Mary R. Gardner, *Deep South: A Social-anthropological Study of Caste and Class* (Chicago, 1941).

* Asterisk indicates book is available in a paperback edition.

*Chief Joseph of the peaceful Nez Percé, who were driven from their
land and forced into a hopeless war with the American army.*

2

RALPH K. ANDRIST

The Death of
the Plains Indians

In early 1973, a group of militant Indians occupied and laid siege
to Wounded Knee, a historic Indian settlement located in South
Dakota. The choice of Wounded Knee by the American Indian
Movement (AIM) was no accident — for it was there, in 1890,
that the Oglala Sioux, the tribe of Red Cloud and Crazy Horse,
were finally subdued by the federal government. The massacre
of two hundred Sioux by the United States Army proved to be
the end of the Plains Indians' resistance to the white man's culture and economy.

The history of the treatment of the Indian by the white man
is not a happy one — nor, from the point of view of the American Indian, an equitable or a merciful one. In the early 1830s,
President Andrew Jackson felt that the Indian problem could be
dealt with best by removing the Five Civilized Tribes — whose
lands were coveted by southern planters and farmers — to territory west of the Mississippi River. By the end of the Civil War it
became clear that the Great Plains, too, had to be cleared of
Indians if the white ranchers and farmers were to flourish in the
region. And so, for more than a quarter of a century, the federal
government employed a variety of techniques to remove the
Indian as an obstacle in the path of the white settler.

The coming of the cattle kingdom and the farmer to the
trans-Mississippi brought an end to the plains culture created by
the Indians. Having created a way of life and an economy based
upon the use of the horse, land in common, and free-roaming
buffalo, the Plains Indians proved no match for the white man's

civilization. Within two decades after the end of the Civil War, the Plains Indians suffered a loss of food, clothing, shelter, household utensils, and military equipment as hunters exterminated what had been estimated in 1866 to be a total of 40 million buffalo. Forced onto reservations, the Indian had to contend with contagious diseases, alcoholism, and incompetent or corrupt federal agents. In 1887, through the Dawes Severalty Act, the Indian lost much fertile and productive land and gained only the right to vote if he chose to become a farmer.

The combination of guile and force that was employed by the federal government in order to deprive these Indians of their land and freedom is graphically described by Ralph K. Andrist in *The Long Death: The Last Days of the Plains Indians*. From his book, we have selected the tragic narrative concerning the fate of Chief Joseph and the Nez Percé, a peaceful tribe that settled, with the blessings and the consent of the United States Government, in the Wallowa country in the northeastern corner of Oregon prior to the Civil War. The nobility of Chief Joseph and the justice of his cause will be found in the last sentence of Andrist's narrative — Charles Erskine Wood's eloquent statement on the occasion of Chief Joseph's death in 1904: "I think that, in his long career, Joseph cannot accuse the Government of the United States of one single act of justice."

The company guidons still snapped in the wind when cavalry patrols passed on the plains just as they had for years, but there was a difference. The patrols no longer really expected trouble. There would be no ambush ahead; there was no chance that they would come on the burned wagons and the scalped bodies of a party of emigrants. Their main call to action was likely to be a request from an Indian agent to round up and escort back a few tribesmen who had wandered off the reservation. The Army on the plains had changed from fighting force into jail warden.

Custody of the Sioux had been returned to the Indian Bureau again, now that the war was over, and the Army had relinquished control. But the military was always close at hand. There were Army posts on almost all the reservations, most of them nearly within shouting distance of the agency and ready for any trouble. The chances of further trouble would appear

Reprinted with permission of Macmillan Publishing Co., Inc., from *The Long Death* by Ralph K. Andrist. Copyright © 1964 by Ralph K. Andrist.

remote, but while most tribes now settled down to empty and frequently hungry existences, a few last flickering fires of resistance born of desperation were to break out during the next several years. Then, and only then, would it all be over, and the white man would at last have conquered and caged every Indian, from sea to shining sea.

The year after the Little Bighorn, it was the turn of the Nez Percés — or rather, a band of nontreaty Nez Percés — to face the United States Army. The Army never fought a more unjust war, nor did it ever oppose so superior a type of Indian foe. If any people deserved well of the United States, they did, and in the end they got less than nothing.

The Nez Percés are a people of the Pacific Northwest, who originally lived in the region where Washington, Oregon, and Idaho meet, in the valley of the Clearwater River and in part of the valleys of the Salmon and Snake. It was — and is — a magnificent country of deep canyons, ridges, evergreen forests, and grassy meadows carpeted in season with flowers of many colors and kinds. They had lived here for hundreds of years, hunters of deer, bear, mountain sheep, and lesser game, eaters of salmon which the rivers supplied bountifully, dwellers in semipermanent lodges. Then about 1760 they acquired the horse, and it worked the same revolution in their lives as it had with so many other tribes. They became superb horsemen and were deeply influenced by the horse-and-buffalo culture of the Plains, to the extent that they actually became buffalo Indians to a degree, crossing the Continental Divide and traveling three or four hundred miles to the nearest buffalo ranges in Montana on hunting trips. They adopted the tepee and a seminomadic way of life, and many other attributes of the Plains people, although in other ways retaining their old culture.

Lewis and Clark came through Nez Percé lands in 1805 on their famous trip to the Pacific, and again on their return when they stopped with the tribe for several weeks while waiting for the snow to melt in the mountain passes. The Nez Percés were hospitable hosts, and it continued to be their claim through succeeding decades and increasing provocations that they had never killed a white man.

At the Council of Walla Walla in 1855, when treaties were made restricting the tribes of the region to reservations, the Nez Percés managed to retain about half the country they claimed, partly because no one was yet interested in such wild and remote country, partly because the government wanted the backing of the powerful Nez Percés in negotiating with other tribes. White indifference to the country disappeared when prospectors came looking for gold, and the Indians, after turning them back for a time, were at last persuaded to let the gold-hunters in — under proper restrictions, of course.

There is no point in detailing the betrayal of the Nez Percés once the whites had an entering wedge. The prospectors spread beyond the limits set for them; settlers followed although it had been a clearly stated part of the agreement that no farmers should enter the Nez Percé lands; Indian fences were torn down, their pastures taken over and they were driven off lands they were farming. When the Nez Percés demanded that the government enforce the 1855 treaty, there was a cry of outrage at such impertinence. The government did at last intervene in 1863 to set things right — which it accomplished by a new treaty taking away three-quarters of the Nez Percé lands. The remaining reservation lay entirely in Idaho on the Clearwater River; the lands in Washington and Oregon were outside the reduced reserve. Despite gaining so much land, however, whites only increased their depredations against what remained.

Two-thirds of the chiefs present at the council had refused to sign the treaty, saying there was no point in a new agreement when the government had not honored or enforced the old one. One of the nontreaty chiefs was known as Joseph, a name he had taken long ago when he had become a Christian. A good and long-time friend of the whites, he now tore up his New Testament and swore to have nothing more to do with white men in whom no trust could be placed. Joseph and his band were more fortunate than many of the nontreaty Nez Percés who were living on land where they were now being pushed around by settlers, because Joseph's home was in the country of the Wallowa River in the northeastern corner of Oregon, a region no white man had yet become interested in. The band was still living there in peace in 1871 when Joseph, very old, died, leaving two sons; Ollikut, a great athlete and warrior, and Hinmaton-yalatkit (Thunder-Rolling-in-the-Mountains), better known as Young Joseph. Young Joseph, the elder son, became Chief Joseph on his father's death. "I buried him in that beautiful valley of the winding waters," Joseph later said. "I love that land more than all the rest of the world."

Love it he might, but keep it he could not. The time came, as inevitably it would, when settlers began moving into the area. They and state officials set up the familiar anguished cries for soldiers to come and take Joseph's band away to the reservation. For a time the Federal government resisted the pressure and set aside part of the Wallowa country as a reserve for "roaming Nez Percés" by presidential order in 1873, but minds were changed two years later and the entire region thrown open to homesteaders.

Chief Joseph, however, continued to maintain that the land belonged to him and his people. His father had not given it up, neither had he parted with it. Old Joseph, in his last days, had told him never to sell the land. "This country holds your father's body," he told his son. "Never sell the bones of your father and mother."

A five-man commission was sent to talk to Chief Joseph. Two members were Army officers, three civilians. One of the officers, whom the Nez Percés were to have considerable to do with very soon, was Major General Oliver O. Howard, who had lost his right arm at Fair Oaks in the early part of the war, and had commanded a wing of Sherman's army during the March to the Sea during the last part. Howard was a man of pinch-nosed religiousness. . . . He was much interested in helping the recently freed Negroes (he was instrumental in founding Howard University for Negroes) but his heart did not go out in a like manner to the Indian in his time of trouble.

Joseph made the commissioners uneasy. He was a man of quiet dignity and commanding presence. He was confident, calm, intelligent, capable of expressing himself with a logic the five white men found difficult to answer. Moreover, he nettled them because there was no trace of obsequiousness in his manner. He acted with the quiet assurance that he was the equal of the white men to whom he was talking — and as every Indian ought to be taught, no red man was the equal of any white. He denied the commissioners' contention that the Wallowa country had been signed away by the Nez Percés in the Lapwai Treaty in 1863. His father had not signed the treaty, said Joseph, and the Wallowa belonged to his father. "If we ever owned the land we own it still, for we have never sold it," Chief Joseph said. . . .

But in spite of Joseph's logic, . . . the five whites decided that Joseph's band should be removed to the Lapwai reservation, by force if necessary, and there receive about sixty plots of twenty acres each (they had about a million acres in the Wallowa country). Just about six months earlier, the other officer on the commission, Major H. C. Wood, had made another investigation of the Wallowa question and had decided that the right was all on Joseph's side, and General Howard had rendered a similar opinion. The truth and right could vary from month to month where Indian policy was involved.

Joseph bowed to the inevitable. He selected land on the reservation on May 15, 1877, and then was given one month by General Howard to bring his band in. Joseph asked for more time. The stock was foaling and calving at that season; the animals were still scattered in dozens of secret valleys and it would take time to round them up. Even more serious, the Snake River, which the band would have to cross — women, infants, aged — was half a mile wide and raging with melt waters. One month, Howard repeated. If the band delayed one day beyond that time — only one day — the troops would be there to drive them in.

The band was in no position to resist — it had only 55 men of fighting age — and the thing was somehow accomplished. Stock was rounded up, although hundreds of head were missed in the haste, and the crossing of the Snake was made without loss of human life, with the very young and the very old of the band towed on rafts through the swift, wide current. More livestock was lost when several hundred head were swept away in the river, and white settlers hanging around the edge of the band like jackals were able to cut out and stampede a large number of horses.

After the crossing, the band stopped to camp for the ten days or so still remaining before they had to come on the reservation. Other nontreaty bands, likewise ordered to settle down, joined them, and the encampment became a lively and cheerful place, considering the circumstances. But some tempers were thin. During a parade two days before the deadline date, someone became irritated by the antics of a young man named Wahlitits who was clowning on a horse and made a waspish comment to the effect that he had not been such a big man when it had come to avenging his father's murder two years before.

Wahlitits's father had died at the hands of a white man who had squatted on his land while he had been away; when the Nez Percé had returned and protested, the white man shot him. The dying man made his son promise not to take revenge, but now, burning from the taunt made at the parade, Wahlitits set out the next day with a cousin and another youth to take belated vengeance. They were unable to find the guilty man but they killed four others, at least two of whom well deserved it. They returned to camp, recruited another fifteen or twenty firebrands, and set out on a carnival of raiding and murder. With the help of liquor which they found and dipped into heavily, they killed fifteen more white men, plundered homes, and assaulted women.

The Nez Percés had always claimed they had never killed a white man, but now they had done in a good number of them, and rather messily, in a few hours. The encampment was shocked at the news, and broke up rapidly as families left to disassociate themselves from the murderers. Many went south, to the canyon of White Bird Creek, a stream emptying into the Salmon River. Joseph had been away from the encampment when the raids had taken place, but he knew that neither that circumstance, nor that none of the murderers were members of his band, was likely to be taken into consideration when retribution was dealt out. He stayed for two days with his wife who had just given birth to a daughter, then the three joined the others at White Bird Canyon.

General Howard, at Lapwai on the reservation, got the news on June 15, and at once sent Captain David Perry with two companies of the 1st Cavalry after the Indians. . . . As the force neared the Indian camp at White Bird Canyon, the Nez Percés sent several men with a flag of truce to meet it, but they were fired on. The Indians were outnumbered; they had only about sixty to sixy-five men, some of them old, some still in sorry condition from too much stolen whiskey the night before, about a third armed with bows and arrows, many of the rest with old muzzle-loaders. But fighting a battle which they improvised as they proceeded, they routed the troops, cut them into sections, pinned one group of nineteen men against a rocky wall and wiped them out, and killed thirty-four and wounded four, while suffering only two wounded themselves. . . .

General Howard moved more cautiously now. He called in more men from posts throughout the entire Pacific Northwest while reserves were brought in from as far as Atlanta, Georgia, to stand by in case the war spread. The Nez Percés picked up some strength, too. Two competent warriors, Five Wounds and Rainbow, returning from a buffalo hunt in Montana, met the fugitives and joined them with their small bands. General Howard, through a stupid act, gave them more recruits. A prominent chief named Looking Glass was camped on the reservation with his band, completely divorced from all the violence that had been occurring. Nevertheless, when wild-eyed settlers brought stories that Looking Glass was preparing to join the hostiles, Howard, without investigating, sent a Captain Whipple with two companies of cavalry against Looking Glass's village. Nor did he direct Whipple to investigate before he took action, so Whipple did not hesitate to launch an attack when he found a peaceful camp. Only three or four Indians were killed in what was a completely treacherous attack, but the village was destroyed. The infuriated Indians thereupon left the reservation and set out to join the hostile force.

While Captain Whipple was making his ill-advised raid on Looking Glass's camp, General Howard had been decoyed across the swollen Salmon River and led on a chase through the rugged, almost trackless country south of that river. Then the Indians doubled back, leaving Howard to flounder about in the wilderness. The Nez Percés headed north to a new camping place on the Clearwater River. . . . At the Clearwater camp, they were joined by Looking Glass and his still-angry band, giving them just under 200 men, and about 450 women and children.

By July 11, General Howard, with his army reinforced and increased to 400 soldiers and 180 scouts, teamsters, and packers, had caught up with the hostile band, who were still camped on the Clearwater, and took them completely by surprise by opening fire from the bluff across the river with a howitzer and two Gatling guns. However, before Howard could get his attack underway, Toohoolhoolzote, chief of one of the nontreaty bands, an elderly man but a noted warrior, dashed across the river and up the bluffs with only twenty-four men to hold the soldiers off until reinforcements could follow and swing around Howard's flanks and rear.

In spite of a numerical advantage of six to one, and despite his possession of artillery, the chagrined General Howard soon found himself completely surrounded and besieged, with his forces drawn up in a hollow square. For more than a day, the Indians kept up the close siege, sometimes coming near enough for hand-to-hand fighting. Then, tiring of the battle, they broke it off, after first giving the camp plenty of time to move on. They had lost four killed and six wounded, the Army thirteen killed and twenty-three wounded.

After traveling a safe distance to the east, the Nez Percés camped to take stock of their situation and decide their future course. They had fought their battle on the Clearwater as five separate bands, each under its own chief (Ollikut, Joseph's brother, had led the Wallowa band) and with no clear idea of what they were fighting for except to defend themselves. Now it was decided that the only course open to them was to leave Idaho Territory and go east across the mountains. There they could join their friends, the Crows, on the buffalo plains in Montana. Chief Joseph objected; he wanted to continue to fight for his beautiful land, to the death if need be, but he was overruled. . . .

The band passed over the high point of the Bitterroots and were moving down its eastern slope into Montana when they found their way blocked by hastily built fortifications manned by about thirty-five regular Army infantrymen and some two hundred volunteers, under the command of Captain Charles C. Rawn. Chief Joseph, Looking Glass, and old Chief White Bird rode forward to parley. They explained that they had no quarrel with anyone but General Howard and would harm no one if permitted to pass. The volunteers knew the Nez Percés well and favorably from their buffalo-hunting trips. They decided that, since they were there only to defend their homes from Indians, and since their homes needed no defending from these Indians, they might as well go home. Most of them did; only thirty volunteers remained with Rawn and his regulars. . . .

The band moved on to Stevensville where supplies were replenished, not by looting and pillage, but by decorous purchase in the town's stores. These strange Indians, who could easily have taken anything they wanted, quietly paid with gold and currency for their sugar, coffee, and tobacco, and at prices which the merchants had raised sky-high for the occasion. There was, however, no buying of liquor because the chiefs had told the town fathers to have all supplies locked up till the band had moved on.

Now they turned south, following the Bitterroot River to its head, then crossed the Continental Divide and passed into the Big Hole Valley just south of it, where at last they set up their tepees for a long rest and to repair some of the ravages of the hard trip. They were sure they were in friendly country now, with nothing to fear. But Colonel John Gibbon had come by forced marches from Fort Shaw on the Sun River, gathering men from other posts as he came, and at dawn on August 9, he attacked the sleeping camp with approximately two hundred men. There was no warning. The shot that killed a solitary horse herder came almost at the same instant as the crash of rifle fire into the lodges and the whoops of charging soldiers. Women were shot without hesitation; children were gunned down; even babies had their heads crushed with a kick or a clubbed rifle. Such, at least, is the testimony of an officer who took part in the campaign.

But despite the overwhelming surprise of the attack, some of the Indians recovered and began to fight back, rallied by doughty old White Bird. One sharp stroke of luck fell their way; the lieutenant commanding Gibbon's left wing was killed, and as the leaderless troops lost purpose, the Indians opposing them organized a counterattack that continued until it had rolled up Gibbon's entire force, which was now giving too much of its attention to plundering. The marksmanship of the Nez Percés was taking a heavy toll (their accurate shooting, unusual among Indians, was remarked in every engagement). Gibbon was soon on the defensive and besieged; Chief Joseph had taken charge of getting the camp packed up and moving, and the weary, never-ending flight was on again.

When a detachment of soldiers attempted to set up a howitzer, a handful of Indians drove them off, seized the cannon, and, since they did not know how to use the weapon, wrecked it. Gibbon, running out of food, water, and ammunition, was saved only by the arrival of General Howard. He had lost thirty-three dead and thirty-eight wounded, including himself. He claimed the Indians lost eighty-nine, and this appears to be correct, or very nearly so, but most of those dead were women, children, and aged. The Nez Percés later said that only twelve warriors died, but they included some of the best, among them Rainbow and Five Wounds.

The Nez Percés buried their dead before withdrawing; Howard permitted his Bannock Indian scouts to dig up the bodies to scalp and mutilate them. This barbarism, coming on top of the savage slaughter of noncombatants, shocked the Nez Percés, who had been fighting by all the rules of so-called civilized warfare. Howard became the most despised man in the world as far as they were concerned, not completely logically, for it was Colonel Gibbon who had been guilty of killing the women and children.

Looking Glass was displaced as war leader because he had let the camp be taken by surprise, his place taken by a chief named Lean Elk who had recently joined the band; he had been buffalo hunting and was camped in the Bitterroot valley with half a dozen lodges when the fugitives came by shortly after the affair of Fort Fizzle. But the stories going out to the country — and the public was by now intensely interested in what was occurring — all credited Chief Joseph with the military leadership of the band. General Howard, recalling Joseph's astuteness in council and his leadership in peace, assumed that he was continuing to guide the Nez Percés in battle. So the legend arose of a rude military genius in the northern mountains, a red-skinned Napoleon, maneuvering his outnumbered warriors so skilfully as to confound, confuse, and defeat, time and again, the trained troops of the United States.

The truth is somewhat less exciting. Joseph was not a war chief, and although he took part in the fighting once or twice, he usually took charge of the camp to see that it was struck, packed for traveling, and on its way, with women and children taken care of. It was an important and necessary function and not to be denigrated — most tribes had peace chiefs and war chiefs — but it lays to rest the myth of the master tactician in moccasins. The Nez Percé victories were due, not to any unusual brilliance in battle, but to a combination of bravery, determination, and the rare ability to stand fast when caught off-balance and then recover and take the initiative. That, along with overconfidence and some fortuitous (for the Nez Percés) mistakes on the part of their white foes.

The fleeing band paralleled the general line of the Continental Divide, which swung in a great arc toward the east. General Howard was pushing them hard. . . .

The fugitives passed on into Yellowstone Park, then only five years old but already attracting a considerable number of hardy tourists. They barely missed one party containing General William Tecumseh Sherman, but swept up another, shooting and almost fatally wounding one man. . . .

The flight continued, through Yellowstone Park and the northwestern corner of Wyoming; then the Indians swung northward where more trouble awaited. Part of the 7th Cavalry, commanded by Colonel Samuel Sturgis . . . tried to head them off, but the Nez Percé band found its way through mountainous country which had been considered impassable for men with horses and came out behind Sturgis on Clarks Fork of the Yellowstone River.

The decision was made to continue the weary journey on to Canada. . . .

. . . Their course took them north across Montana, as far as a low range called the Bear Paw Mountains which rose from the plains in the northern part of the Territory. There, only thirty miles from the Canadian border, the fugitive band made camp to rest and to hunt and lay in a supply of dried meat and buffalo skins against the coming winter.

Once again they had reckoned without the telegraph. Colonel Nelson E. Miles was hurrying up from Fort Keogh on the Yellowstone with six hundred men. . . . Another day and the Nez Percés would probably have made it to Canada, for most of the pack animals already had their burdens lashed on and the band was making ready to move again when Miles's scouts sighted their lodges on the morning of the last day of September.

Colonel Miles ordered an immediate attack, hoping to smash the Nez Percés with a single charge. But he had begun the charge a good four miles away, and the Indians had that much warning; old White Bird quickly posted his men in front of the camp, and as the onrushing battle line of troops came within range, it met a withering fire which killed two officers and twenty-two men, and injured another four officers and thirty-eight men. The charge stopped as though it had been poleaxed, and the men took shelter behind rocks and in gullies. But they did not retreat; the camp remained under fire.

White Bird had only 120 men against Miles's six hundred. . . . When the soldiers gave up the pursuit, many of the warriors turned back, too, and slipped into camp.

Two brave leaders, Chief Toohoolhoolzote and Ollikut, were among the good men who died in the first confused fighting. Chief Joseph and his twelve-year-old daughter had been with the horse herd when the attack came. He told the girl to catch a horse and join those who were cut off from the camp. Then he galloped his horse through the line of soldiers, unharmed, though his horse was wounded and his clothes pierced many times. His wife met him at the entrance of his lodge and handed him his rifle. "Here is your gun. Fight." . . .

On October 4, General Howard arrived with more troops, making the situation of the Nez Percés hopeless. Negotiations were begun through two treaty Nez Percés who had come with Howard as interpreters. The few remaining chiefs were told that Howard would treat the band with honor if they surrendered and would send them back to the Lapwai reservation in the spring, when the mountains were clear of snow again. Looking Glass and White Bird wanted to fight on, but Chief Joseph insisted that they must make their decision for the freezing women and children crouching in the pits that had been dug for shelter from Miles's howitzer.

Just as the council broke up, brave Looking Glass fell dead, struck in the head by a chance bullet. For four months, and over a trail 1,300 miles long, the Nez Percé band had fought and fled, to be caught only thirty miles from freedom. A short distance still remained for Chief Joseph to travel, the ride from the camp to the hill where General Howard and Colonel Miles were waiting, but for him it would be the longest part of the journey. He had already sent his message of surrender ahead with Captain John, one of the Nez Percé interpreters, who had carried it to General Howard and repeated it with tears in his eyes.

> . . . I am tired of fighting. Our chiefs are killed. Looking Glass is dead. Too-hoolhoolzote is dead. The old men are all dead. It is the young men who say yes and no. He who led the young men [Ollikut] is dead. It is cold and we have no blankets. The little children are freezing to death. My people, some of them, have run away to the hills, and have no blankets, no food; no one knows where they are — perhaps freezing to death. I want to have time to look for my children and see how many I can find. Maybe I shall find them among the dead. Hear me, my chiefs, I am tired; my heart is sick and sad. From where the sun now stands, I will fight no more forever.

About two hours later, Joseph rode over, with several of his men walking beside him. He dismounted and handed his rifle to Howard, who motioned that he should give it to Colonel Miles. Thereafter, he was treated as a prisoner of war.

Chief White Bird escaped to Canada that night with a handful of followers. . . . A few more than 400 were captured of about 650 who had started on the long trip; probably close to 200 died during the flight or on the plains. But Joseph's fears that his own children might be dead were groundless; of his six children, only the baby born on the eve of the long journey remained with him at the time of the surrender, but all were later found safe.

The captives were taken to Fort Keogh, a logical place to hold them until they could be returned to Idaho in the spring. But soon an order came from General Sheridan to send them to Fort Abraham Lincoln. It would be too expensive, he said, to maintain them at Fort Keogh through the winter. Colonel Miles, after making a futile protest, put most of his prisoners on flatboats to make the long trip down the Yellowstone and Missouri without military guard or escort except for one enlisted man on each boat. The able-bodied men and some of the women marched overland with Miles and his troops. All arrived safely.

When Miles arrived in Bismarck with the overland contingent of Nez

Percés, a remarkable thing occurred. Bismarck, it will be remembered, was still a frontier community, and most of its people were convinced of the basic rightness of Sheridan's dictum, "The only good Indian·is a dead Indian." Not only that, it was at Fort Abraham Lincoln, near Bismarck, that the 7th Cavalry had been stationed. Many of the townspeople had had friends who had died only a year before with Custer.

Bismarck would, in short, seem an unwise place to bring a group of Indians who had lately been at war with the Army. But as the column rode through the main street, with Chief Joseph on horseback beside Colonel Miles and the rest of the Nez Percé following, enclosed by a protecting square of soldiers, crowds of townspeople surged out into the street and against the cordon of troops. However, there was no hate and no violence intended; they carried food, and broke through the square of troops to give it to the Indians. Only when the people had exhausted all their gifts was the column able to proceed on to Fort Lincoln.

Two days later an even more remarkable event occurred. The good ladies of Bismarck were hostesses at a dinner at which Chief Joseph and the other chiefs were guests of honor. But these were the only two bright spots in their treatment by white people since their war began and would be just about the last. Two days after the dinner, they were on a train, headed for Fort Leavenworth, with Indian Territory as their eventual destination. Colonel Miles and General Howard protested this betrayal of the promises made by Howard to the Nez Percés at the time of the surrender, but the higher powers in Washington felt under no kind of obligation to honor the promises. General Sherman, while refraining from talking about extermination in this case, announced that the Nez Percés must be suitably punished to discourage other tribes who might feel moved to defend their rights.

The Nez Percés were settled in a low, malarial part of Indian Territory, especially deadly to these highland people whose resistance to disease had been lowered by their recent hardships and suffering. Within a few months, more than a quarter of them were dead. They got along fairly well after they became somewhat acclimated to their new surroundings and even prospered in a small way through their skill at stock raising, but they remained hopelessly homesick for their mountains. Strong public sentiment had been aroused by their magnificent retreat and by the way they conducted themselves during it, and the public was not permitted to forget their story. Colonel Miles (brigadier general after 1880), a firm friend of Joseph since the end of the war, regularly recommended that the Nez Percés be permitted to return.

A few widows and orphans were allowed to go to the Lapwai reservation in 1882, and the rest were sent north three years later. Slightly more than half went to Lapwai; the rest, among them Joseph, were for some reason sent to the Colville reservation in northern Washington to live among the several small tribes there. None of Joseph's six children returned north with him; he had buried them, one by one, in alien soil, victims of the climate and disease of the south.

Chief Joseph, during the rest of his life, asked to be permitted to return to the Wallowa country, of which he had said, "I love that land more than all the rest of the world." But where the rest of the country had come to admire Joseph, the ranchers in his former home opposed his return, and the government supinely gave in to their wishes. Joseph died, still grieving for his lost country, in 1904. Charles Erskine Wood, aide to General Howard during the Nez Percé War, wrote what might be Joseph's epitaph: "I think that, in his long career, Joseph cannot accuse the Government of the United States of one single act of justice."

STUDY GUIDE

1. Trace the stages in Chief Joseph's relationship with the white man, explaining the occasion for each encounter, the agreements made, and the course of action taken by the federal government following each of these meetings.

2. What were the attitudes of the whites toward the Indians? Fear? Hatred? Admiration? Contempt? Can you generalize for all whites and at all points in the narrative? If not, why not?

3. What role did the federal government play in subduing the Indian? What instruments were employed, and how?

4. Placing the Plains Indians on reservations appears to have been unjust and even cruel. Were there any alternatives? If not, how could reservation life have been made more tolerable than it was for Chief Joseph?

5. Can you explain why the United States Army pursued the Nez Percé to the Canadian border? Why were the Indians not permitted to cross into Canada and to freedom?

6. Considering the entire question of Indian-white relations, was there anything in our historical experience that would have prepared white Americans for dealing sympathetically or equitably with the Plains Indians? Did Americans deal with one another more humanely? If so, how would you explain the brutality of the Civil War or the violence of the Pullman and Homestead strikes in the late nineteenth century?

BIBLIOGRAPHY

A number of books provide further reading on the Indian and the impact of the white man's civilization on Indian life. A brief introduction to the subject is William T. Hagan, *American Indians* * (Chicago, 1961). An informed survey of the culture of the American Indian, incorporating historical material as well, is Ruth M. Underhill, *Red Man's America* (Chicago, 1953). A widely read and classic indictment of the white man's treatment of the Indian is Helen Hunt Jackson, *Century of Dishonor** (New York, 1885) and more recently the following: Gary E. Moulton, *John Ross, Cherokee Chief* (Stillwater, Okla., 1974), and H. Craig Miner and William E. Unrau, *The End of Indian Kansas* (Lawrence, Kan., 1978). The treatment of Indians by the United States Army is covered in Robert M. Utley, *Frontier Regulars: The United States Army and the Indian* (New York, 1973) while interpretations of the impact on Indian life and education of Protestant reformers is contained in several volumes: Henry E. Fritz, *The Movement for Indian Assimilation, 1860–1890* (Philadelphia, 1963); Francis Paul Prucha, *American Indian Policy in Crisis: Christian Reformers and the Indian 1865–1890* (Norman, Okla., 1975); and Robert W. Mardock, *The Reformers and the American Indian* (Columbia, Mo., 1971). Several volumes by Mari Sandoz — *These Were the Sioux** (New York, 1961), *Crazy Horse: Strange Man of the Oglalas** (Lincoln, Neb., 1961), and *Cheyenne Autumn** (New York, 1962) — offer a sympathetic view of the Indian's plight in the face of the cruelty and the superior technology of the white man. In a similar vein is Dee Brown's popular, but controversial, volume, *Bury My Heart at Wounded Knee** (New York, 1971). Should you want to know more about the Nez Percé, you can consult Merrill D. Beal, *I Will Fight No More** (Pullman, Wash., 1963), and Mark H. Brown, *The Flight of the Nez Percé** (New York, 1967), as well as the book from which the preceding selection was taken, Ralph K. Andrist, *The Long Death** (New York, 1964).

* Asterisk indicates book is available in a paperback edition.

The cowboy is a heroic figure of the American past.
Here a cowboy of 1894 poses in full regalia.

3

PAUL HORGAN

The Last Frontiersman

The cattle kingdom flourished first in Texas and then farther north on the open range from the end of the Civil War to the end of the 1880s. A number of factors contributed to the growth of the cattle industry, including the presence of large herds of unbranded cattle in and around Texas, the huge tracts of grazing land on the High Plains, and the ever-increasing demand for beef by a nation transforming its economy from an agricultural to an industrial one. A ready market for beef had developed during the Civil War and expanded after the war as a result of the growth in the nation's urban population, and the need for a steady supply of beef by the soldiers, railroad gangs, miners, and others in the West. More Americans looked to the open range for one of the principal items of their daily diet. By the late 1860s a head of beef in Texas sold for approximately four dollars; the same beef when sold in St. Louis or in other states to the north and east of Texas commanded a price of forty dollars a head. The cattle kingdom — which grew to thousands of herds roaming the Western plains by the 1880s — rose and fell in an effort to profit from this highly profitable trade.

Legend and lore have preserved and romanticized many aspects of the cattle kingdom. Life on the open range has become a staple of American short stories, Western novels and movies, and weekly television programs. From the tales of Zane Grey to the popular TV episodes of "Bonanza," Americans have been fascinated and entertained by the various elements of the cattle kingdom — the chuck wagon and the long drive along the Chisolm Trail, the cattle towns of Abilene and Dodge City, Indian fights, and the struggles between the ranchers and the farmers for control of the open range. At the center of this segment of the American past is the cowboy. In the next selection, Paul Horgan provides us with a historical perspective on the American cowboy and a psychosocial and economic portrait as well. The strength of his essay lies in its synthesis of realism and romance.

Ever since the eighteenth century the raising and tending of large herds of beef cattle had been practiced on the [Rio Grande's] wide, flat borderlands. All descended from animals brought to Mexico in the sixteenth century by Spaniards, there were several types of cattle on the river plains, of which the most distinctive had tremendously long horns doubled up and backward for half their length; heavy thin heads; tall legs, and narrow, powerful flanks. They were haired in various colors, with white patches. By the hundred thousand, wild cattle roved at large over the uninhabited land on both sides of the border, and constituted its prevailing form of wealth. As such they were always prizes for Indians, Mexicans and Americans who in an unbroken tradition of border violence raided the herds — preferably those already gathered into ownership by other men — and drove away thousands of animals to sell on the hoof, or to kill for their hides which were bailed and sold to traders, while the carcasses were left to carrion, and the bones to workers who gathered them up and hauled them for sale as fertilizer to Texas farming towns.

Even in the face of such hazard a few cattle traders drove herds east to New Orleans, north to Missouri, and west even as far as California, before the Civil War. But the trade was unorganized, and the principal markets, New Orleans and Mobile, were supplied by cattle steamers that sailed out of the Texas Gulf ports. The longhorn cattle they carried were called "coasters" or "sea lions." The coastwise cattle trade was limited by a monopoly held on Gulf shipping by the Morgan Line. "To anyone outside of the ship company," wrote an early cattle trader, "an enormous rate of freight was exacted, practically debarring the ordinary shipper." And when the Civil War took levies of manpower from the cattle business, the trade was further constricted. In consequence of such conditions, "for a quarter of a century or more," the trader remarked, "the herds of Texas continued to increase much faster than the mature surplus was marketed. In fact, no market accessible existed sufficiently to consume this surplus, and of course the stock [became] less valuable in proportion as it became plentiful." But shortly

From *Great River* by Paul Horgan. Copyright 1954 by Paul Horgan. Reprinted by permission of Holt, Rinehart and Winston, Publishers.

after the Civil War the cattle trade was revived, and by the 'seventies the herds of Texas owners were the largest in the United States. Of these some of the largest belonged to great companies operating where the nation's range cattle industry had its origin — along the Rio Grande between the Pecos and Mexico Bay.

It was the brasada, the brush country, stretching from the Nueces to the Rio Grande. It was profuse in growths — but almost all were thorned. It was either swept with gray dust borne on blistering winds or beaten by deluges that hissed as they first struck the hot ground or raked by blizzards that came whistling out of the north. In its interlocking thickets that enclosed small clearings where grew curly mesquite grass, cattle could graze by thousands and hardly be seen by horsemen who sought them. There cicadas sang of the heat, and sharp-haired peccaries rooted among the thorns, and blue quail ran amidst the wiry shadows, and rattlesnakes sought the cool and sometimes were drummed to death by wild turkey gobblers at whose destroying wings they struck and struck with no effect on nerveless quill and feather. It was a land of hard secrets, the best kept of which was the location of water. Its few rivers ran in abruptly cut trenches walled with pink or yellow or slate blue limestone, and could not be seen except from their very brinks. In every direction the wilderness looked the same. There were no distant mountains to be seen. The land swelled away toward the white sky in slow rolls and shimmered in the heat that blended the ashen color of the ground with the olive greens of the brush until across the distance there seemed to hang a veil of dusty lilac.

It was astonishing how much human activity there was in a land so hostile to man's needs. It was the scene of habitual Indian travels, and of the military campaigns of the Mexicans and Texans in their wars, and of the United States Army in its Rio Grande movements, and of travelling traders, missioners and criminals. In its thickets there was even an occasional small ranch, locked in isolation by sun, distance, and the poverty of its occupants, who possessed even fewer wishes. And it became the scene of organized work in the cattle business. Animals born and grown there were taken in herds to the milder prairies above the Nueces, and across the rest of Texas and Oklahoma to beef markets in the north. ". . . The cow boys, as the common laborers are termed," said a cattleman who saw the industry develop, "go in squads of four or five scouting over the entire range, camping wherever night overtakes them, catching with the lasso upon the prairies every young animal found whose mother bears their employer's brand." It was "legal and a universal practice to capture any unmarked and unbranded animal upon the range and mark and brand the same in their employer's brand, no matter to whom the animal may really belong, so be it is over one year old and unbranded. . . ."

The cow boy was the last of the clearly original types of Western American to draw his general tradition and character from the kind of land he worked in, and the kind of work he did. His forerunners were the trapper of the mountains and the trader of the plains. Of the three, he left the fullest legacy of romance and to see him as he first was, it would be necessary in a later century to clear a way back to him through a dense folk literature of the printed page, the moving picture film and the radio that in using all his symbols would almost never touch the reality that supported them.

His work was monotonous in hardship and loneliness, and occasionally it was shot through with excitement that rose from danger. The country where he worked was in its dimensions and character his enemy; and yet it was also in an intimate way almost a completion of his nature, that revelled in vast vacant privacies, and fixed its vision on the distance as though to avoid any social responsibility. He had for his most constant companion not a man or a woman, but an animal — his horse, on whom his work and his convenience and even at times his life depended. His duties took him endlessly riding over range country, where he sought for cattle to capture, calves or yearlings to brand, herds to drive to water, individual cows or bulls of a proper age or condition to cut out of a herd for segregation into another group. Such a group would then be driven to another location — a different pasture or a market.

In dealing with cows through the consent of his horse, the cow boy needed to know much of the nature of both animals. Through experience he learned to anticipate the behavior of cattle, and to judge the effect upon them of every stimulus. He saw that the laws that governed them were the laws of the crowd; and he developed extraordinary skill in handling great crowds of cattle at a time. His horse, broken to riding, and subject to his will, he had to know as an individual creature, and dominate relentlessly its nature by turns sensitive, stubborn and gentle. Living with these two animal natures, the cow boy seemed to acquire in his own certain of their traits, almost as though to be effective at living and working with them, he must open his own animal nature to theirs and through sympathy resemble them. If he could be as simple as a cow, he could also be as stubborn; as fearless as a wild mustang, and as suspicious of the unfamiliar; as incurious as an individual bull, and as wild to run with a crowd when attracted. Even in his physical type, the cow boy might tend to resemble his animal companions — a certain flare of nostril and whiteness of eyelash could recall the thoughtless face of a calf; a leanness of leg and arm was a reminder of a horse's fine-boned supports and further suggested the physique best adapted to, and developed for, the horseman's job — the hard, sinewy body, light of weight but powerful, tall for high vision over the animal herd, long-legged for gripping the mount around its breathing barrel. His state of body and nerve had to be ready to fight, for his job sometimes included battle, when Indians or organized cattle and horse thieves came down upon his herd. Then like any soldier he had to shoot to kill, under the sanction of his duty. For his labors, he was paid in the 1870s from fifteen to twenty dollars a

month in gold or silver. He saw himself at his task, and his self-image survived in his anonymous folk literature:

> All day long on the prairie I ride,
> Not even a dog to trot by my side;
> My fire I kindle with chips gathered round,
> My coffee I boil without being ground.

In any group of nineteenth century cow boys, more were bearded than
clean-shaven. Their costumes were much alike, though with individual
variations. But all their garments were "coarse and substantial, few in number and often of the gaudy pattern." The cow boy wore a wide-brimmed
hat with its crown dented into a pyramid or flattened. If the brim in front
was sometimes turned up off his face, it could be turned down to protect
him from the pressing light of the sky under which he spent all day. Around
his neck he wore a bandana of tough silk. It served many purposes. Tied
over his face it filtered dust before his breath. It served to blindfold a calf
or tie its legs. It was a towel, a napkin, a bandage, a handkerchief, or simply
an ornament. His shirt was of stout cotton flannel, in a bright color or loud
design of checks or stripes or plaids. Over it he sometimes wore a cloth or
leather vest but rarely a jacket. His trousers were either of heavy denim, dyed
dark blue, sewn with coarse yellow thread, and reinforced at points of great
wear with copper rivets; or were of odd colors and materials, mostly dark,
that could stand tough use. They fitted tightly. The trouser legs were stuffed
into boots that reached almost to the knee. At work, the cow boy often wore
leggings of thick cowhide. They were made after the pattern of Indian
leggings — two long tubes, with wide flaps at each side cut into fringes or
studded with silver disks, that reached from ankle to groin, and were tied
to a belt as though to the string of a breechclout. Their purpose was to
shield him against thorns in the brush he rode through, and the violent
rub of haired animal hides, and the burn of rope when he pulled it against
his leg as he turned his horse to control a lasso'd creature. On his boots, he
wore large spurs, of silver or iron. He wore gloves to work in, and around
his tight hips he wore a cartridge belt from which depended his pistol —
most often a Colt's single-action, .45 caliber revolver called the Peacemaker.
He had no change of clothing. He went unwashed and unbathed unless
he camped by a stream or a pond. "I wash," he said in his multiple
anonymity,

> I wash in a pool and wipe on a sack;
> I carry my wardrobe all on my back. . . .

Like the object of his work and its chief instrument — the cow and the
horse — his Texas saddle, in its essential form, came from Spain. Its high
pommel and cantle, heavy stirrups and great weight suggested the squarish,
chairlike saddle of the jousting knight, though its design was modified by

Mexican saddlers until all contours were rounded and smoothed, and the pommel, of silver or other metal, was developed to serve as a cleat about which to secure the lariat whose other end was noosed about a captive cow or horse. When not in use the lariat was coiled and tied to the saddle. There was little other baggage on the saddle, except now and then a leather scabbard containing a short rifle. If two cow boys travelled together they carried their camp equipment and bedrolls on a pack animal. Otherwise, when a large group worked daily out of a central camp, their equipment was carried in the camp wagon to which they returned during the day for meals and at night for fire, food and companionship.

The wagon, pulled by four horses and driven by the camp cook, was a roving headquarters for the grazing party. Its form was invented by Charles Goodnight in the 1850s, who adapted an Army vehicle to the needs of the cow camp. Rolling in movement, it had a compact look, with its sheets over bows, that concealed the contents, which consisted of bedrolls for the workers and at its free end a high, square chest standing upright. Parked, free of its horses, and with its tongue propped level to serve as a rack for harness, and with its sheets extended and supported by poles to make a generous pavilion of shade to one side, the wagon seemed to expand into several times its own size. It was amazing how much it carried, and how much immediate ground its unpacked equipment could cover. The chest at the rear was faced with a wooden lid which when opened downward became a worktable supported by a central leg. Then were revealed in the chest many fitted drawers and hatches in which the cook kept every necessity for cooking and every oddment, including medicines. Behind it in the wagon bed, along with the bedrolls, he carried his heavy pots and skillets and tin dishes. Beneath the wagon frame hung buckets and to its sides were lashed water barrels.

The cooking fire, which at night served also to give its only light to the camp gathering, was made a few feet from the wagon and its profuse scatter of equipment. There the cook prepared his meals, always the same. If brush or wood were scarce, he made his fire of dried animal droppings, like the Spanish soldiers who centuries before had found these the only useful product of fabled Quivira. If he had no matches he could start his fire by pouring gunpowder into his pistol, wadding it loosely, and firing it with its muzzle close to a scrap of cloth or other dry kindling. He prepared a great pot of coffee boiled from whole beans. A cow boy drank a quart or more every day. Of such coffee it was said that "you would hesitate, if judging from appearance, whether to call it coffee or ink." It was drunk without cream or sugar. There was a kettle full of stew in which using his pocket-knife — his only table service — the cow boy probed for a lump of meat. With thick biscuit or cornbread he soaked up the gravy and like an Indian ate from his fingers. There were no green vegetables to be had. A pot of kidney beans finished the meal. The cow boys squatted near one another, or stood idling by the wagon, and ate in silence and with speed. A meal was not an occasion of social interest. It was an act of need, disposed of without grace or amenity. Inseparable from it were the taste and smell of dust and cowhair and horse sweat and leather — sensory attributes of everything in the cow boy's working life.

> For want of an oven I cook bread in a pot,
> And sleep on the ground for want of a cot.

But before the bedrolls were opened up from their heavy canvas covers, and the work party went to sleep, there was a little while for talk and other diversion. Such a miniature society created its own theatre. There was always someone who would be moved to perform, while the rest gazed at the intimate, never-failing marvel of how one whom they knew — a man just like them — became before their very eyes somebody else. The campfire put rosy light over the near faces of the gathered men and their cluttered possessions, and threw their shadows like spokes out on the flat ground until the immense darkness absorbed all. At the very center of light a fellow rose. He had a joke to tell. He acted it out. It may have been well known to all, but they listened in fixity. It was likely to be an obscene jape. The cow boy, observed a cattleman of the 'seventies, "relishes . . . a corrupt tale, wherein abounds much vulgarity and animal propensity." His delight was a practical joke on one of his fellows. The joke was good if it made a fool of someone. It was better if it mocked the victim's personal peculiarity, and it was even better if it played upon "animal propensity" — for the sake of symbolic relief of the enforced continence under which the work party lived on the range.

There were other stories to hear — many dealt with experiences in the Civil War, to which the early cow boys were still close in time. There were wrestling and other trials of strength to perform. There were songs to sing, some of whose texts were lewd parodies of sentimental ballads. All knew the songs of the cattle trail, and could sing them together. If in one of his cubbyholes the cook carried a violin for its owner, there would be fiddle music of an astonishing legerity that yet managed to seem tuneless, while a cow boy danced a clog in firelighted dust, and the rest clapped hands. Often a mournful piety stirred in someone, and when he began to sing a hymn, others joined him, and like a sigh of innocence, their united voices rose over their lonely fire where they camped, a little knot of men with every potentiality, to one or another degree, for every human attribute. The bedrolls came out of the wagon and were spread. Nobody had a book to read, and in any case, the firelight was dying and would soon be down to coals.

> My ceiling's the sky, my floor is the grass,
> My music's the lowing of herds as they pass;
> My books are the brooks, my sermons the stones,
> My parson a wolf on his pulpit of bones. . . .

As his artless song implied, the cow boy belonged to the type of man who was not, actually, domesticated. He chose freedom in the wilds over responsibilities of hearth and home. He thought more about work than he did of a family. He made love on almost a sesaonal schedule, as though in a rut. He visited a prostitute, or took a sweetheart, only to leave her, with sighs about how he must go roaming, as though all would understand his natural state. He departed for work or went off to fight wherever he would find other men like himself. He preferred the society of men to that of women: for only with men could he live a daily life that was made up of danger, and hard exposure, and primitive manners. These did not seem like disadvantages to him, for he liked them for themselves, and, further, they brought into his life excitement, freedom and wilderness, all of which he sought.

If he saw himself as a simple creature, and if tradition so accepted him, both were wrong. His temperament and character were full of tempestuous contradictions and stresses. The life he chose resembled the Indian's more than any other, but it lacked the sustaining spiritual power of the Indian's nature-mythology, and so it could not really hold for him the unquestioned dignity of a system that tried to explain — in whatever error — the whole of human life. He was close to the frontiersman many of whose ways he repeated, but he was neither innovator, builder nor explorer. His love of hardness and primitive conditions could be turned either to serve his comrades in unbreakable loyalty, or lead him, as it did in individual cases, to a career as gunman or cattle thief. His longing for love was so great that he felt an exaggerated chivalry for womankind, but in his worship he made women unreal; and yet through his song literature he lamented, ". . . between me and love lies a gulf very wide." He sanctioned his state by romanticizing it in ballad and story; but he refuted it symbolically by his periodic violent outbreaks of gunplay, drunkenness and venery. And with all his hardness, he gave in to a soft core of sentiment whose objects were the animals he worked with, and the comrades who worked with him.

"I and they were but creatures of circumstance," said a cow boy of his fellows in his domesticated old age, " — the circumstances of an unfenced world." From their unfencedness came their main characteristics. Solitude was put upon them by their chosen environment, which thus modified their character. "Adhesiveness," in the jargon of the nineteenth-century parlor science, was a human trait. The nearest living being to whom the cow boy could turn with affection was his horse. It was his daylong companion and helper. It obeyed his orders and made him master of distance and took him in and out of danger. Responding to his signals, it seemed to him to possess more than animal intelligence. His horse, a masterpiece of anthropomorphism, joined him in a partnership, and was paid every honor due to such a position. "My horse," continued the retired cow boy, "my horse was something alive, something intelligent and friendly and true. He was sensitive, and for him I had a profound feeling. I sometimes think back on . . . remarkable horses I owned in much the same way that I think back on certain friends that have left me. . . . I went hungry sometimes, but if there was any possible way of getting food for my horse or if there was a place to stake him, even though I had to walk back a mile after putting him to graze" — and cow boys hated to walk — "I never let him go hungry. Many a time I have divided the water in a canteen with a horse." If it was expedient to take care of his horse in order to assure his own mobility and safety, and if it was ordinary human kindness to care for a dumb creature, there was yet more than such promptings in the cow boy's devotion to his mount, as many a song and story attested. The professional cow boy rarely had a cultivated mind; and in his incurious thought he was lowered and his horse was elevated until they drew together in common identity. It was a process typical of a juvenile stage of character, and it may have suggested why the cow boy and his legend should appeal forever after as a figure of play to little boys. In much the same sort of emotion the cow boy felt a mournful fondness for the animals he herded — the little "dogies" to whom he sang on the trail to keep them quiet, and to whom he attributed something of himself as they were objects of his vigilance and labor, day and night. In its innocence and pathos his system of projected sentimentality for his animals suggested that only by making of them more than they were could he have survived his lonely and arduous duty with them. One of his songs said of the cow boy that "his education is but to endure. . . ."

Another song celebrated the life of cow boys together in their wandering yet coherent community. "The boys were like brothers," they sang of themselves, "their friendship was great. . . ." Alike in their extreme individualism, their self-reliance, their choice of a life wild, free and rude, the companions of the cow camp gave to one another an extreme loyalty. It seemed like a tribute to the hard skills they had to master to do their jobs. A man who proved himself able at it deserved membership in a freemasonry unlike any other. Its physical tasks caused a high value to come upon the life of action, in which there was no place for the values of mind and spirit. These were relegated to the world of women; and in the towns and cities that later completed the settling of the last frontier West, for the better part of a century it would be the women's organizations that would try to rescue the fine arts, education, religion, and social amenity from being held as simply irrelevant to civilized life — an attitude even more withering to mankind's highest expressions than one of mere contempt. For its purpose in its time, the brotherhood of the cow camp was all that was needed to make an effective society. Diverse like all individuals, and sprung from various backgrounds and kinds of experience, the cow boys taken together seemed to merge into a type more readily than most workers in a common job. Their environment directly created the terms of their work, and their work in its uncomplicated terms created their attitudes and points of view. And if they were like one another in their principal traits, it was because so many of them chose their calling for the same general reason.

This — it was attested to again and again in the cow boy's anonymous ballad literature — this was flight from one kind of life to another. Many cow boys left home, "each," said a ballad,

> "Each with a hidden secret well smothered in his breast,
> Which brought us out to Mexico, way out here in the West."

In this lay a suggestion of doom, a rude Byronism that was echoed in other songs by allusions to unhappiness, guilt, escape. Some were driven to the new society of the cow range by a faithless girl at home, or a dissolute life, or a criminal past; others by inability to become reconciled to their home societies following the Civil War, or by bitterness in family life, or even by a cruel stepmother. Romantic conventions of behavior in the nineteenth century could move the cow boy, who punished those who had betrayed him. "I'll go," he threatened,

> ". . . to the Rio Grande,
> And get me a job with a cow boy band."

He did not mean a band of musicians, for not until the next century would the cow boy's public identity be chiefly that of an entertainer who in a commercial adaptation of the cow boy costume would spend more time with a microphone than with either horse or cow. No, with companions on the cattle range, the cow boy, deaf to dissuasion by loved ones who had proved faithless, promised to go

> ". . . where the bullets fly,
> And follow the cow trail till I die."

Unable for whatever reason to accept the bindings of conventional society, within the one he sought and helped to make on the last frontier, he was capable of sure dependability in any cause for the common good of his comrades, whom he did not judge, even if sometimes a propensity to go wrong should overtake them in the very land where they had thought to escape their doom. Who knew when a man might encounter the moral frailty of one of his friends of the brushlands?

> As I walked out in the streets of Laredo,
> As I walked out in Laredo one day,
> I spied a dear cow boy wrapped up in white linen,
> Wrapped up in white linen as cold as the clay.

It was a dirge for a young man who in his dying words revealed a longing for a gentler land than the dusty empire of his work, and confessed his errors. "Oh," he said,

> "Oh, beat the drum slowly and play the fife lowly,
> Play the dead march as you carry me along;
> Take me to the green valley, there lay the sod o'er me,
> For I'm a young cow boy and I know I've done wrong."

Unashamed of their grief that sprang from their close living, his bearers saw themselves in him, and if he had sinned, they could not condemn him.

> We beat the drum slowly and played the fife lowly,
> And bitterly wept as we bore him along;
> For we all loved our comrade, so brave, young and handsome,
> We all loved our comrade although he'd done wrong.

For here was a clan feeling, a solidarity, with a realistic view of character and its capacity for error. Idealizing one another in the all-male society of their work and play, the cow boys remained loyal above, or even because of, the weaknesses they shared and assuaged with violence. In conclusion, the dirge moved from the individual to the group.

> Then beat your drum lowly and play your fife slowly,
> Beat the Dead March as you carry me along;
> We all love our cow boys so young and so handsome,
> We all love our cow boys although they've done wrong.

In another valedictory the cow boy spirit, after reciting the perils of "some bad company" which could only lead to being "doomed for hell," ended in the presence of the hangman with an admonition to morality.

> It's now I'm on the scaffold,
> My moments are not long;
> You may forget the singer
> But don't forget the song.

In the cow boy's lonely character there were extremes of feeling and behavior. If in his work there seemed to be a discipline of dedicated stead-fastness, a purity of vocation, then when he went to town, he threw himself into indulgence. Perhaps the town was a reminder of the coherent social life he had fled at home, and perhaps it was now a guilty joy to outrage it by his behavior. Certainly the town was the very opposite of the desolate open range from which even the cow boy needed periodic change.

His best chance for it came when men of the range party were told off to drive a herd of cattle to the marketing and shipping towns. The main trails along which he drove went north from the Texan Rio Grande to Kansas, and another — the Goodnight-Loving Trail — led westward to New Mexico and California. It passed to Pecos River at Horsehead Crossing about a hundred miles above the Rio Grande, and presently divided into two forks. One pointed north to Colorado. The other crossed the Rio Grande at Las Cruces and followed the old road to San Diego.

The cattle made trails that showed many narrow grooves side by side — marks of the strict formation in which the animals in their thousands were driven for upwards of a thousand miles. A cow boy said that trail life was "wonderfully pleasant" — this in spite of continuing hazards. There still might be trouble with Indians. All the cattle were wild, and were easily stampeded by attacks, or by thunderstorms, or by hail. If the weather was wet, rivers rose, and to take thousands of cattle across swollen waters was at best a tedious job, and often a perilous one. Against the drovers on the move there pressed at one period a whole organized enterprise of thievery. Outlaws captured drovers, tortured them, sometimes killed them, and stole their herds. When one drover was captured, he tried to talk his way out of his trouble, but the bandits were immovable and a reporter of the incident said bitterly that "it was like preaching morality to an alligator."

But in swelling volume the animal trains passed through to their destina- ions, and the cow boys were happy on the trail. They played tricks on one another, and shot game on the prairies, and after supper sang, told stories, danced to a fiddle, lay back to look at the stars and speculate about them, and listened for the sounds of the herd settling down for the night. "I do not know anything more wholesome and satisfying," mused a cow boy long after his trail days, "than seeing cattle come in on their bed ground at night so full and contented that they grunt when they lie down." It was like a communion of creature comforts in which man and animal could meet. Three shifts of night guards were posted over the herds. A sleepy cow boy rubbed tobacco juice in his eyes to keep awake. Morning must come, and another day to be spent at the pace of cattle walking with odd delicacy in their narrow grooved trails, and after enough such days, the shipping town would take form like a few scattered gray boxes on the severe horizon, and the cow boy would feel his various hungers begin to stir.

It was in town that he got into most of his trouble. Every facility was there to help him do it. As a cattle shipper observed, in frontier towns "there are always to be found a number of bad characters, both male and female; of the very worst class in the universe, such as have fallen below the level of the lowest type of brute creation." These pandered to the cow boy's howling appetite for dissipation.

Sometimes he rode into town and without cleaning himself or changing his clothes but just as he had dismounted in hat, damp shirt, earth-caked trousers, and boots and spurs, he strode into a dance house, seized a "calico queen" or a "painted cat," as he called the dancing women, and with Indian yells and a wild eye went pounding about the dance floor under a grinding necessity to prove in public, most of all to himself, that he was at last having a good time. The music to which he danced was "wretched . . . ground out of dilapidated instruments by beings fully as degraded as the most vile. Few more wild, reckless scenes of abandoned debauchery can be seen on the civilized earth," remarked the cattle shipper, "than a dance house in full blast in one of the many frontier towns. To say they dance wildly or in an abandoned manner is putting it mild. . . ."

And sometimes the cow boy, at large in town with his accumulated pay, went first to improve his looks. In a barbershop he had a bath, and then had his three to six months' growth of hair trimmed, and his full beard cut down, shaped and dyed black. In a clothing store he bought completely new

clothes, from hat to boots, and then, strapping on his pistol, he was ready
to impose himself like shock upon the town. Gambling rooms, saloons, a
theatre, a row of prostitutes' quarters like cattle stalls, dance houses — from
one to the next the cow boy could make his explosive way, to be catered to
by "men who live a soulless, aimless life," and women who had "fallen low,
alas! how low . . . miserable beings." Among the conventions of the cow
boy's town manners was free use of his firearm, whether he might harm anyone or not. The pathos of folly long done and half forgotten would make
his murderous antics seem unreal to later view. But they were real enough
in the frontier towns of the 1870s. "It is idle," sighed the cattle shipper in
that decade, "it is idle to deny the fact that the wild, reckless conduct of the
cow boys while drunk . . . have brought the *personnel* of the Texan cattle
trade into great disrepute, and filled many graves with victims, bad men
and good men. . . . But by far the larger portion of those killed are of that
class that can be spared without detriment to the good morals and respectability of humanity. . . ." And "after a few days of frolic and debauchery, the
cow boy is ready, in company with his comrades, to start back to Texas, often
not having one dollar left of his summer's wages." All he had was a memory
that found its way into one of his songs, about "The way we drank and
gambled and threw the girls around. . . ."

The cow boy triumphed at a lonely work in a beautiful and dangerous
land. Those of his qualities that did the job were the good ones — courage,
strength, devotion to duty. His worse traits, exercised for relief, were not
judged in relation to his task. All aspects of his complex nature entered into
his romance. He saw himself for his own achievement, and like the earliest
individuals of the frontier, he consciously created his character and his tradition, and whether his emotion was honest or not, it was so energetic that
by it he made his nation see him in his own terms. In him, the last American to live a life of wild freedom, his domesticated compatriots saw the end
of their historical beginnings, and paid him nostalgic tribute in all their
popular arts. Soon, like them, he would lose his nomadic, free and rough
form of life before the westward sweep of machine technics by which
Americans made their lives physically more easy — and socially less independent and self-reliant. In the very exercise of their genius for convenience
in living, the Americans sacrificed to the social and commercial patterns of
mass technics some part of the personal liberty in whose name the nation
had been founded. The cow boy in his choice of solitude held on to his
whole liberty as long as he could. But domestication of his West by machine technics began in the 1860s and, once started, went fast.

For in response to such technics, the cattle industry grew with sudden-
ness, and then became stabilized. The first of these was the westward advance of the railroads with which the northbound cattle drives could make
a junction. It was not easy to arrange for the earliest rail transport of
western cattle. A young Illinois cattle shipper who was the first to establish
a livestock market in Kansas was astonished to have his new idea rejected

by two railroad presidents and the leading businessmen of several Kansas towns to whom he went in turn. Finally the Hannibal & St. Joe Railroad gave the young shipper a contract "at very satisfactory rates of freight from the Missouri River to Quincy, thence to Chicago." He selected Abilene, Kansas, as the site for his stockyards, and in 1867, the first cattle were driven there from Texas. During the next four years 1,460,000 head of cattle were brought to Abilene. Other trails and shipping centers were soon established, and it was estimated that during a period of twenty-eight years nearly ten million cattle worth almost a hundred million dollars were moved from the Texas ranges to market. In the process of developing so great a business, the whole practice of cattle raising became formalized through changes that sought greater efficiency.

One of these used a technical machine product that soon conquered the open range where wild cattle once drifted according to weather. It was barbed wire, first used in 1875 to fence pastures in which with fewer and less skillful cow boys the herds could be restricted and more easily managed. When land was enclosed, ranch dwellings were needed. Permanent headquarters buildings followed. Cattle no longer were driven to rivers but found their water in earth tanks supplied by dug wells, with still another machine product to keep it flowing — the metal windmill. The main trunk lines of the railroads ran east to west across the continent; but soon feeder lines were built — sometimes following the flat terrain of the old trails — and machine transportation reached nearer and nearer to the great ranches of the border where the whole cattle industry had had its beginnings. The Missouri, Kansas and Texas Railroad was the great Texas cattle line. It tapped the Rio Grande brush country ranges. The Atchison, Topeka and Santa Fe main line crossed New Mexico and a branch line ran from Belen on the Rio Grande all the way down the valley to El Paso. The Texas and Pacific reached eastward from San Diego to El Paso in 1877, and bridges now came back to the Rio Grande to stay. The whole river empire was soon tied to the rest of the nation by rails. When packing houses were established at Kansas City, Fort Worth and other Southwestern cities, the final pattern of the organized beef cattle industry was realized. In it there was little room for the figure, the temperament, of the original cow boy, with his individual lordship over great unimpeded distances and his need of freedom as he defined it. His cow camp literature recorded yet another stage — the last — of his history. "The cow boy has left the country," he could sing, "and the campfire has gone out. . . ."

On barbed wire fences, like symbols of the new order of affairs over the controlled range lands, dead, skinned coyotes were impaled in a frieze — twenty or thirty of them at a time. They were stretched in midair with a lean, racing look of unearthly nimbleness, running nowhere; and their skulled teeth had the smile of their own ghosts, wits of the plains. In the dried varnish of their own amber serum they glistened under the sun. The day of unrestrained predators was over.

STUDY GUIDE

1. Where did the cattle kingdom originate and what assured its financial success?

2. The author writes: "The cowboy was the last of the clearly original types of Western Americans to draw his general tradition and character from the kind of land he worked in." What evidence do you find for this in the essay?

3. The cowboy's dress appears to have been a bit unusual. Can you explain the practical advantages of the kind of costume he wore?

4. The author suggests that the cowboy's life was beset by "contradictions and stress." Explain and document.

5. What impression do you get of the cowboy and his life from the songs cited by the author?

6. What evidence is there for the author's contention that the cowboy was truly "The Last Frontiersman?"

BIBLIOGRAPHY

Serious reading on the West, the ecological relationship between the settlers and the natural environment, must begin with Walter Prescott Webb, *The Great Plains* * (New York, 1931) and W. Eugéne Hollon, *The Great American Desert: Then and Now* (Lincoln, Neb., 1966), an updating of Webb's classic study. Also worthwhile is Richard A. Bartlett's *The New Country: A Social History of the American Frontier, 1776–1890* * (New York, 1974). The life of the western settlers has been the subject of a number of studies by Everett N. Dick: *The Sod-House Frontier, 1854–1890* (Lincoln, Neb., 1954); *Tales of the Frontier* * (Lincoln, Neb., 1964); and *Vanguards of the Frontier: A Social History of the Northern Plains and Rocky Mountains from the Fur Traders to the Sod Busters* * (Lincoln, Neb., 1941). Mining on the frontier is well treated in Rodman Wilson Paul's *Mining Frontiers of the Far West, 1848–1880* (New York, 1963). On the subject of the cattle kingdom one might begin with Lewis E. Atherton's *The Cattle Kings* (Albuquerque, N.M., 1961), Robert R. Dykstra's *The Cattle Towns* * (New York, 1968), and J. Frank Dobie, *The Longhorns* * (New York, 1941). The cowboys is the subject of Joe B. Frantz and J. E. Choate, Jr., *American Cowboy: The Myth and the Reality* (Norman, Okla., 1955), Philip Durham and E. L. Jones, *The Adventures of the Negro Cowboys* * (Des Plaines, Ill., 1966), and Ramon F. Adams, ed., *The Best of the American Cowboy* (Norman, Okla., 1957). The coming of the farmer to the West is fully explored in Fred Shannon, *The Farmer's Last Frontier* * (New York, 1945), which also surveys late nineteenth-century farming in general.

* Asterisk indicates book is available in a paperback edition.

II INDUSTRIAL AMERICA

For the American people, the industrialization of our economy was the most significant development of the closing decades of the nineteenth century. The factors that enabled the United States to become the world's leading industrial power were many: a Yankee tradition of trade and commerce that provided both the skill and the capital required for industrial expansion; a commitment to private property and the profit system that gave the Rockefellers, the Morgans, and the Carnegies the incentive to build corporate empires; an abundant and skilled labor supply; political institutions and a constitution that fostered the growth of business and prohibited tariffs within the boundaries of the United States; immense and easily accessible raw materials; excellent natural and man-made transportation facilities; and expanding markets at home and abroad.

The statistics on the growth of industry in the late nineteenth century are awesome — some industries recording a tenfold increase in production within a period of two or three decades. But production figures provide only a small segment of the total picture of a nation being transformed from one of wood and stone to one of steel and concrete.

More interesting, perhaps, is the impact of this process on the social aspects of American life — where Americans lived, how they earned their livelihood, and how they related to one another. In these years, home-made or custom-made clothing gave way to ready-to-wear suits and dresses; horsedrawn transportation gave way to the railroad and later to the automobile; and improved transportation combined with developments in communications to provide the enterprising businessman with a nationwide market for his products and services.

This section touches upon a number of facets of the Gilded Age, Mark Twain's name for this period of excessive ornamentation and ostentation. The first essay deals with life in the small towns of America, communities made affluent by industrialism but little touched by its negative consequences. The next two selections, on the urban centers of the nation and on the shooting of the Lattimer miners, bring the impact of industrialization and urbanization into sharper focus. The final selection explores the growing puritanism in the sexual relationships of middle-class Americans.

*Parades provided diversion and a sense of community
for small-town Americans.*

4

LEWIS E. ATHERTON

The Small Town
in the Gilded Age

Perhaps someday a historian will write a history of the United
States in terms of the rise and decline of specific regions, developing the notion that certain regions seized the leadership of the
country at particular periods in its history. In the first two decades
of the nineteenth century, our presidents were drawn from the
"Virginia dynasty"; later the center of power shifted westward,
with the rise to political eminence of Andrew Jackson, Henry
Clay, Abraham Lincoln, and Stephen A. Douglas in the North and
John C. Calhoun and Jefferson Davis in the South.

In the decades between the end of the Civil War (1865) and
the turn of the century, the locus of economic growth and political leadership in the United States was undoubtedly the Midwest,
along the Middle Border and the states that comprised it: essentially the states of the Old Northwest plus Minnesota, Iowa, and
the eastern fringes of Kansas, Nebraska, and the Dakotas. A
survey of our nation's economy in the Gilded Age demonstrates
in clear-cut terms the central importance of this region: lush
prairie harvests of corn and wheat; flour milling in Minneapolis;
the manufacture of farm implements and the meat-packing industries in Chicago; the steel mills of Gary, Indiana, and the Ohio
Valley; and the remarkably profitable and efficient network of
transportation that integrated the region as an economic unit in
order to feed, house, and move the nation. In the political arena,
the Middle West — and more specifically the state of Ohio —
provided the nation with the majority of its presidents and served
as the crucial battleground for the success or the failure of the

major political parties. This era, as David Graham Hutton has so felicitously described it, was "The Midwest at Noon."

Lewis Atherton's essay offers us a portrait of small-town America at the turn of the century. His is a somewhat idealized vignette, focusing on the relatively comfortable middle class, omitting the unattractive small-town life of the newly arrived immigrants, the unskilled laborers, and the others who were part of the unfranchised segments of these communities. Enough truth remains in Atherton's description, however, to enable us to see the sharp contrast between life in small-town America of the Gilded Age and life in the tenements of New York City or the shanties of Homestead.

Since citizens knew the color and shape of every home in town, and could even direct strangers by such means, streets and houses went unmarked until towns grew large enough to obtain house-to-house mail delivery, at which time federal regulations required people to post street names and house numbers. Here was tangible evidence of the closely knit character of village life, of the satisfaction of being so well-known as to need no identifying numbers, of belonging to a neighborhood, of achieving membership in a community simply by living within its boundaries. Early in the twentieth century, and just before the debunking era, Zona Gale published her popular Friendship Village Love Stories, in which she eulogized village life:

> . . . The ways of these primal tribal bonds are in my blood, for from my heart I felt what my neighbor felt when she told me of the donation party which the whole village has just given to Lyddy Ember: — "I declare," she said, "it wasn't so much the stuff they brought in, though that was all elegant, but it was the Togetherness of it. I couldn't get to sleep that night for thinkin' about God not havin' anybody to neighbour with." . . .

Many small-town citizens were less enamored of the "togetherness" of their existence. When a door-to-door salesman in late summer, 1898, sold sixty dollars' worth of house-numbers to Gallatin, Missouri, women, the local editor immediately criticized them for being taken in by the "numbers game," which, in his opinion, was "as covered with moss as lightning-rod deals." According to him, women who disliked to live in country towns used house numbers to show that they understood city ways. Although the

From *Main Street on the Middle Border* by Lewis E. Atherton. Copyright © 1954 by Indiana University Press. Reprinted by permission of the publisher.

editor was correct in saying that not one citizen out of ten knew the names of Gallatin streets, and that residents had no need for signs and numbers to direct them, his sharp criticism of dissatisfied women undoubtedly made them no happier over having to live in a community which assumed the prerogative of telling them how to decorate their homes.

Thoughtful writers have noted the influence of "togetherness" on small-town personalities. In his stories of Winesburg, Ohio, Sherwood Anderson included the half-witted town character, Seth Smollett, the wood chopper, who went out of his way to wheel his cart of wood down Main Street for the sheer joy of being shouted at and of returning the hoots and catcalls. They proved that he belonged and had a place in local society. Anderson also described the farm boy who, after moving to town with his father to open a store, learned to dread the attitude of Winesburg people. They called his family queer, or, at least, he thought they did. Under the circumstances, he longed to return to farm life:

> When we lived out here it was different. I worked and at night I went to bed and slept. I wasn't always seeing people and thinking as I am now. In the evening, there in town, I go to the post office or to the depot to see the train come in, and no one says anything to me. . . . Then I feel so queer that I can't talk either. I go away. I don't say anything. I can't.

In Anderson's story this boy "escaped" to Cleveland and hid himself in city crowds. Solitude existed on the farm and in cities, but no one could escape the "togetherness" of village life. . . .

Village people rose early in the morning and set a pace which saw them through a long working day without exhausting their energies. A leisurely tempo with slack periods gave time to enjoy others and to engage in talk, the most pervading of all social activities. Women deserted their canning, washing, and housecleaning to gossip over the back fence or to rock in another's home while they discussed departures from routine patterns of neighborhood and town life. Marriage, birth, accidents, and death were common topics of conversation. Reports on those ill circulated each morning, and rumors of moral derelictions were passed from home to home. Retired farmers, down town for the morning mail, discussed crops and weather, which had shaped their daily activities for so many years, and then deaths and marriages. These were fitted into family and community relationships. Ancestral backgrounds, family connections, property holdings, and highlights of the career of any recently deceased member of the community were recalled and placed in their proper niche in the oral history of the village, thus giving a sense of continuity.

Town loafers who worked intermittently or not at all gathered at another spot to squat against the wall of a business building or to sit hunched over on the ledge extending from the foundation. They alone failed to speak to women passing by on shopping trips to the business section, feigning instead a blindness to matron and girl which was belied by the shifty glance of appraisal and interest in the female body.

At the post office and within the stores conversation was more general and yet more restricted because of the presence of both sexes and of all age groups. Everywhere it concerned people and things. Since art, literature, and abstract ideas were beyond the daily experience of those engaged in making conversation, individuals sought esteem by telling how they had warned another of the proper method of handling some situation which resulted badly through failure to follow seasoned experience. Illness or distress were quickly known and evoked a warmly sympathetic response because people were flesh-and-blood neighbors; wrongdoing or snobbishness aroused an equally quick condemnation for much the same reasons. Gossip served as informal judge and jury, and it sat daily to pass on every individual in the town. . . .

The structure and functioning of nineteenth-century midwestern village life confirm European critics in their assumptions that people must have a sense of belonging to the larger society around them and also in their convictions that a mobile, equalitarian age struggles hard to find a sense of permanence and stability. But European critics have misread American history when they assert that we have achieved such ends and must achieve them by being a nation of joiners, for nineteenth-century villagers were satisfied with a limited number of organizations which admitted *all* members of the community. Before automobiles permitted people to seek distant associations, they had to find them locally. "Togetherness" before 1900 came from a few community-wide organizations, from informal community life, and from local association. Americans are not necessarily "joiners"; they do want to "belong."

Churches and lodges were the focal points of organized social life before the 1890s, and they were open to all. Many did not belong, it is true, but only because they preferred to find their social outlets through informal, community activities. The few formal organizations had no rules which excluded a portion of the community, and since membership was a matter of choice and not of necessity, little stigma was attached to limiting one's participation to affairs involving the whole community.

On Sunday morning church bells were heard throughout the town, a reminder that religion had passed beyond the usual informality of village social life and functioned throughout the year. Morning and evening preaching services on the Sabbath, Sunday school, and midweek prayer meeting were common among Protestant sects by 1865. Unlike twentieth-century arrangements, however, Sunday school might follow preaching, and varied enough among churches as to meeting time to enable gregarious individuals like William Allen White [the nationally prominent newspaper editor] to display their knowledge of the "Golden Text" in several different places every Sunday. Though parents sometimes left infants at home with older children or the hired girl, the basic church services stressed family worship. All could paritcipate in Sunday school, and babies were put to sleep on back benches during evening services. Young ladies attended Sunday-night preaching and the midweek prayer service as a means of meeting their beaus. When the services ended, boys gathered at the church door or along the walk to escort their favorite girls home.

Sunday school has remained fairly standardized in the smaller churches since 1865. Then, as now, the Sunday-school superintendent called the group together for opening exercises, generally a prayer and a song, and then the classes, sectioned according to age or sex, adjourned to their assigned places in the main auditorium, which in the small churches constituted the one and only meeting place. Though some churches had curtains to separate classes, they did little to deaden the low drone of voices from the various groups. As individual teachers got discussion of the lesson under way, a symphony of sound like that of several hives of bees swarming at one time rose throughout the auditorium. The secretary-treasurer moved from class to class to receive pennies and nickels. Total attendance and total contributions were announced when the superintendent brought the groups together again for a final word pointing up the lesson, another hymn, and a prayer of dismissal. Louis Bromfield remembered the Biblical pictures on the walls, the small chairs, and tiny children marching twice around the room to the tune of "Onward Christian Soldiers," but he obviously belonged to a congregation rich enough to afford separate Sunday school rooms which permitted greater individuality.

Sunday-school teaching left much to be desired. All could memorize the Golden Text, and all could listen to someone comment verse by verse on the scriptural subject matter of the lesson. All were expected to carry away with them a central thought or principle, generally moralistic in nature, but this objective often failed of realization. Teachers of adult classes concentrated on colored maps of the Holy Land and translated shekels and cubits into American money and inches. But if an inquiring youngster asked who made God, he was likely to have a scriptural passage — such as, "In the beginning God created the heavens and the earth. And the earth was waste and void; and darkness was upon the face of the deep. And the Spirit of God moved upon the face of the waters" — read to him in explanation.

Church women maintained a Ladies Aid or a missionary society, and supported temperance groups like the W.C.T.U. [Women's Christian Temperance Union]. While young people's groups like Christian Endeavor and Epworth League became popular around the 1890's, churches did not begin to stress auxiliary organizations of men and boys before the turn of the century.

Various fund-raising and social activities were popular everywhere. One was the donation or pound party . . . to collect money or foodstuffs for the minister. Socials or sociables also were common. On such occasions, whole families met at some private home, at the parsonage, or in the church for entertainment and fellowship.

Churches used still another type of activity, the festival, to raise money. At Chatfield, Minnesota, in 1876, Presbyterian ladies held a centennial festival in "Ye Whytee's Halle," at which they presented "ye Courtship" of Miles Standish. Also, "Ye Musicke of ye Olden Tyme." Doors opened at "Earlie Candleliting" and admission was fifteen pennies.

The Unitarians, Universalists, Episcopalians, and Catholics often combined dancing with a church dinner as a means of raising money. In February of 1867, some 200 Chatfield people attended a festival of that type. About half of them engaged in dancing but the rest limited themselves to the "delicious refreshments." In reporting the event, the local editor said that all local churches sent delegations and that none seemed unduly shocked at the dancing going on at one end of the hall. Nevertheless, it took a generous and liberal spirit for some to approach so close to wickedness, and the editor was pleased at their courage.

"Festivals and fairs," or, simply, "fairs," as they were sometimes called, were the most ambitious of all church undertakings. On such occasions, the church women sold food, entertainment, and articles donated by members and friends. When the Ladies Sewing Circle of the Algona, Iowa, Baptist Church in 1867 staged a festival and fair to help complete their church building, they raised almost a hundred dollars on a cold, blustery day by selling tea and coffee, and a choice of oysters or meat at the Harrison hotel, and music, entertainment, and donations of quilts, clothing, books, pictures, nuts, and candies at the town hall.

Catholics and Protestants of less rigorous bent also used lotteries as a part of their fund-raising activities at festivals and fairs. The Catholic young ladies at Lacon, Illinois, in 1884 visited local political meetings to sell chances on articles which they had collected for their fair at Rose's Hall. They had donated a clock for that purpose, the Sisters of Mercy had given a set of silver teaspoons, and Father O'Brien a rug and table. Many local Protestants must have grumbled at such brazen gambling being permitted within the city limits.

Fraternal organizations appeared very early on the town frontier. Masons and Odd Fellows remained most numerous, even after insurance programs of the various orders of Woodmen began to exert a strong appeal around the 1890's. Although a Masonic Eastern Star auxiliary was organized in 1867, it achieved great popularity only after social cliques and clubs began to grow in numbers a generation later. Lodge halls in second-story rooms above business buildings served as regular meeting places for the conduct of routine business and initiation of new members. Lodges were popular in part because they emphasized mutual help and accepted respectable men regardless of wealth or prominence. The religious and moralistic nature of their rituals appealed to churchmen, and even to many who believed in God and morality without being affiliated with churches.

Lodges engaged in a variety of activities. At Monroe, Wisconsin, in 1869 the Masons celebrated St. John's Day with an afternoon and evening program of speeches, toasts, a dinner, and a grand ball. The Odd Fellows of Algona, Iowa, welcomed the New Year in 1877 with a musical and dancing party, an indication of the greater liberality of lodges in regard to dancing. Lodge anniversaries called for something special. The fiftieth anniversary of the founding of Odd Fellows was commemorated at Monroe, Wisconsin, in 1869 by a street parade and banquet, at which toasts, speeches, and tableaus entertained the diners and any citizens who cared to pay twenty-five cents to look on from the gallery. Lodges frequently held public installations of officers, and lodge members occasionally attended church as a group to hear a sermon in their honor. They also made much of funeral ceremonies, one of their strongest appeals. The emphasis on fellowship and informality in modern-day service clubs, like Rotary, contrasts sharply with the dignity and solemnity which dominated nineteenth-century lodge meetings. As one writer has said, the difference is seen in the modern tendency to address a fellow member as "Bill" instead of "Worshipful Grand Master."

Although they deferred to the "togetherness" of village life by freely admitting applicants to membership, lodges and churches represented a beginning drift toward our highly organized, twentieth-century social life. For the time being, however, most social relations followed a simple, informal pattern. For the individual, this involved birth, marriage and death as assured moments of prominence in the life cycle. For the village, it meant adjustment to seasons of the year and to state and national holidays. For all, it meant activity involving the whole community — celebrations in which individuals participated without waiting for invitations from various inner circles to join in setting social boundaries. And for all it meant that most social life was so informal as to need no organization to make it work.

Rank-and-file citizens were honored at various times. Relatives and neighbors were invited to family birthday dinners, where they joined the honored member in eating and visiting, usually without thought of presents or candles and cakes. Although weddings were scheduled to interfere as little as possible with the groom's job and honeymoon trips were for the few, dinner with the bride's parents, an "infare" visit to the home of the groom's family, and perhaps a charivari [a very noisy mock serenade] by neighbors honored newly married couples. Golden Wedding celebrations had great appeal partly because the death rate prevented so many couples from reaching that goal, but also because people liked to think that Golden Weddings proved the greater stability of marriages in small towns. . . .

Death touched an entire community because virtually all knew the deceased. Before undertakers built their lavish parlors, a death called for many activities on the part of relatives and friends. The corpse must be washed and laid out, with its hair combed, and in its best suit or dress. A cabinet maker got busy on a casket, unless some furniture dealer carried ready-made stock. Friends began pouring in to the bereaved home as soon as the news reached them, and members of the family seated in the living room received their condolences. Each caller tiptoed into the parlor to see the corpse, as everyone was expected to perform that rite, and all commented on how natural and peaceful it looked. Cakes and pies and meats began to appear in the kitchen in profusion, the gifts of friends and neighbors. A summer death was always easier to honor because home-grown flowers were available, but even in winter one could count on a five-dollar wreath from the lodge. Some member of the family hurriedly arranged for black-edged cards announcing the hour and place of the funeral to be run off at the printing office for display in business houses. A spray of flowers or black ribbon on the front door and small groups of neighbors sitting at night in a dimly lighted room with the corpse signified that death prevailed within.

Since custom favored large funerals, citizens generally turned out in numbers. While the bereaved family would not have had things otherwise, they were in for a rough hour. A long eulogy by the preacher and doleful hymns by a quartette only served to weaken those closest to the deceased and to leave them defenseless for the final ordeal at the grave. White gloves for pallbearers and a plumed hearse gave solemn pageantry, which often was enhanced by uniformed GAR [Grand Army of the Republic, the victorious Northern army] or lodge groups participating in the funeral ceremony. Unseemly haste must be avoided at all costs, and horses in the funeral processions were not permitted to move faster than a walk. When the mourners returned home, they generally found that neighbors had swept and dusted and restored a semblance of order to the house. In return for such neighborly services they inserted a card of thanks in the local newspaper informing all of their appreciation for help in their time of trouble. Widows then donned black mourning garb for a year and widowers moved with circumspection, for the sympathy which had been so evident early in the bereavement could quickly disappear if they departed in the slightest from community customs involving respect for the dead. . . .

In spite of ups and downs, a well-recognized annual calendar of events geared to national holidays and weather conditions prevailed in small-town Mid-America. Year after year from January 1 to December 31 this pattern repeated itself with varying intensity but with sufficient emphasis to enable all citizens to know what lay ahead in the way of social life and recreation. As early as 1862, for instance, Iowa followed the national pattern in making January 1 a legal holiday, along with July 4 and December 25. In 1880 Memorial Day was added to the list, in 1890 Labor Day, and in 1897 Washington's Birthday. Not until 1909, the hundredth anniversary of his birth, was Lincoln's Birthday given the same recognition in Iowa. With the exception of Lincoln's Birthday, Iowa followed the pattern of federal statutes, and other midwestern states did much the same. Of these legal holidays, only July 4, December 25, and Memorial Day were observed with any degree of consistency in small towns, and even then business houses remained open part of the day.

New Year's Eve and Day meant little to the small fry except that they were free from school and could ice skate, go sledding, or hunt rabbits to sell to local produce dealers. For teen-agers and adults it was a different story. Drunkards continued their Christmas spree through the New Year's since winter weather and the holiday season provided only casual labor, if any at all, for the element most heavily addicted to the bottle. Respectable people could choose among a number of well-recognized activities. Retired farmers and their wives generally limited themselves to a dinner with relatives and friends on New Year's Day, although some broke over and attended the New Year's Eve watch party at a local church. Methodists most often observed this practice. Such parties kept respectable people up beyond their usual bedtime hour, however, and differed very little from the regular church services to which they were accustomed. The Monroe, Wisconsin, editor in 1884 reported that sermons, songs and prayers had kept the brethren and sisters awake at a number of watch meetings in the local churches. Though lacking in novelty or excitement, the watch party continued to have a place in village life.

Oyster suppers and dances provided a more lively time for those who had no religious scruples to the contrary. A program at Monroe, Wisconsin, in 1883 started off with musical numbers by the young people and then dancing. The Universalist ladies served supper to the group during the evening. At the hour of midnight all paused to welcome the New Year, and then, it being Leap Year, the season was inaugurated with a grand waltz, the ladies having the choice of partners. All over the Midwest church groups with liberal leanings, lodges, young ladies intent on celebrating Leap Year when they could, and even "club" dances, sponsored by temporary groups formed for that purpose alone, added to the tendency to "trip the light fantastic" on New Year's Eve. Since teen-agers from pious homes could not engage in dancing, most of them ended up at the church watch party in a disgruntled state of mind.

Fortunately, many devout church members permitted their offspring to participate in play parties. Even though group singing eliminated the need for musical instruments in party games, and the tempo of action was somewhat less than in dancing, they came close to being an adequate substitute. . . . A whole series of party games were well known everywhere: Skip-to-My-Lou; Pig in the Parlor; Here We Go Round the Mulberry Bush; Oats, Peas, Beans, and Barley Grow; Needle's Eye; London Bridge; Miller Boy; and King William was King James's Son were among the more popular. Some were combined choosing and kissing games and others depended primarily on group rhythm for their appeal. Youngsters could forget the strictures of strait-laced parents when they became immersed in these along with the partner of their choice. . . . Such games seem to have had a rural origin and were popular longest in isolated farming communities, but they also lightened the gloom of village youngsters who could not take part in outright dancing.

From George Washington's administration to January 1, 1934, when Franklin Roosevelt suspended the practice, the President always held a public reception on New Year's Day. Midwestern country towns imitated this custom with varying degrees of intensity, but it was sufficiently common to merit attention in many local papers. Printers encouraged the idea of receptions in order to sell calling cards, and some advertised that they would remain open to print orders until noon on New Year's. . . .

Though January and February were cold, raw months on the Middle Border, they failed to halt social life. At Coffeysburg and Jamesport, Missouri, in 1893 the temperature dropped to twenty-one below zero, and village boys found the daily chore of filling the wood box after school more time-consuming than usual. Still, the correspondents of those two villages had much to report to the county paper — marriages, deaths, chicken pox among the children, and hog cholera. Harness makers were busy preparing for spring trade, and one of the postmasters received a new stock of notions to occupy his time when not handing out mail. Boys braved the cold to kill rabbits, for which they received ten cents from the local produce dealers. A Christian Endeavor Society was organized at one of the churches. Farm sales were common. Burt Ford moved into Grandma Coffey's place, since she intended to live with her children the rest of her days. The GAR gave a bean supper; young people attended informal parties in private homes; and a citizen captured a bald eagle measuring seven feet from tip to tip. The ground hog failed to see his shadow on the second of February. Preaching services, lodge meetings, and an occasional itinerant lecturer helped to vary life in the dead of winter.

Valentine's Day provided an excuse for a dance and for the sending of sentimental greetings or ugly, joshing caricatures, depending on one's age and inclinations. Volunteer fire companies and other local organizations gave dancing parties on Washington's Birthday, but otherwise it seems not to have been widely observed.

March and April could be bitter cold, but they also were likely to bring sudden shifts to mild, clean-smelling days when all the earth seemed ready to burst with lush, new vegetation. Small towns like Jamesport and Coffeys-burg, Missouri, began to turn to outdoor activities. March first was moving day for farm renters who were thinking of sowing spring oats, and townsmen cleared away debris so gardens could be plowed and prepared for early vegetables. Spring thaws meant a battle with mud. People were both amused and sympathetic toward the two sisters who suffered accidents in the spring of 1893 — one receiving a mouthful of mud kicked up by the horse which she was driving; the other a scorched back from dropping a curling iron with which she was frizzing her curls. Though revival meetings, oyster suppers, birthday parties, and sociables were common, the approaching termination of school left no doubt that activities were shifting to the outdoors.

Easter Sunday was the only occasion consistently and widely observed in these two spring months. Some women made a practice of growing flowers to decorate their churches at the Easter season. Special music, new dresses and hats for the ladies, and sermons prepared with greater care than usual combined with callas, ferns, gloxinias, and Easter lilies to make Easter Sunday a memorable day. Even before the Civil War children looked forward to dyeing Easter eggs. William Dean Howells remembered the soft, pale green colors obtained by boiling eggs with onions, and most of all the calico eggs which resulted from boiling them wrapped in multi-colored calico cloth.

Youngsters had to have their fun on April Fool's Day. In 1869 the Tiffin, Ohio, editor recommended concealing a stone under an old hat on the sidewalk for passers-by to kick. In his estimation, All Fool's Day gave every sort of license to play tricks on one's friends, and no one had any right to be angry at the custom. Some village schools celebrated Arbor Day, of Nebraska origin, and editors occasionally urged citizens to plant trees in honor of the occasion.

Most of all, people looked forward to freedom from hovering within the small areas of heat generated by stoves in homes and public buildings. During the winter it was possible to be warm in front or behind, but uniform temperatures were unknown. Approaching freedom from school and access to woods, caves, and swimming holes within walking distance of town gave the small fry a feverish itch to be about their summer business of foraging, the activity best remembered by writers who spent their childhood in midwestern villages. The antics of Huckleberry Finn and Tom Sawyer, as seen through the eyes of Mark Twain, have immortalized this phase of village life, and here indeed was the glory of small-town existence for youngsters. Farm boys had too many chores, too few companions, and too much nature to enjoy it to the limit; city boys lacked the opportunity. But no one complained of the vistas which lay before village youngsters who could be in open country or the woods in a matter of minutes.

The pattern of childhood activity within the village itself was set before the Civil War. William Dean Howells remembered the sequence of events in Ohio towns — marbles in early spring, followed by foot races, tops, and swimming, and then kites during the sweltering heat of summer. Though Howells became a literary dictator in Brahmin New England with the passage of the years, he never forgot the pets of his youth — coons, dogs, goats, rabbits, and chickens around the yard, and fish and turtles in the hogshead of rain water at the corner of the house. Howells owned a pony for a time, which he stabled in part of the family cow shed. Since guns were scarce, seven or eight boys took turns shooting a muzzle-loader on hunting trips. Howells went to the woods with others to obtain May apples, blackberries, chinquapins, red haws, pignuts, black walnuts, and sugar water from maple trees. As fall approached, boys built a cart and planned to haul in several bushels of nuts, but like all foraging activities the planning of this was more important than the execution.

Thomas Hart Benton [distinguished American painter and lithographer] revelled in similar pleasures at his home town of Neosho, Missouri, in the 1890's. Neosho had creeks where the gang learned to swim, and on whose banks they practiced chewing and smoking, and added to their linguistic powers. A railroad siding near Neosho enabled youngsters to steal two-mile rides on passing trains. There were caves to explore, horses to ride, cottonmouth moccasins and copperheads to kill. In the autumn, Benton took part in possum hunts west of town, where one ran with a kerosene lantern in hand, trying to beat his companions to the treed possum, with only the bark of the dogs as a guide. A large barn on the Benton lot was a magnificent place for amateur shows and circuses.

Although William Allen White was never a great outdoors man, his small-town boyhood made him fond of nature. Besides his family home, White listed three major influences on his childhood. One was the family barn, with its trapeze, haymows, ancient lores and skills. A second was the river, which provided fishing, swimming, rowing and skating. And the third was "roaming" — roaming in the timber, trapping quail and songbirds, foraging for nuts, and exploiting the changing seasons of the year.

Nostalgia for one's youthful kinship with the spirit of Tom Sawyer never departed from adults who grew up in midwestern country towns. When Herbert Hoover later spoke of the swimming hole under the willows by the railroad bridge near his boyhood home in West Branch, Iowa, of trapping rabbits with box traps, of fishing with willow poles, and of spitting on the bait to assure success, he plumbed the very heart of the Midwest.

Girls were more limited in their play, but they too enjoyed the pets which inhabited outbuildings of the family home, found a ready circle of neighborhood friends, and joined the boys in the nightly game of hide-and-seek. When parents called their children in after dusk of a long summer evening, boys and girls found kinship in a common fatigue and in wondering at the unreasonableness of adults who wanted youngsters to wash their feet after a day of barefooted play.

May and June quickened the tempo of outdoor life still more for all ages. Men and older boys discussed the prospects for baseball, which had become the great American game by the 1860's. In December of 1865 delegates from Illinois, Indiana, Michigan, and Iowa met in Chicago and adopted the name "Northwestern Baseball Convention," with the intention of obtaining for western clubs some voice in the national movement. State associations were formed in Iowa and Minnesota in 1867, and league play rapidly developed among larger towns all over the Middle West.

Though smaller places were unable to maintain regular schedules, they participated to the extent of their ability. In May of 1867, for example, the Algona, Iowa, paper asked those interested in forming a local team to meet on the public square at three the next Saturday afternoon. Before the end of the month a diamond had been laid out and practice games were under way. Plans for the summer called for games at five on Wednesdays and at two on Saturdays. By the 1870's small towns like Washburn, Illinois, were holding three-day baseball tournaments at the close of the summer season, with cash prizes for the winning team. In general, teams operated on a purely amateur basis and on the smallest possible margin of cost. In 1897 the Croswell, Michigan, Grays beat Center, Michigan, on the latter's diamond fifteen to thirteen, although earned runs stood only five to three. "Jollying, singing, and jostling" helped the Croswell team forget its muddy ride to Center for the contest. After dinner at the Center hotel and a stroll around the village, the team reached the playing grounds at three. As the contest got under way, a drummer drove by and inquired what was going on, a ball game or a yacht race, and was rewarded by a jeer from the small boys hugging the sides of the diamond — "ball, you d — d fool."

Baseball did little to cement good will among competing towns. If one can believe reports in small-town newspapers, umpiring changed little over the years, for the beaten team and its supporters almost invariably agreed that decisions had been intentionally biased. Towns accused one another of playing ringers, of employing crooked umpires, and of unfair noise-making to rattle opponents at crucial moments. But Babe Ruth never equalled the slugging record of many a midwestern small-town team. Freeport beat Monroe, Wisconsin, on July 5, 1869, by a score of sixty-six to thirty-nine. In explaining the loss, the Monroe editor pointed out that the score was thirty-all at the end of the fifth, but since Freeport had three pitchers and Monroe only one, the latter naturally dropped behind in the later innings.

May and June encouraged villagers to live outdoors. Churches and lodges held so many ice cream and strawberry lawn festivals that papers merely noted the hour and date. Children's-day Sunday-school exercises were occasionally held as early as 1869, and had become fairly common by the 1880's. May-day customs, including baskets for sweethearts and picnics, appealed only to a scattering of towns, but all observed Memorial Day. First proclaimed in 1868 by General John A. Logan, commander-in-chief of the recently formed Grand Army of the Republic, Memorial Day rapidly developed as a major ceremonial occasion.

Two heavy fieldpieces on the river bank fired a sunrise salute at Lacon, Illinois, on Memorial Day in 1884, and shortly thereafter country people began to arrive. At one o'clock the Peru band, a military company, fifty veterans, and citizens on foot and in carriages went in procession to the local cemetery, where eight little girls placed sprigs of evergreen on graves of Union soldiers. Prayers, songs by a quartette, and the firing of a military salute completed the cemetery program, after which the group marched to a grove to hear more band music, more singing, and the orator of the day. Several short talks were also made, one of which stressed the politically useful, time-honored theme of the Republican party — that the Democrats were traitors and that Jeff Davis should have been hanged at the close of the Civil War. Elaborate celebrations of this type were costly, flannel for the powder sacks, and powder and gun primers alone costing fifteen dollars. The program at Minonk, Illinois, the same year showed that Memorial Day celebrations were similar everywhere, and yet the variety of details that could be worked in. The Minonk procession contained a brass band, a drum corps, a wagon holding an organ and a quartette, 200 school children carrying flowers for the graves, the usual assortment of veterans, and forty carriages of civilians. An additional crowd, estimated at one thousand people, straggled along the sidewalks on foot. After visiting the cemetery, the group returned to the local opera house for music and recitations by school children and an oration by a local preacher. The day closed with an "elocutionary entertainment" to raise $150.00 to pay for the celebration.

Memorial Day rapidly surpassed even the Fourth of July as the outstanding ceremonial honoring American national traditions, partly because of the great strength of the Grand Army of the Republic and its auxiliaries like the Women's Relief Corps. Perhaps, too, the "Boys in Blue," and their honored dead, symbolized American conviction that preservation of the Union had ended the last threat to national safety. Since America, and especially the Midwest, was heading toward an era of peace and constantly increasing material growth, one needed only to honor the dead who had made this possible. An occasional citizen like William Allen White's father, irritated by the constantly increasing pension raids and GAR bias toward the Republican party, muttered that Memorial Day parades included "a lot of damn bounty jumpers." But Memorial Day remained supreme until national and world events, starting with the Spanish American War, and the thinning ranks of the GAR, encouraged Americans to divide their attention more evenly among national holidays.

American seaboard villages began to observe the Fourth of July early in the nineteenth century with public prayer, a reading of the Declaration of Independence, and a patriotic speech by an "orator of the day." Many villages also held public dinners at which leading citizens drank patriotic toasts. Although music and entertainment were not wholly eliminated, these early celebrations were basically commemorative in nature. As native-born Americans moved on into the Middle West it was only natural for them to adopt the same kind of program. . . .

Elaborate celebrations were held less frequently after 1876. In 1886 Luverne, Iowa, welcomed the Fourth with a sunrise cannon salute which was audible three miles away. An oration, band music, and fireworks featured the day-long celebration. Algona repeated much the same pattern as in 1876, except that the cannon blew up from an overload of gunpowder through failure to discover that someone had choked its mouth with clay, and a "bowery dance," staged in a brush-covered arbor competed with one at the courthouse.

More and more, towns took the day at a less strenuous pace or turned to sheer amusement. At Centreville, Michigan, in 1888 people used the daylight hours for fishing and picnics, and waited until sundown to drift downtown to hear the band and see the fireworks. The Centreville program on July 4, 1897, revealed the changed emphasis when towns celebrated elaborately. The mayor issued a proclamation asking citizens to display large flags and to wear smaller ones or strips of red, white, and blue cloth in their lapels. The program consisted almost wholly of contests — running, jumping, vaulting, catching a greased pig, and egg, sack, and wheelbarrow races, with prizes for winners in each. Because of the current bicycle craze, the largest prizes were given to winners in that division. Within another few years, small-town, Mid-America, responded to the national crusade for a safe-and-sane Fourth in protest against a yearly toll of youngsters maimed by exploding firecrackers and to protect adult nerves. By then, however, the whole pattern of life was shifting.

As torrid heat began to settle over the Middle Border, and more and more farm crops were laid by or harvested, farmers and townsmen alike slowed to a snail's pace in response to a brassy sun by day and humid nights. The Protestant churches of Monroe, Wisconsin, even started union services in the courthouse park for the remainder of the summer in July, 1876, but Baptists at Centreville, Michigan, in August of 1879 still boasted of "Baptists not yet on Vacation" to show that they could endure two regular Sunday preaching services in hot weather. Lawn socials and Sunday-school picnics increased in popularity at this time of year as did railroad and steamboat excursions for those who could afford the expense. Small boys found the scum and stagnant water of their favorite swimming holes less inviting and spent more time resting on the muddy banks, unwittingly storing strength to meet the penalty of illness which many of them would pay. The eastern Chautauqua movement was beginning to invade the Middle

West, and citizens of Iowa and Wisconsin towns began to attend the Monona Lake Assembly, while others within easy driving distance went to the Old Salem Chautauqua grounds in Illinois to hear inspirational lectures. . . .

County fairs survived because they could be modernized from time to time to meet shifting interests and changed conditions. The period preceding the 1870's has been called the golden age of midwestern fairs because of its heavy emphasis on educational activities, with amusement strictly subordinated to instruction. Midwestern county seat towns awarded generous premiums on farm exhibits, and serious-minded farm folk looked forward to vying with one another for prizes and to visiting with neighbors.

Between 1870 and the turn of the century considerable change occurred. Increasing co-operation with newer educational agencies, like agricultural colleges and farmers' institutes, and more scientific methods of stock judging gained widespread approval. Other changes were more debatable. Horse racing became more prominent and racing circuits were arranged to coincide with a series of county fairs. Opponents of horse racing argued that it had nothing to do with the real business of agriculture; instead, it absorbed an undue proportion of premium funds, distracted attention from farm exhibits, and encouraged gambling. Defenders were not lacking, however, and their arguments impressed a countryside that loved horse racing. They insisted that the development of fine horses of all kinds was a legitimate branch of stock breeding, and that gambling could be controlled, if people really wanted to check it. Moreover, attendance would decline, especially among townsmen, if racing was eliminated. . . .

County fairs continued to draw large crowds to the turn of the century in spite of criticism. Some towns held a short, spring racing program, at which grandstand weddings, mule races, and ladies' riding contests vied with the pacers and trotters for attention. The main fair came in the early fall, with a program lasting from two to three days. Directors of the Algona, Iowa, fair in 1877 required all exhibitors to have their entries in place by Wednesday, September 12. Thursday morning was devoted to showing brood mares, jacks, and mules, and to a shooting match with glass balls as targets. The afternoon program opened with an exhibition of horses, which was followed by a pulling contest at two, and then trotting and running races. Awards on farm produce, stock and machinery were announced at ten on Friday, and the rest of the day was given over to horse racing. . . .

The midway asked only for room to pitch its tents and stalls, which moved from fair to fair during the season. As early as 1875 fairs had balloon ascensions, glass works, monkey shows, shooting galleries, and minstrel troupes. In time the midway featured attractions for every age. All bought "candy cream," long strips of a sweet confection which were cut with scissors and wrapped in tissue paper as they emerged from vending machines. Music from a wheezy hand organ — often the same tune over and over — and the thin, shrill whistle of a small steam engine, which emitted puffs of black coal smoke in its efforts to move a heavy load of customers, drew attention to the merry-go-round. Burly countrymen, bashful but proud of their strength, fell easy prey to barkers who challenged them to bet a dime against a good cigar that they could sledge-hammer a lead weight into ringing a gong topping a pole.

Even the most abject gained confidence as they gave way to the frenzied spirit of the midway. Boys twirled canes won at some booth and purchased feather dusters to poke into girls' faces, and were showered with confetti in return. The more daring donned hatbands with snappy slogans and purchased soft rubber balls fastened to India-rubber strings, which enabled them to pop a girl and retrieve the balls virtually in one motion. Small boys exchanged information about sideshow freaks and the strength of the lemonade before investing their nickels and pennies. And all stood in line for access to the one shallow tin cup attached to the fairground pump, even though individuals far back in the milling mob tried to drive other parched throats away by yelling that a dead cat had been found in the well. . . .

During the early fall some churches staged Harvest Home festivals to show their gratitude for bountiful crops, and lyceums and literary societies resumed their winter tempo. Sportsmen who had hunted deer and elk near Algona, Iowa, and other midwestern towns in the 1860's now turned to smaller game or even to trapshooting. Thanksgiving-morning union church services, turkey dinners, and visiting among relatives and friends were common from the 1860's on. But Christmas remained the last and greatest festival of all the year. . . .

Local schools dismissed for as much as a week, which alone would have endeared Christmas to children. College boys, schoolteachers, and distant relatives arrived to spend the vacation with their families; dances, marriages, and drinking increased; and youngsters drilled on their songs and recitations for the Christmas program. Already filled with wonder and excitement, children saw fairyland when they entered the church door holding to their parents' hands. There, at the front of the church, stood a magnificent tree, reaching almost to the ceiling, its branches strung with ropes of beauty made from threading pop corn kernels and cranberries alternately on twine. Tinfoil streamers, tapers, and a gold star at the very top added to its splendor. Even the odor of the place seemed changed, a mixture of the smell of wet snow on clothing, of evergreens, of wax and tinsel, of oranges, all nicely mixed and flavored by drafts of hot air from stove or registers and the sharply biting cold which swept inside each time the door was opened. . . .

In just a few more days the annual cycle of social life would start over again and citizens would have to decide whether to attend the Methodist watch party or a dance on New Year's Eve. By the 1890's small-town social clubs were growing in numbers, state federations of women's clubs were joining the national federation, and the "togetherness" of nineteenth-century country towns was shifting toward a twentieth-century pattern. For the time being, however, citizens automatically belonged to neighborhood and to community, around which social life revolved.

STUDY GUIDE

1. Define what Atherton means by "togetherness." Does he consider this a virtue or a shortcoming? What does he mean when he asserts that small-town Americans wanted to "belong," but were not "joiners." Does this hold true today as well? If not, why not?

2. Atherton lists a host of activities and organizations within the church structure. How many of these remain in the church or synagogue? Can you account for the differences?

3. Are fraternal organizations popular in your community? If so, are the reasons for their popularity the same as those advanced by Atherton? If not, can you suggest why not?

4. Compare and contrast the rites of death described by Atherton to those familiar to you.

5. Atherton lists a number of holidays observed by small-town Americans in the Gilded Age. Which, in your opinion, continue to be observed and which have been dropped or drastically altered in meaning and observance? Can you suggest, for each of the holidays and observances, why?

BIBLIOGRAPHY

You may want to round out Atherton's treatment of the small town in the late nineteenth century with David Graham Hutton's, *The Midwest at Noon* * (Chicago, 1946). The influence of the country school on the lives of the inhabitants of the Middle Border is perceptively treated in chapters 4 and 5 of Solon T. Kimball and James E. McClellan, Jr., *Education and the New America* (New York, 1962). Two volumes provide excellent surveys of the nation as a whole. Lewis Mumford, *The Brown Decades* * (New York, 1931), is a pioneering yet very useful study of the country's material and cultural landscape in the Gilded Age. See also Howard Mumford Jones's more up-to-date study, *The Age of Energy; Varieties of American Experience, 1865–1915* * (New York, 1971).

A survey of the cultural climate in various regions can be obtained from a number of other fine books. C. Vann Woodward, *The Origins of the New South, 1877–1913* * Baton Rouge, La., 1951) has an excellent chapter on Southern culture in this period. New England culture in the late nineteenth century is the subject of Van Wyck Brooks, *New England: Indian Summer* * (New York, 1940). The way of life of the people who settled on the Great Plains has been treated in a number of highly readable books by Everett Dick, including *The Sod-House Frontier, 1854–1890* (Lincoln, Neb., 1954) and *Vanguards of the Frontier: A Social History of the Northern Plains and Rocky Mountains from the Fur Traders to the Sod Busters* * (Lincoln, Neb., 1941).

* Asterisk indicates book is available in a paperback edition.

By 1895, New York's Seventh Avenue had street lights and convenient public transportation facilities.

5

ARTHUR M. SCHLESINGER, SR.

The City in the Gilded Age

In contrast to European cities such as London, Paris, and Rome, which are looked upon as possessing historical and even aesthetic worth, American cities have found little favor with intellectuals and have traditionally been considered a source of social problems. Thomas Jefferson warned the nation not to abandon the farm for the town; Henry David Thoreau sought peace and creativity at Walden Pond; and Frederick Jackson Turner, the historian of the American West, located the origins of political democracy and social equalitarianism on the frontier — not in the city. Despite these typically negative assessments of life in the city, Americans have been moving to the city in greater and greater numbers since the eighteenth century. Indeed, as one historian has noted, America was born on the farm and moved to the city.

The movement from the farm to the city was especially great in the closing decades of the nineteenth century. Although the spread of urbanism could be found in all regions of the country, the cities of the East and the Middle West surpassed all others in their rate of growth. New York's population, a million in 1880, burgeoned to a million and a half within ten years. Chicago's population leaped from a half-million in 1880 to more than a million in 1890. Minneapolis and St. Paul, the twin cities, trebled in size in the same period, and other cities in the Middle West — Detroit, Milwaukee, and Cleveland — were not far behind in their rate of growth. Much of this urban growth was a result of two developments: the mechanization of farming and the growth of industry. The first freed many from the time-consuming work on the farm and, at the same time, produced a high volume of farm products to feed the growing multitudes in the city; the second — industrialism — brought job opportunities and wealth to those who were venturesome enough to abandon the countryside for the new metropolitan centers. In addition to the native Americans who were rapidly migrating from the farm to the cities of the nation, a tide of "new immigrants" — from Southern and Eastern Europe — flocked to the cities of America during this period. In 1890, there were as many immigrants as native-born Americans living in Chicago. In that same year, a quarter of the people of Philadelphia were foreign born and a third of the population of Boston were immigrants. In the city of New York, four out of five residents were either of foreign birth or of foreign parentage.

In *The Rise of the City: 1878–1898,* Arthur Meier Schlesinger, Sr., traces the growth of urbanism in American life in the late nineteenth century and the many social, religious, and cultural implications of this phenomenon. The chapter we selected from the Schlesinger volume focuses on the cities' early attempts to provide such essential services as lighting, hygiene, transportation, sanitation, and sewage for their rapidly increasing populations. The record of the nation in making the city a habitable environment, Schlesinger points out, was by no means a negative one. "No other people," this distinguished historian concludes, "had ever met such an emergency so promptly or, on the whole, so successfully."

In America in the eighties urbanization for the first time became a controlling factor in national life. Just as the plantation was the typical product of the *antebellum* Southern system and the small farm of the Northern agricultural order, so the city was the supreme achievement of the new industrialism. In its confines were focused all the new economic forces: the vast accumulations of capital, the business and financial institutions, the spreading railway yards, the gaunt smoky mills, the white-collar middle classes, the motley wage-earning population. By the same token the city inevitably became the generating center for social and intellectual progress. To dwell in the midst of great affairs is stimulating and broadening; it is the source of a discontent which, if not divine, is at least energizing. In a

From *The Rise of the City, 1878–1898* by Arthur M. Schlesinger, Sr. Reprinted by permission.

populous urban community like could find like; the person of ability, starved in his rural isolation, might by going there find sympathy, encouragement and that criticism which often refines talent into genius.

Moreover the new social needs created by crowded living stimulated inventors to devise mechanical remedies — appliances for better lighting, for faster communication and transit, for higher buildings — which reacted in a thousand ways on the life of urban folk. Density of population plus wealth concentration also facilitated organized effort for cultivating the life of mind and spirit. In the city were to be found the best schools, the best churches, the best newspapers, and virtually all the bookstores, libraries, art galleries, museums, theaters and opera houses. It is not surprising that the great cultural advances of the time came out of the city, or that its influence should ramify to the farthest countryside. . . .

But the heirs of the older American tradition did not yield the field without a struggle. To them, as to [Thomas] Jefferson, cities were "ulcers on the body politic." In their eyes the city spiritual was offset by the city sinister, civic splendor by civic squalor, urban virtues by urban vices, the city of light by the city of darkness. In politics they sought to preserve or restore their birthright of equality by stoutly belaboring their capitalistic foe embattled in his city fortress; but against the pervasive lure of metropolitan life, felt by their sons and daughters, they could do no better than invent sensational variations of the nursery tale of the country mouse and the city mouse. Urban growth evoked a voluminous literature of bucolic fear, typified by such titles as *The Spider and the Fly; or, Tricks, Traps, and Pitfalls of City Life by One Who Knows* (N.Y., 1873) and J. W. Buel's *Metropolitan Life Unveiled; or the Mysteries and Miseries of America's Great Cities* (St. Louis, 1882). It may be questioned, however, whether such exciting accounts with their smudgy but realistic pictures did more to repel than entice their breathless readers to partake of the life they depicted.

To traveled persons familiar with the distinctive personalities of European centers American cities presented a monotonous sameness. Apart from New York, Boston, Washington, New Orleans and a few other places [James] Bryce believed that "American cities differ from one another only herein, that some of them are built more with brick than with wood, and others more with wood than brick." Most places possessed the same checkerboard arrangement of streets lined with shade trees, the same shops grouped in much the same way, the same middle-class folk hurrying about their business, the same succession of unsightly telegraph poles, the same hotels with seedy men lounging in the dreary lobbies. Few foreign visitors stopped to think, however, that American cities were the handiwork not of many national states but of a fairly uniform continent-wide culture. If they lacked the colorful variety of ancient European foundations, they also lacked the physical inconveniences and discomforts which picturesqueness was apt to entail. But it could not be gainsaid that a tendency toward standardization, as well as toward higher standards, was one of the fruits of American urban development.

While in the European sense there was no single dominant city in America — no city both metropolis and capital — yet all agreed in according the foremost position to New York. Nowhere else were there such fine buildings, such imposing financial houses, such unusual opportunities for business and recreation. No other place had such an air of rush and bustle, the streets constantly being torn up, dug up or blown up. To New York an unending stream of visitors discovered some pretext to go each year; in it many foreign travelers, going no further, found material for pithy, if ill-informed, comments on the whole American scene. "The streets are narrow," wrote one observer in 1883, "and overshadowed as they are by edifices six or more stories in height, seem to be dwarfed into mere alley-ways." At that time the well-populated district did not extend much beyond Fifty-ninth Street; and Madison Square at the intersection of Broadway and Fifth Avenue had recently supplanted Union Square as the nerve center of New York life. But the period of growth and expansion was at hand. The corporate limits, which before 1874 had not reached beyond Manhattan Island, spread rapidly until in 1898, as Greater New York, they embraced Bronx County, Kings County (Brooklyn), Richmond County (Staten Island), and a portion of Queens County (on Long Island).

As earlier, Broadway was the main artery of New York life, lending itself successively to wholesale trade, newspaper and magazine publishing, retail shopping, hotels and theaters, as it wended its way northward from the Battery. Manhattan's other famous thoroughfare, Fifth Avenue, offered a continuous pageant of "palatial hotels, gorgeous club-houses, brownstone mansions and magnificent churches." Different from most American cities, the finest residences stood side by side without relief of lawn or shrubbery; only on the striking but as yet unfinished Riverside Drive, with its noble view of the Hudson, was architecture assisted by nature. Merchant princes and Wall Street millionaires vied with one another to sustain Fifth Avenue's reputation of being the most splendid thoroughfare in America, "a very alderman among streets." During the 1880's a dark brown tide swept up the avenue. The late A. T. Stewart's marble palace at the corner of Thirty-fourth Street, long a magnet for sightseers, was eclipsed by the newer brownstone mansions of the Vanderbilts and others farther up the avenue, inclosed by forbidding iron fences. In the late afternoon Fifth Avenue churned with "a torrent of equipages, returning from the races or the park: broughams, landaus, clarences, phætons . . . equestrians in boots and corduroys, slim-waisted equestriennes with blue veils floating from tall silk hats." . . .

The New Yorker was already famed for his provincialism: his proud ignorance of the rest of the nation and lofty condescension toward cities of lesser note. Yet foreign tourists found much to interest and detain them in these other centers, and at least one felt a native New Yorker to be "less American than many Westerners born on the banks of the Oder or on the shores of some Scandinavian *fjord.*" Boston charmed with the quiet tenor of her life, her atmosphere of intellectuality, her generally English appearance. With the reclamation of the Back Bay, a great engineering project completed in 1881, the city acquired over a hundred acres of filled land which made possible its expansion southward and the development of straight, wide thoroughfares to Copley Square and beyond.

Even more than Boston, Philadelphia impressed her visitors as a city of homes, with row upon row of prim brick houses with white wooden shutters, owned by their occupants. "If there are few notable buildings, there are few slums." In Washington the traveler found America's most beautiful city, "one of the most singularly handsome cities on the globe." Its parks and wide shaded avenues, its spacious vistas, the dazzling white of its public edifices, were reminiscent of great European capitals. In the absence of an army of factory workers the general tone was one of dignified ease in pleasing contrast to the feverish anxiety typical of other cities. "The inhabitants do not rush onward as though they were late for the train . . . or as though the dinner-hour being past they were anxious to appease an irritable wife . . . ."

Farther to the west lay Chicago, "the most American of American cities, and yet the most mongrel," a miracle city risen Phœnix-like from its great fire of 1871. Its business and shopping district, rivaling New York's in high buildings, noise and impressiveness, was fringed by three residential areas: the north side, its broad streets lined with handsome abodes, churches and club houses overlooking the lake; the south side, a newer and hardly less aristocratic section, studded with stately mansions and spacious parks; and the vast west side, more populous than the other two combined, where dwelt the immigrants and laboring folk. Like every other great city, Chicago offered a study in contrasts: squalor matching splendor, municipal boodle contending with civic spirit; the very air now reeking with the foul stench of the stockyards, now fresh-blown from prairie or lake. A "splendid chaos" indeed, causing the roving [Rudyard] Kipling to exclaim, "Having seen it, I urgently desire never to see it again." . . .

Certain problems growing out of crowded living conditions vexed all municipalities, differing among them in degree rather than in kind. None was more important in 1878 than that of adequate traffic facilities. Even in the major cities streets were ill paved, if paved at all, and in the business sections were apt to be choked with rushing, jostling humanity. "The visitor is kept dodging, halting and shuffling to avoid the passing throng . . . ," asserted one timid contemporary. "The confusing rattle of 'busses and wagons over the granite pavement in Broadway almost drowns his own thoughts, and if he should desire to cross the street a thousand misgivings will assail him . . . although he sees scores of men and women constantly passing through the moving line of vehicles. . . ." Cobblestones and granite blocks were the favorite paving materials in the East because of their local availability, just as wood blocks were in the Middle West. . . .

In . . . twenty years the streets of America were greatly improved, though the civic conscience did not regard it essential that good streets should be kept clean. By the end of the century Washington and Buffalo had become the best-paved cities in the world while Boston and the borough of Manhattan in New York were not far behind. Chicago remained the Cinderella of great American municipalities, closely rivaled by Baltimore. In 1890 only 629 of Chicago's 2048 miles of streets were paved at all, about half with wood block, the rest with macadam, gravel, stone block, asphalt, cinders or cobblestones. Despite the civic lift given by the World's Fair of 1893 the situation was but little better at the close of the decade.

Since most large cities were intersected by waterways, the needs of rapidly growing municipalities required an adequate system of bridges. The problem appeared in its most acute form in New York where hordes of people must cross over each day to their places of work on Manhattan Island. . . .

When finished, Brooklyn Bridge was the longest suspension bridge in the world. The formal opening on May 24 [1888] was attended by President [Chester A.] Arthur and his cabinet, the governors of nearby states and many other distinguished persons. The only discordant note in the chorus of rejoicing came from Hibernian New Yorkers who denounced the choice of Queen Victoria's birthday for the grand occasion. Majestic in the sweep of its great cables from tower to tower, the completed structure was over a mile long, with a central river span of nearly sixteen hundred feet and a passageway wide enough for two rail lines, two double carriage lanes and a footpath.

Though the traffic relief was considerable it was not sufficient. Between 1886 and 1889 Washington Bridge was built over the Harlem River, its two great steel arches each over five hundred feet in span, and in 1896 a second bridge, the Williamsburg, was begun to link Brooklyn and New York. Other cities wrestled with the same problem. Thus Pittsburgh built the Seventh Street suspension bridge over the Allegheny River in 1884, Philadelphia completed a cantilever bridge carrying Market Street over the Schuylkill two years later, and Richmond, Indiana, spanned the Whitewater River with a suspension bridge in 1889.

Horse cars, omnibuses, cabs and other similar vehicles had suited the needs of simpler days, but the age of the great city called for swifter conveyance. The old "bobtail" cars, modeled on the stagecoach and pulled by horses or mules, did not suffice for moving an enormous mass of people to and from their places of work at about the same hours of the day. Already New York had shown the utility of an overhead railway, four-car trains being drawn by diminutive steam locomotives which scattered oil and live ashes on the heads of unwary pedestrians. . . . Kansas City also elevated some of her tracks in the mid-eighties, and Brooklyn built an extensive system the same decade. But Chicago did not open her first line until 1892, and Boston, which meantime had begun to burrow underground, not until 1901.

The slow adoption of the overhead system was due partly to its ugliness and noise, but even more to the initial cost of construction. Of greater popularity in the eighties was the cable car, first contrived by a Scotch immigrant, Andrew S. Hallidie, in 1873 to solve the problem of transit over the hilly streets of San Francisco. The car moved by means of a grappling device which descended from the floor to an endless steel cable moving in a slotted trench between the tracks. After a few years the system was taken over by cities which lacked San Francisco's peculiar need. In 1882 Charles T. Yerkes laid a cable road in Chicago, achieving not only a success for the city but a fortune for himself. Philadelphia followed the next year and New York in 1886. By the mid-nineties Eastern cities had one hundred and fifty-seven miles in operation, the Middle West two hundred and fifty-two, the Far West two hundred and seventeen and the South six.

While the cable system was yet in its heyday, this generation made its most substantial contribution toward solving the problem of urban transit. For many years — at least since 1835 — inventors in America and abroad had been working on the idea of an electrical railway. Until the development of a practicable dynamo in the 1870's, however, they had been baffled by the lack of an adequate supply of cheap current. The 1880's saw the launching of trial lines at points as far removed as Boston and Denver, but the credit for the first American electric railway successfully operated for profit over city streets belongs to Lieutenant Frank J. Sprague. In 1887–1888 he installed two and a half miles of track in Richmond, Virginia, the cars securing their current from an overhead trolley wire fed from a central power house.

Its instant success started a veritable revolution in urban transit. Not only were electric-propelled cars fast and comfortable but they were relatively cheap to construct and maintain. Fifty-one cities installed the new system by 1890, and five years later eight hundred and fifty lines were in operation, mostly in the East and Middle West, with a total mileage of ten thousand. Though horse and cable cars lingered on many streets, their doom was sealed. European cities lagged far behind those of America in adopting electric transit. At the close of the century Germany, with a trackage as great as all other European countries combined, possessed only one ninth the mileage of the United States.

Traffic congestion, however, kept even pace with the new facilities for dealing with it. The tangled situation in down-town Boston, whose narrow crooked streets exemplified the old adage that one good turn deserves another, led to the final effort of this generation. Taking a leaf from the experience of London and Budapest, Boston between 1895 and 1897 constructed a subway line a mile and a half long under Tremont Street. It was a notable engineering feat costing the city four and a quarter million dollars. Plans were at once made for extensions, and New York, as was fitting, projected a much more ambitious tunnel system which, however, did not open to the public until 1904. Except for these last two instances, the varied and heroic endeavors made during these twenty years to clear the city streets were all carried out under private auspices.

Hardly less urgent than the need for better transit was the need for readier communication. In 1878 the recently invented telephone was hardly more than a scientific toy. To use it a person, after briskly turning a crank, screamed into a crude mouthpiece and then, if the satanic screechings and groanings of static permitted, faintly heard the return message. There was no central exchange station, telephone users being directly connected with one another by separate wires. Besides these disadvantages the sheer novelty of Bell's miracle made it unpopular. People felt "a sense of oddity, almost of foolishness," in using the instrument. "The dignity of talking consists in having a listener and there seems a kind of absurdity in addressing a piece of iron. . . ." For a number of years [Alexander Graham] Bell traveled about the country exhibiting his invention. On one such trip he offered Mark Twain stock in the enterprise at twenty-five, but that usually gullible humorist "didn't want it at any price," though before the year was out he put up the first telephone wire in Hartford, Connecticut, connecting his home with the *Courant* office. . . .

In 1880 eighty-five towns had telephone exchanges with nearly fifty thousand subscribers and about thirty-five thousand miles of wire. Ten years later the number of subscribers had grown fivefold and the wire mileage sevenfold. From the first intercity line joining Boston and Lowell in 1879, the reach of the telephone grew constantly greater until by 1892 Boston and New York were talking with Washington, Pittsburgh, Chicago and Milwaukee and a few years later with Omaha. And presidential candidate [William] McKinley sat in his home at Canton, Ohio, and talked with his campaign managers in thirty-eight states. When in 1893 the patents owned by the Bell Company expired, many independent companies sprang up, especially in the smaller towns of the Middle West where the Bell system had not found it worthwhile to extend its service.

Nearly eight hundred thousand phones were in use by 1900, one for every ninety-five persons as compared with one for every nine hundred and twenty-three twenty years before; the United States had twice as many telephones as all Europe. In two decades Bell's invention had, from a mechanical curiosity, become a necessity of American life. That it added to the speed of living and the breaking down of personal privacy cannot be doubted. That it helped make the American people the most talkative nation in the world is likewise clear. On the credit side of the ledger, however, must be put the enormous gains resulting from the facilitation of social and business intercourse and from the extension of urban influences into areas of rural isolation.

Largely because of the greater utility of the telephone the telegraph expanded slowly during these years. In 1874 [Thomas Alva] Edison had doubled the carrying capacity of the wires by his invention of quadruplex telegraphy, which allowed two messages to be sent simultaneously from opposite ends of the same line. Actual wire mileage, however, grew but fourfold between 1878 and 1898. By the mid-nineties only one telegram per person per year was being sent in the United States while the people were using the telephone ten times as much. The telephone far outstripped its elder sister even for long-distance use; only in submarine communication did the telegraph continue to reign unchallenged. In the closing years of the decade, however, new vistas opened for it in a field in which it was thought the telephone could never compete. This was wireless telegraphy, the invention in 1896 of Guglielmo Marconi, an Italian engineer. Still in the experimental stage, the chief use of "wireless" before the coming of the new century was for ocean vessels. . . .

Improved lighting was almost as great a necessity as improved communication, for the new conditions of city life required something better than the dim rays shed from gas lamp-posts on the streets and the yellow glow of kerosene lamps or open-flame gas jets indoors. For years inventors in many countries had been seeking to harness electricity to the service of illumination, but success, as in the case of the trolley car had to await the development of the modern dynamo. Though the Russian engineer, Paul Jablochkoff, in 1876 devised an arc lamp which was used with some success to light the boulevards of Paris, his achievement was quickly eclipsed by the ingenuity of Charles F. Brush, a young Ohio engineer, who in 1879 illuminated the public squares of Cleveland, Ohio, by means of a system which could maintain sixteen arc lamps on a single wire. The superiority of the new device won immediate public favor. Soon the hissing, sputtering noise of the carbons and the brilliant glare of the lamp were familiar sights on American city streets, San Francisco leading the way by setting up a central power plant the same year as the Cleveland trial. The Brush system quickly spread across the Atlantic and presently, too, to the cities of Japan and China.

Satisfactory as was the arc lamp for outdoors it proved of little use for interior illumination. For this purpose some method had to be found of minutely subdividing the electric current so as to produce lights corresponding to gas jets in size and cheapness. Inventors on both sides of the Atlantic labored at the problem; but success came first to Thomas A. Edison, whose wizardry in the domain of electricity was already presaged by his improvements on the telegraph and the telephone. Edison was at this time thirty-two years old, "a pleasant looking man, of average size . . . with dark hair slightly silvered, and wonderfully piercing gray eyes," who was apt to be found "with acid-stained garments, dusty eyebrows, discolored hands and dishevelled hair." Since 1876 he had been conducting his experiments in a great laboratory at Menlo Park, New Jersey; but this establishment had been acquired only after years as a tramp telegrapher and mechanical tinker had led him by devious paths from his native town of Milan, Ohio, to Boston and New York, where his inventions won generous financial backing.

The problem of incandescent lighting quickly reduced itself, in Edison's mind, to finding a suitable filament which, when sealed in a vacuum bulb, would burn more than a few hours. . . . His incandescent lamp was patented on January 27, 1880. It not only gave a steadier, cooler and brighter light than gas, but he had also solved the problem of switching lamps off without affecting others on the same circuit.

The public gazed with wonder at the new illuminant in Edison's show-room at 65 Fifth Avenue. In 1882 central lighting stations were erected in London and New York. Perhaps no mechanical invention ever spread so swiftly over the world. The new light first entered American homes at the residence of J. Hood Wright in New York; it began to burn in American hotels at the Blue Mountain House in the Adirondacks; it first appeared in a theater when six hundred and fifty bulbs lighted up a performance of Gilbert and Sullivan's opera "Iolanthe" at the Bijou in Boston on December 12, 1882. The number of central electric stations for all purposes — incandescent and arc lighting, traction power, etc. — rose from thirty-eight in 1882 to nearly six hundred in 1888 and to approximately three thousand in 1898. . . .

Improved lighting not only dispelled much of the darkness of urban night life but also many of its dangers. By helping erase the difference between day and night it lengthened the working hours for intellectual toilers, made possible continuous operation of factories and, at the same time, gave an enormous stimulus to after-dark amusements and the theater. Better illumination also meant less eye strain, though this advantage may have been offset by the constant temptation to overwork on the part of the studious. The vastly increased productivity of mind and mill in this period owes more than has ever been recognized to the services of Brush, Edison and [Carl Auer von] Welsbach.

Municipalities were less successful in coping with the problem of waste elimination. Since the middle of the century and earlier, places like New York, Boston and Chicago had had public underground conduits for discharging sewage into near-by bodies of water. But their facilities lagged behind the growth of population and most other cities employed village methods of surface-draining their streets and of using private vaults and cesspools for family wastes. In 1877 Philadelphia had eighty-two thousand such vaults and cesspools, Washington fifty-six thousand and Chicago, despite its sewerage system, thirty thousand. Two years later a noted sanitary engineer called proper sewage disposal "the great unanswered question of the day." Its solution involved grave problems of community health, for dense populations made private uncleanliness increasingly a public concern.

In the two decades following, however, sewerage facilities were greatly extended, while important improvements were effected in sewer construction and in methods of ultimate disposal. This last problem was an especially difficult one. Cities with water fronts usually discharged their sewage into sea or river with always a danger of water pollution, especially where there was a tidal backwash; elsewhere filter beds and farm irrigation systems were commonly used. Progress was very uneven. While Boston and Washington spent millions in improving their sewerage works during these years, Philadelphia and St. Louis had at the close of the period little more than half as great a mileage of sewers as of streets, and Baltimore, New Orleans and Mobile continued to rely for drainage mainly on open gutters. The allied problem of garbage disposal was taken care of hardly better. In New York, Boston and other ports such matter was carried in scows and barges several miles out to sea and discharged upon an outgoing tide. A common practice in inland towns was to contract for its collection by farmers who fed it to swine. Since animals so fed were subject to trichinæ, with a consequent danger to meat eaters, after 1885 furnaces began to be introduced, especially in Middle Western cities, for the reduction of garbage by fire.

The growing volume of urban wastes complicated the problem of a potable water system. This generation, however, gave less heed to the quality of the water than to its quantity. Only about six hundred cities had public waterworks in 1878, but in the next two decades their number grew nearly sixfold. At the same time some of the greater cities enlarged their existing facilities. Thus between 1885 and 1892 New York, at a cost of twenty-four million dollars, constructed the New Croton Aqueduct with a carrying capacity of nearly three hundred million gallons a day.

Gradually, however, as a result of European example and the advance of the germ theory of disease, attention was also given to the purity of the water. The Massachusetts board of health in 1886 was granted by law general oversight of all inland waters of the state with power to advise municipal authorities in regard to water supply, sewage disposal and methods of preventing pollution. Within the next few years careful investigations were also made by the state health boards of Connecticut, Minnesota, New Jersey, New York, Ohio and Rhode Island. Cities differed greatly as to the purity of their water supplies, and public-health guardians were not slow in pointing out corresponding differences as to mortality from typhoid fever. Between 1880 and 1890 about half as many people proportionately died of typhoid fever in New York and Boston, where the water was comparatively pure, as in Philadelphia and Chicago, where the supply was contaminated. Pollution by sewage and manufacturers' wastes was especially serious in the case of cities drawing their water from rivers or other natural sources.

The activity in developing municipal water plants was in part caused by the greatly increased fire risks which resulted from the crowding together of buildings and the extensive use of electric wiring. This generation was resolved to have no such conflagrations as those of Chicago and Boston in the early seventies. Though they succeeded in this aim, scarcely a year passed without one or more million-dollar fires and the waste of thousands of lives. The estimated total fire losses in 1878 were over sixty-four million dollars. In 1883 they passed permanently beyond the hundred-million-dollar mark and in 1892 and 1893 rose above one hundred and fifty million.

That the situation was no worse was due to the new methods devised for combating the danger. While small towns and the more backward cities still clung to the volunteer system of fire fighting, with sometimes a nucleus of professional firemen, the large places possessed full-time paid departments, though Philadelphia's dated only from 1871 and St. Paul did not have one until ten years later. With more efficient organization appeared improved apparatus and equipment. Swinging harness for hitching the horses to the fire wagons came into use in the seventies, as did also the fire boat, the fire-alarm signal box and the water tower. In the next decade chemical engines were introduced in Chicago, Milwaukee, Springfield, Ohio, and elsewhere. The invention of the Grinnell automatic fire sprinkler in 1877, added to the widening use of fire-resistant building materials — concrete, terra cotta, brick, steel, asbestos — helped further to reduce fire hazards, particularly in factories and office buildings. Though wide differences continued to exist among cities, the fire departments in general compared favorably with those of any other country. Chicago, for example, had twice as many men and horses and half again as many steam fire engines as London, a city three times as populous.

Conditions of lodging varied as widely as types of people and differences in income. For well-to-do transients the great cities offered hotels constantly increasing in number, size and sumptuousness. . . .

Such hotels, gorgeously decorated and furnished, with a steadily diminishing emphasis on the "steamboat style," made a special appeal with their private baths, electric elevators, electric-call service and other up-to-the-minute conveniences. Though the incessant "tinkle, tinkle, tinkle of the ice-pitcher" proved "positively nauseous" to the British compiler of *Baedeker,* he otherwise thought well of the American institution and had even a word of praise and commiseration for that "mannerless despot," the hotel clerk. Every large city also had hotels of second and third class or of no class at all, falling as low in New York as lodging places in Chatham Street (now Park Row) and the Bowery where one could secure sleeping space for a few pennies a night. In general, hotels in the South were apt to be poorer than in any other section, while in the West, even in the newer towns, they were unexpectedly good. . . .

In contrast to this agreeable picture must be placed another, that of the living conditions of the less prosperous classes and particularly of the immigrants. Of the great cities of the land Philadelphia and Chicago were least scarred by slums. Boston, Cincinnati, Jersey City and Hartford had badly diseased spots, but the evil was most deeply rooted in New York City, where land rentals were highest and the pressure of immigrants strongest. In all Europe only one city district, in Prague, was half as congested as certain parts of Manhattan. Bad as conditions had been earlier in New York, they became worse in 1879 with the advent of a new type of slum, the "dumbbell" tenement, so called because of the outline of the floor plan. This became virtually the only kind erected there in the next two decades.

Five or six stories high, the bleak narrow structure ran ninety feet back from the street, being pierced through the center by a stygian hallway less than three feet wide. Each floor was honeycombed with rooms, many without direct light or air and most of them sheltering one or more families. Almost at once such barracks became foul and grimy, infested with vermin and lacking privacy and proper sanitary conveniences. The sunless, ill-smelling air shafts at the sides of the building proved a positive menace during fires by insuring the rapid spread of flames. In rooms and hallways, on stairs and fire escapes, in the narrow streets, dirty half-clad children roamed at will, imbibing soiled thoughts from their soiled surroundings. The dense slum district bounded by Cherry, Catherine, Hamilton and Market streets was known as "lung block" because of the many deaths from tuberculosis. No wonder such rookeries were nurseries of immorality, drunkenness, disease and crime. The real surprise is, as the state tenement-house commission pointed out in 1900, that so many of the children grew up to be decent, self-respecting citizens. . . .

Remedial legislation, following the first tenement-house statute of 1867, was passed in 1879, 1887 and 1895. But in spite of the reformers the laws contained loopholes and enforcement was sporadic. The tenement-house commission of 1900 felt that, on the whole, conditions were worse than they had been fifty years before. Yet one year later a comprehensive statute was adopted which showed that the humanitarian energies of this generation had not been spent in vain. The act of 1901 not only insured real housing reform in New York, but prompted other states and municipalities to a fundamental attack on the evil. . . .

Criminologists and publicists pointed with alarm to the portentous increase of lawlessness in the United States. A census inquiry disclosed a fifty-percent rise in the number of prison inmates from 1880 to 1890. . . .

Yet it seemed to an acute observer like James Bryce that the Americans were at bottom a law-abiding people. Indeed, in the absence of adequate data for earlier periods, it is possible that crime, being mainly concentrated in the cities, had become merely more conspicuous rather than greater in volume. However this may be, all agreed that the evil was accentuated by lax law enforcement. The official guardians of society only too often were in league with the antisocial elements, passively or actively. In most large centers a crook could secure police "protection" provided he agreed to hunt his prey elsewhere or, if operating locally, to share his profits with the authorities. It was the opinion of the widely experienced Josiah Flynt that, from Maine to California, the aim of police departments was merely "to keep a city superficially clean, and to keep everything quiet that is likely to arouse the public to an investigation." Beyond that point they felt no genuine concern. . . .

If we consider only the sordid aspects of urban life the American city of the period seems a cancerous growth. But the record as a whole was distinctly creditable to a generation which found itself confronted with the phenomenon of a great population everywhere clotting into towns. No other people had ever met such an emergency so promptly or, on the whole, so successfully. The basic facilities of urban living — transit, lighting and communication — were well taken care of by an outburst of native mechanical genius which helped make these years the Golden Age of Invention. Some places moved forward faster than others, of course, and all lagged in some respects while advancing in others. If the rural spirit of neighborliness was submerged in the anonymity of city life, there developed in its place a spirit of impersonal social responsibility which devoted itself, with varying earnestness and success, to questions of pure water, sewage disposal and decent housing for the poor, sometimes taking the extreme form of municipal ownership. Moreover, what the great cities felt obliged to do under the whip of necessity, smaller towns undertook in a spirit of imitation, so that the new standards affected urban life everywhere. What most impresses the historical student is the lack of unity, balance, planfulness, in the advances that were made. Urban progress was experimental, uneven, often accidental: the people were, as yet, groping in the dark. A later generation, taking stock of the past and profiting by its mistakes, would explore the possibilities of ordered city planning, not only in the interests of material welfare and community health but also with an eye to beautification.

STUDY GUIDE

1. Do you agree with the author that there is an "agrarian bias" — a prejudice in favor of the country over the city — in American thought? Does this bias show itself in our contemporary culture? What is your evidence one way or the other?

2. How do you account for the differences that Schlesinger appears to have found among various cities? To what degree are these variations a result of: (a) historical factors; (b) economic conditions; (c) geography; and (d) ethnic factors?

3. Schlesinger appears to feel that the cities, on the whole, made good progress in finding solutions to a number of the problems that confronted them.

Consider the following problems and rank them from 1 to 6 according to how successfully each was dealt with in the cities: (a) housing; (b) transportation; (c) lighting; (d) communication; (e) sanitation; and (f) crime. Would you agree that problems that lent themselves to material solutions were more easily solved than those requiring alterations in human behavior?

4. How many of the problems (a) to (f) just listed have been completely solved today? Is it possible to find final solutions to these problems? How would you grade our recent performance in comparison to accomplishments of the American people in the period described by Schlesinger?

BIBLIOGRAPHY

The urbanization of the United States, and American attitudes toward the city, are the subjects of a large number of books on American history. Morton and Lucia White, *The Intellectual Versus the City* * (Cambridge, Mass., 1962) is an excellent survey of antiurbanism, or the "agrarian bias," in American thought. A very scholarly and detailed study of the city in late-nineteenth-century America is Blake McKelvey, *The Urbanization of America, 1860–1915* (New Brunswick, N.J., 1963). *Street Car Suburbs: The Process of Growth in Boston, 1870–1900* * (New York, 1969), by Sam Bass Warner, Jr., is a path-breaking analysis of an important development in this period — the emergence of the suburb as a response to the new forms of urban and interurban transportation. For those interested in the impact of the city on the religious life of the nation, the introductory chapter in *The Church and the City* * (Indianapolis, Ind., and New York, 1967), edited by Robert Cross, is well worth reading. The impact of the city on our nation's political life is the subject of Carl Degler, "American Political Parties and the Rise of the City: An Interpretation" in *The Journal of American History,* Vol. LI (June 1964), pp. 41–59. Two other general books on urbanism may be of interest: Charles N. Glaab and A. Theodore Brown, *A History of Urban America* * (New York, 1967), which includes a bibliography on the subject, and Zane L. Miller, *The Urbanization of Modern America* * (New York, 1973), which is similar to Glaab and Brown's book but restricted to recent times.

* Asterisk indicates book is available in a paperback edition.

Charles H. Burg Collection, Division of Archives and
Manuscripts, Pennsylvania Historical & Museum Commission

On their way to the Lattimer Mines.

6

MICHAEL NOVAK

Labor in the Gilded Age

The security and well-being enjoyed by the American worker since World War II stand in sharp contrast to the insecurity and deprivation that characterized the life of the workingman in the closing decades of the nineteenth century. Collective bargaining sessions between big business and big labor today may center on the size of retirement benefits, the number of days to be granted for sick leave, and the amount of money to be put by industry into unemployment compensation or an upgraded program of medical insurance for the worker, the worker's spouse, and their children. The advances of the American worker, particularly since 1940 — in pay, job security, and other benefits — stand as a tribute to the productivity of our capitalistic system, the courage of American labor leaders and workers, and the enlightenment, albeit belated at times, of American industrialists.

The selection that follows, taken from Michael Novak's account of the massacre of nineteen Slavic miners in an eastern Pennsylvania coal town in 1897, provides us with a portrait of labor conditions quite different from those of our own time. The tragedy at the Lattimer Mines, like other instances of labor violence in the late nineteenth century, grew out of a number of basic grievances — intermittent unemployment, low wages, and high prices — and the workingman's search for a more equitable share of the growing wealth of the nation. In their efforts to find some remedy for these and other grievances, workers, both native- and foreign-born, were confronted by a formidable adversary — the modern corporation that had the capacity to hire strikebreakers and private police and to influence the actions of local sheriffs, state legislatures, the Congress, the courts, and those who served as presidents of our country in the Gilded Age.

Labor responded convulsively to these developments and foes, most often with little success. In the summer of 1877, a combination of state militias and federal troops broke a nation-wide railroad strike called to protest the wage cuts that followed the panic of 1873; in 1892, at Homestead, Pennsylvania, and in 1894, at Pullman, Illinois, labor suffered similar defeats in its effort to improve working conditions through a combination of unionization, collective bargaining, and the strike.

The Lattimer massacre constituted a repetition of this basic pattern. In the trial that followed, the sheriff and his deputies were declared not guilty by a jury that failed to give serious con-sideration to the evidence presented at the month-long trial. Although several newspapers were critical of the verdict, the majority felt otherwise; for the New York *Sun* — no doubt speak-ing for many in the country — the verdict was proof that "Ameri-can civilization is safe under the protection of the law."

Lattimer, however, proved to be a turning point. Within a year after the shooting, John Mitchell became the head of a re-vitalized labor union, the United Mine Workers of America; by 1902, with the help of Theodore Roosevelt, he led his union toward recognition from the coal operators and better pay and shorter hours. By the 1930s, under another Roosevelt — Franklin Delano — the United Mine Workers led the American worker to a level of unionization that has been a source of protection and security to this day.

On Friday morning, the sun rose brilliant. A gang of the breaker boys from Harwood planned to go swimming. By the time the men began to assemble for the march to Lattimer Mines, some had already been out over the hills in Butler Valley to pick berries. At nine o'clock, John Hlavaty, a Slovak from Lattimer, came to the home of Thomas Racek in Harwood and said again that the men at Lattimer planned to walk out that afternoon if the men from Harwood would come to call them out. Racek took Hlavaty to Jacob Sivar's house, and they called the men together. There was still dis-cussion as to whether a large crowd should go to Lattimer or whether they should just send a committee. Some said everyone should go, or else the com-

From *The Guns of Lattimer: The True Story of a Massacre and a Trial, August 1897–March 1898,* by Michael Novak, © 1978 by Michael Novak, Basic Books, Inc., Publishers, New York.

pany might blacklist the men on the committee. This idea was generally approved.

The men recalled John Fahy's instructions of the night before about the sheriff and his armed men. Fahy had warned them not even to take marching sticks, like the garden fence poles that walkers in these parts usually carried. He instructed them about the rights of free assembly, but also about the sheriff's use of the riot act. Yesterday, he told them, the sheriff's men had fired warning shots and were reported to be more and more hostile; great caution was necessary. Fahy did not plan to accompany the marchers to Lattimer. He said he would be posting signs in nearby Milnesville; he would come over to Lattimer later. He never took part in marches.

John Eagler, who was to lead the march, was excited. He had sent a message to Alex McMullen inviting the McAdoo men to come along. McMullen said no. Echoing Fahy, he warned Eagler again not to march without an American flag. So Eagler told the men to hold off until he could find a flag to carry. With three companions, Andro Sivar, Joseph Michalko, and August Kosko, he hiked over to Humboldt.

Those who waited behind decided that the youngest boys would not be permitted to march. It would be twelve miles or more, round trip, under a broiling sun. Only boys over fifteen would be allowed to accompany the men; these were sent inside to put on shoes and decent dress. Some of the men may have fortified themselves with a little whiskey; in any case, the sheriff was later to allege so. Meanwhile, unknown to the marchers, someone from Harwood — possibly an employee at the company store — telephoned Sheriff Martin about the plan of march, its route, and destination.

In the days just before the march, visible signs of conflict frightened some of the American women of Harwood, who nervously embroidered on them at the trial. Thus, for example, Mrs. Catherine Weisenborn heard one foreigner threaten another: "If you don't come, we'll kill you." She also testified she heard some strikers threaten people like her: "We'll show the *white people* what we'll do when we come back!" . . .

By the time John Eagler got back, the men had had time for an early lunch. A cheer went up when they saw Eagler and Sivar return with not one, but two, flags. Stragglers poured out of the houses. Steve Jurich kissed his pretty bride, and the others teased them both. The older men waved good-bye to their families. At almost every doorway and out in the street women and children waved and shouted as the men moved into position. Eagler and Joseph Michalko walked down the line, telling individuals to discard their walking sticks and suggesting that they start out four abreast. There were between 250 and 300 men. They started from two separate locations and met at the picnic grounds. Joseph Michalko and Steve Jurich walked out in front with the American flags snapping in the breeze. A crowd of breaker boys fell in behind the flags, but their elders sent them unhappily away. As this unarmed band got themselves organized to answer the request of their Italian brothers at the Lattimer Mines, many were taking part in the first civic act of their lives. Most had not been in the previous marches; Eagler hadn't; Cheslak hadn't. Most had never laid eyes on Sheriff Martin; none, perhaps, had seen the guns of the deputies. It was just after one when the command "Forward march!" was shouted by Michalko.

As they walked along, they picked up new recruits. They did not aim to create a big crowd, and they did not plan to have a large rally. Frequently, they called out to friends lined up to watch them on their route. . . . The men were relaxed and festive. For the past year, most had worked only one day out of every two, and the activities of the strike — giving promise of some small but basic changes in their lives — seemed far preferable to being out of work.

The night before, the strikers had formulated three grievances and taken them to the superintendent at Harwood. They demanded a pay raise of 10¢ a day, a reduction in the price of powder from $2.75 a keg to $1.50, and an end to the company store and the company doctor. They particularly resented the prices at the company store: a dozen eggs that cost 13¢ at an independent store cost 23¢ from the company; butter at 8¢ a pound elsewhere cost 26¢; and the powder they needed for their work came from the manufacturer at 90¢ to $1.00 a keg. On the average, excess charges to miners in the Hazleton region worked out to $217.50 per capita per annum.

Their ranks swollen by recruits from Crystal Ridge and Cranberry, four hundred men were now raising a cloud of dust on their way toward Hazleton, jackets over their arms, their handkerchiefs often in use to wipe their necks and brows. No effort was made on this day, as there had been on others, to close down other breakers as they passed. They passed the Cranberry breaker, calling to their friends, shouting threats to scab workers. The marchers were unarmed and determined to be peaceful, in order to avoid trouble with the sheriff.

The strikers felt patriotic under the flag. They also felt protected. Marching down into the valley and up the opposite hill, the thin yellow dust rising in the still air behind them, many felt a surge of purpose and accomplishment. John Eagler, at nineteen, although walking at their head, was not really in charge; neither was Michalko. Older leaders like Anthony Novotny, Mike Cheslak, Andrej Sivar, and others quite naturally talked things through and decisions emerged among them by common consent. Each had been carefully reared not to be boastful, assertive, or proud. No one should be in the position of attracting criticism. The traditions of serfdom and peasant life operated like censors upon anyone who might stand out too far above the group. Oppression from above had been internalized. The community cut would-be leaders down to size.

Harwood lay two miles southwest of Hazleton. The plan was to proceed by the road at the bottom of Buck Mountain and on up through the city of

Hazleton. This would be the shortest route to Lattimer Mines on the far northeast side of town. Even so, the march would be about six miles.

It was almost two when the marchers in the front line çaught sight of armed men hurrying toward them in West Hazleton. . . .

Deputy Ario Pardee Platt boasted of ancestors who had fought in the Revolutionary War, in the War of 1812, and in the Civil War. (During 1861–65, little Hazleton had supplied almost two thousand men to the Union cause.) Platt was the chief bookkeeper of the Pardee company, and the general manager of its company stores in Hazleton, Harwood, and Lattimer Mines. It made his blood boil to see all these foreigners carrying the flag his ancestors had championed. Platt was looking for action, he had wanted action all along and was not happy with the overcareful way the sheriff had been handling things.

Thomas Hall, another deputy, was a leader in the Coal and Iron Police. He was a man who had organized the posse for the sheriff and who directed it in the sheriff's absence. Before the strike had even begun, as far back as August 12, the owners of the mine companies had called a meeting in Hazleton to discuss their dissatisfaction with the performance of the Coal and Iron Police. Even without a strike looming up before them, they were complaining that they were paying for one hundred policemen, paying well, too, and not getting the protection they needed. The police were spending too much time at Hungarian weddings, they said, and not enough time protecting property. They were paying for protection and they intended to have it. The tenor of the meeting was then leaked to the newspapers. So now, only one month later, Thomas Hall was not of a mind to occasion any further dissatisfaction from his employers. It would be his task to teach Sheriff Martin the way things were done in the lower end of the county and to keep the pressure on him to do them. His own neck was at stake.

Deputy Alonzo Dodson was a miner who lived in Hazleton. He was heard to say, "We ought to get so much a head for shooting down these strikers. I would do it for a cent a head to make money at it."

Deputies George and James Ferry — the latter known to everyone as Pinky — were also heard to say at McKenna's Corner that they would blow the strikers' brains out. Perhaps it was the power of suggestion that was working on the consciousness of the deputies, for one of them, Harry Diehl, even threatened to blow out the brains of Herman Pottunger, if he did not get off the road. Pottunger himself heard Deputy Wesley Hall say of the marchers: "I'd like to get a pop at them." . . .

Also among the deputies were Robert Tinner, the superintendent of the Central Pennsylvania Telephone and Supply Company, Willard Young, a lumber merchant and contractor, and Samuel B. Price, who held the contract to build a new breaker in Harwood, work on which was being held up by the strike. All in all about forty deputies had accompanied Sheriff Martin to West Hazleton. Nearly all these men owed their livelihood, or a portion of it, to the mining companies. Other deputies were waiting for the marchers at Lattimer.

Sheriff Martin's fondest hope seems clearly to have been to put an end to the march right at West Hazleton. But he was in something of a spot. He knew he didn't have jurisdiction inside the city, at least not without consultation, and the marchers had already reached McKenna's Corner. He was being pressured to "teach the strikers a lesson" that would get them off the roads. His own inclination still seemed to be to keep matters peaceable and under his control.

The sheriff walked directly toward the two men carrying flags, Andro Sivar and Joseph Michalko. He had his pistol in one hand. He took the nearest man, John Yurchekowicz, by the coat, brandishing the revolver in his face, and announced vigorously: "I'm the sheriff of Luzerne County, and you cannot go to Lattimer."

Steve Juszko pushed past Yurchekowicz, saying defiantly, "Me no stop. Me go to Lattimer."

The sheriff again said: "If you go to Lattimer, you must kill me first."

John Eagler, who had been fifty paces back in the line when it stopped, walked forward and now spoke up in a reedy voice: "We ain't goin' to. We are going to Lattimer. We harm no one. We are within the law."

Before the words were fully out of Eagler's mouth, Anthony Kislewicz [variants: Kascavage, etc.] bent over for a flat rock (he later said) to strike a match for his pipe during the halt. One of the deputies brought the butt of his rifle down viciously on Kislewicz's arm. Then Deputy Hall moved toward Steve Juszko, who had stepped forward, and swung through the air twice with his rifle butt, crunching across the two arms the boy raised to protect himself and hitting his head. Blood flowed. Both arms hung limp.

The sheriff pointed his pistol right and left as though holding off a legion.

Ario Pardee Platt, fired up by the bloodshed, ripped the flag from Joseph Michalko's hands, broke the stick across his knee, and stood there shredding the flag with contempt. He dropped the torn rags in the dust.

John Eagler, watching Deputy Cook raise his gun, stopped to pick up a stone. The sheriff waved his pistol and Eagler dropped the stone. Other deputies mixed it up briskly with the marchers.

Deputy Cook fired a shot into the air and the hillside reverberated. The marchers did not move. They were baffled.

John Eagler stepped forward to obtain the name of the deputy he had seen hit Juszko. Sheriff Martin held Eagler with a gesture and pulled a paper from his pocket. The sheriff had seen disorder and now had his opportunity. "This is my proclamation and you can't go any farther. It's against the law."

Then Chief of Police Jones walked forward shouting to John Eagler and the sheriff, and Sheriff Martin put his paper back in his pocket. Jones told the sheriff the strikers had a right to march peacefully, and he, the sheriff, knew it. To Novotny the chief said he had confidence in the way the marchers were conducting themselves; he would let them march around the edges of West Hazleton but not go through the city. He was willing to show them how they could go, so as to continue on to Lattimer in peace. . . .

Murderous joking, meanwhile, seems to have gripped the deputies. They had talked all morning about shooting and killing. Herman Pottunger heard a deputy say quietly to a friend: "I bet I drop six of them when I get over there." August Katski and Martin Lochar stood near the trolley car as the departing deputies were boarding. Two deputies went after them and hit them, but one said: "Let them go until we get to Lattimer and then we'll shoot them." It may have been a form of macabre humor, intended only to frighten.

William A. Evans, the reporter, arrived just after the confrontation, while the men were still standing on opposite sides of the road. He saw one of the strikers picking up a stone as Ario Pardee Platt tore the flag. No stone was actually thrown.

Doctor John Koons of Hazleton was called by the chief of police to treat the two wounded men in the jail. One of the men — Juszko — had to be examined by force. His scalp wounds required nine stitches. Juszko appears to have been listed the next day as among the wounded in the hospital. Six months later, he was still unable to use his arms.

Chief Jones did, as he offered, point the way for the marchers to cut through West Hazleton, adding another mile or so to the trip. It was after 2:30 when the marchers returned to their original plan. Now only one American flag waved in the sun, but the men were feeling vindicated and safe under the law. Mike Krupa from Crystal Ridge had joined them in West Hazleton with several of his friends, and the marchers made Krupa and his friends throw away their walking sticks. George Yamshak also joined them and was told to throw away the small stick he was carrying. The marchers had learned that their best protection was lack of arms. . . .

Later, the editorialists were not to overlook the symbolism of the day and the hour. It was almost three o'clock and the detachment of deputies assigned to wait at Lattimer was restless. A mile away, at Harleigh, Sheriff Martin and the deputies who had seen action at West Hazleton sat in the trolley and waited. Some removed plug hats to wipe away the sweat under their hatbands. Others fingered their Winchesters. A few of them were later to claim that they believed then that the miners had guns in their pockets; some even may have believed it. . . .

For the deputies sitting on that trolley in front of Farley's Hotel in Harleigh, the waiting was almost over. In a cloud of dust, the marchers were beginning to appear around the bend, the lone American flag still at their head. The deputies watched the strikers pause while eight men or so from the first two lines huddled. The other marchers broke ranks to drink water from a pump. The question for the huddled leaders, posed by John Eagler, was whether to march first to breaker Number One in Lattimer Mines or to breaker Number Three. Finally the strikers started walking again. John Laudmesser, the hotel-keeper, counted the marchers as they passed, there were 424....

In the past, strikers had often changed plans in unexpected ways, and the sheriff was taking no chances. He ordered the trolley to stay right alongside the marchers. For almost a mile, deputies and strikers went along eyeing one another. A few insults may have been exchanged. At the last fork in the road, when it was plain that the strikers could be taking no other road except into Lattimer, the sheriff ordered the trolley to speed up and race ahead to the village.

In Lattimer there was by now considerable commotion. The colliery whistle sounded a warning. Those deputies and private police who had already been waiting in Lattimer had made their preparations. One of them told Mrs. Craig, "Go inside, as there may be some shooting today." Trolley cars shuttled in from Milnesville, Drifton, and points north. Doors slammed. Some mothers hurried to the school to bring their children home. Fear of the foreigners had been intense ever since the Tuesday before, when a band of noisy strikers had marched through the village.

On his arrival by trolley, Sheriff Martin took command of the assembling deputies. His force, bolstered by some of the new deputies from Drifton, now numbered almost one hundred and fifty. Some of them stood guard at the breakers and the superintendent's office. He divided the others into three companies, under Samuel Price, A. E. Hess, and Thomas Hall. He called the men down off the trolley bank and stationed them across the single road leading into Lattimer, just before it forked into Main Street and Quality Row, with the schoolhouse lane above. Dissatisfied, he then ordered all of them off the road to take up positions in an enfilading crescent on the lower, north side of the road. In this way, they would be able to cover the entire length of the march as it filed in front of them. The Craig house on the end of Main Street was surrounded by a white picket fence. Inside, Mrs. Craig fretted nervously. Outside, across the street, stood a tall gumberry tree, later to become known as "the massacre tree." Almost in its shade, Sheriff Martin stood near the house with the white fence and looked up the empty road toward Harleigh. As he did so, A. E. Hess was showing his men one last time how to fire their guns.

From where the sheriff stood, the road swept gently upward over the brow of a distant hill. Not far from where it came over the hill, the trolley track crossed over it and continued to parallel it on the south but on a raised embankment. The marchers would come over the hill and then be caught between the embankment and the line of Winchesters. In addition, the road then gradually curved closer and closer to the deputies down toward the house where the sheriff was now standing. Thus, if the marchers kept coming, their first rank would be no farther than fifteen yards from the line of deputies, and those in the last ranks would be no farther than thirty or forty yards. The sheriff was satisfied and strode up the line a little, nearer to the center of his deputies. . . .

At last the marchers came over the hill. Next door to the Craig house, John Airy watched from his home as the unarmed marchers walked in rank toward him. As at West Hazleton, so at Lattimer the marchers felt secure under the law. In the first two rows were Steve Jurich, carrying the flag, John Eagler, John Pustag, Michael Malody, Mike Cheslak, wearing an odd pointed cap, Andro Novotny, and George Jancso. All were from the two counties of Sariš and Zemplin in Slovakia.

After dismissing their students when anxious mothers came to gather their youngsters, Charles Guscott and Grace Coyle, the teachers, stood at the doorway of the schoolhouse, and watched the slow-motion drama unfold. They stood about one hundred yards from the gumberry tree. About sixty of the ninety men in the deputies' line, they later recalled, had their rifles raised in firing position as the strikers, led by the flag, began to file past them.

Sheriff Martin told Hess and Price to keep an eye on him. He said he would find out the marchers' intentions. "If they say they are not going to do anything I may let them go on and we will go along with them." When the flag had come about two-thirds of the way past the far flank, Sheriff Martin strode forward as he had now done on four previous occasions to see if he could handle the situation alone. He had his revolver drawn. He held up one hand. The men kept coming as he advanced and he had has hand almost in their faces when he announced in official manner: "You must stop marching and disperse." Those a few ranks back could not hear him at all, and the others behind them could not see him. "This is contrary to the law and you are creating a disturbance. You must go back. I won't let you go to the colliery."

The front ranks stumbled, trying to halt. Someone from behind called out in English, "Go ahead!" The marchers behind kept coming. The front row was pushed forward.

Angered, the sheriff reached first for the flag. But Steve Jurich pulled it erect. Then the sheriff reached into the second row and grabbed Michael Malody by the coat, thinking that he was the one who had said, "Go ahead!" The sheriff didn't know which man was the leader. Frightened, Malody insisted he hadn't said a word. Andro Novotny, who was next to Malody, intervened in his defense. The sheriff then grabbed Novotny with one hand and pulled his revolver up, aiming it at Novotny's chest. By now, the sheriff had pulled four or more men to the deputies' side of the road. The other marchers continued on. Eagler was among those pushed partially forward down the road. Those near the sheriff — including, now, men from the rear like John Terri and Martin Shefronik (Šefronik) — were afraid and puzzled.

"Where are you going?" the sheriff asked, pulling on Novotny and beginning to panic. The front of the column was getting farther and farther past him. Novotny said in English, "Let me alone!" He swept his arms up and pushed the barrel of the sheriff's revolver away from his own chest.

George Jancso reached in and pulled the sheriff's other hand free from Novotny. The sheriff then grabbed Jancso's coat and pointed his pistol at Jancso's forehead; Jancso and Eagler heard the pistol snap — Sheriff Martin also felt it snap — but it did not fire.

In that instant, the sheriff's second in command, Samuel Price, left the line of deputies and stepped forward to come to the surrounded sheriff's assistance. Other deputies frantically called him back, since he was now in the line of fire. He stepped back.

Mrs. Kate Case from her third-floor window heard someone shout "Fire." She thought the deputies were firing over the marchers' heads. Then she saw some marchers fall. She screamed.

Novotny heard the sheriff command, "Fire," and Jancso heard him shout "Give two or three shots!" Some witnesses thought that in the struggle the sheriff had fallen briefly to his knees; others said he remained standing. His body was directly between the deputies and Jancso when a shot rang out, then three or four in unison. The sheriff raised both arms as though to stop the action. But a full volley rang out again and again.

Watching from the schoolhouse, Charles Guscott saw the first puff of smoke come from the fourth or fifth man from the farthest end of the deputies' line, Hess's men. It seemed to those closer that the whole line erupted with fire.

Steve Jurich had held the flag and was the first to fall. "O Joj! Joj! Joj!" he cried in the ancient Slovak cry to God. "Enough! Enough!" Bullets shattered his head and he died as he bled.

John Eagler saw Cheslak drop, his peculiar peaked hat falling from his head, so he, too, dropped to the ground. Eagler saw trickles of blood flowing in the dust toward him from Cheslak's head. He realized then that the deputies were not using blanks.

John Terri threw himself on the ground. Another striker fell on him, dead. Terri saw Cheslak beside him and tried to speak to him. Cheslak's eyes were open but he did not speak. Then Terri got up and ran.

Andro Sivar, in the fourth row, turned his back at the first shot. When the man beside him caught a bullet in the back, Sivar fell with him. Michael Kuchar, nineteen, was about ten yards from the sheriff and could neither hear nor see what was happening in front; at the loud shouting, he threw himself down. George Jancso tore himself from the hands of the sheriff and ran to throw himself in a ditch as flat and close to mother earth as he could press himself.

Martin Shefronik stood close to Jurich, and saw blood spurt out the back of Jurich's head and also from his mouth. As he dropped, Jurich was completely drenched with blood. Shefronik ran toward the schoolhouse, until he was thrown forward by the impact of a bullet in his shoulder. John Putski of Harwood also ran toward the schoolhouse until a bullet in his right arm and another in his leg spun him to the ground. Andrew Jurechek ran toward the schoolhouse and almost reached safety before a bullet struck his back and exploded through his stomach.

Watching from the schoolhouse, teachers Charles Guscott and Grace Coyle had looked on in horror as dust and acrid gunsmoke filled the air. "They're firing blanks," Miss Coyle said. "No, see them dropping," Guscott said. The firing went on for two or three minutes. Some deputies turned, wheeled, and followed running men, shooting some down at a distance of 300 yards. Many men ran toward the schoolhouse; one was hit, spinning, just before he reached the terrified teachers. Other shots crashed into the schoolhouse sending showers of splinters. Running toward the teachers, Clement Platek clutched his side; he too was crying: *"O Joj! Joj! Joj!"* The teachers saw, in addition to those mentioned: the brains of one man splattered forward; still another hapless man shot through the neck so that his head was almost severed. Grace Coyle ran forward to help Andrew Jurechek, who was clutching at the entrails slipping from his stomach and who cried out to her: "No! Me want to see wife. Before die." He died before her eyes. His wife was heavy with child.

Mathias Czaja had been standing ten or twelve feet from the sheriff. He had seen the sheriff pull his revolver and point it at the man with the flag. He had heard him say, "If you go any farther, I will shoot you." He had been frightened. He did not hear the order to fire. His back was blown open by a bullet.

Michael Srokach (Srokač) saw eight deputies run forward thirty yards or so to gain better shots. From the public road, the miners fled backward toward the trolley line and up over its bank, either up the hill west toward Harleigh or east toward the schoolhouse.

One man fled as far as a telephone pole on the trolley line when he was hit. He pulled himself up, holding to the pole. As other shots poured into him, his body buckled two or three times. He slid to the earth.

William Raught and another deputy, according to several witnesses, broke from the line of deputies in order to pursue the fleeing strikers. In order to get a line of fire, Raught and the other man climbed up on the trolley tracks, still firing. Srokach heard some deputies answer pleas from the wounded with the shout: "We'll give you hell, not water, hunkies!" Others heard: "Shoot the sons of bitches!"

The smoke from the first volley was thick. Dust was raised by men running. For a while it was difficult to see. From his home, John Airy saw deputies take careful aim and pick men off as they were running to get in the shelter of the hillside. "They shot man after man in the back," he reported. "The slaughter was awful." He estimated that the deputies fired "at least 150" shots. "They kept firing for some time. Men fell on the ground and screamed in agony and tried to drag themselves from the murderous guns. At last it was all over."

Cries of pain, groans, and shrieks remained. Andro Sivar got up from a circle of dead and wounded. Andrew Meyer — seventeen-year-old breaker boy — pleaded for help for his shattered knees. John Slobodnik, wounded in the back of the head just above the neck cried out for water. Slobodnik and John Banko, also shot in the head, were carried by friends to Farley's Hotel in Harleigh, looking for medical attention of some kind. John Eagler ran, bent over, for 150 yards before he turned. He saw one of the men from Crystal Ridge bleeding from his arm and back. The man asked him: "Butty, loosen me suspenders and collar, they hurt me much." Eagler pulled down the man's shirt and saw a big hole in the back of his neck spouting thick blood. He pushed a handkerchief in the hole. Then he bent to help Frank Tages. He pulled off his own coat, put it around his friend, led him to a trolley car for a ride to the hospital. Sick and afraid, Eagler saw some of the deputies begin to offer water to the wounded. Then he started on the long walk back to Harwood. In shock, he could not comprehend what had just happened.

Cornelius Burke was eleven years old and lived in Lattimer II, the next settlement up from Lattimer. During recess from school, he was overcome by curiosity about the commotion in town and ran down to Lattimer to see the excitement. He was part way up Main Street when he heard the terrific crack of rifles. When he got up to the site, he recalls, ". . . Oh, my God, the poor fellows were lying across the trolley tracks on the hillside, some had died and some were dying. Some were crying out for water." Connie picked up a little can and carried water to one of the dying miners. "It was a terrible sight and so much confusion existed. Everyone was running in all directions. They searched the men who were shot and found they carried no weapons."

One of the deputies, George Treible, was wounded by a bullet that creased both his arms. The Wilkes-Barre *Times* reported that he believed he was shot by one of his own men, who had wheeled to fire after the dispersing strikers. Bullets flew, Treible said, in every direction. Some of the deputies at the right end of the crescent (farthest from Lattimer), who seem to have fired most of the shots, were shooting back toward Lattimer at the strikers fleeing toward the schoolhouse. "The deputies," said the paper, "were not under control. The odor of smoke inflamed them."

The fury of some was not yet spent. Some of the deputies walked among the fallen, kicking them and cursing them. A. E. Hess told one bystander who was crying shame, "Shut up or you will get the same dose." John Terri, who had fallen beside Cheslak, went through the smoke of battle to find water for his wounded uncle and cousin. Asked for water, a deputy named

Clark said, "Give them hell," grabbed Terri, kicked him, and held him prisoner for an hour. Joseph Costello, a Hazleton butcher, saw Hess kick a prostrate victim (who was in fact Andrew Meyer) and denounced Hess for the butchery. Hess told him, too, to shut up. Grace Coyle, the schoolteacher, upbraided Hess for his manner among the fallen, with his cigar in his mouth. Hess did not defend himself.

John Welsh saw Sheriff Martin after the shooting and asked him how he was.

"I am not well," Sheriff Martin said.

The sheriff was pale and shaken. He turned his revolver over to a detective. Many of his deputies had fled and some went into hiding. Some of the others were lifting the wounded into conveyances. But John Airy witnessed the most saddening scene of all: "The trolley car in which the sheriff and his deputies came was right in front of my house and the officers got in it. They were laughing and telling each other how many men they killed." Another bystander also heard them: "Yes, and one of them said he took down a dozen 'Hunks,' and knew what he was shooting at every time. He was boasting of what a fine shooter he was. They sat there for some time, joking and laughing about it, and then they rode back to the city."

STUDY GUIDE

1. What impression do you get of the relationships in this mining town — between the workers and their employers, the workers and the law enforcement officers, and among the workers?

2. Is there any nativistic (anti-immigrant) sentiment in the community? If so, what evidence is there for it; if not, how do you account for its absence? Also, do the nativistic tendencies appear to be universal in the community?

3. What is the attitude of the workers toward their adopted country — the United States? Document your answer.

4. What impression do you get of the degree of professionalism of the deputies?

5. Do you feel, on the basis of the narrative, that the verdict of the jury (see the Introduction to the selection) was a fair one? If so, why; if not, why not?

6. Turn to the author of the narrative. (a) Is he dispassionate in his account, or do you sense that he has some strong feelings about what happened? Document your answer — either way. (b) Does it surprise you to learn that he is a spokesman for ethnicity in our country, the founder of a movement to promote ethnic pride among immigrant groups and their descendants? (c) What evidence is there in this essay of ethnic pride on Novak's part? Is it, in your opinion, justified, or to put the question this way: did the

miners, in your opinion, act in a legal and patriotic manner? If so, on what evidence; if not, on what evidence?

BIBLIOGRAPHY

The conditions of American workers described by Michael Novak did not go unchallenged by labor or labor leaders in the late nineteenth and early twentieth centuries. Should you want to learn more about labor organizations as well as the opposition to them, begin by reading the entirety of *The Guns of Lattimer* (New York, 1978), by Michael Novak. Other books that focus on specific strikes are equally informative, especially in their conclusions about the attitude of the courts and government toward labor's effort to organize and bargain collectively: Robert V. Bruce, *1877: Year of Violence* * (Indianapolis, Ind., 1957), the story of the nationwide railroad strikes of that year; Henry David, *The History of the Haymarket Affair* * (New York, 1936); Almont Lindsey, *The Pullman Strike* * (Chicago, 1942); Wayne G. Broehl, Jr., *The Molly Maguires* (New York, 1964); and Leon Wolff, *Lockout: The Story of the Homestead Strike of 1892* (New York, 1965). For an account of an important strike of the early twentieth century, see David Brody, *Labor in Crisis: The Steel Strike of 1919* * (Philadelphia, 1965). General histories of the efforts of labor to organize include Foster Rhea Dulles, *Labor in America: A History* * (New York, 1949); Henry Pelling, *American Labor* * (Chicago, 1960); and Joseph Rayback, *A History of American Labor* * (New York, 1959).

An 1874 woodcut of Victorian courtship — with chaperone.

7

JOHN S. HALLER
ROBIN M. HALLER

Sex in Victorian America

Women's rights have not progressed steadily from the colonial period to our own time. Some evidence indicates that women in the colonial and revolutionary periods enjoyed a less restricted status, economically and otherwise, than women experienced in the nineteenth century. The narrow and confining Victorian mode contrasts with the greater freedoms enjoyed by women in the seventeenth and eighteenth centuries on one hand and in the twentieth century on the other.

Several developments account for the significant role of women in the early history of the country. One factor was revolutionary fervor, which led Abigail Adams, Mary Wollstonecraft and others to demand equal rights with men. The enhanced status of women in the colonial period was reinforced by the shortage of women on the frontier, Puritan opposition to idleness, and the need of an underdeveloped country for everyone, male and female, to work. Women, whether young girls, married, or widowed, worked, some at home and others at trades outside the home. It was not unusual for women in pre-1800 America to be silversmiths, gunsmiths, and butchers, or to supervise the operation of mills and plantations. This provided the colonial woman with legal rights not enjoyed by women in Europe.

This favorable status for women was reversed between 1800 and 1860 and in the Gilded Age. The egalitarian thrust of the American economy and American society in the antebellum decades was accompanied by upward mobility and individual advancement; it provided opportunities — but for males only. As historian Gerda Lerner pointed out in her study of the status of women, in these decades women were forced into one of two roles, neither of which led to personal fulfillment or to socio-economic advancement. Women of low status went into low-paying, dead-end jobs, "women's work," in the factories that had begun to dot the landscape; women of high status became genteel ladies of fashion, economically unproductive and confined to a narrow and superficial role in the middle-class home. Losing the skills and the trades that they had enjoyed in the colonial period, by the mid-nineteenth century women were reduced to the status of an unskilled "mill girl" or placed on a pedestal as a domesti-cated "lady."

In the following selection, John S. Haller and Robin M. Haller describe the impact of these developments on love and marriage. They detail the emergence of a middle-class sex code that de-prived the woman of her sexuality and her husband of a partner-in-marriage who could help him fulfill his sexuality.

Few women understand at the outset, that in marrying, they have simply cap-tured a wild animal, and staked their chances for future happiness on their capacity to tame him. He is beautiful physically very likely, of pleasing man-ners and many external graces, and often possessed of noble qualities of mind and heart; but at the core of his nature he cherishes still his original savagery, the taming of which is to be the life-work of the woman who has taken him in charge. It is a task which will require her utmost of Christian patience, fidelity, and love.

[Anonymous], *Letters from a Chimney-Corner*, 1886

The same society which placed such great emphasis upon race progress, national improvement, and material prosperity could only see sexual promiscuity and the break up of the home circle as the most serious threat to the advance of civilization. For Victorian America, sexual promiscuity was an ominous indication of national decay, not a sign of progress or of women's liberation. It represented a pandering to the lower instincts, a lessening of family structure, and a serious weakening of society's order and stability. The "twilight talks" for men and women concealed in manuals of hygiene and ethics, religious pamphlets, medical articles, and etiquette books were thus calculated to impress their readers with sentiments of virtue and

Reprinted by permission of The University of Illinois Press from *The Physician and Sexuality in Victorian America* by John S. Haller and Robin M. Haller. Copyright © 1974 by the Board of Trustees of the University of Illinois.

chastity, and offered the notion that physical love somehow interfered with the realization of society's greater objectives. Discussions of sex predisposed the Victorians to an assortment of inferences in which sexual urges were somehow at variance with the search for morality and the proper definition of virtue. Love, like nature, proceeded according to an established set of laws or principles which, when carefully observed, would prevent the sexes from yielding to the lower passions. Love had a certain order and harmony which manifested the infinite wisdom of the Deity and which, when platonic, appeared to express its most perfect form; only under the most stringent rules did the physical aspects of love include similar attributes of beauty and goodness. Though Victorians admitted the power and value of sex, they interpreted its use in terms of its function in the species' evolutionary advance. Just as race progress demanded a higher specialization of man's talents in both the arts and sciences, so the purpose of sex was less a means of personal enjoyment than a specialized function of race and national development. The same providence that watched over America in its victories and peace was similarly engaged in the management of the Victorians in their capacity as preservers of the species.

Sex as described in the manuals of Victorian America became middle class, with all the marks of sobriety, propriety, modesty, and conformity, and supplied for rural and working-class America much the same function it provided for urban America looking across the Atlantic for cues to correct behavior. From another point of view, the sex-in-life manuals were a carry over from the dabblers of the mid-nineteenth century society in the areas of pseudo-science, liberal Christianity, Transcendentalism, and perfectionist tendencies. With the sex manuals the clergy, who were declining in their function as moral advisors . . . , and the physicians, who were attempting to widen their function as spiritual as well as physical healers, met to reform both medicine and morals. . . . With a strong undercurrent of Old Testament vengeance, the purity literature of the late nineteenth century portrayed sex as the most primitive human tendency . . . , the aberrations of which were invariably detected and punished through disease and mental anguish.

The seventeenth- and eighteenth-century manuals of love and marriage contrasted sharply to those of the later Victorian period. The most obvious difference lay in their emphasis on "pleasure." . . . An anonymous author in 1719 suggested, for example, that "when young persons are not early happy in their conjugal embraces as [they] may wish to be, and it is suspected from a coldness, and insufficiency upon that account on either side," the use of either Strengthening Electuary or Restorative Nervous Elixir would not fail "to render their intercourse prolific, as it actually removes the causes of impotency in one sex, and of sterility, or barrenness, in the other." Another popular manual encouraged sexual pleasure by demanding that both sexes meet "with equal vigour" in the conjugal act. The woman's interest in sex as well as her ability to conceive depended entirely upon pleasurable reciprocity. The clitoris, which achieved an erection similar to the male penis ("yard" or "codpiece") as a result of stimulation, "both stirs up lust and gives delight in copulation, for without this, the fair sex neither desire mutual embrace, nor have pleasure in them, nor conceive by them." Noted medical scientist John Hunter (1728–93) had identified the clitoris as the reciprocal organ of the male penis: "There is one part in common to both the male and female organs of generation, in all the animals that have the sexes distinct; in the one it is called the penis; in the other the clitoris. Its special use, in both, is to continue by its sensibility, the action excited in coition till the paroxysm alters the sensation." . . .

Love manuals written during the first half of the nineteenth century treated women as potentially equal partners in the marriage bed, but they were not nearly as explicit in their discussion of sex as those of the previous century. For one thing, authors tended increasingly to limit the pleasurable aspect of sexuality. While encouraging healthy persons to exercise the sexual instinct, they cautioned against too frequent satiation of the senses. Although there was to be a definite decorum in the privacy of the bed-chamber, marriage manuals allowed that normal sexual relations could be enjoyed four or five times a week without difficulty, and the wife should experience orgasm along with the husband. . . .

One of the first significant changes in marital advice came with the writings of Sylvester Graham (1794–1851), whose health crusade during the 1840s demanded certain rules regarding the frequency of intercourse for married couples. Graham observed that American men were suffering from increased incidence of debility, skin and lung diseases, headaches, nervous-ness, and weakness of the brain — all of which he blamed on sexual excesses in marriage. Believing as so many others in his day that an ounce of semen equaled nearly forty ounces of blood, Graham concluded that sexual excesses lowered the life-force of the male by exposing his system to disease and premature death. . . .

The publication of William Acton's *Functions and Disorders of the Reproductive Organs* (1857) was responsible for much of the subsequent medical justification for the changing role of women in marriage. Speaking as a physician with countless hours of private consultation, Acton observed that women had little sexual feeling, and in fact, remained indifferent to the physical aspects of marriage. Only out of fear "that they would be deserted for courtesans if they did not waive their own inclinations," Acton wrote, did passionless women submit to their husbands' embraces. Woman's indiffer-ence to sex was naturally ordained to prevent the male's vital energies from being overly expended at any one time. For a century which was beginning to focus exclusively upon the male as the center of force and vitality, the role of woman in the personal sexual relationship could only be a supportive position, conserving male strength by matching the brassy edges of his ego with submissive femininity. According to Acton, since the sexual act was such an enormous drain on the nervous system, the male should perform this function in as short a time as possible, preferably a few minutes. The female's lack of complementary satisfaction only helped to preserve the male's vital energies for other more serious responsibilities. "I should say that the majority of women (happily for society) are not very much troubled with sexual feeling of any kind," he remarked. "What men are habitually, women are only exceptionally. . . . There can be no doubt that sexual feeling in the female is in the majority of cases in abeyance, and that it requires positive and considerable excitement to be roused at all: and even if roused (which in many instances it never can be) it is very moderate compared with that of the male." . . .

The attitude of the medical profession toward women's sexuality, however, was in no way monolithic. Although most manual writers alluded to woman's lack of sexual desire, physicians like Elizabeth Blackwell challenged Acton's thesis, maintaining that most female repugnance for sexual passion resulted from terror of pain, fear of injury from childbirth, and past experiences with awkward or brutal conjugal encounters. These women, for whom the sexual act was devoid of both romance and pleasure, and was, in fact, a source of discomfort, found sexual abstinence and frigidity an "easy virtue." . . .

Unfortunately, the views of Acton remained dominant among physicians who were unwilling to make the connection between the clitoris and the woman's feeling for excitement. "There is an ingrained and inborn prudery prevailing," wrote one distraught physician, "which stifles the few and hesitant endeavors of medical men who occasionally feel impelled to speak of this subject." By the 1870s, purity authors had begun to monopolize marriage manuals and extolled frigidity in the female "as a virtue to be cultivated, and sexual coldness as a condition to be desired." As one manual suggested in 1876, women had "more of the motherly nature than the conjugal about them. . . . Their husbands are to them only children of larger growth, to be loved and cared for very much in the same way as their real children. It is the motherly element which is the hope, and is to be the salvation of the world. The higher a woman rises in moral and intellectual culture, the more is the sensual refined away from her nature, and the more pure and perfect and predominating becomes her motherhood. The real woman regards all men, be they older or younger than herself, not as possible lovers, but as a sort of step-sons, towards whom her heart goes out in motherly tenderness."

To restrain the aggressive nature of the male, purity authors advised women to remain cold, passive, and indifferent to the husband's sexual impulses. Careless and amative acts destroyed the "innate dignity" of the wifely role and led to the misuse of the sexual function in immodest responses in the male. It was part of nature's plan, wrote Mary Wood-Allen, M.D., . . . national superintendent of the Purity Department of the Woman's

Christian Temperance Union, for women to "have comparatively little sexual passion." Though women loved, and while they gladly embraced their husbands, they did so "without a particle of sex desire." For Wood-Allen, the most genuine sort of love between man and wife existed in the lofty sphere of platonic embrace. As a passive creature, the wife was to endure the attention of her husband in a negative sense, if only to deter the greater weakening of his "vital forces." Late nineteenth-century moralists likened the sexual role of women to that of the flower — motionless, insentient, passive, and inanimate. Women must follow nature, and like the flower, lie "motionless on [the] stalk, sheltering in a dazzling tabernacle the reproductive organs of the plant." In contrast to the writers of the eighteenth- and early nineteenth-century love manuals, purity authors agreed that the experience of "any spasmodic convulsion" in coition would interfere with conception — the primary function of the marriage act. "Voluptuous spasms" in the woman, wrote one author, caused a weakness and relaxation which tended to make her barren.

Nearly all purity literature condemned the romantic novel as responsible for the increase in sexual neurasthenia, hysteria, and generally poor health among American women. Not only did sentimental novels tempt them to impurity, but the emotional stimulation that accompanied novel reading tended "to develop the passions prematurely, and to turn the thoughts into a channel which led in the direction of the formation of vicious habits." Whatever stimulated emotions in the young girl caused a corresponding development in her sexual organs. Overindulgence in romantic stories produced a flow of blood to certain body organs causing "excessive excitement" and finally disease. For this reason, children's parties, staying up late, puppy love, hot drinks, "boarding-school fooleries," loose conversation, "the drama of the ballroom," and talk of beaux, love, or marriage were contributing causes to unnatural sexual development. The physician's duty was to oppose novel reading as "one of the greatest causes of uterine disease in young women." . . .

Doctors advised parents to prevent "silly letter-writing" between boys and girls in their early school years. "We have known of several instances," warned John Harvey Kellogg, M.D., in his *Ladies Guide in Health and Disease* (1883), "in which the minds of pure girls became contaminated through this channel." Kellogg, famous for his health foods (he helped to found the W. K. Kellogg cereal company) and rest homes for the century's neurasthenics, campaigned for "eternal vigilance" and enjoined parents to guard the chastity of daughters in all their relations. This vigilance included the prohibition of tea and coffee until they were at least eighteen years of age. These "comforting properties" were addictive and sometimes led the young woman to seek stronger tonics to satisfy her craving for stimulants.

Like novels and letter-writing, dancing was another source of impurity.

Kellogg, for example, claimed that the dance had caused the ruin of three-fourths of the degenerate women in New York City. One young lady confessed that the waltz had awakened a "strange pleasure" in her constitution — her pulse fluttered, her cheeks glowed with the approach of her partner, and she "could not look him in the eye with the same frank gayety as before." According to Sylvanus Stall, author of a sex-in-life series in 1897 which sold more than a million copies and was translated into a dozen or more foreign languages, the male transferred his physical emotions to the woman through animal magnetism. Not the dance itself, nor even the intentions of the male dance partner, caused the woman pleasure; rather, the female absorbed the male's more domineering and passionate nature through magnetic contact. Thus, wrote a ruined and repentant girl, "I became abnormally developed in my lowest nature."

The proper training of girls, their personal hygiene, their relations with other children, their reading habits, and the embarrassing problem of masturbation (variously called the "solitary vice," "self-pollution," "self-abuse," or the "soul-and-body-destroyer") dominated a major portion of the sex manuals of the day. Manual writers cautioned girls never to handle their sexual organs, for, while it gave temporary pleasure, the habit left "its mark upon the face so that those who are wise may know what the girl is doing." The misuse of the sexual organs brought inevitable disease and severe complications in later life. "The infliction of the penalty may be somewhat delayed," wrote one physician, "but it will surely come, sooner or later." The young girl who practiced the solitary vice would never escape the consequences of her indiscretion. She would become subject to a multitude of disorders such as backaches, tenderness of the spine, nervousness, indolence, pale cheeks, hollow eyes, and a generally "languid manner." Her attitude, once pure and innocent, would turn peevish, irritable, morose, and disobedient; furthermore, she would suffer loss of memory, appear "bold in her manner instead of being modest," and manifest unnatural appetites for mustard, pepper, cloves, clay, salt, chalk, and charcoal. . . .

The mistaken notion of delicacy left many girls unprepared for the physiological changes at puberty. One doctor remarked that nearly a fourth of his female patients were ignorant of the significance of bodily changes, and many of them were "frightened, screamed, or went into hysterical fits." However, part of the problem was surely due to the manuals themselves, which touched ever so gently on the subject of menstruation. Jules Michelet, in *Love* (1859), for example, explained that for a period of fifteen or twenty days out of twenty-eight, the woman was "not only an invalid, but a wounded one." It was woman's plight, he wrote, to ceaselessly suffer "love's eternal wound." . . .

In their relations with males, purity authors constantly advised girls to play a passive role. "The safest and happiest way for women," wrote one author, was "to leave the matter [of courtship] entirely in his hands." Though matrimony was a great and noble vocation, it was "an incident in life, which, if it comes at all, must come without any contrivance of [the woman]." And in all relations with the wooer, the girl was to maintain a strict modesty in order to guard against personal familiarity. She was never to participate in any "rude plays" that would make her vulnerable to a kiss. She was not to permit men to squeeze or hold her hand "without showing that it displeased [her], by instantly withdrawing it." Accept no unnecessary assistance, one author cautioned, "sit not with another in a place that is too narrow; read not out of the same book; let not your eagerness to see anything induce you to place your head close to another person's." . . .

Manuals cautioned the woman to passively await the male's declaration of matrimonial intentions before expressing the slightest evidence of reciprocating love. To allow herself even a "partially animal basis" during courtship was to fall prey to the evils of blighted love which weakened not only her modesty but also her most important organs. Trifling with love was immoral as well as damaging to the physical and mental balance of the woman's delicate structure. When a gentleman engaged the affections of the woman, his amorous attentions caused those special organs of her sex (bosom and reproductive organs) to quicken in their development. Love not only enhanced charm and virtue, but also brought womanly functions to sexual fruition. One writer described the woman in love as one whose breasts "rise and fall with every breath, and gently quiver at every step." But when the male suitor broke off the relationship (usually as a result of the woman's immodest actions), he destroyed her charm and attractiveness, and because of the "perfect reciprocity which exists between the mental and physical sexuality," he crippled the physical organs of her sex, causing deterioration as well as disease. . . .

Young girls were also to avoid the hazards of early marriage. Premature love robbed the nerve and brain of their natural needs and blighted the organs of sex. It was consummate folly, wrote one author, for girls to "rush into the hymeneal embrace" since it would only exhaust the love powers, and precipitate disease and an early grave. To prevent this, young women were to place themselves on "high ground" apart from "gushing affections," holding their love as the "choicest treasure," not conferring even the smallest degree of affection to the male wooer. This etiquette would promote in the male a higher understanding of love, as he expressed "upon the bended knees of confession and solicitation" only the purest form of veneration. . . .

Although physicians were divided on the question of birth control, the majority of those who published books or pamphlets on the subject took a strict view of conjugal pleasures and remained publicly opposed to the use of contraceptives. Doctors wrote of weak, scrofulous, and even monstrous children born of parents who had brought the devices of the street prostitute into their homes, of husbands who were despondent and subject to impotency or involuntary losses of semen as a result of their fraudulent efforts, and of women whose fear of pregnancy led to horrible disorders of the uterus. Not without reason, then, medical practitioners were particularly critical of coitus interruptus ("pull back" or "withdrawal") and referred continually to men and women who suffered physically and psychologically from the practice. Specifically, the male's withdrawal the moment before ejaculation caused the sexual act to stop before the vas deferens completely emptied of semen. Enough of the fluid remained "to tease his organs and to kindle in him desires too importunate to tolerate any self-control." Thus men indulged in repeated venereal excesses to satisfy unfulfilled desires, leading to a constant drain on the "life-giving fluid" and a continual expenditure of the "nerve-forces." And for the wife, conjugal onanism, or what the French called a "coup de piston," prevented the "bathing" action of the semen upon the uterus. For many years, the medical profession was almost unanimous in its belief that measures taken to prevent the comingling of the male and female fluids resulted in tumors, uterine colics, neuroses, polypi, and even cancer. Wives were known to become hysterical because their wombs had not been "refreshed and soothed" by a teaspoonful of seminal secretion. In the 1870s, however, Bertillion, in his *Hygiene Matrimoniale,* argued that there were no scientific grounds for the assertion that the spermatic fluid vitalized the membranes of the uterus. Similarly, Ely Van de Warker, one of the foremost gynecologists of the century, published "A Gynecological Study of the Oneida Community" in the *American Journal of Obstetrics* demonstrating that the nonejaculation of the male in no way hindered the health of the woman. The women of the Oneida community, some of whom had sexual relations oftener than seven times a week without the discharge of semen into the vagina, did not suffer from uterine disease.

Besides withdrawal, probably the most common contraceptive other than a woman's headache, was the condom, which Madame de Stael once described as "a breast plate against pleasure and a cobweb against danger." Doctors condemned the device as deterring sexual enjoyment, and most doubted its effectiveness. One physician remarked that "at any moment it is liable to rupture and place the wearer in the position of the virtuous swain, who used an eel-skin as a prophylactic and neglected to sew up the eye holes." "Male continence" was yet another form of contraception in vogue during the late nineteenth century, and although its main adherents were the members of the Oneida community, medical journals as well as some marriage manuals discussed its applicability. The founder of the Oneida community, John Humphrey Noyes, had divided the sexual act into three stages: the presence of the male organ in the vagina, the series of reciprocal motions, and last, the ejaculation of semen. Since the only uncontrollable portion of the sexual act was the final orgasm, he claimed that with sufficient mental control, the male could voluntarily govern the first two stages, prolonging the motions of sex so that mutual satisfaction could be obtained without orgasm. Certain members of the medical profession looked enviously on the ability of the Oneida communitarians to prolong carnal pleasures, but most agreed that the mental discipline was far too demanding for the ordinary man, and that its effectiveness would probably be obvious to those who practiced the technique in nine months. In addition, doctors suspected that prolonging the sexual act without proper ejaculation induced discomfort, atrophy, urethritis, insomnia, impotency, melancholia, and severe spermatorrhea. The only result of Noyes's sexual experimentation, claimed one skeptic, was the substitution of "wet dreams" for natural ejaculation.

Since complete intercourse was thought to expend a large amount of vital force, J. H. Greer, M.D., in his *Woman Know Thyself* (1902), suggested an alternative to Noyes's technique of "male continence" called Zugassent's Discovery. The husband and wife united as in intercourse but refrained from orgasm, achieving "magnetic harmony" through the exchange of vital magnetic currents. Similarly, Ida C. Craddock, the author of *Right Marital Living* (1899), divided the sexual organs into "love organs" and those intended for procreation. With proper control, she wrote, the husband could achieve orgasm without ejaculation of semen, thus reabsorbing the semen into the system and conserving male vitality. . . .

During the first half of the nineteenth century, druggists reported more purchases of abortive drugs than contraceptive devices and germicides. . . . By the 1870s, however, the trade changed to contraceptive devices such as the pessarium occlusivum, which Annie Besant advertised in private circulars to women. Besant's "womb veil" or "tent" consisted of a small rubber cap surrounded at the rim by a flexible ring. Women sometimes used vaginal injections of carbolic acid to prevent conception and avoid venereal contagion, a solution popular in many houses of prostitution. Other contraceptive douches consisted of injections of cold or warm water, solutions of bicarbonate of soda, borax, bichloride of mercury (which, improperly used, caused mercurial poisoning), potassium bitartrate, alum, dilute vinegar, lysol, creolin, and other agents to remove or sterilize the sperm. Tampons of sponge, cotton, and other substances were retained in the vagina for as long as twenty-four hours after intercourse to prevent conception. Physicians who recommended "prevention" sometimes prepared vaginal suppositories of cocoa butter and boric acid to be applied before intercourse to act as a germicide. Tannic acid and bichloride of mercury were also used in place of boric acid, while olive oil or glycerin were substitutes for the cocoa butter. Another contraceptive device consisted of borated cotton pledgets which were attached to a piece of string and pushed into the vagina against the cervix. Women who were less knowledgeable employed handkerchiefs to cleanse the vagina after intercourse, and one physician recalled a patient who was accustomed to wiping out her uterus with a crochet needle around which she attached a piece of cloth. One popular belief was that if a woman engaged in vigorous exercise (usually dancing or horseback-riding) after intercourse, she would avoid conception. . . .

To be sure, there were more exotic forms of contraception. Karl Butten-stedt in *Happiness in Marriage* (1904) and Richard E. Funcke in *A New Revelation of Nature* (1906) maintained that if a husband continued to suck his wife's breasts after a child was weaned, natural contraception would be continued, and give "everlasting life for humanity." The woman's milk was an "elixir of life" for the male partner as well as a contraceptive. As Funcke wrote: "Thou shalt not leave thy vital force unutilized; thou shalt not menstruate unless thou hast the firm will and desire to become pregnant; thou shalt allow thy vital force in the form of milk to flow from thy breasts for the benefit and enjoyment of other human beings." . . .

Most Protestant church leaders ignored the question of contraception altogether. While condemning feticide, they seldom dealt with the problem of prevention, preferring to leave the matter to private conscience. As one Presbyterian minister wrote in 1899, "the sin [of prevention], if sin existed, must be a purely physiological one, and in physiological matters the clergy must sit at the physicians' feet as learners." The Catholic clergy, on the other hand, was united in its condemnation, despite the fact that its laity represented a significant percentage of patients requesting prevention information. Although many medical men agreed with the church's position, they seldom expressed public support because of medical repugnance to the church's cast-iron position against craniotomy, which had for decades antagonized the moral sense of doctors who favored the life of the mother over the life of the fetus. . . .

Most American Victorians were aware of contraceptive devices but, for a variety of reasons, clung to the rigid sexual mores of the day. Women authors of purity manuals were even more vocally opposed to birth-control practices. While there were, of course, feminists like Annie Besant and later Margaret Sanger who sought greater sexual freedom through birth-control techniques, most sex-in-life authors chose the route of "marital continence," which they hoped would lessen women's role as sex objects. Marital continence meant the "voluntary and entire absence from sexual indulgence in any form, and having complete control over the passions by one who knows their power, and who, but for his pure life and steady will, not only could, but would indulge them." Women reared under the influence of the WCTU and other purity-minded organizations felt that artificial birth control would destroy the sanctity of the home circle by bringing into it the tools of the street prostitute, and within the framework of nineteenth-century male guardian-ship would perpetuate in a most licentious manner women's continuing role as sex objects. Moreover, manual writers shied from talk of birth-control techniques after the legislative successes of purity fanatic Anthony Com-stock, secretary of the New York Society for the Suppression of Vice, and the subsequent passage of anticontraceptive laws in some twenty-four states after 1879. The American attitude toward the discussion of sex (which George Bernard Shaw called "Comstockery") forced manual writers to broach the subject in only the vaguest language, for public morality judged such practices as unnatural and illegal. For these reasons, most married couples either avoided the issue completely by leaving the problem to chance or practiced variations of marital continence.

In reply to those Malthusians who advocated limitation of families without contraceptive devices, women responded with the demand for total abstinence, prohibiting coition except when there was a desire for parenthood. "No pandering to sexual indulgence" or "gratification of the lower nature" was permitted as long as the slightest unwillingness for parenthood existed. Those not wishing to have children had to have a "proper manly and womanly Christian temperance in those things." Too many marriages were nothing more than licensed prostitution in which the lower natures of both man and wife were "petted and indulged at the expense of the higher." Since the sexual act caused an expenditure of vital force in the male body, any release of seminal fluid "prostituted to the simple gratification of fleshy desire" weakened the husband and endangered the well-being of his physical and mental state. He should conserve his seminal fluid for limited coition only — the implication being that the vital energy not expended in the sexual act would then be diverted to the "mental and moral force of the man." According to purity advocates, the conservation of sperm illuminated the mind and soul through its assimilation by the brain, where it was expended in thought. . . .

Purity manuals expressed hope that married couples would accept strict continence as a standard in marital relations. If parents would assure their children that sexual powers in the human species were properly used only for reproduction, "the whole veil of mystery would be blown away and the subject would then be presented in a beautiful and ennobling light." There would be no further necessity for prostitution, no need for governmental regulation of vice, no white slave traffic, nor further reason for the degradation of women. The world would be safe from the greatest social evil of life, and men and women would meet "upon the basis of intellectual congeniality" without the perplexing issue of sex, and, for the first time, "the delight of friendship, now practically unknown, could be enjoyed to the fullest extent." If sexual continence prevailed in marriage, the husband and wife would not have to live as "comparative strangers" in separate bedrooms, in constant fear of inflammatory desires. "If the human body were always held in thought as a sacred temple," wrote Wood-Allen, "its outlines would be suggestive of nothing but the purest and holiest feelings." . . .

Delos F. Wilcox dedicated his *Ethical Marriage* (1900) to youths and maidens "who do what they think they ought to do, admitting no ideal that is impractical, and omitting no duty that is seen." Using a Spencerian formula, he, like Henry Finck, argued that the institution had undergone an evolution from brute savagery to nomadic marriage, and finally to ethical marriage. The new ethical family was founded on the principles of love, intelligence, and duty, and would perpetuate only those traits which it considered of "superior social value." Evolutionary law ruled that sexual intercourse "should be had at long intervals and during a limited portion of adult life." Any nonprocreative sexual union was contrary to nature's laws. In practice, this meant that married couples ought to be "loyally affectionate" until they chose to have children, at which time they "should have a single complete sexual congress. . . . Time should then be given to ascertain whether or not conception has taken place. Normally menstruation ceases during pregnancy. If the menses are not interrupted, the probabilities are strong that conception has not taken place, and then another copulation will be necessary. Intercourse may take place once a month until there is reason to believe that the woman is pregnant, or until the season favorable to reproduction has passed. After impregnation has been secured there should be no more intercourse until another child is desired."

Wilcox, whose ideas reflected a confusing mixture of eugenics, the perfectionist tendencies of Shaker Mother Ann Lee, and the crusading vengeance of Anthony Comstock, believed that continence was a practical answer to the sexual passions in marriage. Speaking from his own experience, however, he argued that the mere desire for sexual continence was not enough; married couples needed to take specific steps to prevent the unleashing of their unhealthy passions. These steps included an understanding that marriage "should make no more immediate difference in their lives than the taking of a roommate does to a student," avoiding a honeymoon, the use of separate beds or sleeping quarters, abstaining from stimulants, encouraging exercise, and finally, the proper education of children to prevent sexual curiosity or abnormal habits. . . .

Nearly all manuals restricted sexual relations during pregnancy. The very fundamentals of Victorian science and morality ruled against this practice. "The submission of an unwilling wife or the sexual irritability that may be engendered through the mother who gives herself up to the indulgences of desire" would jeopardize the physical and moral future of the child. The upheaval of the child's embryonic home "through gusts of passion" left an indelible mark on his character. Coition during pregnancy, according to one physician, predisposed children to epilepsy. "The natural excitement of the nervous system in the mother by such a cause," he wrote, "cannot operate otherwise than inflicting injury upon the tender germ in the womb." Kellogg believed that the mental and nervous sensations of the mother molded the brain of the fetus, and when the mother indulged in sexual relations, she increased the chances of the child's developing an abnormal sexual instinct. "Here is the key to the origin of much of the sexual precocity and depravity which curse humanity," wrote Kellogg. "Every pang of grief [or passion] you feel," added Orson S. Fowler in his book on maternity, "will leave its painful scar on the forming disk of their soul."

The child's future depended upon his mother's conduct during pregnancy, a conduct that concerned not only her diet, but also her reading material, relations with her husband, and her most private thoughts. Martin Luther Holbrook, M.D., in his book *Stirpiculture,* explained why some children were more virtuous and beautiful than others. A Darwinian who crusaded for healthy marriages on the basis of community-controlled eugenics and high ethical behavior, he pointed out that the child's character, morals, and even physical appearance depended on how the parents conducted themselves during the pregnancy. "In my early married life," confessed one mother, "my husband and I learned how to live in holy relations, after God's ordinance. My husband lovingly consented to let me live apart from him during the time I carried his little daughter under my heart, and also while I was nursing her." These were the happiest days in her life. "My husband and I were never so tenderly, so harmoniously, or so happily related to each other," she exclaimed, "and I never loved him more deeply than during these blessed months." As a result of the parents' relationship, the child born at this time was beautifully formed, and grew to be virtuous, healthy, and extremely happy. Several years later, wrote Holbrook, the same mother became pregnant with a second child, but during that period, her husband "had become contaminated with the popular idea that even more frequent relations were permissible during pregnancy." Yielding to her husband's rapacious demands, the wife became "nervous and almost despairing." The child was born sickly and nervous, and after five years of constant difficulty, died "leaving them sadder and wiser." . . .

The Victorian era has pictured itself to later generations in terms of stereotypes, sometimes conflicting, often grossly overdrawn. In many cases, however, the gap between the stereotypes handed down to twentieth-century America and life in Victorian society only reflects the disparity between the pretensions of a middle-class society and the reality it often chose to ignore. In one sense, there seems to be a certain status-suffix evident in its aspiring view of the role of sex. The sex-in-life manuals were an arena for imaginative writing in nineteenth-century society, and appear at times to shroud the urban middle class in a romantic arcadia set apart from the lusty vernacular of urban immigrants and city slums. The manuals were caricatures of subjective prejudices and assumptions concerning middle-class values and behavior. The romanticization of family and marriage portrayed in the manuals was not so much a plea for reshaping the marriage relationship as it was a technique for explaining the incongruity that existed between middle-class "principles" and reality. The middle class measured its greatness not only by its achievements but also by its principles — a situation which allowed it to blame any discrepancy upon a gallery of villains. Manual writers stalked the victims of sexual deviation in the empirical reality of the "lower races" and working classes, where disease, poverty, and depravity seemed to spawn the world's problems.

As moral pronouncements of society, the sex-in-life manuals became documentaries of middle-class myths seeking both to justify the prevailing social and moral fabric of Victorian America and to explain, without a sense of personal guilt, the survival of a less imaginative reality. The history of the century's manuals of love and marriage reveals an effort to interpret and grapple with the lack of tradition in urban life, and to reach for an understanding of sexual relationships in a way that would give added relevance to the class consciousness of middle-class America. A sense of pretension, along with a very real sense of educational, ethical, and economic superiority to the rawness of working-class America, combined to create a thinly concealed romantic moral code, steeped in fictitious parables and impossible ideals, struggling to assert a new and imaginative perspective for the American class structure. The aspirations of the middle class form a vital link in a proper understanding of sexual attitudes of the nineteenth century. It was this group in America which, in the absence of a hereditary class system, sought to create a moral and ethical barrier between themselves and the working class. And it was perhaps the rising expectations of the working class which allowed such pretensions to go unchallenged in spite of an obvious discrepancy between pretensions and reality.

STUDY GUIDE

1. What role did Victorians assign to the sexual urge according to the authors? How did their view of sex fit into the evolutionary theory they believed in?

2. Contrast the view of women's role in sex in the early nineteenth century with their role after mid-century.

3. What preparations for a passive sex life for the woman were made before she reached maturity? How would you contrast this regimen with the advice on child-rearing offered today by Dr. Benjamin Spock or other physicians? Do any of the taboos listed by the Hallers still hold?

4. The authors appear to disapprove both of the various birth-control techniques used by middle-class Victorians and of their practice of marital continence. Given the primitive contraceptives available to these men and women and their desire — for purposes of economic and social mobility — to limit family size, what alternatives to continence were available? Explore.

5. At the end of their essay the Hallers point out that the rigid sex code prescribed by these manuals served a moral and social function for middle-class Americans. Explain.

BIBLIOGRAPHY

Further information on the relations between the sexes in nineteenth-century America will be found in the following: G. J. Barker-Benfield, *Horrors of the Half-Known Life* (New York, 1976); Carroll Smith-Rosenberg, "The Hysterical Woman: Sex Roles and Role Conflict in Nineteenth-Century America," *Social Research,* Vol. 39 (Winter 1972), pp. 652–678, and "The Cycle of Femininity: Puberty and Menopause in Nineteenth-Century America," *Feminist Studies,* Vol. I (Winter-Spring 1973), pp. 58–72, and, with Charles Rosenberg, "The Female Animal: Medical and Biological Views of Women in Nineteenth-Century America," *Journal of American History,* Vol. LX (Sept. 1973), pp. 332–356; and Ann Douglas Wood, "The Fashionable Diseases: Women's Complaints and Their Treatment in Nineteenth-Century America," *Journal of Interdisciplinary History,* Vol. IV (Summer 1973), pp. 25–52. Related studies include Isaac Harvey Flack's survey of gynecology, *The Eternal Eve: The History of Gynecology and Obstetrics* (New York, 1951); Lawrence Lader's *Abortion* (Indianapolis, Ind., 1966); Norman E. Himes, *Medical History of Contraception* (Baltimore, 1936); David J. Pivar's *Purity Crusade: Sexual Morality and Social Control, 1868–1900* * (Westport, Conn., 1973), a study of antivice reformers; James C. Mohr, *Abortion in America* (New York, 1978); and James Reed, *From Private Vice to Public Virtue: The Birth Control Movement and American Society since 1830* (New York, 1978).

The classic treatment of the American family is Arthur W. Calhoun's *Social History of the American Family from Colonial Times to the Present,* 3 vols. (Cleveland, 1917–1919). Brief, yet scholarly, surveys of the status of women in American society will be found in Mary P. Ryan, *Womanhood in America: From Colonial Times to the Present* * (New York, 1975); Gerda Lerner, *The Woman in American History* * (Reading, Mass., 1971); and Lois W. Banner, *Women in Modern America: A Brief History* * (New York, 1974). A judicious anthology of articles on the role of women in various periods of American history will be found in Jean E. Friedman and William G. Shade, *Our American Sisters: Women in American Life and Thought* * (Boston, 1976); and another on the family in Michael Gordon, ed., *The American Family in Social-Historical Perspective* * (2nd ed., New York, 1978); and Mary S. Hartman and Lois Banner, eds., *Clio's Consciousness Raised* * (New York, 1974).

III PARADOXES OF PROGRESSIVISM

The two decades between the opening of the twentieth century and the end of World War I were dominated by strenuous efforts on the part of a large number of Americans to improve the quality of life at home and abroad. Progressive reformers assumed that behavior could be altered and the performance of institutions improved. As Eric F. Goldman wrote in *Rendezvous with Destiny,* Progressives believed that "an environment ... made by human beings ... could be changed by human beings."

Until 1914, Americans concentrated largely on domestic reforms. At the grass-roots level, there were numerous programs to improve municipal government and administration. Some reform mayors — Tom L. Johnson in Cleveland and Samuel M. "Golden Rule" Jones in Toledo — sought to reduce trolley-car fares and inaugurate municipally owned utilities to compete with those that were privately owned. Seth Low in New York and James D. Phelan in San Francisco were more concerned with efficiency than equality and consequently set about modernizing the collection of taxes and the budgetary procedures of their municipal administrations. Still other Progressives sought to enact legislation for urban zoning, the inspection of the milk supply, or the improvement of public education. Reforms on the state and national level followed and paralleled these early local efforts. And while the ultimate worth of these efforts is being reassessed by historians, many of the instrumentalities through which our public utilities are regulated and our bank system coordinated originated in the legislation of the Progressive era.

Activism dominated our foreign policy as well in the Progressive period. Following the end of the Spanish-American War in 1898, the American people turned their attention outward. The student of American history can draw a line from the assertiveness of Theodore Roosevelt's acquisition of the Panama Canal in 1903 to Woodrow Wilson's intervention in Mexico and our entry, in 1917, into World War I. The ebullient confidence with which we entered the Great War — in Wilson's words, "to make the world safe for democracy" — is closely related to the profound disillusionment that set in after the war. The failure of Wilson to achieve at Versailles the realization of his Fourteen Points, in many ways a Progressive program for international affairs, led the nation to reject the treaty and the League of Nations written into it.

The selections that follow illustrate the realities and the paradoxes of the Progressive era. A typical immigrant enclave, the Greek ghetto in urban America, is the subject of the first essay. The second, on the settlement house, describes one of the principal institutions through which Progressive reformers sought to acculturate the immigrant. Far less attention was paid by the Progressive reformers to the blacks in the South or, as the third selection makes amply clear, to those making their way North as well. The final selection offers a glimpse of another negative aspect of the Progressive era — the violations of the constitutional rights of native and foreign-born Americans in the witch-hunt called the Red Scare of 1919.

Theodore Saloutos

A Greek-American (c. 1910) attired in the uniform of the evzones, an elite Greek army unit, topped with an American straw hat.

8

THEODORE SALOUTOS

The Greek Ghetto

The United States is a nation of immigrants. Some, like the English and the Scotch-Irish, came in large numbers prior to the Revolution of 1776; others, like the Germans and the Scandinavians, came in the nineteenth century, while still others — the Italians, the Slavs, the Poles, and the Russo-Polish Jews — came at the very end of the nineteenth century and in the first three decades of the twentieth. Some thirty million immigrants came to the United States in the nineteenth and twentieth centuries — five million from 1815 to 1860, ten million from 1860 to 1890, and fifteen million from 1890 to 1924.

After the turn of the century, social scientists and historians divided the immigrants into two principal categories: the "old" and the "new." The first group included those born in Northern and Western Europe, while the "new" immigration had its sources in Southern and Eastern Europe. Unfortunately, a number of native Americans favoring immigration restriction made unfair comparisons between these two immigrant groups. With little justification, the "old" immigrants were described as having come to America out of idealistic motives and as having an inborn instinct for freedom and liberty; while the "new" immigrants, they charged, came to the United States for material gain and would make little contribution to the democratic ideals and institutions of our country. Those who opposed America's policy of unrestricted immigration won their fight with the passage of the Immigration Restriction Act of 1924. This legislation limited immigration from Europe to a maximum of 150,000 and provided that the overwhelming majority of these immigrants come from the British Isles and Northern Europe. The gates were shut in 1924, but not before many immigrants from Europe established ghettoes for themselves in the nation's urban centers. These ethnic enclaves provided a measure of security in an alien, and sometimes hostile, environment.

From Professor Theodore Saloutos' *The Greeks in the United States,* we have selected a description of the Greek ghetto in a typical metropolis shortly after the turn of the century. The ghetto experience, the institutions, and the old-world values described by Professor Saloutos can easily be translated into the cultural context of other ghettoes — those enclaves established in the same decades and often in the same neighborhoods by the Italians, the Poles, the Slavs, and the Russo-Polish Jews. Those groups, like the Greek-Americans described in this essay, were trying to fuse the old and the new, to preserve aspects of their European past in order to ease the process of their inevitable Americanization.

The first immigrants attempted to graft the social and cultural life of the Old World onto the environment of the New. And to a considerable extent they succeeded. During the early 1900s, living within relatively compact areas bred a special community spirit. The Greeks built churches; they sponsored schools, social events, church programs, theatrical and musical productions; and the men continued that most ubiquitous and popular of all Greek institutions — the coffeehouse.

The perpetuation of the Greek language became a prime concern. Community leaders, priests, the press, all joined in the demand that children born of Greek parents learn the language that "gave light to the world." This was a mission that had to be carried out, as well as a heritage that had to be preserved. The missionary zeal shown for the study of the parent language probably explains why so many children before the First World War learned to speak Greek before they learned English.

An immigrant with a family to rear faced the dual task of learning to speak English himself and of instilling an appreciation for the Greek language in his children. In this he faced an uphill, and eventually a losing, struggle; for, despite the risk of antagonizing his children, he sometimes placed greater emphasis on Greek than on English. In this respect the immigrant had greater foresight than those critics who advised him against it, for he himself needed an avenue of communication. He knew that his children could learn English in the public schools, but who could teach them Greek? With him it was a matter of necessity as much as it was one of culture. This was an unusual situation. For here was an immigrant parent who, for the most part, had little or no formal education, worrying lest his children reach adulthood in ignorance of the native tongue. He was haunted by this fear. Patriotic organizations, the press, the parish priest, and letters from the homeland kept drumming it into his ears. On the other hand, he was harassed by critics, Greek and non-Greek, frequently his own children, who kept telling him that since he had come to the United States he was obliged to speak English and forget Greek.

The church community, as a rule, accepted the responsibility of offering instruction in the Greek language. This occurred as soon as a sufficient number of families had settled in a district, and after a core of small merchants and tradesmen had taken command. The community school normally made its appearance after the church had been established. Often the parish priest served as the first teacher.

Beginning late in the afternoon — after the public-school day had come to an end — and continuing into the early evening, the Greek school was conducted in the most convenient quarters available. Children of various ages, sometimes as young as five and six, gathered in a rented hall, a vacant store, the basement of a church, or a community center to commence their study of Greek. Maintaining the interest of the child was a challenging and frequently frustrating experience, which taxed the ingenuity of even the most dedicated teacher. The objectives of these schools varied little. Most commonly stressed was the need of perpetuating the modern Greek language and of preventing the child from being raised in complete ignorance. The latter was particularly true when so many of the first immigrants still dreamed of returning to Greece. The more patriotic — the ardent nationalists — spoke of the need of rearing the children as Greeks, and as one well-drilled youngster put it: "If you want Greeks give us Greek schools." Another spoke of the urgency "to imbue our American-born children with . . . the greatness of our race . . . teach them the Greek language and impose upon them the Greek character and Greek virtue." This would mark the beginning of a new era, the emergence of a new kind of citizen, one who would be proud of both the United States and Greece. . . .

Experience bore out that more than oratory and strongly worded resolutions were needed to support the language schools. Finding satisfactory central locations for the schools, securing properly trained teachers, raising the necessary finances, weathering controversies and shifts in policies — these problems taxed the patience of parents, pupils, and priests. When the immigrants began dispersing, the problems multiplied. Finding qualified teachers of modern Greek who understood the needs of children born in the United States was an endless quest. In many instances the classroom teacher was the community priest, whose knowledge of the United States and the English language was about as limited as that of the parents of his pupils. Sometimes a graduate of a Greek gymnasium or, on rare occasions, a former student from the University of Athens was available. For the child, attending public school during the day, in which he was taught by an American-born, American-educated teacher, and then attending a Greek school in the late afternoon, presided over by a Greek-born, Greek-educated teacher, was often a contradictory and confusing experience.

The Greek school scene in Chicago in 1914, which probably was typical of conditions in other cities, must have been a shock to many people's patriotic sentiments, for very few of the city's estimated five hundred children born of Greek parents participated. The classes were held in dark and dreary rooms; the instruction was dull and uninspired; the children were unhappy over having to attend a Greek school after a full day of classes; cooperation between teachers and parents was lacking. The two Chicago schools were so inadequately equipped with desks and materials that many parents withdrew their children after a brief attendance. In 1915, according to one observer, the two schools graduated one child for every five attending the city's public schools. . . .

The formation of fraternal societies was as much a part of community life as was the establishment of Greek-language schools. Perhaps the prominence of these societies and the conspicuous role they performed is best illustrated by the comforting letter that a candidate for mayor of a town in Greece received from his son: "Father, do not feel very badly because of your failure to become the mayor of our town, for I have been elected president of our lodge here in America." Here he touched on one of the most delicate phases of community life. The immigrants demonstrated a mania for forming local, or *topika,* societies that many Americans found difficult to understand. It appears that every village and minute parish in Greece was represented in the United States by a society with an impressive array of banners, lengthy constitutions, and high-sounding names. The majority of these organizations, at least in the beginning, were composed of fifteen to thirty people and governed by councils of twelve to fifteen. Gold tassels and buttons adorned the officers' uniforms, which were worn on every possible occasion. An essential part of their equipment was the organization seal, whose use was confined exclusively to the president and the secretary. About one hundred such societies were in existence in the United States as early as 1907; in New York alone there were thirty.

Onlookers undoubtedly found it difficult to understand this zeal for societies. Four, five, and even more persons lived in cheerless rooms and denied themselves the ordinary comforts of life. Yet they formed societies, paid dues, elected officers, carried on endless debates, and raised money to aid their villages. When one curious American asked the meaning of this, the reply was: "Every organization has a president, a vice-president, a secretary, and a treasurer, and that's something." Of course, there was more than the usual quest for status and recognition behind these efforts. They reflected the localism and provincialism of a naturally provincial people, and these traits were transplanted to the United States. Greece was a country of small valleys and plains shut off by mountains, making communications between different parts of the country extremely difficult. This proved contagious, and it bred organizations of a local character in America as well as in Greece. . . .

The immigrants' organizations were also, of course, characterized by activities: mutual aid, charity, and humanitarianism. These bodies came into existence before many of the members knew how to speak English; they were, as indicated, organized according to villages, towns, districts, and islands. They collected money to build schools, bridges, waterworks, churches, roads, and other public works in their native villages. They also furnished a meeting place for old acquaintances and for the formation of new friendships, entertainment, political activities, and outlets for those floods of oratory that flowed so profusely from every Greek.

The localism manifested in the societies also was reflected in the railroads, mines, and factories in which Greeks labored. A Lacedemonian, a Thessalian, an Arcadian, a Macedonian, or a Cretan could generally be found working with compatriots from the same village or province. The same divisions were observed among the coffeehouses and restaurants; the Lacedemonians had theirs, as did the Macedonians, the Arcadians, the Messinians, the Stereoladitans. The Greeks tended to work, sleep, eat, and drink according to villages, districts, and provinces. . . .

Also founded on a local, though more permanent, basis was the *kinotitos,* or community. The kinotitos was the governing body of the group. It provided for the establishment of a church and school; arranged for the election of officers; administered funds; hired and fired priests, teachers, and janitors. This community-wide organization was the equivalent of the New England town meeting (which all patriotic Greeks would agree was Hellenic in concept).

Such a community organization was headed by a board of directors, elected by dues-paying members. In the beginning the actions of this organization were a true barometer of community opinion. But unfortunately they also set the stage for ceaseless feuds that rocked colony after colony to the very foundations; sometimes they resulted in harsh and long lawsuits that left deep scars. These community-wide quarrels on some occasions were instigated by priests; on others, by lay leaders seeking to shape and guide the policies of the community. They usually were fought out in the open, for undercover feuding was foreign to the average immigrant. The disputes revolved around the qualifications of priests, teachers, and board members, the political affiliations of rival leaders, the use of funds, church and school policies, construction projects, the use of the English language, and kindred topics. For a time, these community organizations were never at a loss for issues over which to argue.

A third kind of organization in this era was national and patriotic in nature, such as the Panhellenic Union. The Union hoped to enroll every Greek in the country; its fees were small, its ceremonies simple, and its promised benefits liberal. The branches in every major city of the country furnished a forum for the expression of Greek national interests, and they attracted considerable attention. The Union was founded in New York in 1907, on the premise that most Greeks would return to their homeland; it would help them perpetuate their faith and language in this country and, when the occasion arose, to help to mobilize them for military service. When the Balkan Wars broke out, the Union assumed the characteristics of a semimilitary order. Its local branches attempted to discharge the duties of recruiting offices.

No account of a Greek community would be complete without reference to one of the most widespread of all immigrant institutions, the *kaffeneion*, or coffeehouse. For it was to the coffeehouse that the immigrant hurried after his arrival from Greece or from a neighboring community. It was in the coffeehouse that he sought out acquaintances, addresses, leads to jobs, and solace during the lonely hours. One could frequently hear him say: "I'll see you at the coffeehouse . . . I went by the coffeehouse . . . I heard it at the coffeehouse."

The coffeehouse appeared whenever a sufficient number of Greeks and an enterprising compatriot had settled in a particular neighborhood. Little capital was needed to start one. A store was rented; a few marble-top tables and wire-twisted chairs, several pounds of coffee, a few narghiles [water pipes], and a dozen or so decks of playing cards were collected; and the coffeehouse became a reality. On the walls the proprietor was likely to hang lithographic portraits of his political favorites and those of his patrons; in communities in which [Eleutherios] Venizelos [Greek republican leader] was the idol, pictures of the kings of Greece were not to be seen. There might also be posted battle scenes of some Greek victory over the Turks, a map of Greece, a military hero, a revolutionary leader, or some modern Greek Hercules. Coffeehouses bore names such as "Acropolis," "Parthenon," "Paradisos," "Venizelos," "Messinia," "Arcadia," "Synantisis," and "Lesche." In the rear of the house was the kitchen in which the proprietor brewed the coffee which he himself served to his patrons. Lokum, baklava, and other Near Eastern delicacies were in evidence, as were bottled soft drinks.

The coffeehouse was a community social center to which the men retired after working hours and on Saturdays and Sundays. Here they sipped cups of thick, black Turkish coffee, lazily drew on narghiles, played cards, or engaged in animated political discussion. Here congregated gesticulating Greeks of all kinds: railroad workers, factory hands, shopkeepers, professional men, the unemployed, labor agitators, amateur philosophers, community gossips, cardsharks, and amused spectators.

The air of the average coffeehouse was choked with clouds of smoke rising from cigarettes, pipes, and cigars. Through the haze one could see the dim figures of card players or hear the stentorian voices of would-be statesmen discussing every subject under the sun. No topic was beyond them. European problems were resolved readily, and all were at their peak when the politics of Greece were discussed. On the marble-top tables one could see diagrams of Near Eastern divisions, military strategies, and imaginary advances or retreats. One might find a plan for the bombing of the Dardenelles or a likeness of Eleutherios Venizelos. Quarrels began and amnesties were declared here. When the subject under discussion was not politics, it was the weather, the stock market, the faults of others, the capabilities or limitations of the community priest and teacher, life in the hereafter and what language departed souls spoke, and the possibilities of a Greek's becoming president of the United States. Few listened, and most talked as though they would explode if they did not talk. On visitors, especially those not understanding Greek, such discussions could have an almost terrifying effect; they could easily have been mistaken for quarrels. But they were all verbal; no blows were delivered, "except those received by the tables or chairs." Greeks, like other southern Europeans, accompanied "their words with multiple gestures of hand and head, maybe even the foot, or the whole body."

The coffeehouse served as a recreation center. Tables were filled with players deeply involved in some card game, frequently the intricacies of *skampili*. The game usually was vociferous, with many exclamations and disputes, loud acclaim on the part of the victor and threatened recriminations on the part of the vanquished. After tiring of cards, a new amusement could be found, sometimes music. Perhaps a violin or two would be brought out, "a bellying guitar of powerful resonance, and a zither-like instrument called the 'santouri.' " After a few minor chords, "a waiting and strikingly mournful cadence" became the signal for two or maybe four *palikaria* to step out on the floor and clasp hands. After the tables were pushed aside, spectators would gather round and shout encouragement as the dancers began their steps. The Greek dances consisted of "many gyrations, leapings, stampings, twisting of the body, alternating with many short steps and breaking and reclasping hands with loud slaps. Now and then a dancer would whirl swiftly on his toe, slapping his leg or the bottom of the other foot." A successful rendering of the dance was rewarded by applause, drinks for the performers, and the inevitable call, *Eis hygeia sas* (To your health). . . .

Less important were strong-man exhibitions, floor shows, and Greek cinema productions. The strong-man demonstrations appealed especially to those with a liking for Tarzan pictures and to youngsters, who gaped at the weightlifting and rod-bending antics of the performers. The strong man generally prefaced his performance with a few preliminary remarks to the effect that he wanted to demonstrate, in person, that the Herculean powers of the ancient Greeks had not disappeared. After displaying his physical prowess with gusto, he concluded his performance by talking about physical fitness. What were called floor shows attracted slight attention, but we may note that they were attended by an all-male audience, were Oriental in flavor (of the "belly-dance" variety), and were staged by females of questionable talent and virtue.

Some of the coffeehouses achieved notoriety by becoming gambling houses that were periodically raided by the police. The police files of a number of cities were filled with the names of persons confined for such activities. Many owners and patrons were fined; some coffeehouses were placed under police surveillance; others were temporarily closed. On one occasion Mayor Carter Harrison of Chicago condemned the coffeehouses as centers of vice and evil, classified them with "dime-a-dance" halls, and opium dens, and suggested placing a heavy tax on them. An uninformed and antagonistic general public that gathered its impressions from reading the daily newspapers, as well as Greek compatriots who were hostile to the coffeehouse on general principle, were prone to agree with the mayor. But the picture portrayed by the mayor was obviously out of proportion. Few would deny that coffeehouses catering to the gambling instincts of lonely and frustrated immigrants should be condemned. But those observers who knew about the gambling knew that it was of the petty variety engaged in by young men away from home for the first time, who craved a kind of excitement that would bring them relief from a drab, humdrum existence.

The raiding of the coffeehouses and the arrest of their patrons had a humorous as well as an embarrassing side. Since many of the houses bore historical or classical names, it was amusing to read in the newspapers headlines such as "Parthenon and Seventeen Greeks Arrested," "Acropolis and Venizelos Taken," "The Acropolis Closed," or "Paradise Is Raided." In such instances the ridicule was worse than the disgrace.

Responsible community leaders and newspaper editors admonished the proprietors and patrons to refrain from practices that brought shame upon their nationality. Young men were urged to shun the coffeehouses, to attend night school, and to improve themselves intellectually, vocationally, and physically. At the same time, the proprietors of clean and well-regulated coffeehouses were praised for providing dignified meeting places and recreational opportunities for their patrons. But the attacks to which the coffeehouses were subjected can easily cause one to overlook their constructive features. After all, they were social gathering places where men could meet and discuss a wide variety of subjects, where information and advice could be obtained, and where the otherwise lonely hours could be spent in the company of compatriots. Coffeehouses became veritable places of refuge for many immigrants who worked hard all day and slept in crowded and cheerless quarters. In some cases they were potent influences in keeping the immigrants content with their lot. Few objected to the closing of the more notorious and disreputable coffeehouses, the gambling dens that preyed on innocent and unsuspecting immigrants; but many, perhaps the majority, would have objected to the closing of all coffeehouses. "Let the gambling houses be closed — but not the *kaffeneia*."

In time the coffeehouse lost its appeal. A better-developed family life, an increased knowledge of the United States, the formation of new friendships, the acquisition of some knowledge of English, and the substitution of other forms of recreation helped bring about its decline. The coffeehouse eventually became a shadow of its former self, a memory of early immigrant days, even though in some communities it has survived to this day. One can only conjecture what the social life of the male immigrant would have been had it not been for the companionship and diversion provided by this very special Greek institution.

The observance of religious holidays, at least in these early years, were another important social outlet. Women often found their way to church on weekdays, as well as on Sundays, in observance of a saint's day or some special religious service. If a man also acquired the church-going habit, he soon discarded it; for attending church on weekdays meant the loss of a day's wages.

The nameday furnished still another occasion for celebration. In accordance with Old World customs, the nameday rather than the birthday was regularly observed. Friends and relatives visited the homes of the namesake to extend good wishes and share in the hospitality of the day. Music, dancing, and food were inevitable parts of these events. In the beginning the tendency was to celebrate them in a fashion reminiscent of the village from which the host came. With the passage of time, these celebrations were observed with declining regularity; only in the homes of the tradition-bound and the newer arrivals were they observed.

Christmas for the early immigrants was more of a religious holiday than a day of gift-giving and fun-making. Solemnity, the offering of greetings, and the singing of carols depicting the nativity predominated. Gift-giving was kept at a modest level. Unlike Christmas, New Year's Day, or St. Basil's Day, was the day for mirth. The zeal with which this was celebrated varied. In cities with large colonies and where tradition was strong, children carolers sometimes visited homes, coffeehouses, and stores singing "Agios Vasileos." They concluded their caroling by extending good wishes for the New Year and receiving small tokens from the listeners. Cutting the *Vasilopita,* or St. Basil's Cake, was also common. The eve of St. Basil's Day, and in some cases the entire holiday season, offered the men an excuse for swarming to the coffeehouses to test their luck at the gaming table.

Easter was far and away the most important holiday of the year. In Greece the pre-Lenten season was observed with much festivity and music, but in the United States this was rare, except perhaps in the earlier years.

Palm Sunday, or *Vaeion,* was accompanied with the customary good wishes to friends and neighbors. During Holy Week, church services were held every night. At the Thursday evening services the priest read from the Twelve Gospels, and on Good Friday (*Megale Paraskevi*) the churches literally bulged with people. This was the one day of the year when the once-a-year churchgoers turned out en masse.

Good Friday also was the day of the procession of the *Epitaphios,* a flower-decorated bier which depicted the entombment of Christ. In a large colony such as Chicago, the stores of Greek proprietors would be draped in purple and black on the night of Good Friday. At the late evening service, the priest would slowly move amidst the flare of hundreds of tapers held by those in attendance, the smoke of the incense, and the sound of chanting, and sprinkle the crowd with scented water. At the appropriate time the *Epitaphios* would be lifted and carried around the church amidst singing. In the larger cities this funeral procession was held out of doors, sometimes assuming the dimensions of a lengthy parade; but later this phase of the ceremony was eliminated.

The religious services for the week culminated at midnight on Saturday, when the mass was celebrated which ushered in Easter. At the approach of midnight, all church lights were extinguished. At the stroke of twelve, the priest appeared with a lighted candle and chanted to the parish: "Arise, and take the flame from the Eternal Lights, and praise Christ Who is risen from the dead!" "Truly He is risen," was the response. Then the congregation responded with the enthusiastic Resurrection Song. Meanwhile, the worshipers had taken light from the burning taper of the priest and passed it around until all the candles in the church were lighted.

In the earlier days, the singing of the Resurrection Song was the signal for the setting off of fireworks in the neighborhood of the church. Skyrockets and firecrackers were symbolic of all the believers in the faith. Inside the church, services continued. After the ceremony, the customary greetings were exchanged — "Christ is risen" and the response "Truly He is risen." The people then returned to their homes where they broke the Lenten fast with a ceremonial breakfast. The chief dish was *mayeritsa,* a stew consisting of tender liver, kidneys, and the intestines of the paschal lamb, seasoned with butter and thyme and covered with egg and lemon sauce. Salads, *retsina* (a cool resin wine), cakes, and sweets rounded out the annual feast. Before the meal, the family usually cracked red-dyed eggs, symbolizing the blood of Christ. The one whose egg best withstood the cracking was expected to have good luck during the year.

The desire for family security led to marriage as soon as the immigrant felt reasonably secure in his job or business. This, in many instances, furnished a feeling of permanence that made it difficult, if not unthinkable, for one return to Greece. It became the turning point in the lives of many. During the early years, when Greek women were scarce, the more tradition-bound of the men either journeyed to Greece in search of wives or else had prospective brides, vouched for by relatives and close friends, sent to the United States. This was a logical if not a very romantic procedure. Those immigrants who felt strongly about secure and indissoluble family ties had a natural preference for a mate of their own nationality and religion, plus an abhorrence of the manner in which so many marriages ended in America.

The attitude of some men, especially during the peak of the immigration movement, toward American women or women of other national backgrounds was one of misinformation, confusion, and poor judgment. Some who should have known better created the impression, through their boastful talk, that Greek women had a monopoly on virtue, homemaking, and belief in the family. They spoke of "American women," in particular, as though they were Amazons determined to rule or ruin their husbands. . . .

Marriage for a Greek woman in the United States meant that, as a rule, her parents were spared the need of providing a dowry. The scarcity of women naturally elevated their status and weakened all efforts to introduce the dowry system into the country. Those exposed to the American scene began viewing the dowry as "a barbarous system" that brought grief, unhappiness, and spinsterhood in Greece, but there were men who, if given their way, would have held fast to the custom. For all practical purposes, however, the tables were reversed in favor of the women.

Wedding receptions were commonplace in many communities. Native dances and music became a standard form of entertainment. The gusto with which they were celebrated sometimes achieved a hilarious note. After one ceremony, the officiating priest was seen with "a shiner on his left eye" and the groom with a head "lumpy from bruises." Originally the custom had been to throw rice at the newlyweds, but for some reason or other hard candy was substituted. Some suspected that the Greek confectioners, who were well represented in the trade, were responsible for this innovation. . . .

The status of women was somewhat improved over what it was in Greece, even though matrimony was almost the only career open to them. If custom had been observed, every boy born of Greek parents in this country would have supported his sister, provided her with financial aid at marriage time, and even made provisions for her after the death of her husband. Considering that in Greece women were kept in near seclusion, they adapted themselves reasonably well in this country. They tended to keep within their circle of Greek friends, but became active in charitable and church work. However, unlike women of other immigrant groups, they rarely worked outside the home unless it was in the family business. This was partly because the husband felt that it was a disgrace for his wife, even his sister, to work, and it was a question of his ability to provide for his family.

The Greek mother preferred the services of a midwife at childbirth; in part this was the result of habit. The midwife usually served as doctor, nurse, and family counselor, which meant preparing the food and caring for the children and husband, as well as the mother and newborn infant. The qualified midwife posed no problem; but those who were unqualified, and they seem to have outnumbered the others, had a demoralizing effect on the useful members of the profession and caused no end of concern to the health authorities.

The father generally was the master of the family, in fact as well as in theory. He believed in exercising his authority: "He is the family head who must be respected and obeyed. Children must submit to his will; womenfolk must uphold his decisions. He . . . governs his affairs according to the precedent laid down by his elders and in strict conformity with the established customs." It was he who put the seal of approval on the prospective marriage of a daughter.

One of the loudest complaints of the immigrant father, especially in the larger cities, were the restrictions imposed on him by American custom and law when he wanted to discipline his children. Many a father wished that he could have momentarily found himself in his native village, where he could handle in his own style an insubordinate son or daughter who had been spoiled by "America." His inability to discipline his children in the fashion he had grown accustomed to and respected, and the social pressures that prevented him from so doing, made him very critical of the "American system of rearing children."

The Greek-language press was a conspicuous and, for a time, very influential part of community life. It carried international news, especially stories about the affairs of Greece, including events in the villages and provinces, as well as about the Greek colonies in the United States. It kept the immigrant with little or no knowledge of English in contact with happenings in the homeland, perpetuated Old World feuds and gave rise to new ones. Greek publishers printed and sold newspapers and books geared to the needs of the people, which filled a useful function as immigrants continued to arrive, communities continued to grow, and the Greek language continued to be used. These newspapers had a rare opportunity to be of public service by acquainting the Greeks with American ways and ideas, but whether they did this is open to question.

In Greece there was a saying: "Either you give me a job or I'll bring out a newspaper." This kind of personal journalism got off to a quick start in the United States, even though newspapers with broader issues were also published. Newspapers, however, did appear for the sole purpose of attacking or praising certain individuals, of exploiting the weaknesses, prejudices, or petty vanities of the naive. Men presuming to be editors wrote vituperative articles against a particular individual, showed these handwritten pieces to rivals of the attacked man, received from them the cost of the newsprint or the salary of the typesetter, and then printed the articles as "newspapers."

There were newspapers engaged in personal journalism of another variety, less venal but equally pointless. Usually having a handful of subscribers, they wrote two- and three-column articles about the wedding of some patron, with laudatory accounts of the bride and groom and numerous other details; or they ascended to unbelievable heights in praising the deeds of some local society or organization. And there were newspapers which on one day would heap praises on Mr. X, calling him a merchant, a man of eminence, a friend of the people, and a patriot, and on the next would denounce him as a nonentity, a traitor, an illiterate, and a bootblack.

These newssheets multiplied rapidly and their activities became widespread. To one observer at least, anyone who knew how to read and write and was unwilling to work issued a newspaper; he cites the ten-line letter of an editor which had more than thirty mistakes in it as proof of this. This same observer, a lawyer and immigrant publisher, adds: "the influence of the press and clergy was so great on the future of the Greeks in America, that were it possible to say who worked most earnestly for the welfare of the immigrants, the latter [the clergy] were not only prototypes of friendly, educated, and progressive citizens, and finally Christians, but virtually angels." . . .

One of the most publicized and ambitious journalistic efforts was *Panhellinios* (The Panhellenic), edited by Socrates Xanthaky, who for ten years was editor-in-chief of *Atlantis*. It appeared in 1908 as a biweekly, was converted into a weekly, and waged five years of unremitting warfare against the newspaper Xanthaky formerly edited.

Chicago was a close rival of New York in the birth and death of newspapers. *Hellas,* the fourth Greek newspaper to be founded in the United States, appeared in Chicago in 1902 and was published until the latter part of 1912. The weekly *Hellinikos Astir* (Greek Star) began its existence in 1904 and is still being published. *Athene* began as a weekly in 1908; after the bankruptcy of *Panhellinios, Athene* was transferred to New York in the hope that it would acquire the patronage of the defunct newspaper and that of people dissatisfied with the policies of *Atlantis. Loxias* (The Blade), a weekly, began publication in 1908 and was issued for approximately ten years. Of longer life was the *Saloniki* of K. Salopoulos, which was a product of the Balkan Wars and an organ for Venizelist sentiments. Shorter-lived was the *Nea Hellas* of Speros Kotakis, who, beginning in 1921, also edited *Kathemerini* (The Daily).

The short lifespans of the Greek-language newspapers had an unsettling effect on the various communities, often arousing suspicion and distrust. To make matters worse, some outcasts from Athenian society and the world of letters posed as agents for various newspapers published in Greece or America, without the knowledge of the papers. As a result, Greek-Americans suffered from numerous bilkings by paying for their subscriptions in advance. It is apparent that more weeklies and dailies appeared than the public could support.

Some readers became very critical of newspapers that published articles in coarse dialect. Literate and status-conscious immigrants, who believed in preserving the "purist tradition," expressed their distaste for this type of journalism. They warned these publishers of *vlachika* that professors and students of the Greek language read Greek newspapers for the sake of retaining their knowledge of the language or gaining a greater familiarity with it. It would be a sad day indeed when the language of the shepherd became the universal language of the Greeks in the United States.

But despite these criticisms, many of which were justified, the Greek-language press rendered services to the members of the first generation that otherwise would have been difficult for them to obtain. It helped perpetuate the Greek language. It served as an intermediary between the immigrant and the New World; it kept him posted on happenings in the old country, even though the treatment of the news often was slanted; it published information on naturalization procedures, printed books and pamphlets that were of direct concern to the newcomer, and in various other ways came to his assistance. Still the role it played in perpetuating Old World quarrels and in fomenting political strife in the United States cannot be ignored. In any event, no treatment of the Greeks in the United States would be complete without an account of the activities of the Greek press.

It is apparent that social and community life, outside the church, . . . revolved around the numerous local societies that came into being, the all-male coffeehouse, the langauge school, the family and neighborhood ties that were being formed, the numerous weddings and receptions, the religious and nameday celebrations, and the discussions and controversies inspired by the Greek-language press. Everything tended to emphasize the idea of preserving a Hellenic identity. And nothing better demonstrated the effects that these community efforts were having than the readiness with which the Greek-Americans sprang to the defense of the mother country during the Balkan Wars of 1912–1913.

STUDY GUIDE

1. The Greeks and other immigrant groups established foreign-language schools. What purposes were they intended to serve and what problems did they confront?

2. Can you see why "societies" of various kinds would tend to be more numerous among immigrants than among native-born Americans? Explain.

3. The coffeehouse appears to have been central to the Greek immigrant community. Did other immigrant groups have similar places to meet? Did native Americans? If so, where; if not, why not?

4. Contrast the holiday observances in the Greek community with those of

small-town Americans described in Lewis Atherton's "The Small Town in the Gilded Age" (pp. 59–76).

5. How did the immigrant experience affect the status of women, marriage, and family relationships?

6. Assess the Greek-American newspapers, describing both positive and negative features.

BIBLIOGRAPHY

The topic of immigration has received a great deal of attention from American historians in recent years. Among the older volumes still worth reading are the following: Carl F. Wittke's *We Who Built America* * (Cleveland, 1939) and Marcus Lee Hansen's *The Immigrant in American History* * (Cambridge, Mass., 1940). More recent surveys include Maldwyn A. Jones's *American Immigration* * (Chicago, 1960) and *Destination America* (New York, 1976), and Philip A. M. Taylor's *The Distant Magnet: European Emigration to the U.S.A.* * (New York, 1971). An important contribution to the literature on immigration has been made in the following books by Oscar Handlin: *The Uprooted: the Epic Story of the Great Migrations That Made the American People* * (Boston, 1951); *Children of the Uprooted* * (New York, 1966); and *Immigration as a Factor in American History* * (Englewood Cliffs, N.J., 1959). Scholarly yet highly readable portraits of particular immigrant groups will be found in Humbert S. Nelli's book *Italians in Chicago: 1880–1930* * (New York, 1970); Moses Rischin's *The Promised City: New York's Jews, 1870–1914* * (Cambridge, Mass., 1962), and in the source of the above selection, Theodore Saloutos, *The Greeks in the United States* (Cambridge, Mass., 1964).

* Asterisk indicates book is available in a paperback edition.

Jane Addams and student, 1931. Settlement workers tried to teach art as well as practical skills to the "new" immigrants.

9

ALLEN F. DAVIS

The Settlement House

Although there is much controversy among historians concerning the precise character of Progressivism — that broadly based movement for social reform that flourished in the first decade and a half of the twentieth century — we can, in retrospect, divide the accomplishments of the Progressive movement into three broad categories: a greater measure of regulation of our economy, the democratization of politics, and what one historian has called a "quest for social justice." From the waning years of the nineteenth century until World War I, numerous programs were launched in order to solve a number of the social problems created by the unbridled industrial and urban growth in the late nineteenth century. Whatever may have been the motives of the Progressives — and here, too, historians disagree — it is clear that a large measure of idealism motivated the men and women who participated in the social-justice movements of this era.

One of the most idealistic and interesting institutions of the Progressive era was the settlement house, established among the immigrants in the nation's urban centers. These settlement houses — devoted to the cultural, artistic, vocational, and psychological uplifting of the immigrants and their families — clearly reflected the humanitarian strain that in part propelled the Progressive movement. The "settlement idea," as it is called by the movement's chronicler, Allen F. Davis, originated in London with the establishment of Toynbee Hall by two Oxford students who hoped, through this kind of institution, to bring culture to the workingmen of that city. Within a few years, the programs offered by settlement houses were broadened and the number of such institutions, in both England and the United States, increased.

Under the leadership of idealistic, yet highly competent and pragmatic pioneers — Jane Addams in Chicago, Robert A. Woods in Boston, and Lillian Wald in New York — settlement houses began to dot the ghettoes of American cities in the East and in the Middle West. In 1891, there were more than a hundred and by the end of the decade, more than four hundred. As Professor Davis's history of the movement in the United States, *Spearheads for Reform,* makes amply clear, the settlement houses touched upon many aspects of the lives of those they served: in addition to providing programs of a vocational, educational, and artistic character, the settlement house leaders agitated for more honest politics, better housing, more parks, schools and playgrounds, improved working conditions for adults, and a ban on child labor. In many instances, the settlement houses were the first institutions to recognize the plight of the urban Negro in the North, and a number of leaders in the movement actively participated in the organization of the National Association for the Advancement of Colored People.

The influence of this idealistic movement went beyond the Progressive era. In the concluding chapter of his book, Professor Davis demonstrates how the ideas and values of the settlement house movement lived on to influence the thought and the programs of the New Deal of the 1930s. Here are his closing words on the subject: "All those who today join the war on poverty or try to rehabilitate the nation's cities are influenced, whether they know it or not, by a generation of settlement workers who dared to dream that American cities could be safe and stimulating for all citizens, and who worked from their bases in urban neighborhoods to make a part of that dream come true."

Many early settlement residents were teachers by training or inclination. Some of them even had classroom experience, but rejected a career in high school or college teaching as too routine and narrow, and too far removed from the pressing problems of an urban, industrialized country. They came to the settlement as educational innovators, ready to cut down the barriers that separated learning from reality. "A settlement is a protest against a restricted view of education," Jane Addams once remarked, and like most settlement workers, she considered education a method of social reform.

From *Spearheads for Reform: The Social Settlements and the Progressive Movement, 1890–1914* by Allen F. Davis. Copyright © 1967 by Oxford University Press, Inc. Reprinted by permission.

Jane Addams and the other settlement pioneers drew heavily on the English settlements and university extension movements. They planned to extend the advantages of a college education to workingmen in order to narrow the gulf between factory worker and college graduate through classes, lectures, and discussions. Stanton Coit patterned his Neighborhood Guild in part on Frederick Denison Maurice's Working Men's College in London, and in 1890 Morrison Swift planned a settlement in Philadelphia that would be a social university. Jane Addams and Ellen Starr began to teach and to lecture as soon as they unpacked at Hull House. Miss Starr organized a reading group to discuss George Eliot's *Romola,* which broadened to include Dante, Browning, and Shakespeare. Julia Lathrop started a Sunday afternoon Plato Club for the discussion of philosophical questions. Vida Scudder and Helena Dudley organized a Social Science Club at Denison House in Boston in 1893, and for a time forty or fifty businessmen, professionals, workingmen, and students gathered weekly to hear lectures and discussions on such topics as "The Ethics of Trade Unions" or "German Socialism." But attendance dwindled after a few months, and the club collapsed after the third year.

Almost every settlement had its lecture series and its educational conferences, and a few like Hull House had university extension classes for college credit. John Dewey and Frank Lloyd Wright were among those who spoke at Hull House. George Santayana once gave a lecture on St. Francis and the beauty of poverty at Prospect Union in Cambridge that left most of the hearers aghast. Some of the lectures and discussions were exciting at least to the residents and students if not to the workingmen in the neighborhood. And although Sinclair Lewis exaggerated in *Ann Vickers* when he described the educational fare in his fictional settlement as composed mostly of "lectures delivered gratis by earnest advocates of the single tax, troutfishing, exploring Tibet, pacifism, sea shell collecting, the eating of bran, and the geography of Charlemagne's Empire," there was an element of the unreal and the esoteric about the early settlement workers' attempts to dispense the culture of the universities to workingmen.

There was also something unrealistic about the attempt to turn settlements into art galleries. . . . Ellen Starr and Jane Addams collected reproductions of great art in Europe before they founded Hull House and took pride in hanging the pictures in the settlement. Miss Starr was the leader in the "attempt of Hull House to make the aesthetic and artistic a vital influence in the lives of its neighbors." She taught classes in the history of art, patiently explaining the meaning of each picture. She also organized exhibitions gathered from the homes of wealthy Chicagoans with the hope of limiting the pictures to those which combined "an elevated tone with technical excellence." Edward Burchard, the first male resident of the settlement, was elected to guard the pictures at night and to carry placards up and down the streets and into the saloons to advertise the exhibitions. . . .

University Settlement in New York also held art exhibitions, but the men in the neighborhood were openly hostile. Edward King reported that many of his friends thought they were "a cleverly disguised trick on the part of the eminent mugwumps in the University Settlement Society to get a grip on the district in the ante-election months." The women were less suspicious. A young immigrant girl hung a reproduction of a Fra Angelico angel on the wall of her tenement. Many workingmen and their families were genuinely interested in art, but they found nothing in the public schools to satisfy this interest; the schools did not even have pictures on their walls.

The first building especially constructed for Hull House contained a gallery, and the settlement continued its art exhibits until the opening of the Chicago Art Institute made them unnecessary. Ellen Starr also led the movement to put art in the schools. She donated a series of reproductions to the school nearest Hull House and helped the Chicago Women's Club form a committee to exhibit pictures in all other schools in the city. Thus began the Chicago Public School Art Society. It was a small beginning that did not revolutionize public education in the city, but it was significant as the first of many experiments tried first in the settlements and then adopted by the public schools.

Art exhibitions, lectures, and university extension classes were fine; they satisfied the desire of many settlement residents to make use of their college training. Moreover they provided intellectual stimulation for "the transfigured few" in the neighborhood capable of abstract thought. Men like Philip Davis, Meyer Bloomfield, Henry Moskowitz, and Francis Hackett found the programs stimulating and were thus inspired to continue their education. In addition, settlement lectures and classes served to bring the real world to a number of university professors (or at least they liked to think so). But it soon became obvious that the great majority of the people in the settlement neighborhood were not interested in extension classes. Although thousands attended art exhibitions they took little away that would vitally influence their lives.

What most people in a working-class neighborhood needed was something useful and concrete, something closely related to their daily lives. This might mean courses in manual training, or homemaking; it might simply mean instruction in English or basic American government and history. Large groups of immigrants made both English-type university extension courses and American public schools inadequate in the urban setting, thus forcing settlement workers, whether they liked it or not, to experiment with new methods and techniques.

They quickly learned that among the most useful things were child care and kindergarten classes for young children whose mothers worked all day. Stanton Coit opened a kindergarten at Neighborhood Guild only a few months after the settlement was organized, and Hull House, New York College Settlement, Chicago Commons, and most other pioneer settlements, established them soon after opening their doors. . . .

The goals of the settlements and the kindergartens seemed so similar that one kindergarten teacher labeled the social settlement "the kindergarten for adults." Most settlements were more than that, but many had actually developed from kindergartens. In Boston a number of neighborhood kindergartens and day nurseries established by Mrs. Quincy A. Shaw in the late 1870's and early 1880's became settlements in the 'nineties. Also in Boston, a group of men and women who sought consciously to combine the principles of the kindergarten and the settlement established the Elizabeth Peabody House. Neighborhood House in Chicago, Kingsley House in New Orleans, and others scattered around the country, developed this same way. Mary McDowell was trained as a kindergarten teacher and directed classes at Hull House before becoming the head resident of the University of Chicago Settlement. Eleanor McMain, who had taught pre-school children, became head resident of Kingsley House in New Orleans. Still others brought some of the kindergarten ideals to the settlement and introduced a large number of college-trained men and women to [Friedrich] Froebel and the possibilities of creative play. Many settlements trained kindergarten teachers in a more formal way. Amalie Hofer, the editor of *Kindergarten Magazine,* and her sister, Mrs. Bertha Hofer Hegner, directed the Pestalozzi-Froebel Kindergarten Training School at Chicago Commons. The Chicago Kindergarten Institute met for several years at the University of Chicago Settlement. Mrs. Alice H. Putnam's Kindergarten Training School used Hull House, and South End House had a kindergarten normal school after 1897.

While the settlements did not originate the kindergarten idea, they played a significant part in popularizing it, especially since they often pressured the public schools to take over their work. Teaching little children could be a thankless occupation, but the idea of developing the whole child through art and music and creative play provided a challenge also to revise the whole educational system. It led to attempts to apply the same principles to adult education; for grown men and women could also learn by "playing." It led to a search for playgrounds, parks, and gymnasiums, and to campaigns against child labor. The kindergarten ideas of Froebel, taken seriously, could lead to reform. In the case of the settlement workers they often did.

The kindergarten classes brought mothers and sisters as well as little boys and girls to the settlement and led naturally to attempts to provide them with something useful and meaningful. Usually this meant classes in homemaking, cooking, sewing, and shopping. Some courses taught useless skills, such as the art of serving tea from a silver service or accepting a calling card on a tray. Many of the women settlement workers were appalled at the way their immigrant neighbors kept house. Their wastefulness and disorderliness bothered those brought up in neat middle-class American homes. Some settlement workers could never quite overcome their feeling of superiority, and these homemaking classes only made the immigrant woman more conscious of differences and deficiencies. But many newcomers, baffled by unfamiliar urban ways of household management, acquired helpful suggestions and new confidence at the settlement. Of course, the immigrants did not always listen; and, indeed, sometimes they knew more than the settlement workers. . . . Settlement workers soon discovered that they could get the attention of neighborhood women by setting up model flats and housekeeping centers similar to tenement apartments. There they taught cooking, cleaning, caring for children, and other household tasks, in a more realistic setting. In this way they tried to relate their teaching to the real problems that their neighbors faced. Eventually the public schools borrowed many of their techniques.

The practical needs of the people in the neighborhood usually dictated the types of classes offered. Many settlements were located near textile factories where women and children could take out work. Skill and speed in making buttonholes or operating a sewing machine was vitally important and meant increased family income. Most settlements attempting to satisfy the real needs of their neighborhoods soon found themselves very much involved in manual training and industrial education. Hartley House in New York maintained a carpentry shop; Boston's South End House had a lace-making shop and, after 1903, a separate building equipped with a stage for plays; carpentry and clay-modeling rooms; and kitchen and kindergarten equipment. Hull House held classes in pottery, metalwork, enameling, wood carving, weaving, dressmaking, sewing, millinery, and cooking. Greenwich House in New York began a handicrafts school and shop in 1907 to teach young women how to make lace, pottery, and other articles, and also to employ the many immigrant women in the neighborhood who already had special skills. Settlement workers combined lectures and visits to museums with the teaching of practical skills in order that the newcomers might see that they were engaged in artistic work that had a long history and real importance. Greenwich House started the shop and school primarily to aid the people in the neighborhood, but after three years it was self-supporting and was taken over as a private enterprise by two young women.

Most settlement workers wanted to do more than just teach practical skills to their neighbors. Borrowing from Ruskin and Morris, they also tried to preserve handicraft skills in an industrial age. Moreover, they were concerned with the wider implications of the teaching and learning process in an urban setting. They saw immigrant women who felt useless and out of place in a strange land. They observed sons and daughters employed in meaningless jobs and rebelling against their parents and the language and customs of the old country. When Jane Addams and Ellen Starr decided to establish the Hull House Labor Museum in 1900 they were anxious to preserve the spinning and weaving art of the Italian women. But they also saw a chance to help the younger generation appreciate this talent, and by teaching the girls something of the history of the textile industry, something of the relationship between raw material and the finished product, they hoped to transform their lives from drudgery to more meaningful activity. . . .

Not all settlement workers were realistic in their educational experiments, and there was something romantic and nostalgic about their attempt to revive handicrafts in the face of increasing industrialism. But they were usually concerned with real problems and tried to satisfy important needs. The early residents who provided art exhibitions and musical concerts for people in the area were aware of a craving for beautiful things on the part of many who lived in those dreary surroundings. But they realized only gradually that this need could be better satisfied and utilized by letting the people themselves create things rather than by having them merely look and listen. A few settlements, therefore, began to hold exhibitions, not of reproductions of great art, but of painting actually done by the neighborhood people, and they asked those skilled in painting or sculpture to teach others. Hull House, Greenwich House, and several other settlements supported successful amateur theaters which provided an artistic outlet for some and helped a great many immigrants learn English. "The number of those who like to read has been greatly over-estimated," Jane Addams decided, and the theater gave these knowledge of the language, and an education in the broadest sense. . . .

Many settlements also utilized and encouraged the musical talent of those in their neighborhood; a few offered musical instruction as well. The Hull House Music School was begun in 1893 under the direction of Eleanor Smith, and the following year Emilie Wagner began giving piano and violin lessons in College Settlement in New York. After 1899 the project was sponsored jointly by University and College settlements and in 1903 a separate organization, the Music School Settlement, was begun. There was no attempt to turn every student into a professional musician, but rather to allow those who loved music to find a way to express themselves through it. Some critics charged that by teaching the children of the poor to enjoy music and the finer things of life the settlement workers would only make them more unhappy and dissatisfied. Thomas Tapper, director of the New York Music School Settlement, admitted that this was occasionally true; he wished it would happen more often for he believed unhappiness was the first step on the road out of the slums.

Most of the immigrants had to struggle desperately to survive and to learn something about their new country. Language was a difficult barrier, and the public schools did little to teach immigrants English: a few conducted evening classes in English or Civics, but these usually treated immigrant adults as American children just learning to read. Grown men read, "I am a yellow bird. I can sing. I can fly. I can sing to you," or "Oh Baby, dear baby,/Whatever you do,/You are the king of the home,/And we all bend to you." Philip Davis remarked that an English primer placed in the hands of the immigrant "should emphasize less the words 'cat,' 'rat,' and 'mat' and dwell more on the words 'city,' 'citizen,' and 'state.' " The settlements often tried to combine the teaching of English with the teaching of citizenship. Because they understood some of the immigrants' needs, settlement workers treated them like adults and tried to relate the problems of language and of government to their experiences.

Kindergarten classes, classes in English for adults, in music, art, handicrafts, and homemaking — all these areas of education settlement workers experimented with before most public schools considered adding them to their curricula. They were important to the individual experiences and needs of the local population. In a sense they were practical courses, although few could earn a living in music or art.

The settlement workers, interested in relating education more closely to life, could not long ignore the pressing problems of training young men and women in their neighborhoods for worthwhile jobs. They knew that they could inspire the few with exceptional ability to go to college, but that the majority could never go. What would happen to them? Would they merely drift into unskilled jobs, or could the settlements do something to prepare them for a meaningful role in the industrial world?

Robert Woods of South End House was perhaps more concerned with this problem than any other settlement worker. . . . We have been "training too much the consumer citizen and too little the producer citizen," he remarked, "and concentrating too much on the two percent who get to college and the eight or ten percent who get to high school." Like Ellen Starr, he was disturbed that industrialism had brought about a separation of cultural and vocational interests. The skilled workman, he believed, "must be helped to gain the position he had in the Middle Ages, when the artisans were poets and artists also." He advocated some manual training for everyone, so that even the lucky ones who went on to college would have an appreciation of the dignity and the difficulties of working with their hands or operating machines. . . .

Woods argued for state-supported vocational training in speeches before the National Education Association and at a meeting of the Harvard Teachers' Association. As early as 1901 he spoke out in favor of public vocational education in an article in the *Boston Globe*. Woods in 1904 investigated the existing facilities for vocational training in Massachusetts and in 1906 served for three months as temporary secretary of a state commission on industrial education which had the authority to set up industrial schools. There was opposition, of course. Labor leaders feared that trade schools would threaten their control of the skilled labor force, and educators were horrified by any attempt to change the curriculum of the public schools. However, other settlement workers joined Woods — Jane Addams, Ellen Starr, and Graham Taylor in Chicago, and Lillian Wald and Mary Flexner in New York — and they were especially insistent to point out the need for training hands as well as minds. When the National Society for the Promotion of Industrial Education was formed in 1906 Robert Woods and Jane Addams served on the board of managers. At the local and the national level settlement workers played a significant part in forcing public schools to take over the industrial and vocational training begun in the settlements.

The settlement workers' interest went beyond vocational education to concern for the school drop-outs. Vocational training, they decided, meant little without vocational guidance, so almost every settlement worker at one time or another advised about jobs and training programs. Some settlements operated an informal employment bureau, but Civic Service House in Boston even went beyond that.

Mrs. Quincy Agassiz Shaw established Civic Service House in the North End of Boston in 1901 to promote civic and educational work among the immigrant population of that area, with Meyer Bloomfield, a young, brilliant, and energetic reformer then fresh out of Harvard, as the guiding force behind the venture. Bloomfield, who had grown up on New York's Lower East Side and had attended clubs and classes at University Settlement, felt he owed something to the recent immigrants still caught, as he had once been, in the slums. He explained his plans for a new settlement to Mrs. Shaw, and she financed the experiment in reform.

Bloomfield was soon joined by Philip Davis, another who had risen from the ghetto. They organized clubs and classes, helped immigrants learn English, and encouraged them to join trade unions. They also began to attract an impressive group of intellectuals and reformers. Students from Harvard and Boston University came in the evening to teach classes in American government, history, and English. Ralph Albertson, an itinerant reformer who had organized the ill-fated Christian Commonwealth in Georgia, drifted to Boston and Civic Service House. One of Albertson's closest friends was Frank Parsons, law professor, municipal expert, prolific scholar, and impassioned reformer. Through Albertson and Bloomfield (who had studied under him at Boston University Law School), Parsons became interested in the new settlement venture. He was especially impressed with Philip Davis's idea for beginning a workingmen's institute at Civic Service House. Having followed the work of Toynbee Hall's Workingmen's Institute in London for some time, Parsons devoted himself to the task of creating a similar institution at Civic Service House.

The Breadwinner's College, as its founders named it, opened in 1905 with courses in history, civics, economics, psychology, and philosophy. Parsons and Albertson were the backbone of the faculty, aided by Philip Davis, Meyer Bloomfield, and Morris Cohen, a philosopher who had experience with a similar school in New York. There was also an occasional lecture by Josiah Royce and Lincoln Steffens, among others. . . .

Some of the students at Breadwinner's College were out of work; others were unhappily toiling at jobs that held no interest, no meaning, and no future. When Parsons invited groups of high school boys to the settlement he discovered that most had no vocational plans or else had plans that were completely unrealistic. Since there was no organization to help them choose the right job and none to help them utilize their latent and about-to-be wasted talent, Parsons created one. In 1908 he asked Mrs. Shaw for more money to support another experiment, a vocational bureau. The bureau began operation on April 23, 1908. Parsons talked with scores of young men eager for help in choosing a career. He emphasized the need for guidance by a counselor carefully trained and armed with industrial statistics and information about job openings. And he wrote down his ideas about an orderly and scientific way to guide young people in their choice of job or profession in his book *Choosing a Vocation,* published in 1909. But Parsons did not live to see the book; he had died from the strain of overwork in the fall of 1908.

Frank Parsons was the founder of the modern vocational guidance movement which might never have been started if Bloomfield had not been ready to step in and take over as director. He expanded the activities, advertised in books like the *Vocational Guidance of Youth,* and *Youth, School and Vocation,* and in lectures at Harvard and elsewhere. Bloomfield helped "sell" the idea of vocational counseling to the school committee of Boston, which became the first city in the country to have such organized, systematic job counseling. Bloomfield also called the first National Conference on Vocational Guidance, which met in Boston in 1910 and led to the organization of the National Vocational Guidance Association in 1913. The experiment begun by a few dedicated men in a Boston social settlement thus stimulated a national vocational guidance movement, with far-reaching and significant results.

Vocational training and vocational guidance were later adopted by the public schools. This was somewhat unexpected because in the beginning, most settlement workers had no desire to alter or reform the public educational system; they saw their function only as supplementing schools. However, as soon as they became aware of the inadequacy of education, especially in the poorer districts of the great cities, the attempt to supplement became an attempt to change.

Some reforms were practical, such as the introduction of school nurses and school lunchrooms. Lillian Wald and her fellow workers at Henry Street Settlement simply demonstrated the need and proposed them as effective solutions to some chronic problems. Miss Wald had been troubled by the number of children she met who were kept out of school because of disease or sickness. Eczema or hookworm could prevent a child from receiving any education at all. Doctors had been inspecting school children since 1897, sending home those with diseases, but no one had made an attempt to treat these children. Ironically, the coming to power of Seth Low's reform administration in 1901 complicated rather than solved the problem, for the inspection of school children was made more efficient and more rigorous. Still, nothing was done in the way of treatment. At this point, Lillian Wald, well acquainted with the Health Commissioner and other officials of the Low administration, offered to show how school nurses could solve the problem by treating the diseases diagnosed by the doctors. First, however, she made the city officials promise that if the experiment proved successful they would use their influence to have the nurses put on a permanent basis with salaries paid out of public funds. The settlement nurses found that by making regular visits to the schools, working with the doctors, and in some cases visiting the families, all but the most seriously ill could be treated and kept in school. After only one month's trial, the Board of Estimate appropriated money to hire school nurses. Soon the experiment was being copied in other cities.

Hot lunches for a penny began in much the same way. In 1905 a number of people in New York were aroused by a widely misquoted statement from Robert Hunter's book, *Poverty*, claiming that 70,000 school children went to school in the city without breakfast (he had said, underfed). Lillian Wald and other settlement workers had tried to get the city to subsidize school lunches as early as 1901. They continued to argue in favor of cheap or inexpensive lunches: "The needs of the body are as imperative as those of the mind, and the successful training of the latter depends upon the adequate nourishment of the former," Miss Wald announced. But for a time the settlement workers' suggestions were ignored. Then the Salvation Army and several restaurants attempted to provide lunches for the children. However, the settlement workers realized that private charity was not the answer; they sought to have the school authorities take over the responsibility of serving hot lunches. Eventually they were successful, and the "homemaking centers" inaugurated by the settlements demonstrated that the idea was practical.

Another pioneer educational project at Henry Street Settlement involved mentally retarded and handicapped children. Settlement workers encouraged the work of Elizabeth Farrell, a neighborhood teacher interested in helping the retarded, and they persuaded the Board of Education to permit her to teach an ungraded class of handicapped children. They furthermore got special equipment for her and convinced the Board of the importance of her work. In 1908 the Board voted a separate department for teaching the retarded. . . .

A settlement worker's concern with local education often led him into broad reform movements, as the example of Florence Kelley illustrates. She taught at night in a nearby public school during her first year at Hull House. Although she had been concerned about child labor even before this, what she saw as a teacher played an important part in her decision to concentrate on winning better child labor laws. The frustration experienced by Jane Addams and others in trying to convince the City Council that the public school in the Hull House district needed enlarging led them to a futile attempt to unseat the local ward boss. They soon discovered that educational reform was closely related to economic and political reform.

While the settlement workers were most influenced by the concrete needs they saw about them, for improved school buildings, practical courses, and school nurses, they were concerned with educational theory, too, and with the implications of their experiments. Indeed, they made important contributions to the development of progressive education. They did not invent progressive education, but often borrowed from the advanced thinking of experts in many fields, frequently adopting the latest theories. They provided the practical testing ground for others' ideas. In their experiments with vocational training and their attempt to relate the work of the school to the reality of the world, through kindergartens, work with immigrants, and by their efforts to tailor the school to the needs of the student, the settlement workers tried to make the student the center of the school and the school the center of the community. Although they were never quite sure whether they sought to adjust the child and the immigrant to society, or whether they meant to transform society to meet the needs of their pupils, they used education as a method of social reform.

The settlement movement and progressive education intertwined at many points, and both drew support from a broad area. The mutual influence of the two movements is most obvious with John Dewey. He was a member of the first board of trustees at Hull House and a frequent visitor at the settlement. He lectured and on several occasions led the discussion at Julia Lathrop's Plato Club. He gave a formal address now and then and sometimes just dropped in to talk, to meet the interesting people who found their way to Hull House, to argue with the socialists, the anarchists, and the single-taxers, and to learn. . . . When he moved to New York and to Columbia University he became associated with Lillian Wald at Henry Street Settlement and became chairman of the educational committee at Mary Simkhovitch's Greenwich House. When he went to Boston or another city he often sought out a settlement house.

Dewey learned a great deal from his contacts with settlement workers. He sympathized with their attempts to broaden the scope of education and widen the impact of the school. Most of all, he learned from watching and participating in educational experiments and from taking part in the give-and-take of discussions.

The settlement workers also learned from Dewey. Possibly his greatest contribution was making them see the meaning and the consequences or implications of their day-by-day educational experiments. "I have always thought that we were trying to live up to your philosophy," Lillian Wald wrote him on one occasion. Jane Addams also saw the implications for social work of Dewey's ideas. "His insistence upon an atmosphere of freedom and confidence between the teacher and pupil . . . ," she wrote, "profoundly affected all similar relationships, certainly those between the social worker and his client." Dewey's writings had a large impact on the settlement movement; in turn, the settlement movement had an important influence on him. In one of his books, *Schools of Tomorrow,* there is a chapter entitled "The School as a Social Settlement." That sums up what Dewey and the settlement workers were trying to accomplish in the city. They were trying to make the schools more like social settlements, and to a large extent they succeeded.

STUDY GUIDE

1. What rationale was developed by the settlement house founders to justify their general cultural and educational programs for immigrants and their art classes and exhibits in particular?

2. What role did the settlement house play in developing the kindergarten, and on what theoretical grounds were kindergartens established?

3. Explain how the settlement house helped the immigrant in the following areas: home economics, arts and crafts, music, vocational instruction, language, health instruction and treatment, hot lunches, and assistance to the unskilled and retarded children. Why do you think what was initially a cultural organization chose to become involved in the more practical problems of day-to-day urban life?

4. One of the nation's leading philosophers during the Progressive era was John Dewey. What was his relationship to the settlements, and what did the settlements contribute to his thinking?

5. Would you say that altruism, rather than self-interest, characterized the motives of the men and women who established the settlement houses? Or do you feel that this kind of social reform was in reality a means of social control — an effort to encourage the immigrants to conform to an accepted Anglo-Saxon pattern of behavior? During and after World War I, many Progressive programs turned into deliberate attempts to force conformity on immigrants. Why do you think such a change took place?

BIBLIOGRAPHY

In addition to *Spearheads for Reform: The Social Settlements and the Progressive Movement, 1890–1914* * (New York, 1967), from which the preceding selection was taken, Allen F. Davis recently published a biography of Jane Addams entitled *American Heroine: The Life and Legend of Jane Addams* (Fairlawn, N.J., 1973). Additional material on the settlement house movement will be found in Josephine C. Goldmark, *Impatient Crusader: Florence Kelley's Life Story* (Urbana, Ill., 1953); in two autobiographical volumes by Jane Addams, *Twenty Years at Hull-House* (New York, 1910) and *The Second Twenty Years at Hull-House* (New York, 1970); in Lillian D. Wald, *The House on Henry Street* (New York, 1915); and in Robert A. Woods and Albert J. Kennedy, *The Settlement Horizon: A National Estimate* (New York, 1922). Other aspects of the social-justice movements are presented in Robert Bremner's factual *From the Depths: The Discovery of Poverty in the United States* (New York, 1956) and Clarke Chambers, *Seedtime of Reform: American Social Service and Social Action* * (Minneapolis, Minn., 1963). Another important book — tracing the evolution of social work from an idealistic activity of laymen to a full-time professional occupation — is Roy Lubove, *The Professional Altruist: The Emergence of Social Work as a Career, 1880–1930* * (Cambridge, Mass., 1965).

* Asterisk indicates book is available in a paperback edition.

Black migrants making their way north.

10

FLORETTE HENRI

Black Migration

Throughout the twentieth century — and at an accelerated pace with each succeeding decade — American blacks abandoned the cotton fields and small towns of the South for the industrial cities of the North. In the last decade of the nineteenth century and in the first of the twentieth, 200,000 blacks came North. Between 1910 and 1920, a half-million more came, and larger and larger numbers migrated North in succeeding decades. They came, as Florette Henri makes clear in the essay that follows, for a number of reasons: some came to sightsee and never returned South; some came to escape the violently racist attitudes of the South; and some came to enjoy the economic opportunities the North afforded. Blacks who came to the North were motivated by the same search for opportunity that drew rural and small-town whites as well as the "new" immigrants to the cities: the millions of jobs for able-bodied men and women made available by a vibrant and ever expanding industrial economy. For many, a job even at the lowest of ranks in the factory provided an income higher than they could earn as sharecroppers or tenant farmers.

Many parallels can be found between the migration of American blacks from the South to the cities of the North and the "new" immigration to the United States from Southern and Eastern Europe between 1880 and 1924. Both groups were abandoning a system of landholding where they were at once tied to the land and landless — blacks as sharecroppers in a system of tenant farming and sharecropping, the Europeans as peasants in a feudal land system. There are other parallels as well: both groups settled, for the most part, in the big cities, not in the rural areas of the country; both were relegated to the unskilled levels of the industrial work force; and both created urban ghettoes as a shield from a strange, and even hostile, environment. But one important difference between these two groups of migrants remained: no white ethnic group had to overcome the barriers of color that confronted the black American.

[The] story of movement in the black population says clearly that many blacks did not sit quietly in one place waiting for things to change under them; that, in fact, they shared in the general American pattern of mobility. But early migrations were dwarfed by the surge of black people northward after 1900, and especially after 1910. According to various contemporaneous estimates, between 1890 and 1910 around 200,000 black Southerners fled to the North; and between 1910 and 1920 another 300,000 to 1,000,000 followed. . . .

What precipitated the mass migration of that period is succinctly expressed in this verse:

> Boll-weevil in de cotton
> Cut worm in de cotton,
> Debil in de white man,
> Wah's goin' on.

Drought, then heavy rains, and the boll weevils that flourish under wet conditions had ruined cotton crops in 1915 and 1916. Tenant farmers and croppers were desperate. Too, injustice, disfranchisement, and Jim Crow — "debil in de white man" — grew more severe and galling each year, until life in the South was intolerable for a black man. And at the same time, finally, there was a reasonable hope of escape from this suffering because of the Great War, as it approached and while it was going on. At precisely the time war production needed all the labor it could get, immigration was sharply curtailed, dropping from 1,218,480 in 1914 to 326,700 in 1915, to under 300,000 in 1916 and 1917, and finally to 110,618 in 1918 — less than 10 percent of the 1914 figure. If immigration had continued at the 1914 rate, almost 5,000,000 more immigrants would have entered the United States by the end of the war, and war production could probably have employed almost all the workers among them. It seems reasonable to believe, therefore, that even if one accepts the top figure of 1,000,000 black migrants during that period, they and the immigrants who did manage to enter the country during the peak production years could not have filled the void. Such friction, then, as developed between black and white workers was probably not based on economic competition so much as on racism.

Excerpted from *Black Migration* by Florette Henri. Copyright © 1975 by Florette Henri. Reprinted by permission of Doubleday & Company, Inc.

Woodson claims that even before the unskilled and semiskilled black laborers went North, there was a substantial movement in that direction by educated and professional-level black people — the group that DuBois named the Talented Tenth — who could no longer bear the violence, intimidation, and suppression that were part of everyday life in the South. The increasing callousness of the Republican administrations of Roosevelt and Taft badly shook their faith in the party of liberation. The Brownsville incident of 1906, when President Roosevelt and Secretary of War Taft arbitrarily punished 167 black soldiers, may have been final proof that blacks were deserted by the federal government and must look after themselves. These political facts may have motivated some of the poor, uneducated blacks also to leave the South, although by and large they clung to their faith in the party of emancipation. When Ray Stannard Baker asked a black man why he was leaving Atlanta (after a riot there in 1908) for Washington, D.C., the answer was: "Well, you see, I want to be as near the flag as I can."

According to several contemporaneous studies of the motives of migrants, most blacks left the South simply to be able to feed themselves and their families. George Edmund Haynes, one of the Urban League founders, reported in 1912 that of southern black migrants in New York City, 47.1 percent had come for better jobs. In a 1917 study made for the Secretary of Labor, again the economic motive came first. In the light of what has been said in previous pages about the condition of southern blacks, a rundown of all the reasons given in that study is interesting:

1. low wages: "The Negro . . . appears to be interested in having some experience with from four to six times as much pay as he has ever had before" even if, in buying power, 50¢ to $1 a day in the South should equal $2 to $4 a day in the North;
2. bad treatment by whites — all classes of Negroes are dissatisfied with their condition;
3. injustice and evils of tenant farming — difficulty of getting a planter to settle accounts, about which his word cannot be questioned; also, the high prices charged by planters and merchants for necessary supplies;
4. more dissatisfaction than formerly with these conditions, in the light of the world movement for democracy.

Poor pay was the leading reason for migration in a survey of 1917 in the *Crisis,* followed by bad treatment, bad schools, discrimination, and oppression. Abram L. Harris, an economist and informed student of Negro migrations, concluded that all the movements away from the rural South, from the Civil War on, were "fundamentally the result of the growth of machine industry, and of the lack of economic freedom and the non-assurance of a margin of subsistence under the one-crop share system of the agricultural South."

There were undoubtedly some migrants who moved about simply for adventure or to see new places. Out of the 400 interviewed by Epstein, 85 said they were just traveling to see the country. Gilbert Osofsky in his Harlem study speaks of some who were just wanderers, criminals, hoodlums, or adventurers. But most evidence shows, as Louise Venable Kennedy wrote in her study of Negro urbanization, that blacks move about for the same reasons as other American groups — for jobs, education, better conditions — and not because of a racial trait of rootlessness, as many believed. John Daniels in his 1914 book on black people of Boston spoke of the "excessive migratoriness which is inherent in the Negro character." He added, "Obstacles in the environment are not opposed by a quality of rootedness," explaining why almost 2,000 blacks left Boston between 1900 and 1910. But such an attack on character was hardly necessary to explain why numbers of blacks left Boston. Daniels himself mentions a notable decrease of interest and tolerance on the part of white Bostonians. Even more important was the scarcity of any but menial jobs in nonindustrial Boston. Howard Odum, also, spoke of migratoriness as a race characteristic of blacks, claiming that they have little attachment to home, siblings, or parents. Dillard, however, said that migration was motivated by an effort to improve their condition of living, and as such deserved "commendation not condemnation." And the Atlanta *Constitution* stated bluntly: "The Negro does not move North because he is of a restless disposition. He would prefer to stay in his old home if he could do so on a wage basis more equitable to his race."

The industrial cities were magnets. To farm workers in the South who made perhaps $.75 a day, to urban female domestics who might earn from $1.50 to $3.00 a week, the North during the war years beckoned with factory wages as high as $3.00 or $4.00 a day, and domestic pay of $2.50 a day. As the Dillard report pointed out, blacks longed to get more money into their hands, even if more went out of them; and though living was higher in the North, it was generally not 400 percent higher, as wages might be. A migrant who had gone to Cleveland wrote that he regularly earned $3.60 a day, and sometimes double that, and with the pay of his wife, son, and two oldest daughters, the family took in $103.60 every ten days; the only thing that cost them more than at home, he said, was the rent, $12 a month.

In Pittsburgh in 1918, black migrants were earning between $3.00 and $3.60 a day; only 4 percent of them had earned that much in the South. A 1919 study showed that only 5 percent of migrants in Pittsburgh earned less than $2.00 a day; 56 percent of them had earned less than $2.00 a day in the South. A migrant working in a Newark, New Jersey, dye plant made $2.75 a day plus a rent-free room, and the company had paid his fare North; back home he would have earned less than $1.00 for a long day's work on a farm. Tenant farmers in the Deep South often made less than $15 a month; in 1920, the average annual income of a rural Negro family in Georgia was $290. Even where there was some industry, as in the foundries around Birmingham, unskilled workers got a top of $2.50 for a nine-hour day, while the same sort of worker could make $4.50 a day in Illinois. In Haynes's survey of Negro migrants in New York City, the great majority reported earning from 50 to 100 percent more than they had in the South.

In the complex of motives active upon most migrants it is hard to assess the weight of better educational opportunities for their children. Letters of potential migrants to Emmett Scott and others often speak of this motive. One such letter, written by a representative of a group of 200 men in Mobile, said the men didn't care where they went "just so they cross the Mason and Dixie line" to "where a negro man can appreshate beaing a man" and give his children a good education. Southern politicians of the Vardaman stamp were constantly trying to reduce the little schooling black children got. As governor of Mississippi, Vardaman told the legislature in 1906: "It is your function to put a stop to the worse than wasting of half a million dollars annually" — the cost of black schools — "to the vain purpose of trying to make something of the negro which the Great Architect . . . failed to provide for in the original plan of creation." The black man had no vote, and without a vote he was not likely to enlist any politician in the cause of black education. When Powdermaker's study of Mississippi was made in the 1930s, black schooling was still brief and inadequate; she found fifth-grade children, in that grade because of automatic promotions, who could not read; and she found black parents, especially mothers, with a burning desire to give their children an education at whatever sacrifice to themselves.

Also, it is hard to assay a motive like wishing to appreciate being a man, or wanting to go "where a man's a man" or any place "where a man will Be anything Except a Ker . . . I don't care where so long as I go where a man is a man." The theme is repeated over and over again, and it is a difficult thing to say, a hurtful thing, much harder than simply saying one wants better pay. But it was possibly the overriding reason for leaving the South. W. T. B. Williams, the writer of the report of the Dillard team and its only black member, pointed out that although better pay was most frequently named as a reason for migrating, "the Negro really cares very little for money as such. Cupidity is hardly a Negro vice." He quoted a Florida woman as saying: "Negroes are not so greatly disturbed about wages. They are tired of being treated as children; they want to be men."

Southern blacks were tired of "bene dog as [if] I was a beast"; of never, never being addressed, as they must always address the white man, with a title of respect. Powdermaker says that in Mississippi whites will address a black grade school teacher as "doctor" or "professor" to avoid the Mr., Mrs., or Miss; the consistent withholding of those titles endowed what is a mere polite form with such symbolic force that blacks felt the values of the whole system were concentrated in that Mr. or Mrs. or Miss, and not to be called so meant to be outcast by the system. The sense of being outside the society was reinforced by the equally consistent practice of better-class whites of addressing even the meanest, most illiterate white laborer or loafer as Mr., a cheap way of flattering him into docility by giving him, through the magic of the title, assurance that he was a white man and that as such he shared the superiority of other white men to blacks. This was most damaging to the black man's sense of who he was; because if he, a respectable black, perhaps well educated and fairly prosperous, was not treated like even the dregs of white society, then perhaps he was a different species, not a man at all.

In the many bitter complaints of blacks that they were never Mr. in the South although the white man always was, and in the boast of a migrant writing home that in the North you didn't have to "sir" the white men you worked with — in these there is the cry of the dispossessed and disinherited, a summing up of all the reasons for the black migration. A black minister in Philadelphia put it this way to Ray Stannard Baker: "Well, they're treated more like men up here in the North, that's the secret of it. There's prejudice here, too, but the color line isn't drawn in their faces at every turn as it is in the South. It all gets back to a question of manhood."

Scott said that fear of mob violence and lynching were frequently alleged reasons for migrating, and Booker T. Washington had said that "for every lynching that takes place . . . a score of colored people leave . . . for the city." In the statements of migrants themselves, however, these reasons are not mentioned nearly so often as jobs, pay, justice, better living, and education. Charles Johnson came to the conclusion that persecution, and its ultimate expression in lynching, were not nearly such dominant stimuli to migration as the hope of economic betterment. He claimed that many black migrants — almost 43 percent of them — had gone not North but Southwest, mostly to Arkansas, Oklahoma, and Texas — where economic opportunities might be better but where mob violence was far from uncommon; and that Jasper County in Georgia, and Jefferson County in Alabama, both with fearsome lynching records, had increases rather than declines of black population during the migration period. Kennedy's findings indicated that insecurity of property and life was more likely a supporting cause of migration than a fundamental one, underlying the frequently named reasons of social and educational inequities, humiliations, and insults. In Dutcher's analysis of changes during the 1910–20 decade is the statement that "social grievances appear never to have been sufficient of themselves to produce any considerable movement of the Negro population," and that economic betterment had much greater force. It is amazing, if true, that fear of lynching should not have been a chief reason for flight, considering that ninety-three blacks were lynched in 1908, and fifty, sixty, seventy, or more each year (except 1917) from then until 1920; but the fear may have been too terrible to be given expression in so many words.

Also, there appears to have been a generation gap that made for different motives among older and younger blacks. Many of the older generation, although desperately in need of financial succor, were not so rebellious against "keeping their place." But their sons, who had some schooling, who could read, did not take kindly to the old customs. They were not going to endure being knocked about and beaten on the job "to an extent hardly believable," as the Labor Department reported, and hit with anything that came to the white man's hand, a tool or a piece of lumber. Particularly they resented abuse when their women were with them, and black women were so terrified of what their men might do and what might happen to them as a result, that often the women defended themselves rather than expose their husbands or male friends to danger. A young black said to his father, who was trying to persuade him not to migrate to Chicago: "When a young white man talks rough to me, I can't talk rough to him. You can stand that; I can't. I have some education, and inside I has the feelin's of a white man. I'm goin'." ...

Those who had left early wrote home about freedom and jobs in the North. Labor agents came South recruiting for the big industrial companies, especially the railroads. The Chicago *Defender* carried northern help-wanted ads and detailed accounts of southern lynchings in its "national edition," widely read in the South, thus both pulling and pushing black people. The idea of "exodus" became surrounded with religious fervor. Many believed that God had opened a way for them to escape oppression. Scott described a group of 147 Mississippi blacks who, when they crossed the Ohio River to freedom, knelt, prayed, and sang hymns; they stopped their watches to symbolize the end of their old life. "Exodus" was a matter of excited secret discussion among southern blacks. Anyone who advised against going was suspected of being in the pay of whites. If a black businessman opposed migration, his customers began to vanish; a minister who preached against it from the pulpit was stabbed the next day. Rumors of jobs and of transportation to them increased unrest. Incautiously, many blacks sold or gave away their belongings and followed any crowd of migrants without an idea of their destination. Some rural areas emptied out so thoroughly that one old woman complained she hadn't enough friends left to give her a decent funeral.

"I should have been here twenty years ago," a man wrote back from the North. "I just begin to feel like a man. . . . My children are going to the same school with the whites and I don't have to humble to no one. I have registered. Will vote in the next election and there isn't any yes Sir and no Sir. It's all yes and no, Sam and Bill." A man wrote from Philadelphia telling of good pay, $75 a month, enough so he could carry insurance in case of illness, and added that there you "don't have to mister every little white boy comes along" and that he hadn't heard "a white man call a colored a nigger" since he'd been North; what was more, he could sit where he chose on the streetcars — not that he craved to sit with whites "but if I have to pay the same fare I have learn to want the same acomidation"; still, this far from rootless wanderer would always "love the good old South," he said. A Columbia, South Carolina, Negro paper reported that a migrant brother had come home for a visit with "more than one hundred dollars and plenty of nice clothes." All this was hallelujah news to the home folks. They could easily ignore the occasional cautionary letter, like one from a Cleveland migrant who warned of loafers, gamblers, and pickpockets and said the city streets weren't safe at night. An unnamed but allegedly widely respected black educator is reported to have said: "Uncle Sam is the most effective [labor] agent at this time. All who are away are writing for others to come on in, the water's fine."

Stimulating the urge to "vote with their feet," as the migration was sometimes called, were the solicitations of northern labor agents. In 1916, the first year of large-scale movement, most agents were representing railroads or the mines. Baker reported: "Trains were backed into several Southern cities and hundreds of Negroes were gathered up in a day, loaded into the cars, and whirled away to the North." For example, in February 1917 a special train was sent to carry 191 black migrants from Bessemer, Alabama, to Pittsburgh at a cost to a coal company of $3,391.95. So great was the excitement, Baker said, that Negroes "deserted their jobs and went to the trains without notifying their employers or even going home." Between 75,000 and 100,000 got to Pennsylvania that way, Baker said, many of them to work for the Pennsylvania and Erie railroads, and still more for the steel mills, munitions plants, and other heavy industries. As might be expected, men so hastily and haphazardly gathered up included a good share of shiftless characters, and in addition, the companies had not prepared for their sudden arrival the necessary housing or facilities; because of this combination of circumstances, many of the labor recruits drifted off the job before they had worked out the railroad fare the companies had advanced.

Some of the labor agents were salaried employees of large industrial companies, and these included some blacks. Others were independent employment agents who charged the migrants from $1.00 to $3.00 for placing them in jobs, and collected from the companies as well if they could get anything. Often the labor recruiters gained access to Negro quarters in the cities where they worked by disguising themselves as salesmen or insurance agents. There were probably some honest men among them, but others were flagrantly unscrupulous in their promises. An agency soliciting workers in the Birmingham and Bessemer areas advertised in such phrases as: "Let's go back north where there are no labor troubles, no strikes, no lockouts; Large coal, good wages, fair treatment; Two weeks pay; Good houses; We ship you and your household goods; All colored ministers can go free; Will advance you money if necessary; Scores of men have written us thanking us for sending them; Go now while you have the chance." Some of the "agents" were downright crooks who collected fees from men wanting to migrate and then failed to be at the depot where they were supposed to rendezvous with their clients. Such was the fate of 1,800 Louisiana blacks who paid $2.00 each to an agent who promised them jobs in Chicago but never made good on the promise. The hardship was greatest when men had quit their jobs in the expectation of leaving the South. Micheaux described one agent who, after collecting $3.00 from a man, sent him to several places in search of imaginary jobs; in the end, the agent refused to refund more than $1.00, although he had done nothing for his client. Another racket was to induce ignorant black girls to sign contracts they could not read that obligated them for the cost of their journey plus a placement fee; in many cases the agents were recruiting for brothels, although what they promised the girls was domestic service.

Alarm spread throughout the white South as farm laborers and city menial and domestic help drifted off in twos, twenties, and two hundreds. State laws and city ordinances were passed to oust or curb the agents who were taking most of the workers. In the light of complaints against the agents by a number of migrants, it seems believable that licensing laws for agents were meant at first to protect black workers as well as their white employers. In South Carolina, for example, an 1891 law requiring all labor agents to pay $500 for a license might simply have been aimed at assuring the reliability of the man promising work out of the state; but when in 1907 the fee was raised to $2,000, it was due simply to panic on the part of whites who saw their cheap labor force dwindling. According to Scott, a license cost $1,000 in Jacksonville, under penalty of a $600 fine and 60 days in jail; in Alabama the state, city, and county fees totaled from $1,000 to $1,250; in Macon, a license cost $25,000, and the applicant had to be vouched for by 10 local ministers and 35 local businessmen, which seems not so much regulatory as prohibitive, as the Atlanta *Constitution* called such licensing. In Montgomery, recruiting labor for out-of-state jobs was punishable by a $100 fine and 6 months at hard labor on a convict gang. Force was not infrequently used to prevent the taking of blacks North, Scott says. Labor agents were arrested. Trains carrying migrants were stopped, the blacks forced to return, and the agents beaten. Blacks might be terrorized or lynched on suspicion of trying to leave the state. "But they might as well have tried to stop by ordinance the migration of the boll-weevil," Baker said; by ordinance, or by hitting them on the head, one by one.

Robert Abbott, editor and publisher of the Chicago *Defender* and himself a migrant from the "Negro town" of Yamacraw, was the loudest single voice calling for the northward flow of black labor, but not the only one. Many other Negro papers also encouraged migration, Baker reported. The Richmond *Reformer* spoke out against Jim Crow, segregation, and living conditions "like cattle, hogs or sheep, penned in" as evils that black people in the South must continue to endure "until they rise up in mass and oppose it openly"; self-respecting Negroes, said the Timmonsville (South Carolina) *Watchman*, should take a hint from a recent lynching and "get away at the earliest possible moment." But it was Abbott who fleshed out the vision of escape, who gave it a definite and dramatic form — even a birthday: the

Great Northern Drive of May 15, 1917. Carl Sandburg wrote in the Chicago *Daily News*: "The Defender more than any other one agency was the big cause of the 'Northern fever' and the big exodus from the South." A Georgia paper called the *Defender* "the greatest disturbing element that has yet entered Georgia." The U.S. Department of Labor said that in some sections the *Defender* was probably more effective in carrying off labor than all the agents put together: "It sums up the Negro's troubles and keeps them constantly before him, and it points out in terms he can understand the way of escape." . . .

Abbott put out a "national edition" of his weekly, aimed at southern blacks. It carried in red ink such headlines as: 100 NEGROES MURDERED WEEKLY IN UNITED STATES BY WHITE AMERICANS; LYNCHING — A NATIONAL DISGRACE; and WHITE GENTLEMAN RAPES COLORED GIRL. Accompanying a lynching story was a picture of the lynch victim's severed head, with the caption: NOT BELGIUM — AMERICA. Poems entitled *Land of Hope* and *Bound for the Promised Land* urged blacks to go North, and editorials boosted Chicago as the best place for them to go. Want ads offered jobs at attractive wages in and around Chicago. In news items, anecdotes, cartoons, and photos, the *Defender* crystallized the underlying economic and social causes of black suffering into immediate motives for flight. Repeated stories of those who were leaving the South or who were already in the North conveyed the excitement of a mass movement under way and created an atmosphere of religious hysteria; the *Defender* called the migration the "Flight out of Egypt" and the migrants sang "Going into Canaan." The more people who left, inspired by *Defender* propaganda, the more wanted to go, so the migration fed on itself until in some places it turned into a wild stampede. Even illiterate people bought the paper, as a status symbol. A black leader in Louisiana was quoted as saying, "My people grab it [the *Defender*] like a mule grabs a mouthful of fine fodder." Sandburg wrote that there was in Chicago "a publicity or propaganda machine that directs its appeals or carries on an agitation that every week reaches hundreds of thousands of people of the colored race in the southern states." . . .

Abbott enlisted the aid of two very mobile groups of black people, the railroad men and the entertainers. Chicago was the end of the North-South railroad lines, and a great junction. Hundreds of Pullman porters, dining-car waiters, and traveling stage people passed through it, some of them on their way to remote whistle-stops in the South. The *Defender* paid many of them to pick up bundles of the newspaper in Chicago and drop them along their routes at points where local distributors would meet the trains, get the bundles, and circulate them. In a town where the *Defender* was unknown, the porters would give copies away to any black person they saw. Stage people took bundles of papers and distributed them free in the theaters. The well-known concert singer Sissieretta Jones, who was called the "black Patti" in the patronizing style of the day, asked the ushers in theaters where she performed to give out free copies to all comers.

By such devices the circulation of the *Defender* soared to 283,571 by 1920, with about two thirds of its readers outside of Chicago. This was by far the largest circulation any black newspaper had ever achieved. If each copy reached five readers, a reasonable guess, about 1,500,000 blacks saw it.

Abbott's master stroke in materializing a migration that in 1916 was more rumored than real was the setting of a date, a specific month and day in 1917, for what the *Defender* called "the Great Northern Drive." The incendiary message spread that on May 15 railroad cars would back into the stations of southern towns prepared to carry North any who wanted to go, at a very low fare. The word struck southern blacks with messianic force. There was to be a second coming of freedom on May 15, and it behooved everyone to be ready. . . .

They went with whatever possessions they could carry, "wearing overalls and housedresses, a few walking barefoot." . . . Although it is hard to see how they took their goats, pigs, chickens, dogs, and cats along, as he claims, they certainly must have carried provisions for their long, long journeys, a thousand miles or more for many of them, days and nights of travel with no prospect of any creature comforts along the way. To Chicago from Savannah was 1,027 railroad miles; to New York from San Antonio, 1,916 miles; to Cincinnati from Jacksonville, 822 miles; to Newark from Vicksburg, 1,273 miles; to Detroit from New Orleans, 1,096 miles; to Cleveland from Mobile, 1,046 miles. Some stopped at Chicago for a time before going to their destinations, but most went straight through: from Florida and Georgia to Pennsylvania and New York; from Alabama, Mississippi, Tennessee, and Louisiana to Illinois and Michigan. Most of these people had probably never been more than twenty miles from their homes. . . .

One cheap way to travel was in a group. The *Defender* encouraged the formation of "clubs" of ten to fifty persons and arranged special fares and travel dates with the railroad companies. Many people wrote to the newspaper that they could bring "about 8 or 10 men" or "a family of (11) eleven more or less" or "15 or 20 good men" or "25 women and men," and so on up to "300 or 500 men and women" and finally "as many men as you want." Some of these correspondents sent stamped return envelopes and asked the paper not to publish their letters — "whatever you do, don't publish my name in your paper" — or asked that, if an answer was sent by wire, there should be no mention of the number of people because "if you say 15 or 20 mans they will put me in jail." "This is among us collerd," says one letter offering to bring 20 men and their families.

With so many concerned for secrecy, many must have been too frightened to write at all. They never revealed the presence among them of labor agents. Migrants described how they had to slip away from their homes at night, walk to some railroad station where they were not known, and there board a train for the North. If they were found to have tickets, the police confiscated them. If three or four blacks were discovered together it was assumed that they were "conspiring to go North" and they would be arrested on some trumped-up charge.

For migrants to New York from a coastal city in the South — and most of those who went to New York were from the South Atlantic States — the cheapest and most direct passage was by boat. Steerage fare from Virginia, from which most New York migrants came, was $5.50 or $6.00, including meals. The Old Dominion Line ran boats twice a week from Virginia to New York, and the Baltimore, Chesapeake & Atlantic Railway ran steamers from Baltimore, Washington, and as far south as Florida. By train it would have cost at least $7.50 from Norfolk to New York City, without meals. So the boat was a good buy, although blacks might find themselves in a separate section of the vessel with the household pets of white travelers.

Toward the end of the peak migration period another category of southern blacks settled in northern cities: soldiers returning from France. Rudolph Fisher, a writer of the period, spoke in a short story of a family of Waxhaw, North Carolina, whose son "had gone to France in the draft and, returning, had never got any nearer home than Harlem." There were many such men whose fare, in a roundabout way, had been paid by Uncle Sam. "How're you gonna keep 'em down on the farm,/ After they've seen Paree?" a popular song asked.

The rapid flow northward of black people, especially from 1916 when war production went into high gear, aroused much concern and discussion among whites and blacks, North and South. The word "exodus" was apparently so current that Octavus Roy Cohen used it as both noun and verb in his spurious Negro stories of the early twenties: "the merrymakers exodusted" from a party, he wrote; and, there was a "complete exodus from Decatur." Census figures show that in 1900 only 15.6 percent of black people (1,373,996) lived in a state other than that of their birth, whereas in 1910 the percentage born elsewhere had increased to 16.6 (1,616,608), and in 1920 to 19.9 (2,054,242). Of the 300,000 to 1,000,000 blacks estimated by contemporaries to have gone North, almost all went to urban centers. In 1900, 22.7 percent of Negroes lived in cities, North and South; in 1910 this had increased to 24.4 percent, and in 1920 to 34 percent, in numbers totaling more than 3,500,000. By 1920, almost 40 percent of the black population in the North was concentrated in the eight cities of Chicago, Detroit, New York, Cleveland, Cincinnati, Columbus, Philadelphia, and Pittsburgh, although those cities contained only 20 percent of the total northern population. The city with the most dramatic percentage increase in black population between 1910 and 1920 was Detroit, by an astounding 611.3 percent; Cleveland came next with a 307.8 percent increase; then Chicago, 148.2 percent;

New York, 66.3 percent; Indianapolis, 59 percent; Cincinnati, 53.2 percent; and Pittsburgh, 47.2 percent. In numbers Chicago gained nearly 65,500 black residents, New York 61,400, and Detroit 36,240.

A question that immediately comes to mind is: what did these southern people know how to do that would earn them a living in the North? Since so much of the South was rural, it is amazing the number of occupations represented by the migrants whose letters are in the Scott collection. But indications are that about half the migrants came from towns, a Labor Department survey found. The largest number said they wanted work as laborers at unspecified common labor, with some longshoremen, stevedores, freight handlers, stokers, miners, packers, and warehousemen; many of these men had experience in southern industries such as lumbering, railroading, iron and steel foundries, sawmills, and turpentine stills. The next largest category was the semiskilled or skilled craftsman: plumbers and roofers, painters and plasterers, cleaners and pressers, hotel waiters, brickmakers and bricklayers, machinists and machinists' helpers, caulkers, carpenters, woodworkers, cabinetmakers, mailmen, auto workers, engineers, blacksmiths, glaziers, lumber graders and inspectors, foundry workers, and a large number of molders. The majority of women who wanted to migrate, and some of the men, sought menial or domestic jobs: cooks, laundresses, baby nurses, housemaids, butler-chauffeurs, janitors. Among the businesses represented by migrants were insurance man, barber, hairdresser, laundry owner, merchant, and packer and mover — memorably, the moving company owner who called himself "the Daddy of the Transfer business" of Rome, Georgia. In the much smaller class of professionals and white-collar workers the majority were teachers, including the Alcorn College graduate who was four feet, six inches tall and weighed 105 pounds — a woman, presumably, as were many of the teachers who wanted to leave the South. There were also a sixty-three-year-old graduate of Howard University Law School, an eighteen-year-old artist and actor, and a fifteen-year-old cartoonist; also printers, a college-educated bookkeeper, and a stenographer-typist. Many of the educated class expressed their willingness to do any kind of work, even common labor, if only they could get jobs in the North. Only a few who wrote of their wish to migrate described themselves as farmers, and two of these wanted to go to Nebraska and Dakota to farm. But probably many of those who were looking for laborers' jobs were tenant farmers, sharecroppers, and farm workers; and probably also many other rural people could not write or were afraid to, so we do not know about them — they simply disappeared off the farms and took their chances of finding work in northern cities. Baker says that whole tenant-farming areas of Georgia and Alabama were emptied of prime-age workers. A small number wound up in the tobacco fields of Connecticut, but the great majority must have gone to industrial cities. The black rural population of the South dropped by almost 250,000 between 1910 and 1920.

As the trains and boats pulled out week after week and month after month, the South began to hurt from a loss of the black labor force, especially the Deep South. For the first time in their history, Mississippi and Louisiana showed a decrease in Negro population between 1900 and 1910; and between 1910 and 1920 Mississippi suffered a loss of 129,600 blacks, Louisiana a loss of 180,800. In that decade the black population of the East North Central states increased by 71 percent, and that of the Middle Atlantic states by over 43 percent, although the national increase was only 6.5 percent.

Contemporary estimates by observers such as Baker and Epstein of a million or so migrants seem wildly out of line with the 500,000 figure to be calculated from 1920 census figures, which were not available to them, but it may be that their estimates were more nearly correct than figures arrived at from census returns. For one thing, it has been and remains a fact, substantiated by recent studies by the Census Bureau of its own operation, that black males are significantly undercounted. . . .

If there was finally a black Joshua it was Robert Abbott, blowing the trumpet call of jobs through a rolled-up *Defender*; his troops were the Pullman porters and road shows, with labor agents as mercenaries. Half a million blacks followed behind. Where the metaphor breaks down is that their Jericho was a dirty, crowded, sickly, dangerous city ghetto, which must often have seemed scarcely worth the trouble of getting to.

But the getting there was a tremendous feat of initiative, planning, courage, and perseverance — qualities never appearing in any catalogue of Negro traits drawn up by white people, yet here demonstrated incontestibly not by one or two "exceptional individuals," as blacks were called who did not fit the stereotype, but by at least five hundred thousand perfectly average southern Negroes. They were not passive reactors, waiting for something to happen to them; they made it happen.

STUDY GUIDE

1. What blacks, according to the authors, tended to come North first — and why?

2. Outline the motives that brought about this mass migration and then find similarities and differences (from your text) between these motives and those of the immigrants from Europe.

3. Were there migratory patterns in the movement from the South to the North and, if so, what were they?

4. Offer a generalization about the following: (a) the attitudes of the blacks toward the South and to the North once they arrived; (b) the means

through which the blacks earned their livelihood in the South and in the North; and (c) the temperament of those who came North.

5. And finally: What role did Robert Abbott play in the Great Migration — and with what motives?

BIBLIOGRAPHY

A number of studies are available on the black experience in America. A scholarly introduction to the entire subject of black history, which includes a well-chosen bibliography, is John Hope Franklin, *From Slavery to Freedom: A History of Negro Americans* * (New York, 1978). Another important work is the classic sociological study of the Negro in the United States by Gunnar Myrdal, *An American Dilemma: The Negro Problem and Modern Democracy* (New York, 1944), condensed in Arnold M. Rose, *The Negro in America* * (New York, 1960). An influential, although in parts controversial, analysis of the relationship between blacks and whites in the United States is C. Vann Woodward, *The Strange Career of Jim Crow* * (New York, 1974). For a comparison of the conditions of the blacks in the cities of the North, see Allan H. Spear, *Black Chicago: The Making of a Negro Ghetto, 1890–1920* * (Chicago, 1967) or Constance McLaughlin Green, *The Secret City: A History of Race Relations in the Nation's Capital* (Princeton, N.J., 1967), a study of black-white relations in Washington, D.C.; and Gilbert Osofsky, *Harlem: The Making of a Ghetto* (New York, 1966).

Federal agents raid the offices of Laisve, *a Lithuanian newspaper suspected of being radical and subversive, 1920.*

11

ROBERT K. MURRAY

The Red Scare

Chauvinism — excessive adulation of one's own country, its in-habitants, and its culture — was often the consequence of nine-teenth- and twentieth-century nationalism. Among Europeans, this tendency to exalt native ways and institutions went hand in hand with the "white man's burden" of British imperialism and, in more extreme and vicious form, with the racist doctrines of the Nazis in Germany. The American people have not been im-mune to nativistic doctrines, and throughout our history there have been intermittent crusades by overly zealous and ultra-patriotic citizens to preserve the alleged purity of our institutions and national purpose. Although nativism in the United States never attained the genocidal proportions reached in some other nations, xenophobic manifestations have from time to time brought injustice — and even violence — to those who, for one reason or another, failed to conform totally to the so-called American way.

In his definitive study of American nativism from the end of the Civil War to the mid-1920s, historian John Higham isolates three varieties of American xenophobia: anti-Catholicism, racism (the belief in the superiority of Anglo-Saxons generally and Amer-ican Anglo-Saxons in particular), and antiradicalism. Each of these nativistic movements crested at one time or another in the last century of American life. The last — a violent fear of radical sub-version — climaxed twice: first in the "Red Scare" led by Attorney General A. Mitchell Palmer after World War I and more recently in the witch-hunts led by Senator Joseph P. McCarthy in the decade after World War II. The following selection, taken from Robert K. Murray's *Red Scare: A Study in National Hysteria, 1919–*

1920, graphically describes the earlier antiradical crusade and its consequences for the American people.

The brief, yet hysterical, post-World War I Red Scare derived from a number of sources: the frenzied drive for conformity and 100-percent Americanism demanded by the administration of Woodrow Wilson to gain national support for participation in World War I; the success of the Bolsheviks in overthrowing the Czarist regime in Russia in 1917; the presence in the United States of native and foreign-born Communists and assorted other radicals; and disillusionment with Wilson's campaign "to make the world safe for democracy." Although the Red Scare had come to an end by the time Woodrow Wilson left office in March 1921, it left a legacy for the decade that followed. The execution of the Italian anarchists Nicola Sacco and Bartolomeo Vanzetti, the passage of the Immigration Act of 1924 that discriminated against Southern and Eastern Europeans, the rise of the Ku Klux Klan, and the anti-Catholic campaign against Alfred E. Smith when he ran for the presidency in 1928 are clear indications that the hatred and violence stirred up by the Red Scare did not disappear in 1921.

Prior to the late fall of 1919, the federal government had moved rather slowly against the domestic Bolshevik menace. Because of the press of other postwar problems and a preoccupation with the League [of Nations] question, most officials in Washington had not been able to concentrate their thinking on the radical danger. To be sure, politicians talked now and again about the evidences of radicalism in the country and the newspapers played up such statements with zeal. But only a few politicians had yet become really demagogical. In fact, there was every indication that most officials in Washington were less concerned about the radical menace than were their constituents. They had not lost their heads, nor for the most part had they espoused hasty or ill-advised action to attack a nebulous Red threat. . . .

The person most responsible for the subsequent action of the federal government was Attorney General A. Mitchell Palmer. Under his direction the federal police power was set in motion so zealously against domestic radicalism that the months of November 1919 to January 1920 have sometimes been labeled "Government by Hysteria" or "Palmer's Reign of Terror." . . .

Robert K. Murray. *Red Scare: A Study in National Hysteria, 1919–1920*. University of Minnesota Press, Minneapolis. © 1955 by the University of Minnesota.

It has often been charged that Attorney General Palmer undertook his subsequent one-man crusade against the Reds to further his own personal political ambitions. The Quaker from Pennsylvania did, without a doubt, have his eye on the White House and along with many other followers of the New Freedom hoped to be the heir apparent. His qualifications were certainly better than average. He was an ardent Wilsonian, he was a strong supporter of the League, and, for the moment at least, he had the confidence of the President. Moreover, he was an able administrator, a diligent worker, and a proof-tested reformer, having consistently opposed the infamous Penrose machine in Pennsylvania.

There is every indication that by the spring of 1920 Palmer played the Red Scare for all it was worth, hoping to use his aggressive stand against the Reds as the primary means by which he could project himself into the presidency. But in the fall of 1919 it appeared that the attorney general began his attack on radicalism partially to satisfy mounting clamor for the government to act and partially to sooth his own very real fear that the Reds were about to take over the United States. As alien property custodian, he had already gained a wide knowledge of anti-American and antidemocratic propaganda, and hence was much more sensitive to radical outbursts than he otherwise might have been. Moreover, in that capacity he had been made acutely aware of the problem of sabotage and fifth-column activity, and therefore was more suspicious than normal. Then, too, as a Quaker, Palmer was especially opposed to both the godlessness and the violence of the Bolshevik program and thus easily developed an abnormal attitude toward it. It would be difficult to estimate accurately the tremendous effect which the bombing of his own home had on his thinking. The June 2 incident unquestionably heightened Palmer's proclivity for exaggerating the radical menace anyway, and it is understandable how he came to scent "a Bolshevist plot in every item of the day's news."

Shortly after the bombing of his home, Palmer asked for and received an appropriation of $500,000 from Congress to facilitate the Justice Department's apprehension of those who sought to destroy law and order. Palmer now began his crusade in earnest. On August 1, he established within the Department's Bureau of Investigation the so-called General Intelligence, or antiradical, Division. As its head he appointed young J. Edgar Hoover, charging him with the responsibility of gathering and coordinating all information concerning domestic radical activities. Under the general guidance of bureau chief Flynn and through the unstinting zeal of Hoover, this unit rapidly became the nerve center of the entire Justice Department and by January 1920 made its war on radicalism the department's primary occupation. In fact, there are some indications that both Flynn and Hoover purposely played on the attorney general's fears and exploited the whole issue of radicalism in order to enhance the Bureau of Investigation's power and prestige. Certainly, the hunt for radicals during the 1919–20 period "made" the Bureau of Investigation and started it on the road to becoming the famous FBI of the present day.

In any event, shortly after the creation of the GID, an elaborate card index system was established; over 200,000 cards contained detailed information concerning all known radical organizations, societies, associations, and publications. Set up by Mr. Hoover on the basis of his earlier experience as an employee of the Library of Congress, this index was so constructed that a card for a particular city not only showed the various radical organizations in that area but also their membership rolls, names of officers, and time and place of meetings. By the late fall of 1919, according to Attorney General Palmer, this index also contained the complete case histories of over 60,000 dangerous radicals and housed "a greater mass of data upon this subject than is anywhere else available."

Under the direction of Hoover, the GID became the Justice Department's personal antiradical propaganda bureau as well as a vast repository of radical information. This was particularly true after the formation of the Communist parties in September. In the ensuing months, the division sent to all major newspapers and periodicals letters signed by the attorney general which began with the statement, "My one desire is to acquaint people like you with the real menace of evil-thinking, which is the foundation of the Red Movement," and ended with exaggerated accounts of domestic Communist activity. The division also distributed copies of the manifestoes of the Third International, the Communist party, and the Communist Labor party and warned Americans against falling for this Bolshevik claptrap. At the same time, the division, with the attorney general's full acquiescence, circulated much propaganda connecting the major fall strikes and the summer race riots with the Communists. It need hardly be added that such propaganda was widely circulated by the general press and that under the circumstances the United States Department of Justice was, itself, one of the major agents fostering Red Scare hysteria in the fall of 1919. . . .

. . . The pressure of ensuing events in the summer and fall of 1919 . . . tipped the scales in favor of more aggressive action, and agitation for the deportation of radical aliens became more vociferous while the failure of the government to deport caused increasing comment. Petitions from state legislatures, business organizations, and patriotic societies flooded Congress demanding that the government do something and that the Justice Department, in particular, be shaken out of its lethargy. Such sentiment became sufficiently strong by early October that Senator [Miles] Poindexter rose in the Senate and publicly denounced the Justice Department for not creating new "Red Specials" and securing the immediate deportation of all radical agitators. Such assaults on the Justice Department reached a climax when, on October 19, the Senate unanimously adopted a resolution which requested the attorney general ". . . to advise and inform the Senate whether or not the Department of Justice has taken legal proceedings, and if not, why not, and if so, to what extent, for the arrest and punishment [or deportation] . . . of the various persons within the United States who . . . have attempted to bring about the forcible overthrow of the Government. . . ."

This resolution, together with mounting public clamor, served as the immediate reason for Palmer's turning from less talk to more action. Realizing that in view of the cessation of hostilities with Germany it would be extremely difficult to proceed against radical citizens on grounds of either espionage or sedition, he centered his efforts on the apprehension of radical aliens who would be subject to the deportation provisions of the Alien Law of 1918. This procedure seemed at the moment to be most expedient anyway since the General Intelligence Division estimated that about 90 per cent of all domestic radicals were aliens, and it was believed that the native-born element, if left alone, would never prove really dangerous. On this basis, orders were sent to Bureau of Investigation agents and confidential informants that their major activities "should be particularly directed to persons, not citizens of the United States, with a view of obtaining deportation cases."

On November 7 . . . Attorney General Palmer gave the public and Congress the action they had been waiting for by unloosing a nationwide raid against the Union of Russian Workers. Founded in 1907, this organization had its headquarters in the Russian People's House, 133 East 15th Street, New York City, and, according to its own statements, was composed of "atheists, communists and anarchists." It believed in the complete overthrow of all institutions of government and the confiscation of all wealth through the violence of social revolution. The estimated membership of the organization was 4000.

Although 250 officers and members of the URW were seized in simultaneous raids in eleven other cities, the main blow fell on the New York headquarters. The People's House raid was conducted with mathematical precision, bureau agents remaining outside the building in parked cars until the signal was given. At that moment, they closed in rapidly and took the establishment by surprise. Several huge truck-loads of radical propaganda were confiscated, and about 200 men and women were violently assisted out of the building by a special riot squad and driven away to Justice Department headquarters at 13 Park Row for questioning. The New York *Times* reported that some of the occupants had been "badly beaten by the police . . . their heads wrapped in bandages testifying to the rough manner in which they had been handled."

As a result of the questioning, only thirty-nine of those seized were finally held. Of the others, a few were found to be American citizens and were immediately released; the rest were simple workingmen of Russian nationality who spoke little or no English and who belonged to the organization for almost every conceivable reason except to promote revolution. Nevertheless, despite their obvious ignorance concerning the real aims of the URW, certain of these prisoners were held for excessively long periods of time before they were given their freedom. This wás particularly true at Hartford, Connecticut, where some arrested members were kept in jail five months before even receiving a hearing. . . .

In spite of the obvious injustices involved and the small catch of truly revolutionary characters, the nation seemed delighted with the raids. To the government, and especially to Attorney General Palmer, went unstinting praise for having acted "In the Nick of Time" and having nipped "a gigantic plot" in the bud. Suddenly, the attorney general became the most popular figure in the nation and found himself enthroned as the third in a triumvirate of great saviors of the country — first Hanson, then Coolidge, now Palmer. His prestige was perhaps all the more enhanced since the government was temporarily leaderless; Woodrow Wilson lay stricken in the White House while the ship of state floundered helplessly in the rough seas of fear and reaction. To the man on the street, Palmer was "running the administration," "a lion-hearted man [who] has brought order out of chaos," and "A Strong Man of Peace." Newspapers excitedly described him as "a tower of strength to his countrymen" and declared that his actions brought "thrills of joy to every American." . . .

. . .

The federal raid of November 7 had proved an excellent laboratory experiment. It had shown that if any raid was to be followed by deportations, close cooperation with the Department of Labor was absolutely essential because of its jurisdiction over deportation matters. Therefore, in laying plans for his new move, the attorney general attempted to bring Labor Department officials into closer harmony with his own views. In this attempt, he was aided by the fact that, at the moment, Secretary of Labor [William B.] Wilson was ill and Assistant Secretary Post was otherwise occupied. This left John W. Abercrombie, solicitor of the Department of Labor, but in reality a member of the Justice Department, to function as acting labor secretary. Naturally, he proved most cooperative. Moreover, the Labor Department's top official on deportation affairs, Commissioner General of Immigration Anthony J. Caminetti, was currently evidencing as much hysteria over the Red menace as was the attorney general. Therefore he also fell easily into line.

After consultation with these men, it was unanimously decided that alien members of both the Communist party and the Communist Labor party were subject to deportation under the 1918 Alien Act. On this basis, Acting Secretary of Labor Abercrombie signed on December 27 more than 3000 warrants for the arrest of known alien adherents to the two Communist organizations and gave such warrants to the Justice Department for execution. Four days later, on the advice of Commissioner Caminetti (who in turn was acting upon a suggestion made to him by one of Palmer's emissaries from the Justice Department), Abercrombie also made an important change in the rule governing the procedure of deportation arrest hearings. Prior to December 31 the rule had read: "At the beginning of the hearing under the warrant of arrest, the alien shall be allowed to inspect the warrant . . . and shall be apprised that he may be represented by counsel." The rule, as changed, read as follows: "Preferably at the beginning of the hearing . . . or at any rate as soon as such hearing has proceeded sufficiently in the development of the facts to protect the Government's interests, the alien shall be allowed to inspect the warrant . . . and shall be apprised that thereafter he may be represented by counsel."

It should be noted at this point that deportation involved no criminal proceeding since it was not regarded as punishment. There was no judge or jury and the case was handled administratively through the secretary of labor by immigration officials who heard the case and rendered the decision. The government was perfectly within its rights in changing the grounds and procedures for deportation hearings at any time, for deportable aliens obviously did not have the protection of the ex post facto clause in the Constitution.

But even though no criminal trial was involved and the whole matter was merely an administrative process, it was generally understood that the alien did have certain safeguards — namely those in the Sixth Amendment such as the "right to a . . . public trial . . . to be confronted with witnesses against him; to have compulsory process for obtaining witnesses in his favor and to have the Assistance of Counsel for his defense." The alien also had two possibilities for relief from an adverse administrative decision. The secretary of labor might personally review the record and reverse any deportation decision, or the alien might obtain a writ of habeas corpus which would bring his case before a federal judge, but only if it could be shown that the deportation proceedings had been manifestly unfair.

For these reasons it becomes obvious why Attorney General Palmer did not try to detect and prosecute actual crimes of radicals against the United States. This would have required an indictment and a trial by jury, whether such crimes were committed by citizens or aliens. Rather, he relied on the administrative process for the apprehension and deportation of radical aliens and therefore circumvented most normal legal procedures. Moreover, by Abercrombie's change in the hearing rule, even under the administrative process the alien's opportunity for an able defense of his position was considerably weakened. Hence, through shrewd collusion with certain Labor Department and immigration officials, Palmer assured himself greater success in his drive on radicalism than if he had elected to arrest radical aliens as criminals and thus subject his whole anti-Red program to the vagaries of the courts of law.

Confident now that all was in readiness and that large-scale deportations offered the best solution to the domestic radical problem, the attorney general set the night of January 2, 1920, as the time for his all-out drive on the two Communist parties. Seven days before, on December 27, Palmer sent specific orders to Bureau of Investigation district chiefs instructing them on exactly what to do. They were told to arrange with their undercover agents, some of whom had quietly slipped into radical ranks and had assumed the role of agitators of the wildest type, to have meetings of the two Communist organizations called for the night set if possible because such action would facilitate the making of arrests. Field agents were instructed to "obtain all documentary evidence possible," to secure "charters, meeting minutes, membership books, due books, membership correspondence, etc.," and to allow no person arrested to communicate with any outside person until permission was specifically granted. Such permission could only come from Flynn, Hoover, or Palmer. Further orders specified that if an individual claimed American citizenship "he must produce documentary evidence of same" and that upon arrest "aliens should be searched thoroughly; if found in groups in meeting rooms, line them up against the wall and there search them."

Resultant action could not have been more stunning or more spectacular. On January 2, more than 4000 suspected radicals were rounded up in thirty-three major cities, covering twenty-three states. Virtually every local Communist organization in the nation was affected; practically every leader of the movement, national or local, was put under arrest. Often such arrests were made without the formality of warrants as bureau agents entered bowling alleys, pool halls, cafés, club rooms, and even homes, and seized everyone in sight. Families were separated; prisoners were held incommunicado and deprived of their right to legal counsel. According to the plan, those suspected radicals who were American citizens were not detained by federal agents, but were turned over to state officials for prosecution under state syndicalist laws. All aliens, of course, were incarcerated by the federal authorities and reserved for deportation hearings.

In the New England area, raids were conducted in such towns as Boston, Chelsea, Brockton, Nashua, Manchester, and Portsmouth. In all, about 800 persons were seized of whom approximately half were taken to the immigrant station in Boston and then shipped to Deer Island in Boston Harbor. In this shifting process, the prisoners were forced to march in chains from the immigrant station to the dock — a fact which newspapers played up as attesting to their dangerous, violent character. Upon arriving at Deer Island the prisoners found conditions deplorable; heat was lacking, sanitation was poor, and restrictions holding them incommunicado were rigidly enforced. One captive plunged five stories to his death, another went insane, and two others died of pneumonia.

The remaining half of the 800 who were not sent to Deer Island were released after two or three days when it was determined they were in no way connected with the radical movement. For example, thirty-nine bakers in Lynn, Massachusetts, arrested on suspicion of holding a revolutionary caucus, were released when it was learned that they had come together on the evening of January 2 for the inoffensive purpose of establishing a cooperative bakery. In Boston, a woman named Minnie Federman, who was mistakenly arrested in her bedroom at 6 A.M. on January 3, was released without even an apology when it was discovered belatedly that she was an American citizen and had no interest whatsoever in revolution.

In New York and Pennsylvania the pattern was the same. In New York City more than 400 individuals were arrested as the Communist party headquarters and the Rand School bore the brunt of the federal raid. Prisoners were rounded up and taken to 13 Park Row where they were questioned by GID agents before being sent on to Ellis Island or released. In these New York arrests it seems that brutality was practiced to an excessive degree. Prisoners in sworn affidavits later testified to the violent treatment they had received. One claimed he had been beaten by a Justice Department operative without any explanation; another maintained he was struck repeatedly on the head with a blackjack. Another alien asserted that his glasses had been knocked off by an agent, who then without the slightest provocation struck him in the face. Still another testified: "I was struck on my head, and . . . was attacked by one detective, who knocked me down again, sat on my back, pressing me down to the floor with his knee and bending my body back until blood flowed out of my mouth and nose . . . after which . . . I was questioned and released."

Meanwhile, in Philadelphia, more than 100 were arrested and the "third degree" was as shamefully practiced as in New York. In the Pittsburgh area, 115 individuals were seized although warrants had been issued for only twenty. Indeed, one Pittsburgh man was missed by his friends for almost a month before they discovered he was in jail, having been arrested without warrant and then held without explanation or bail.

In New Jersey, such towns as Jersey City, Passaic, Newark, Hoboken, Paterson, and Trenton experienced similar Red roundups. Altogether, about 500 arrests were made, but the majority were finally released for insufficient evidence. Again many arrests were made without warrant. For instance, one man was arrested about 10 P.M. while walking along Newark's Charlton Street simply because he "looked like a radical." Another, much to his surprise, was seized when he stopped to inquire what all the commotion was about. This zeal to ferret out dangerous radicals caused government agents not only to make many unjust arrests such as these but also to jump to ridiculous conclusions. In New Brunswick, while a Socialist Club was being raided, the drawings of a phonograph invention were found and were immediately forwarded to demolition experts because the raiders thought they represented "the internal mechanism of various types of bombs."

In the Midwest, the raids at Chicago and Detroit were particularly severe. In the Detroit raid about 800 persons were arrested and imprisoned from three to six days in a dark, windowless, narrow corridor in the city's antiquated Federal Building. The prisoners were forced to sleep on the bare floor and stand in long lines for access to the solitary toilet. Some, unable to wait, were forced to urinate in the corridor itself, and, as the custodian later testified, "Before many days . . . the stench was quite unbearable." It was later discovered that the prisoners were denied all food for the first twenty-four hours and thereafter were fed largely on what their families brought to them. Including among their number "citizens and aliens, college graduates and laborers, skilled mechanics making $15 a day and boys not yet out of short trousers," these 800 prisoners were closely questioned by bureau agents who finally released 300 by the end of the sixth day when it was proved that they had not even a cursory interest in the domestic radical movement.

Meanwhile, about 140 of those remaining were transferred from the Federal Building to the Detroit Municipal Building. En route these individuals, who had been unable to shave or bathe for almost a week, served as excellent subjects for press photographers, and local Detroit newspapers ran their pictures as examples of the unkempt, dirty, filthy Bolshevik terrorists the government had netted in its raids. Upon their arrival at the Municipal Building, the prisoners were placed in a room twenty-four feet by thirty feet which originally had been designed to hold offenders no longer than three to four hours. This "bull pen," as it was called, had only one window, a stone floor, and several wooden benches; yet the men remained here a whole week and were fed almost solely on food sent to them by their relatives. Indeed, conditions under which these prisoners lived were actually so wretched that even the Detroit press finally displayed some sympathy for them, and a citizens' committee was created to investigate their situation. This committee subsequently discovered that most of these "dangerous radicals" were but plain, ignorant foreigners who were completely unaware of why they were being so treated.

In Chicago, a most peculiar set of circumstances arose. For five months, state and city officials had laid careful plans for their own drive on radicalism in the Chicago area, and had finally decided on January 1 as the date for such a move. Much to their dismay they then learned that the Justice Department had planned its foray for January 2. Cook County officials persisted in their desire to conduct a raid of their own, and, as a result, raids were held a day apart on radicals in that area.

The state raid of January 1 involved some seventy or more radical clubs or gatherings and netted between 150 and 200 prisoners. As a result of these incursions, some eighty-five Communists, among them "Big Bill" Haywood and Rose Pastor Stokes, were arraigned in Chicago on criminal anarchy charges.

The federal raid which followed on January 2 was therefore somewhat anticlimactic. However, federal officials did nab 225 additional suspected radicals and after questioning held about 80 for deportation. One interesting sidelight on the Chicago raids was a riot which broke out in the municipal jail shortly after the various arrests were made. It seems that the jail's "patriotic" prisoners took violent exception to the fact that Reds were being thrown in the same cells with them. Remarked the Seattle *Times,* "There are some things at which even a Chicago crook draws the line."

In the West and Far West, while raids were conducted, they were not especially significant. Most radicals of any importance, particularly in the Far West, had already been apprehended in the various state raids following the Centralia massacre. Hence, the present forays were carried out only in a cursory manner and arrests were few in number. In Los Angeles, one was arrested; in Portland, twenty; Denver, eight; and Des Moines, sixteen. Only in Kansas City was there much activity, and there 100 were taken and 35 held.

The January raids dazzled the public. The mass of Americans cheered the hunters from the sidelines while Attorney General Palmer once again was hailed as the savior of the nation. In view of the obvious abridgement of civil liberties which the raids entailed, such support can only be explained on the basis that the public mind was under the influence of a tremendous social delirium — a colossal fear which condoned monstrous procedures and acts. Against a background of the three major fall strikes, the Centralia murders, and exaggerated press and official claims, that fear seemed so real it was positively overpowering. Said the Washington *Evening Star,* "This is no mere scare, no phantom of heated imagination — it is a cold, hard, plain fact." As far as the deleterious effect on civil liberties was concerned, the Washington *Post* exclaimed, "There is no time to waste on hairsplitting over infringement of liberty. . . ."

Agreeing therefore that the raids were a cause for satisfaction and willing to overlook the many dangers and injustices involved, most journals were now quick to counsel a rapid follow-through. The immediate deportation of the prisoners, variously described as "the kind of cranks that murder Presidents" or "send bombs through the mails to statesmen," was forcefully demanded. In fact, such action was regarded "as necessary as cauterizing a wound to prevent gangrene." Under such headlines as "ALL ABOARD FOR THE NEXT SOVIET ARK," the press advocated that "ships be made ready quickly and the passengers put aboard."

As to the success of the raids, Palmer and the Bureau of Investigation spoke in glowing terms. The attorney general claimed the raids "halted the advance of 'red radicalism' in the United States," while Flynn maintained they marked the beginning of the end of organized revolutionaries in this country.

As a matter of fact, the raids did have a devastating effect on the domestic radical movement. James Cannon later maintained that the movement disintegrated for the time being. Benjamin Gitlow testified the raids struck terror into the hearts of alien members of the two Communist parties and hurt membership tremendously. It was true that for many weeks after the government action the radical press ceased its activities and meetings of the Communist organizations were suspended. Perhaps the best indication of the effect of the raids can be seen in a report made in February 1920 by the American delegate to the Amsterdam meeting of the Bureau of Propaganda of the Third International. He claimed at that time that the January raids had so wrecked the Communist movement in the United States that it could not be counted on to exert any influence whatsoever.

While satisfied up to this point with the success of his antiradical program, Attorney General Palmer now allowed no lag to develop. With the aid of Flynn and Hoover, he intensified the department's propaganda campaign until it reached its height in late January 1920. Large numbers of antiradical articles and cartoons were sent to the nation's newspapers and magazines without charge, the postage being prepaid by the Department of Justice itself. A sample cartoon, secured by the Justice Department from the New York *Tribune* and used with its permission, depicted Uncle Sam as a farmer weeding up thistles, each one of which had a Bolshevik head, while in the background a woman named "America" was replacing the thistles with pure "American" grass seed. "Give the American Bluegrass a Show," it said.

At the same time, Palmer vigorously continued his drive to secure some kind of peacetime sedition legislation in order to give the federal government the power necessary to deal with citizen radicals effectively. Shortly after the January raids, he appealed to Congress for such legislation, underlining the potential danger which such citizens presented to the country.

Palmer also promised the nation more action to rid the country of all alien agitators. He declared there would be more raids and that on the basis of what already had been done there would be at least 2720 deportations. Like a barker in charge of a colossal sideshow, the attorney general promised New Yorkers, in particular, the exhilarating spectacle of "a second, third, and fourth Soviet Ark sailing down their beautiful harbor in the near future."

STUDY GUIDE

1. Offer an assessment of the magnitude of the threat the so-called radicals represented to American institutions on the basis of this essay.

2. Can you explain why Attorney General A. Mitchell Palmer, a reform-minded Progressive prior to 1919, launched a reactionary campaign to persecute and prosecute men and women whose only crime, in some cases, was being born overseas?

3. What were the precise roles of the following in promoting the Red Scare: (a) President Wilson; (b) A. Mitchell Palmer; (c) J. Edgar Hoover; (d) the Congress; (e) the press; and (f) public opinion?

4. What impression do you have of the legality or the fairness of the government's actions? Can you think of parallels from more recent history? Consider, for example, the role played by the state authorities and the federal government in the relocation of the Japanese-Americans during World War II. From information you can find in your text, list some similarities or differences between the relocation of the Japanese in 1942 and the anti-radical campaign of Palmer.

5. Consider the following question: Is it possible to conduct a war abroad (or a civil war) without a curtailment of the liberty of the individual at home? Consult your text or other sources for information regarding the repression of individual freedom during: (a) the Civil War; (b) the two World Wars; (c) the Korean War; and (d) the protracted war in Vietnam in the 1960s and 1970s.

6. Can you see a relationship between the actions of the government during the Red Scare and the activities of the White House "plumbers" who broke into the office of Daniel Ellsberg's psychiatrist during the administration of Richard M. Nixon? What are the similarities? Are there any differences?

BIBLIOGRAPHY

The most comprehensive study of American nativism since the end of the Civil War is John Higham, *Strangers in the Land: Patterns of American Nativism, 1860–1925* * (New Brunswick, N.J., 1955). Segments of the overall nativistic theme are treated in a number of other books. In addition to the book from which the preceding selection was taken, *Red Scare: A Study in National Hysteria, 1919–1920* * (Minneapolis, Minn., 1955), and subsequent studies: Julian F. Jaffe, *Crusade against Radicalism* (Port Washington, N.Y., 1972), and Murray B. Levin, *Political Hysteria in America* (New York, 1972). See, too, Paul L. Murphy's article on "The Source and Nature of Intolerance in the 1920's" in the *Mississippi Valley Historical Review,* Vol. LI (1964), pp. 60–76. The action taken by the federal government over the years in the suppression of radicalism is described well in William Preston, Jr., *Aliens and Dissenters: Federal Suppression of Radicals, 1903–1933* * (Cambridge, Mass., 1963). The McCarthy witch-hunt of the early 1950s — often called "the second red scare" — is passionately dealt with by Elmer Davis, a newspaperman deeply dedicated to the cause of civil liberty, in *But We Were Born Free* (Indianapolis, Ind., 1954), and in the following, more recently published: Earl Latham, *The Meaning of McCarthyism* (Boston, 1965); Robert Griffith, *The Politics of Fear* (Rochelle Park, N.J., 1971); and Fred Cook, *The Nightmare Decade* (New York, 1971).

* Asterisk indicates book is available in a paperback edition.

IV THE TENSIONS
OF PROSPERITY

As the Republican candidate for the presidency in 1920, Warren Gamaliel Harding promised the American people "not nostrums, but normalcy." Harding proposed that the idealism of the Progressive era and the moralistic fervor evoked by Woodrow Wilson give way to a more prosaic and less exalted vision of American life.

But the 1920s, in retrospect, were neither prosaic nor exalted. An accelerated rate of social change characterized the "Prosperity Decade," and it provoked Americans to wonder whether "progress" was a virtue or a sin. From the end of World War I to the onset of the Great Depression, there were those committed to the values, social practices, and institutions of native, rural, nineteenth-century, Protestant America; and there were those — largely the "new" immigrants and middle-class city dwellers — who saw no value in maintaining this older, agrarian, and puritanical way of life. The trend toward economic consolidation in the 1920s did little to reduce the great social division of that decade.

The issues that polarized the nation were many and bitterly fought. In addition to the "Red Scare" of 1919 and the controversy that surrounded the Sacco-Vanzetti case, the nation debated immigration policy. Nativists wanted an end to unrestricted immigration; they wanted to make certain that most future immigrants to the United States would be Anglo-Saxons rather than Southern and Eastern Europeans. The Immigration Act of 1924 made both these demands law. Other controversies concerned the teaching of evolution in the public schools and the fitness of a Catholic for the office of President of the United States. John T. Scopes was sentenced to jail for teaching evolution to his students in Tennessee in 1925; and the defeat of Alfred E. Smith in the presidential campaign of 1928 can, in part, be attributed to a distrust of Catholics.

The following selections offer you a sense of the divisiveness of the American experience of the 1920s. The first — on the activities of the Ku Klux Klan — deals with one of the nativist movements that divided the nation in the twenties; the second examines the lifestyle of college youth; and the last is on the illegal, yet lucrative, bootlegging trade. By 1929, with the crash of the stock market and the onset of the Great Depression, most Americans could no longer afford to concern themselves with the activities — and style of life — these essays so vividly describe.

A legacy of bigotry and violence — for today and tomorrow.

12

ROBERT COUGHLAN

The Klan in Indiana

The 1920s were marked by strong social divisions and ideological differences between various segments of the American nation: between native Americans and immigrant Americans, between rural-born Americans and those raised in the city, between blacks and whites, between fundamentalists and modernists, and between Protestants, on the one hand, and Catholics and Jews, on the other. These divisions manifested themselves in many regions of the country and brought a number of social movements into being. One of the most frightening was the reappearance of the Ku Klux Klan — a reincarnation of the lily-white organization that had played a part in overthrowing the Radical Republican rule of the southern states and in terrorizing the ex-slaves during the Reconstruction era after the Civil War.

A number of similarities between the Ku Klux Klan of the Reconstruction period and the Klan of the 1920s should be noted: both were anti-Negro, both used violence and intimidation to achieve their ends, and both were comprised of white, native Americans. There were important differences, however: unlike the nineteenth-century Klan, the Klan of the 1920s served as a source of profit to its leadership (through the sale of insurance along with memberships), flourished in the Middle West, the Southwest and on the Pacific Coast in addition to the South, and broadened the focus of its hatred to include Catholics and Jews as well as Negroes. The first Klan constituted a response to the defeat of the South in the Civil War and the threat of integration and equality between blacks and whites after the war. The Klan of the 1920s grew out of a fear that forces of change would destroy the values and way of life created by native, Protestant, Anglo-

Saxon Americans in the nation between the end of the Civil War and the outbreak of the First World War.

The next selection, "Konklave in Kokomo" by Robert Coughlan, is a recollection by a Roman Catholic youngster of a Klan revival meeting in the summer of 1923 in rural Indiana. While the author, a journalist by profession, provides the reader with a history of the Klan — including its rise and fall in the 1920s — the real strength of his narrative lies in his vivid characterization of the Klan membership and leadership and the emotional tone of the Klan gathering in crossroads Indiana in the mid-1920s. The world view of the Klansmen, as portrayed by Coughlan, stands in sharp contrast to the mentality of the generation of college youth who participated in the social revolution described by Paula S. Fass in the selection following this one. The Klansmen represented an effort to hold back the forces of change — the influence on American culture of the city, of science, of Catholics, Jews, and blacks — while the generation described by Fass was the forerunner of changes that would influence the entire cultural and social landscape of the nation in the 1960s and 1970s.

On a hot July day in central Indiana — the kind of day when the heat shimmers off the tall green corn and even the bobwhites seek shade in the brush — a great crowd of oddly dressed people clustered around an open meadow. They were waiting for something; their faces, framed in white hoods, were expectant, and their eyes searched the bright blue sky. Suddenly they began to cheer. They had seen it: a speck that came from the south and grew into an airplane. As it came closer it glistened in the sunlight, and they could see that it was gilded all over. It circled the field slowly and seesawed in for a bumpy landing. A bulky man in a robe and hood of purple silk hoisted himself up from the rear cockpit. As he climbed to the ground, a new surge of applause filled the country air. White-robed figures bobbed up and down; parents hoisted their children up for a view. A small delegation of dignitaries filed out toward the airplane, stopping at a respectful distance.

The man in purple stepped forward.

"Kigy," he said.

"Itsub," they replied solemnly.

With the newcomer in the lead the column recrossed the field, proceeded along a lane carved through the multitude, and reached a platform decked out with flags and bunting. The man in purple mounted the steps, walked forward to the rostrum, and held up his right hand to hush the excited crowd.

"My worthy subjects, citizens of the Invisible Empire, Klansmen all, greetings!

"It grieves me to be late. The President of the United States kept me unduly long counseling upon vital matters of state. Only my plea that this is the time and place of my coronation obtained for me surcease from his prayers for guidance." The crowd buzzed.

"Here in this uplifted hand, where all can see, I bear an official document addressed to the Grand Dragon, Hydras, Great Titans, Furies, Giants, Kleagles, King Kleagles, Exalted Cyclops, Terrors, and All Citizens of the Invisible Empire of the Realm of Indiana. . . .

"It is signed by His Lordship, Hiram Wesley Evans, Imperial Wizard, and duly attested.

"It continues me officially in my exalted capacity as Grand Dragon of the Invisible Empire for the Realm of Indiana. It so proclaims me by Virtue of God's Unchanging Grace. So be it."

The Grand Dragon paused, inviting the cheers that thundered around him. Then he launched into a speech. He urged his audience to fight for "one hundred per cent Americanism" and to thwart "foreign elements" that he said were trying to control the country. As he finished and stepped back, a coin came spinning through the air. Someone threw another. Soon people were throwing rings, money, watch charms, anything bright and valuable. At last, when the tribute slackened, he motioned to his retainers to sweep up the treasure. Then he strode off to a near-by pavilion to consult with his attendant Kleagles, Cyclopses, and Titans.

That day, July 4, 1923, was a high-water mark in the extraordinary career of David C. Stephenson, the object of these hysterics; and it was certainly one of the greatest days in the history of that extraordinary organization the Knights of the Ku Klux Klan. The occasion was a tri-state Konklave of Klan members from Illinois, Ohio, and Indiana. The place was Melfalfa Park, the meeting place, or Klavern, of the Klan chapter of Kokomo, Indiana, the host city. Actually, although planned as a tri-state convention, it turned out to be the nearest thing to a rank-and-file national convention the Klan ever had. Cars showed up from almost every part of the country. The Klan's official estimate, which probably was not far wrong in this case, was that two hundred thousand members were there. Kokomo then had a population of about thirty thousand, and naturally every facility of the town was swamped.

The Konklave was an important day in my life. I was nine years old, with a small boy's interest in masquerades and brass bands. But I was also a Catholic, the son of a Catholic who taught in the public, schools and who consequently was the object of a good deal of Klan agitation. If anything worse was to come, the Konklave probably would bring it. Every week or so the papers had been reporting Klan atrocities in other parts of the country — whippings, lynchings, tar-and-feather parties — and my father and his family were logical game in our locality.

Nevertheless, in a spirit of curiosity and bravado, my father suggested after our holiday lunch that we drive out to Melfalfa Park, which lies west of the town, to see what was happening. My mother's nervous objections were overcome, and we all got into the family Chevrolet and set out for West Sycamore Road. We saw white-sheeted Klansmen everywhere. They were driving along the streets, walking about with their hoods thrown back, eating in restaurants — they had taken the town over. But it was not until we were well out toward Melfalfa Park that we could realize the size of the demonstration. The road was a creeping mass of cars. They were draped with flags and bunting, and some carried homemade signs with Klan slogans such as "America for the Americans," or "The Pope will sit in the White House when Hell freezes over." There were Klan traffic officials every few yards, on foot, on motorcycles, or on horseback, but they were having a hard time keeping the two lanes of cars untangled and moving, and the air was full of the noise of their police whistles and shouts. The traffic would congeal, grind ahead, stop again, while the Klan families sat steaming and fanning themselves in their cars. Most of them seemed to have made it a real family expedition: the cars were loaded with luggage, camping equipment, and children. Quite a few of the latter — even those too young to belong to the junior order of the Klan — were dressed in little Klan outfits, which did not save them from being smacked when their restiveness annoyed their hot and harassed parents. The less ardent or more philosophical Klansmen had given up and had established themselves, with their picnic baskets and souvenir pillows, in shady spots all along the road and far into the adjoining fields and woods. From his gilded airplane, D. C. Stephenson must have seen a landscape dappled for miles around with little knots of white.

Since there was no way of turning back we stayed with the procession, feeling increasingly conspicuous. Finally we came to the cross road whose left branch led past the entrance to Melfalfa. We turned right and started home.

So we missed seeing the Konklave close up. But the newspapers were full of it, and people who were there have been able to fill in the details for me. The program gave a good indication of what the Klan was all about, or thought it was about. The Konklave started in midmorning with an address by a minister, the Reverend Mr. Kern of Covington, Indiana. The Reverend Kern spent most of his time warning against the machinations of Catholics and foreigners in the United States. When he finished, a fifty-piece boys' band from Alliance, Ohio, played "America" and the crowd sang. Then a band from New Castle, Indiana, played the "Star-Spangled Banner" and the Reverend Everett Nixon of Kokomo gave the invocation. These preliminaries led up to a speech by Dr. Hiram Wesley Evans, the national leader of the Klan, who had come all the way from headquarters at Atlanta, Georgia. Dr. Evans commented gracefully on the fact that the center of Klan activities seemed to have shifted from Atlanta to Kokomo, and then talked on "Back to the Constitution." In his view, the Constitution was in peril from foreigners and "foreign influences," and he urged his audience to vote for Congressmen who would legislate "to the end that the nation may be rehabilitated by letting Americans be born into the American heritage." By the time Dr. Evans finished it was lunch time, and the Klan families spread their picnic cloths through the leafy acres of Melfalfa Park. Block-long cafeteria tables lined the banks of Wildcat Creek. From these, the women's auxiliary of the Klan dispensed five thousand cases of pop and near-beer, fifty-five thousand buns, twenty-five hundred pies, six tons of beef, and supplementary refreshments on the same scale.

It was after lunch, at about 2 P.M., when the crowd was full of food and patriotic ecstasy, that D. C. Stephenson made his dramatic descent from the sky.

The rest of the day, after Stephenson's speech, was given over to sports, band concerts, and general holiday frolic. That night there was a parade down Main Street in Kokomo. And while an outside observer might have found a good deal to be amused at in the antics of the Klan during the day, no one could have seen the parade that night without feelings of solemnity. There were thirty bands; but as usual in Klan parades there was no music, only the sound of drums. They rolled the slow, heavy tempo of the march from the far north end of town to Foster Park, a low meadow bordering Wildcat Creek where the Klan had put up a twenty-five-foot "fiery cross." There were three hundred mounted Klansmen interspersed in companies among the fifty thousand hooded men, women, and children on foot. The marchers moved in good order, and the measured tread of their feet, timed to the rumbling of the drums and accented by the off-beat clatter of the horses' hoofs, filled the night with an overpowering sound. Many of the marchers carried flaming torches, whose light threw grotesque shadows up and down Main Street. Flag bearers preceded every Den, or local Klan chapter. Usually they carried two Klan flags flanking an American flag, and the word would ripple down the rows of spectators lining the curbs, "Here comes the flag! Hats off for the flag!" Near the place where I was standing with my parents one man was slow with his hat and had it knocked off his head. He started to protest, thought better of it, and held his hat in his hand during the rest of the parade.

Finally the biggest flag I have ever seen came by. It must have been at least thirty feet long, since it took a dozen or more men on each side to support it, and it stretched almost from curb to curb. It sagged in the center under a great weight of coins and bills. As it passed us the bearers called out, "Throw in! Give to the hospital!" and most of the spectators did. This was a collection for the new "Klan hospital" that was to relieve white Protestant Kokomoans of the indignity of being born, being sick, and dying under the care of nuns, a necessity then since the Catholics supported the only hospital in town. It was announced afterward that the huge flag had collected fifty thousand dollars. . . .

It may be asked, why . . . did the town take so whole-heartedly to the Klan, which made a program of misdirected hate? And the answer to that may be, paradoxically enough, that the Klan supplied artificial tensions. Though artificial, and perhaps never quite really believed in, they were satisfying. They filled a need — a need for Kokomo and all the big and little towns that resembled it during the early 1920's.

In 1923, Kokomo, like the rest of the United States, was in a state of arrested emotion. It had gone whole-hog for war in 1917–18. My own earliest memories are mostly of parading soldiers, brass bands, peach pits thrown into collection stations on Main Street to be used "for gas masks," Liberty Bonds, jam-packed troop trains, the Kaiser hung in effigy, grotesque drawings of Huns in the old *Life*. But it was mostly a make-believe war, as it turned out, and by the time it was well started it was all over.

The emotions it had whipped up, however, were not over. As Charles W. Furgeson says in *Confusion of Tongues*: "We had indulged in wild and lascivious dreams. We had imagined ourselves in the act of intercourse with the Whore of the World. Then suddenly the war was over and the Whore vanished for a time and we were in a condition of *coitus interruptus*." To pursue the imagery, consummation was necessary. With the real enemy gone, a fresh one had to be found. Find an enemy: Catholics, Jews, Negroes, foreigners — but especially Catholics.

This seemingly strange transmutation was not really strange, considering the heritage of the times. Anti-foreignism has been a lively issue in American history since before the Republic. It became a major issue from the 1830's on, as mass migrations took place from Ireland, Germany, Scandinavia, Italy, Poland, Russia, and the Far East. Before immigration was finally curbed by the quota laws, many old-stock Americans in the South and Central West had been roused to an alarmed conviction that they were in danger of being overrun. The "foreigners" with their different ways and ideas were "ruining the country"; and hence anything "foreign" was "un-American" and a menace.

Another main stream in American history was anti-Catholicism, for the good and sufficient reason that a great many of the founding fathers had come to this continent to escape Catholic persecutions. This stream ran deep; and periodically it would emerge at the surface, as in the Know

Nothing Party of the 1850's and the American Protective Association of the 1890's. It was submerged but still strong as this century began, and it came to a violent confluence in the 1920's with the parallel stream of anti-foreignism. The conscious or unconscious syllogism was: (1) foreigners are a menace, as demonstrated by the war, (2) the Catholic Church is run by a foreign Pope in a foreign city, (3) therefore the Catholic Church is a menace. Here was a suitable enemy — powerful, mysterious, international, aggressive.

To some extent, of course, the violence with which the jaws of this syllogism snapped shut was a result of parallel thinking in Washington. Wilson had been repudiated, and with him the League and the World Court, and internationalism had become a bad word. The great debates accompanying these events had stirred the country as it had not been stirred since the days preceding the Civil War, and things said then by the isolationists had been enough to frighten even normally sensible people. The exact sequence is a conundrum like that of the chicken and egg: whether the isolationist politicians led the people or whether the people drove the isolationist politicians. The postwar disillusionment that swept all ranks, including the new generation of authors, would seem to indicate the latter. Great men might have controlled the tide, but they were not to be found in the administrations of Harding and Coolidge.

There were other factors too: the deadly tedium of small-town life, where any change was a relief; the nature of current Protestant theology, rooted in Fundamentalism and hot with bigotry; and, not least, a native American moralistic blood lust that is half historical determinism, and half Freud. The Puritan morality . . . gained new strength, in fact, in the revulsion against the excesses of frontier life. But Puritanism defies human nature, and human nature, repressed, emerges in disguise. The fleshly appetites of the small townsman, when confronted by the rigid moral standards of his social environment, may be transformed into a fanatic persecution of those very appetites. The Klan, which sanctified chastity and "clean living" and brought violent punishment to sinners, was a perfect outlet for these repressions. It is significant that the favored Klan method of dealing with sexual transgressors was to strip them naked and whip them, an act of sadism.

This sexual symbolism could, with not too much effort, be made to dovetail with anti-foreignism and anti-Catholicism. Foreigners were notoriously immoral, as proven by the stories the soldiers brought back from wicked Paris. The Catholic Church, the "foreign church," must condone such things; and besides, who knew *what* went on among the priests and nuns! A staple in pornographic literature for at least one hundred years had been the "revelations" of alleged ex-priests. The Klan made use of these and other fables, such as the old and ever popular one about the mummified bodies of newborn infants found under the floor when a nunnery was torn down. . . .

Thus the Catholic Church very easily assumed, in the minds of the ignorant majority, the proportions of a vast, immoral, foreign conspiracy against Protestant America, with no less a design than to put the Pope in the White House. The Knights of Columbus were in reality a secret army pledged to this aim. They kept their guns in the basements of Catholic churches — which usually had high steeples and often were located on the highest ground in town, so that guns fired from the belfries could dominate the streets. Not all Catholics were in on the plot: for example, the Catholics you knew. These were well-meaning dupes whom one might hope to save from their blindness. My parents were generally considered to be among them. . . .

Kokomo first began to hear about the Klan in 1920. In 1921 the local Nathan Hale Den was established, and within two years the town had become so Klannish as to be given the honor of being host city for the tri-state Konklave. (Of course its name helped: the Klan loved alliterative K's.) Literally half the town belonged to the Klan when I was a boy. At its peak, which was from 1923 through 1925, the Nathan Hale Den had about five thousand members, out of an able-bodied adult population of ten thousand. With this strength, the Klan was able to dominate local politics. In 1924 it elected the mayor, a dapper character named Silcott E. "Silk" Spurgeon, a former clothing salesman, and swept the lists for city councilmen. It packed the police and fire departments with its own people, with the result that on parade nights the traffic patrolmen disappeared, and traffic control was taken over by sheeted figures whose size and shape resembled those of the vanished patrolmen. It ran the town openly and insolently.

As in most of the thousands of other towns where the Klan thrived, there was a strong undercurrent of opposition. But as in most towns, few men were brave enough to state their disapproval openly. The Klan first appealed to the ignorant, the slightly unbalanced, and the venal; but by the time the enlightened elements realized the danger, it was already on top of them. Once organized in strength, the Klan had an irresistible weapon in economic boycott. The anti-Klan merchant saw his trade fade away to the Klan store across the street, where the store window carried a "TWK" (Trade with Klansmen) sign. The non-Klan insurance salesman hadn't a chance against the fraternal advantage of one who doubled in the evenings as a Kladd, Nighthawk, or Fury. It takes great courage to sacrifice a life's work for a principle.

It also takes moral conviction — and it is difficult to arrive at such conviction when the pastor of one's own church openly or tacitly takes an opposite stand. Kokomo's ministers, like her merchants and insurance men, swung with the tide. Most of them, in fact, took little or no swinging, since they saw in the Klan what it professed to be: the militant arm of evangelical Protestantism. There were a few holdouts, but they remained silent; and their silence was filled by the loud exhortations of others such as the Reverend Everett Nixon, Klan chaplain and Klan-sponsored city councilman, and the Reverend P. E. Greenwalt, of the South Main Street Methodist Church, who whipped a homemade Klan flag from his pocket as he reached the climax of his baccalaureate sermon at the high school graduation exercises. Other ministers, while less fanatic, were perhaps no less sure that the Klan was doing God's work. They found that it stimulated church attendance, with a consequent and agreeable rise in collections. They found their churches visited in rotation by a Klan "team" which would appear at the door unexpectedly, stride up the aisle with Klan and American flags flying, deposit a money offering at the foot of the pulpit, and silently depart. Generally, while this was going on, the ministers would find it in their consciences to ask the choir to sing "Onward, Christian Soldiers."

And so it went in Kokomo and in its equivalents all over the Middle West and South. The Klan made less headway in the big cities, with their strong foreign, Catholic, Negro, and Jewish populations, but from the middle-sized cities down to the country villages it soon had partial or full control of politics and commerce. Indianapolis, with a population of some two hundred thousand, was dominated almost as completely as Kokomo. D. C. Stephenson, the Grand Dragon, had his headquarters there, in a suite of offices in a downtown business building, and from there he ran the state government. "I am the law in Indiana," he said, and there was no doubt about it. He owned the legislature; he owned the Governor, a political hack named Ed Jackson; he owned most of the Representatives and both United States Senators. . . .

Stephenson in turn took his orders, after a fashion, from Atlanta, Georgia, where Dr. Evans presided over the Invisible Empire from a sumptuous Imperial Palace on fashionable Peachtree Road. Dr. Evans was a dentist by trade and an Imperial Wizard by usurpation. He had unhorsed the previous Wizard and founder, "Colonel" William Joseph Simmons, several months before the Kokomo Konklave. It was in Kokomo, incidentally, that Evans made his first Imperial appearance before a really large Klan audience, thus giving that event an extra significance for history, since it was during his Reign that the Klan was to have its greatest triumphs and sink finally almost to its nadir.

However, in understanding the place of the Klan in American life, Dr. Evans' significance is less than "Colonel" Simmons'. Evans was shrewd, aggressive, and a good administrator, but he stepped into a going concern. The concern existed because of Simmons. And it was going through the efforts not of either Evans or Simmons but those of an obscure couple named Edward Young Clark and Mrs. Elizabeth Tyler.

The tangled story of the Klan's twentieth-century rebirth opens officially in 1915, but stems back to a day in 1901 when Simmons was sitting on a bench outside his home. The future Emperor at that time was a preacher, but wasn't doing very well at it. As he sat gazing into the sky, watching the wind drive masses of cumulus clouds along, he noticed an interesting formation. As he watched, it split into two billowy lengths, and these in turn broke up into smaller clouds that followed one another in a procession across the sky. Simmons took the phenomenon as a sign from God, and fell to his knees with a prayer.

A devotee of Southern history, Simmons was even more familiar than most Southerners with the legends of the old Ku Klux Klan. Founded in 1866 in Pulaski, Tennessee, by a group of young Confederate troopers home from the war and with time heavy on their hands, it had started out simply as a social club — a device, significantly enough, to recapture some of the lost wartime excitement and comradeship. The young ex-soldiers picked their name from *Kuklos,* the Greek word for "circle," which they transformed to Ku Klux, and framed a fantastic ritual and nomenclature for their own amusement. The idea spread, and as it spread it found a serious purpose in restoring the South to home rule. Eventually the best manhood (and much of the worst) of the South took part, with General Nathan Bedford Forrest as Imperial Wizard. Finally it degenerated into mere terrorism, and General Forrest disbanded it in 1869, but not until the Carpetbaggers had been dispersed and the Klan had become immortalized in Southern memory. It was the old Klan that the convulsed mind of Reverend Simmons saw in the clouds. . . .

What Simmons called forth was not the old Klan, however, but a greatly distorted image of it. For all its excesses, the original Klan had some constructive purposes. Its prescript shows that it was devoted to restoring Constitutional rights to white Southerners, to the proection of Southern womanhood, and to the re-establishment of home rule. It operated in secrecy for the good reason that its members would have been shot or imprisoned by federal troops had they been found out.

The new Klan adopted the costume, the secrecy, and much of the ritual of the old, but very little of the substance. Its purposes are indicated in the Kloran, or book of rules and rituals:

1. Is the motive prompting your ambition to be a Klansman serious and unselfish?
2. Are you a native born, white, gentile American?
3. Are you absolutely opposed to and free of any allegiance of any nature to any cause, government, people, sect, or ruler that is foreign to the United States of America?
4. Do you believe in the tenets of the Christian religion?
5. Do you esteem the United States of America and its institutions above all other government, civil, political, or ecclesiastical, in the whole world?
6. Will you, without mental reservation, take a solemn oath to defend, preserve, and enforce same?

7. Do you believe in clannishness, and will you faithfully practice same toward Klansmen?
8. Do you believe in and will you faithfully strive for the eternal maintenance of white supremacy?
9. Will you faithfully obey our constitution and laws, and conform willingly to all our usages, requirements, and regulations?
10. Can you always be depended on?

Only in "white supremacy" did the aims of the old and new Klans coincide, aside from the banalities about unselfishness, patriotism, and dependability. By questions 2 and 3 Simmons excluded foreigners, Jews, and Catholics, all of whom had been accepted into the original Klan, and thereby set his course in an altogether new direction.

While appropriating much of the ritual of the original, Simmons also added some mumbo-jumbo of his own. The old plus the new enveloped his converts in a weird and unintelligible system of ceremonies, signs, signals, and words. The Klan had its own calendar, so that July 4, 1923, for example, became "The Dismal Day of the Weeping Week of the Hideous Month of the year of the Klan LVII." The local "dens" were governed by an "Exalted Cyclops," a "Klaliff," "Klokard," "Kludd," "Kligrapp," "Klabee," "Kladd," "Klagaro," "Klexter," "Klokann," and "Nighthawk," corresponding respectively to president, vice-president, lecturer, chaplain, secretary, treasurer, conductor, inner guard, outer guard, investigating committee, and proctor in charge of candidates. The Klansmen sang "klodes," held "klonvocations," swore blood oaths, burned crosses, muttered passwords ("Kotop," to which the reply was "Potok," both meaning nothing), and carried on "klonversations." The latter were an exchange of code words formed from the first letters of sentences.

Ayak	Are you a Klansman?
Akia	A Klansman I am.
Capowe	Countersign and password of written evidence.
Cygnar	Can you give number and realm?
No. v *Atga*	Number one Klan of Atlanta, Georgia.
Kigy	Klansman, I greet you.
Itsub	In the sacred, unfailing bond.

They would then *Klasp* left hands (Klan loyalty a Sacred Principle). If a known non-member approached at this fraternal moment, the one who spied him first would break off the klonversation with a warning, "*Sanbog.*" (Strangers are near. Be on guard!)

Non-members were "aliens," and remained so until they were "baptized" as "citizens of the Invisible Empire," whereupon they received the "Mioak," or Mystical Insignia of a Klansman, a little red celluloid button bearing the inscrutable words "Kotop" and "Potok." Having taken the sacred oath, the new member was reminded by the Exalted Cyclops that "Mortal man cannot assume a more binding oath; character and courage alone will enable you to keep it. Always remember that to keep this oath means to you honor, happiness, and life; but to violate it means disgrace, dishonor, and *death*. May happiness, honor, and life be yours." The member's subsequent duties included absolute obedience to the Imperial Wizard, who was described in the Kloran as "The Emperor of the Invisible Empire, a wise man, a wonder worker, having power to charm and control."

Thus equipped, the Reverend Simmons set about creating his Empire. It was uphill work, however. Five years later he had enrolled only a few thousand subjects. The times, perhaps, were not quite right, but in addition the Emperor himself lacked two mundane qualities — executive ability and calculating greed. Both of these lacks were supplied in the spring of 1920, when he met Mr. Clark and Mrs. Tyler.

This couple were professional fund raisers and publicity agents whose accounts had included the Anti-Saloon League, Near East Relief, the Roosevelt Memorial Fund, and others of similar scope. Simmons' Ku Klux Klan was almost too small to be worth their attention, but they decided that it had possibilities. As Southerners, they saw in the anti-foreign, Catholic, Jewish, Negro provisions the raw material with which to appeal to four deep prejudices among other Southerners. After they took the project on Clark became King Kleagle, or second in command, and head of the promotion department, and Mrs. Tyler became his chief assistant. Simmons was left in the misty heights as Imperial Wizard and Emperor, where he was happy. Thereafter, between them, Clark and Mrs. Tyler systematized the appeals to racial and religious hatred and organized the sale of Klan memberships on a businesslike basis.

They divided the country into eight "domains," each headed by a Grand Goblin, and subdivided it into "realms," or states, each in charge of a Grand Dragon, such as Stephenson. The initiation fee was $10 of which $4 went to the Kleagle, or local solicitor, when he signed up a recruit, $1 to the King Kleagle, the state sales manager, 50 cents to the Grand Goblin, and $4.50 to Atlanta. Robes, which were made by the affiliated Gate City Manufacturing Company at a cost of $3.28, were sold for $6.50. Newspapers, magazines, Klorans, and other Klan printed matter was turned out at a substantial profit by the Searchlight Publishing Company, another Klan enterprise, and miscellaneous real estate was handled by the Clark Realty Company. The local Klaverns were supported by dues of a dollar a month, part of which was sent to the state organization. It was somewhat like a chain letter; almost everyone seemed guaranteed to make money.

Within a year and a half, this system had netted more than a hundred thousand members. It had also, according to the New York *World,* caused four killings, one mutilation, one branding with acid, forty-one floggings, twenty-seven tar-and-feather parties, five kidnapings, and forty-three threats and warnings to leave town. The *World's* exposé pricked Congress into an investigation in October, 1921. Emperor Simmons was called, but proved to be a slippery witness. The atrocities ascribed to the Klan were, he said, the work of imposters. The Klan did not permit violence, he assured the Congressmen, and cited instances wherein he had rebuked dens which disobeyed this rule by withdrawing their charters. The Klan was "purely a fraternal organization," dedicated to patriotism, brotherhood, and maintenance of law and order. Although circumstantial evidence was strong, the investigators could find no legal evidence that the Klan's national organization had caused the outrages or even approved of them, and the inquiry petered out.

However, the *World's* detective work did have one notable result. Shortly before the Congressional investigation got under way, the paper printed an account of how, two years before, Clark and Mrs. Tyler had been "arrested at midnight in their sleeping garments, in a notorious underworld resort at 185 South Pryor Street, Atlanta, run by Mrs. Tyler," and hauled off to jail, to be charged with "disorderly conduct" and possession of liquor. In the resultant furor Clark submitted his resignation to Simmons, which inspired Mrs. Tyler to issue a statement calling him "a weak-kneed quitter" and repudiating him. Simmons, who was well aware of what the couple had accomplished for the Klan, refused to take action against them. Instead, the propaganda department began to grind out denials, the *World* was branded as a "cowardly and infamous instrument of murder . . . against fair woman!" and the scandal was smoothed over.

But it left a scar. As the moral custodians of their communities, the rank-and-file Klansmen were deeply shocked by the story. Some of them were not convinced by the denials. Along with the evidence presented during the Congressional hearing, it gradually fermented into a basis for an insurgent movement within the ranks. This faction grew under the loving eye of Dr. Evans, who had deserted dentistry to become Grand Dragon of the Realm of Texas, and who had ambitions to the throne. . . .

. . . By the time Dr. Evans took over, [the Klan] was adding thirty-five hundred members a day, and the national treasury was taking in forty-five thousand dollars a day. Within a year Evans could boast, probably with fair accuracy, of a membership of five million. Being in possession of that many adult voters, he and his henchmen naturally turned their thoughts to politics. Principles, they announced, were important to the Klan, not party labels; and accordingly the state and local organizations adopted whichever of the two major parties was stronger in its region. In the South, the Klan was Democratic, in the North, Republican. But since the Republicans were dominant nationally, both the arithmetic of membership and the ends of expediency dictated a stronger drive within that party. But 1924 was a poor year to interfere in Republican affairs. Calvin Coolidge was not only an extremely popular President, but represented in his person many of the parochial virtues that the Klan endorsed, and there was no point in contesting or even trying to bargain over his nomination. The Democratic convention was much more promising. The strongest candidate was Alfred E. Smith, Catholic, Tammany, wet, and a big-city product — in short, a symbol of everything the Klan was against. The Klan came out fighting for William Gibbs McAdoo and managed to split and stalemate the whole proceedings. It finally lost, but it also prevented Smith's nomination; and after many angry hours and smoke-filled meetings John W. Davis, a J. P. Morgan lawyer, was served up as a compromise. The Harding scandals were fresh in the minds of everyone, and 1924 logically should have been a Democratic year, but Davis lost. Considering later events, it is easy to speculate that the Klan's battle in the 1924 Democratic convention was a decisive event in United States and world history.

For Dr. Evans and his Goblins and Dragons it was an encouraging show of strength, despite their failure to nominate their man. They looked forward to 1928. Then, suddenly, there was a disaster. D. C. Stephenson, the Grandest Dragon of the Empire, made a mistake.

"Steve" — as he was usually known — kept a bust of Napoleon on his desk. And like Napoleon, he knew what he wanted. He wanted money and women and power, and later on he wanted to be President of the United States. . . .

Not much is known about his early life. He was born in 1891, evidently in Texas, and spent part of his youth in Oklahoma. He was a second lieutenant in World War I but saw no service overseas. He was married twice, but had divorced or abandoned both women by the time he moved to Evansville, Indiana, shortly after the war. There he began organizing veterans, and this took him into politics. In 1920 he entered the Democratic Congressional primary as a wet. Defeated by the Anti-Saloon League, he promptly became a dry Republican and at the same time joined the newly rising Ku Klux Klan. He became an organizer for the Klan. By 1922 he had succeeded so well that he was made organizer for the State of Indiana, and shortly afterward for twenty other states, mostly Midwestern. After a short period in Columbus, Ohio, he moved his offices to Indianapolis, and on July 4, 1923, at Kokomo he officially added the Grand Dragonship of Indiana to his portfolio. By that time he was well on his way to his first million dollars. . . .

One of the women he knew, but not very well, was Madge Oberholzer. She had a small job at the State House in the office of the State Superintendent of Public Instruction. She was not particularly attractive. Unmarried at twenty-eight, which in Indiana means ripe spinsterhood, she was a buxom 145 pounds, had a rather long nose, and wore her hair in an exaggerated upswing that hung over her forehead. But for some reason Steve, whose taste usually ran to ripe beauties, was interested in Madge.

He took her to several parties, and once, when the legislature was considering a bill that would have abolished her state job, he gallantly killed it for her.

On the night of March 15, 1925, Madge came home about ten o'clock from a date with another man. Steve had been telephoning, and when she called him back he told her he was going to Chicago and wanted her to come and see him on an important matter before he left. He would send Earl Gentry, one of his bodyguards, to escort her.

She found Steve drinking when she arrived at his home, and according to her later testimony he "forced" her to drink with him. Three drinks later he asked her to go along to Chicago. When she refused, Steve motioned to Gentry and Earl Klenck, another bodyguard, who produced guns; the three men then led her outside and into Steve's waiting car. They drove to the railroad station and boarded the midnight train to Chicago. Steve, Gentry, and Madge went into a drawing room. Gentry climbed into an upper berth and Steve shoved Madge into the lower. "After the train started," her testimony says, "Stephenson got in with me and attacked me. He held me so I could not move. I . . . do not remember all that happened. . . . He . . . mutilated me. . . ."

The next day in Hammond, Indiana, where Steve had the presence of mind to get off the train to avoid the Mann Act, Madge managed on a pretext to get hold of some bichloride-of-mercury tablets. She swallowed six of them. By the time Steve discovered what she had done she was deathly ill. Steve tried to get her to a hospital, then offered to marry her, and finally drove her back to Indianapolis. He kept her in a loft above his garage with the threat that she would stay there until she agreed to marriage. She still refused and finally he had her taken to her home, where she died several weeks later. Before her death she dictated the full story to the prosecuting attorney, William H. Remy, who was one of the few officials of Marion County that Steve did not control. . . .

Steve's crude mistake was a disaster for the Klan not only in Indiana but everywhere. His trial was a national sensation, and his conviction [of second-degree murder] was a national indictment of the organization. It became too absurd and ironic for any Goblin or Dragon to proselytize in the name of morality. The Bible Belt might dismiss the Clark-Tyler episode as malicious gossip, but it could hardly dismiss the legal conviction of one who was probably the Klan's most powerful local leader. The Klan began to break up rapidly, leaving political chaos in its wake. . . .

The Klan died hard, however. It took a new grip on life in 1927–28, with the nomination of Al Smith again in prospect, and the old cries of "Keep the Pope out of the White House!" were heard again. Although it could not prevent Smith's nomination this time, the new wave of religious prejudice it stirred up, and the backwash of intolerance it had created in the years before, were important factors in defeating Smith for the Presidency. Therafter it subsided again, and by the end of the decade it had only a tiny fraction of its former strength. Here and there, during the next years, one heard of it: a whipping, a castration, a cross burning. The propaganda line changed with the times. During the thirties, emphasis switched from Catholics, Negroes, Jews, and foreigners to Communism and "labor agitators." It was an unrewarding strategy, for although it may have gained contributions for employers, especially in the South, it won back few members. . . .

When a new bogey appears on Main Street to take the place of the Pope, and a new organization arises to take the place of the Klan, one can only hope that the new generation will turn out to be less ignorant than the old.

STUDY GUIDE

1. Put yourself in the place of the young Catholic child living in a tiny prairie town totally dominated by people of another, and hostile, religious faith. How would you feel? Are there still pockets of old line Americanism where a non-Protestant could feel intimidated in the 1970s? If so, where? If not, why not?

2. Relate the display of Klan prejudice in the 1920s to the emotions stirred up in the "Red Scare" of 1919. How were the fears that nurtured these movements similar? How were they different?

3. What role did Protestant theology and social values play in the rise of the Klan? Were there nonreligious benefits in being a Klansman in Kokomo?

4. In considering the activities and the careers of Edward Young Clark, Elizabeth Tyler, and D. C. Stephenson, can you explain the comment of one historian, who said that many members of the Klan were privately fascinated and attracted by what they publicly condemned?

5. Compare the Klan revival of the 1920s with other nativistic movements of that decade. What might connect the Klan with (a) the movement for prohibition; (b) the passage of the Immigration Act of 1924, which discriminated against Southern and Eastern Europeans; and (c) the anti-Catholic campaign conducted against Alfred E. Smith when he ran for president in 1928?

BIBLIOGRAPHY

An excellent introduction to some aspects of American nativism in the 1920s will be found in the chapter entitled "The Tribal Twenties" in John Higham, *Strangers in the Land* * (New Brunswick, N.J., 1955). There are a number of books on the Klan. David M. Chalmers, *Hooded Americanism: The First Century of the Ku Klux Klan* * (Garden City, N.Y., 1965) and Arnold S. Rice, *The Ku Klux Klan in American Politics* (Washington, D.C., 1962) are both useful surveys of the origins of the Klan and the motivations and activities of its members. An interesting aspect of the operation of the Klan in the 1920s is explored in Kenneth T. Jackson, *The Ku Klux Klan in the Cities, 1915–1930* (New York, 1967).

* Asterisk indicates book is available in a paperback edition.

The cigarette and lighter — symbols of feminine rebellion.

13

PAULA S. FASS

Symbols of Liberation

Parallels between the 1920s and the 1960s are many and obvious. Both decades were marked by a high level of prosperity and a strong tendency toward the consolidation of industry. Both were punctuated by social tensions — and even violence — of an ethnic, racial, and generational character. And in both decades, a cultural revolution erupted against an inherited way of life — bringing new reason for fear to those conservatives who wanted to preserve the values and the behavior patterns of the past and an exhilarating rebelliousness to the young and the radical who led the demand for social change. In the 1960s there were many who felt that rock music, marijuana, and long hair would destroy the moral fiber of American youth — much as there were those, in the 1920s, who felt the same about the consequences of jazz, gin, and bobbed hair.

Trying to explain the reason for the cultural and social revolution of the 1920s is as difficult as trying to explain the emergence of the counterculture of the 1960s (see essay 19 by William Manchester). Several historians — most notably Henry F. May — have contended that the breakdown of the nation's genteel, Victorian culture and somewhat puritanical moral code preceded World War I and was not a consequence of it. In his book *The End of American Innocence*, Professor May stresses the internal weakness of the nation's nineteenth-century "credo" (its beliefs and attitudes) that contributed to its ultimate demise. A contrary view — one that accents an external event, American participation in World War I, in the breakdown of nineteenth-century norms and social values — was advanced by Frederick Lewis Allen, the author of *Only Yesterday*, the first comprehensive account of the 1920s, and later by William E. Leuchtenburg in his volume *The Perils of Prosperity*.

A somewhat different and, perhaps, more useful explanation of the youth rebellion of the 1920s has been advanced by Paula S. Fass in her study of college youth, *The Damned and the Beautiful*. Noting the tendency to conform as well as the rebelliousness of college youth in the 1920s — again, much like the conformity of dress and behavior that characterized those who participated in the youth movements and counterculture of the 1960s — Fass suggests that far from seeking liberation from society, American youth of the 1920s sought, by petting, smoking, drinking, and dancing, to create a peer culture that would, on the one hand, express their rejection of parental norms and, on the other, prepare them to take their place in the nation's business culture and society. "They were," Fass concludes, "a generation in tension. In a culture slowly moving toward the future, they were caught between those encroaching Main Street roles they would soon assume and those innovations that had twisted their lives in new directions." To a degree, much the same may be said for many of the rebels and dropouts of the 1960s as they made — and will continue to make — their way through the 1970s and 1980s.

Youth's exhilarated self-awareness and delight in the expansive possibilities of a changing world can easily be confused with a sense of freedom, and indeed the youth of the twenties often talked as if they were a newly free generation. In fact, however, to describe them as free would be to misunderstand the reality of their lives and, more significantly, to lose sight of their historical role and influence. They were bound — tightly bound — to family, to school, to each other, and to the many social conditions that held them fast to a specific time. Still, their sense of liberation was quite real. So was their sense of themselves as liberators, for they helped to free a whole range of behaviors and beliefs from older constraints, traditional prohibitions, and conventional assumptions. This was the case in sexual behavior, for example. It was true as well in such areas as smoking for women, dancing and music forms, and social drinking. We think of these today as trivial matters concerned with manners or style. It is easy to forget that not so long ago they were issues weighted with moral taboos and sexual proprieties. It was from these older associations that the youth of the twenties liberated these (to us) minor indulgences. For them, each carried a large burden of history and convention, and in separating them from the old assumptions they also helped to rip apart an older world view. As they adopted these behaviors, first as part of their own lives and then as part of the culture they were helping to create, the young carved out a whole new territory to be governed by personal style, preference, and taste. Ironically, in so doing, they transformed the consequential into the trivial. But they also redefined the public and the private. And part of their historical significance lies precisely in the fact that by differentiating custom from morality, taste from propriety, the youth of the twenties set the stage for a new pluralism in behavior and the rhythm for rapid change in cultural forms.

Smoking was perhaps the one most potent symbol of young woman's testing of the elbow room provided by her new sense of freedom and equality. Prostitutes and women in liberated bohemian and intellectual sets had been known to flaunt their cigarettes publicly and privately before the twenties. But in respectable middle-class circles, and especially among young women, smoking, like rouging, was simply not done. Throughout the twenties, smoking could still provoke heated commentary, and for many young women, to smoke in public was a welcome form of notoriety. Although young women in college did not initiate the smoking habit, they increasingly took advantage of the cigarette as a symbol of liberation and as a means of proclaiming their equal rights with men. More importantly, within the college community they had the support of peer-group opinion. Among the young, smoking for women became widely accepted during the twenties, and while smoking remained an issue, as the decade wore on it became an acceptable and familiar habit among college women.

Smoking is not a sexual activity in itself. In the abstract, it is morally neutral. In the context of the specific values of American society, however, it was both morally value-laden and sexually related. Like cosmetics, smoking was sexually suggestive and associated with disreputable women or with bohemian types who self-consciously rejected traditional standards of propriety and morality. College administrators objected to smoking because it undermined an ideal of proper female behavior and decency. As the Dean of Women at Ohio State University noted, smoking was simply not "done in the best circles," and it was, in the words of the Dean of Rhode Island State College, "an unladylike act." In 1920, when four girls were dismissed from a female seminary in the Midwest, the administration admitted that smoking did not make them "bad girls" but claimed that such behavior would undermine commonly accepted standards of decency and might lead to other socially objectionable practices. The implication was clear. The objection to women's smoking was based on traditional criteria of proper conduct for women; once one of these was questioned, all of them would be questioned.

The right to smoke was denied to women as part of the double standard of morality. The implicit fear was that smoking would have an immoral effect on women because it removed one further barrier from the traditional differentiation of the roles and behaviors of the sexes. Smoking implied a promiscuous equality between men and women and was an indication that women could enjoy the same vulgar habits and ultimately also the same vices as men. It further eroded a tradition that held women to be morally superior to men. Moreover, the kind of woman who smoked in the period before the twenties was disreputable or defiant, and smoking was therefore associated with immorality. Thus, one correspondent to the UCLA paper objected to popular cigarette ads featuring women smoking because they lowered the moral "tone of the paper." Those who objected to smoking could give no specific moral definition to the habit. They were forced instead to argue that smoking was simply "unladylike." The opponents of smoking were ultimately helpless when the young rejected the insincerity and dubious distinctions of such conventions.

These associations and conventions underlay the almost unanimous reaction to what became a *cause célèbre* in the twenties, the lifting of the no-smoking ban at Bryn Mawr College. That action brought the issue out into the open and reflected the growing acceptance of smoking in the college community. When in 1925 President Marion Edwards Park, in response to pressure from the student body, opened smoking rooms at various points on the campus, the day of the smoking young woman had dawned. The Bryn Mawr gesture was, of course, more symptomatic than revolutionary, but it was important nevertheless because it provided official sanction to what had been unofficially countenanced by the peer group and because it came in response to community demands. That it occurred at Bryn Mawr, one of the bastions of prestige and respectability, made the action all the more powerful in the public imagination. Bryn Mawr was, in fact, not the first school to permit women to smoke on campus, but President Park had done her deed with a flourish of publicity and well-poised liberality. Similar requests for smoking rights by Vassar and Wellesley students and by women at Brown had been rejected by school officials. . . .

Park's liberal gesture provoked consternation among deans of women throughout the country. In effect, she had given official recognition to the prevalence of the habit among college women. The reactions were predictable, for they reflected the disparity between traditional perceptions and newly accepted habits. Administrators reacted by linking custom to morality. The young severed custom from morality and regarded the antipathy to smoking for women as a meaningless convention, long overdue for revision. At Kansas State Teachers College, President W. A. Brandenberg reacted with anger: "Nothing has occurred in higher education that has so shocked our sense of social decency as the action at Bryn Mawr." At Northwestern University, the Dean of Women announced that should a girl be found smoking anywhere on the campus, in town, or even at her home, she would be summarily dismissed for immoral behavior. In her view, "nice girls" did not smoke. "Any girl I catch smoking anywhere and at any time will not be permitted to remain in college," declared the Dean at Rhode Island State College after dismissing two girls who were caught. When the Dean of Women at Minnesota heard about the action at Bryn Mawr, she quickly formulated a policy; "Smoke and leave school." When asked whether she would ever follow Bryn Mawr's lead and permit women at the University of Minnesota to smoke, Dean E. E. Nichols answered unequivocally, "Never." So pressing did the urgency of the issue now appear that in 1925 the presidents of the Eastern women's colleges met to discuss smoking rules.

But the young rejected the standards of propriety that governed the actions of the administrations. . . . Starting first in the East and then becoming general on the West Coast, the new freedom penetrated to the heart of the Midwest, and even into the South where women were probably viewed more traditionally than elsewhere. At the University of Texas, for example, between 1920 and 1925 there was a marked increase in smoking among coeds and an important liberalization of opinion among male and female students about whether smoking was wrong for women. By 1927, North Carolina's Duke *Chronicle* carried a large ad for Old Golds in which two young women were portrayed eagerly enjoying their smokes. By the end of the decade, smoking for women had become legitimate. . . .

It is impossible to know how many young women smoked habitually or occasionally during the twenties. Precise statistics are unavailable, but it is clear that smoking was becoming more popular among college women. At Ohio State one-third of the coeds admitted smoking at least occasionally, and an ad-hoc survey of weekending women at Bowdoin College revealed that there were as many women who smoked one brand, Luckies, as all those who did not smoke at all. One knowledgeable fraternity leader at Rhode Island State College declared, "Practically all the girls smoke." But this seems unlikely. In many ways, knowing how many women smoked is unnecessary. Smoking is no more a necessary expression of female freedom than sexual intercourse alone is a gauge of sexual activity. More important than the extent of smoking was the increasing sense that women could smoke if they chose to and the breaking away by the young from traditional proscriptions governing female behavior and connecting smoking with immorality. In 1925, noting that the Dean of Women at the University of Texas was surprised and outraged to find that coeds were smoking, the editor of the *Daily Illini* chided, "The girls are beginning to smoke! Good Gracious, Annabelle! They have been smoking for months and years. One only has to be a boy and answer the continued demands for 'a drag' or a cigarette to know that smoking has with the fair young co-eds long ceased to be a practice. It is an art, and one of their most perfectly practiced ones. All co-eds at the University do not smoke but neither do all the boys." . . .

Women and men on the campuses of the twenties proclaimed that women had a right to smoke if they pleased: "If a man can enjoy his coke more by smoking as he drinks it, why isn't it logical to assume that a woman can enjoy hers more when it is accompanied by a cigarette?" asked one woman correspondent at Illinois. "Why shouldn't a woman have a taste for cigarettes just as a man has? It is not the smoking that breaks down the bonds of convention between men and women . . . a woman can command just as much respect with a cigarette in her mouth as without." At New York University women claimed their rights by announcing that they would hold a smoker rather than a traditional tea. The Dean was outraged and prohibited the event, but the women went ahead with their plans anyway. Blanchard and Manasses found that 80% of the young women they questioned approved of smoking for women. In marked contrast, only 26% of the parents approved.

Except for occasional facetious comments about lost male prerogatives, women's smoking generally received the approval of college editors on two grounds. In the first place, the papers took a critical attitude toward all attempts to reform or regulate conduct in the name of moral uplift. Invariably hostile to the pseudo-reforms that abounded in the twenties with the prevailing fears about moral degeneration, editors thus defended the rights of men or women to smoke as an expression of their right to self-determination in morals and behavior. Editors were quick to point out that those who objected to drinking would soon find in smoking another fertile realm for regulation. Smoking for men and women was for the young a personal issue of preference, not morality.

Second, the specific question of women's smoking was defended on the broad grounds of female equality and a woman's inherent right to indulge her tastes just as men had always done. "In this day," one Illinois correspondent asserted, "one has a perfectly good right to ask why men should be permitted to smoke while girls are expelled for doing it." In this, editors and correspondents went beyond the smoking issue to object to discriminatory regulations of all kinds that restricted women's freedom to a larger degree than men's. "Paternalism in colleges," the editor of the *Ohio State Lantern* announced, "is nowhere as pronounced as maternalism. It seems that in nearly every coeducational college in the country, the regulations affecting co-eds are far more drastic and far more circumscribing than the regulations for men. . . . Is this 'new freedom' and 'equality of the sexes' a chimera? Are men really better able to take care of themselves than women? Is the co-ed an inferior sort of person who must have a guardian as if she were feeble-minded or insane? Almost every coeducational school in the country answers 'No' in its classrooms but 'Yes' in its regulations." The double standard, not completely dead even among the young, was quickly losing its theoretical rationale and with that its efficacy as a guide to behavior. . . .

Youth in the twenties denied that certain kinds of behavior were worse for women than for men and they rejected the notion that smoking involved a question of morality or propriety. Undoubtedly, many women began to smoke in the twenties because it was a glamorous affectation and somewhat naughty. They thus welcomed the sexual connotation that lingered around smoking and incorporated such sexual suggestiveness as part of their right. By the end of the decade what had been risqué became merely another sphere of permissible behavior and, like the rights to sexual expression, it had been appropriated by women in their newer sense of freedom and the expanded concept of social equality.

In the twenties, young men and women danced whenever the opportunity presented itself. Unquestionably the most popular social pastime, dancing was, of all potentially questionable and morally related behaviors, the least disreputable in the view of the young. For most youths dancing was not even questionable but a thoroughly respectable and almost compulsory form of socializing. Even at denominational schools, where dancing continued to be regarded as morally risky by officials, students clamored for a relaxation of the older bans as they asked officials to give up outdated "prejudiced feelings" and respond to "the bending of current public opinion." A dance was an occasion. It was a meeting ground between young men and women. It was a pleasurable recreation. But above all it was a craze.

The dancers were close, the steps were fast, and the music was jazz. And because popular forms of dancing were intimate and contorting, and the music was rhythmic and throbbing, it called down upon itself all the venom of offended respectability. Administrative officials as well as women's clubs and city fathers found the dancing provocative and indecent and tried at least to stop the young from engaging in its most egregious forms, if not from the dances entirely. But the young kept on dancing.

They started during the war years, and they danced through the decade. Dancing would leave its stamp on the twenties forever, and jazz would become the lingering symbol for an era. But whatever its symbolic value during the twenties and thereafter, dancing and jazz were forms of recreation, even a means of peer-group communication, that youth appropriated to itself. Dancing was, in the words of one survey of student life, the "chief social diversion of college men and women," and school officials unanimously acknowledged that it was the most popular and universally indulged social activity. Almost all fraternity and university social affairs revolved around mixed dancing. Advertisements for dancing instruction appeared in most college papers. At the high schools, too, dancing was a prime occasion for socializing. One simply had to know how to dance to be sociable, and to be popular one had to know how to dance well. The ability to dance was both a sign of belonging to the world of youth and a necessary accomplishment if one wished to take part in the activities of that world. "I adore to dance" was a common remark among high school girls. When asked what her favorite recreation was, the Vice President of the Associated Women Students at UCLA answered quickly, "Of course, I adore dancing, who doesn't?" The fact that a man was a "divine dancer" made him an attractive date and added much to his social reputation, whatever his other possible assets or liabilities.

The dances the young enjoyed most were the ones most criticized by adults. The shimmy and the toddle, which had become popular during the war, started the decade and the young on their dancing way. They were followed by the collegiate, the charleston, the black bottom, the tango. The dances brought the bodies and faces of the partners too dangerously close for the comfort of the older folks. Dimmed lights added to the mood. Because of the novelty of the rhythms and the "indecent" motions involved, most of the adverse comments came at the beginning of the decade. As the era progressed, less was said, but not because the dancing stopped. The dancing went on, probably becoming more and not less popular and certainly more hectic. While the steps changed in fad fashion and increased in variety, they remained basically the same — exciting, sensuous, and always to the accompaniment of jazz. The older generation was no less opposed, but by working through the public opinion of the young they found a means of controlling what they considered its most indecent extremes. The young tempered the extremes to meet the adult criticism, but they were really calling the tune. . . .

The young made jazz music and jazz dancing a part of their social world and identified with the jazz medium. It became not dancing itself that demonstrated conformity to the peer group but a certain kind of dancing. As a would-be versifier put it,

> Jazz and the bunch jazz with you
> Dance and you're by yourself,
> The mob thinks its jake
> To shimmy and shake,
> For the old fashioned stuff's on the shelf.

. . . In an editorial entitled "Heaven Protect Jazz," the *Illini* observed: "A college existence without jazz would be like a child's Christmas without Santa Claus." "Jazz conglomerates are second nature to us now. We have them after every meal in every fraternity and boarding house, on scores of phonographs during the off hours of the morning, at the movies in the afternoons and evenings, at the game, in the music shops, at the dance halls. . . . Without the assurance of jazz from September to June it would be folly to matriculate." College students, the *Ohio State Lantern* noted, were "jazz inebriates." . . .

By agreeing to regulate themselves, the young defined the medium within which that regulation took place. They did not conform to the administrative view of what kind of dancing and music was aesthetically attractive or morally wholesome. They took upon themselves the task of defining the sphere, and within that sphere they imposed regulations of their own. At the University of Minnesota, for example, couples who were dancing in an objectionable fashion were given a card, distributed by the Women's Self-Government Association and the Association of Minnesota Upperclassmen, which read, "We do not dance cheek-to-cheek, shimmy or dance other extreme dances. You must not. A second note will cause your public removal from the hall. Help keep the Minnesota Standard." Occasional disregard of the rules on the dance floor was noted and condemned in the papers with the wise warning that should such behavior continue and become general the whole enterprise would be endangered. At Ohio State, an editorial entitled "Watch Your Step" made this clear: "Recent rumpus over dancing should make clear to students that they are being watched, constantly, closely and critically." . . .

By agreeing to impose rules against extreme varieties of dancing, the young had, however, approved what authorities could not logically approve and what, consistent with an older standard, most denominational schools continued to resist — the jazz medium that was offensive to traditional concepts of decency. The young had, in effect, redefined what was proper according to their own tastes. Dancing for the youth of the twenties was not merely a pleasurable recreation; it was a way of assimilating to their own uses one of the truly new artistic forms of twentieth-century America. It was a form that expressed the uninhibited quality of the new century, its accelerated pace and attention to sensuous movement. The young were surely not alone in their approval, but in identifying with jazz, they both expressed their right to make the choice and as significantly (and symbolically) gave respectability to the content. What was involved was style and sensibility, not philosophy or ideology, but it was a profound redirection all the same. In the name of decency the young mellowed the rhythms and smoothed out some of jazz's more raw passions, transforming the rude into the stylish. But the jazz embraced by the young in the twenties was also an expression and an outlet for the new tempo of American culture, its heterogenous sources, and its more open sexuality.

Drinking for youth in the twenties was unlike sex, smoking, or dancing, because the young labored under a specific legal ordinance forbidding alcoholic indulgence of any kind. Prohibition was an anomaly in an age of increasing freedoms. Students had been permitted to drink at least off-campus before the passage of the Eighteenth Amendment and the Volstead Act, and beer drinking had been a regular form of celebration and socializing among male students. Prohibition cut off a former freedom. Moreover, unlike the other moral issues of the twenties, drinking was a male-centered problem that secondarily involved women. Drinking had always been a male prerogative. Respectable women were effectively barred from indulgence by tradition. Drinking among youths during the twenties therefore involved a number of distinct issues: the attitude toward the moral code, the attitude toward the law, and the question of female roles.

Drinking on most campuses in the twenties was clearly a problem. Student editors and administrators admitted that there was drinking, especially at homecoming time, but also generally at fraternity houses, mixers, and other social functions. Administrators, eager to defend Prohibition, played down the extent of drinking on campus in the public press, hoping thereby to prove that Prohibition was justified. But rarely did they deny that the problem existed. Students were suspended for drinking throughout the decade, and fraternity houses were frequently raided. At the University of Michigan, for example, the problem was so severe that President Little instituted a patrol system whereby a faculty member could enter a fraternity house at any time should he suspect that students were drinking or stocking liquor.

It is difficult to determine how many students actually drank during the twenties and what the significance of their behavior was. By the end of the decade, the polls of the Congressional Hearing on the Repeal of the Prohibition Amendment presented overwhelming evidence that men and women students drank in a proportion close to two drinkers to every non-drinker. This was the case in all parts of the nation. . . .

Coming at the end of the decade, the Congressional survey reflected the campus situation when anti-Prohibition sentiment had reached a peak. But the college newspapers suggest that there were changes over the course of the decade in the amount and style of drinking. Drinking among the young appears to have been greatest at the very beginning and again in the second half of the twenties. There was a short period between 1921 and 1924 when the amount of drinking was kept to a minimum, the result of initial attempts by the young spurred on by the administration to control drinking, especially at official university parties and at fraternity dances. . . . In the second half of the decade, however, there was a marked increase in the agitation for repeal or modification of Prohibition and a general decrease in the commitment with which the now formal injunctions against drinking were issued. This happened first at the Eastern schools, which appear to have had a shorter dry spell, and gradually affected the Midwest. . . .

Students were openly contemptuous of the kind of moral reformers who had succeeded in passing Prohibition. Self-righteous moralists trying to impose their own standards on everyone were the butt of derision. The *Daily Princetonian* struck just the right tone of contempt: "If the projects of the crusaders for virtue and purity are realized . . . once more the tottering world and western civilization will be made safe for unsullied virgins and old ladies above sixty. The absurdity of such efforts is second only to the presumption with which they are undertaken by . . . certain self-styled upholders of public morals. . . . To presume that one can define decency or legislate virtue is folly." The young dismissed the idea that morality or propriety could be imposed from above. Even in the early period, when editors urged students to give Prohibition a chance, it was based on the belief that an anti-drinking ethos might evolve from the people themselves and not on the principle that such an ethos could or should be imposed from without. "No law which makes criminal a thing which has not, hithertofore, found an analogous condemnation in the code of morals common to all men, can look for the popular accord necessary to its enforcement," observed the *Cornell Sun*, which went on to predict that law-breaking would become a normal pattern because Prohibition rested solely on the righteous conviction of the few and not on the sentiment of the many. . . .

This new drinking spirit was peer-sanctioned, and drinking was, in general, most prevalent in the fraternities where peer pressure was most intense. At one school a coed noted, "Some fraternities won't pledge a man unless he carries a flask," and the freshman handbook at the University of Chicago noted that "in order to be collegiate, one must drink." Bootleggers, according to the *Daily Illini*, made regular calls on fraternity houses, and these were more fraternity dances with drinking than without. Furthermore, many men now regarded "fraternity formals as an occasion upon which to get drunk." A former Duke student similarly blamed the fraternities for setting the drinking standard. The fraternities "have got more money to spend, more of what is called 'social position,' and hence greater temptations and a greater opportunity to play the part of gilded youth." He went on to declare that "if the leading men in the Greek letter fraternities . . . took a genuine, sincere stand against the use of alcohol, drinking would immediately cease to be a problem." That drinking was most common in fraternities was generally acknowledged by school officials, who usually tried to control drinking on the campus as a whole by working through fraternity leaders. In 1928 the President of the University of Washington tried to do just that by calling together a large gathering of fraternity and sorority members. They were "the chief sinners on the campus," and "six times as bad as non-fraternity members." The positive attitude toward drinking in fraternities and the power of fraternity leadership in the drinking issue illustrate the potent influence of peer sanction in regulating drinking behavior. Drinking was most common in fraternities because peer sanctions were most immediate and effective. At the same time, the fraternities helped to make drinking smart on the campus as a whole. University officials knew that fraternities alone could effectively control it because they set the standards that condoned it.

By the second half of the decade most of the energy of student editors was expended not to urge that Prohibition be enforced but to have the law repealed or modified. There were no more mass meetings like that at Wisconsin calling for a boycott of functions where there was drinking. Peer opinion had effected a change in drinking habits and attitudes. Social drinking had become acceptable, and the cocktail or hip flask shared by men and women had replaced the beer consumed by men at an inn or surreptitiously in the stadium. This does not mean that all men drank, and certainly not all women did, but the peer society now sanctioned a new kind of drinking behavior. Students applied themselves to having the law changed so that they could drink legally. . . .

Youth's attitude quite clearly ran counter to the officially prescribed behavior of the 1920's. Most students believed that Prohibition had not stopped drinking and some that it had, in fact, increased the incentive to drink by making it dangerous and exciting. . . . The editor of the *Wisconsin Daily Cardinal* asserted, "Without doubt, prohibition has been an incentive for young folks to learn to drink. . . . The expense of the Volstead experiment has been an exploitation of youth, and a general breaking down of respect for national law in the minds of the people who are law abiding citizens at heart. Briefly, we feel that the Eighteenth Amendment has accomplished nothing but the ruination of our gastronomic organs, our taste, and our one time respect for federal law. The Volstead law has been an ineffective weapon to stop drinking. Its failure shows that it is impossible to legislate morals." . . .

What was important, however, was not just that the young imitated adult models but the kind of models they emulated. These were the models not of conventional conduct or propriety but of glamor and liberated behavior. The young ridiculed righteous moralists who urged a return to traditional standards and conventions and turned instead to modern or deviant pacesetters. If the young were merely following traditional forms in spite of the contemporary law, they would have restricted their drinking to conform with the traditional code which prevailed on campus in the pre-Prohibition days — that is, occasional and minimal drinking among men. But the drinking code had itself changed. Thus the young were deviating not only from the laws but from traditional canons of propriety.

To some extent drinking like smoking or petting became a necessary demonstration of conformity, but this should not obscure the fact that the young believed that drinking should be left to the taste of the individual. It was a personal preference that should not be denied on the basis of law or convention. Drinking, like smoking for women and dancing, was a way by which the young adjusted traditional standards of morality to express their sense of freedom to engage in various kinds of behavior and their self-conscious modernity. All of them were linked to sex, because the traditional sensibility saw them as indications of promiscuity and a further demonstration of a growing license in moral behavior. Prohibition got in youth's way because it was, in fact, an anachronism that made the young law-breakers in spite of themselves.

Was youth's flamboyant behavior and flouting of convention merely capricious or did it function to express individual and group needs? To pretend that the behavior of these youths can be neatly squeezed into a streamlined functionalism would be to miss much of its petulant naughtiness and spirited frivolity. "It takes nerve to rise in collegiate circles," remarked a Trinity College editor; "the freshman who stopped by the English office and asked for a match to light his fag is assured of any position he wants." Part of their excitement and vitality lay in youth's self-conscious naughtiness, their dare-devil antics, and their conspicuous modernity. But by the same token to deprive their behavior of regularity and direction would be to confuse what was contingent in that behavior with what was vital and necessary. It was not caprice that made the moral reformer seem the malicious fool on their cultural horizon, nor was it caprice that made them question traditional proprieties in sexual morality and in such areas as smoking, drinking, and dancing. These the young defined as the private sector, as a sphere for personal expression to be governed by need and taste rather than by law and morals. This differentiation was clearly enunciated in their view of Prohibition — the law had no business regulating personal tastes. It was also implicit in their views on music, dancing, and smoking, which they saw as arenas for expressive style and not for moral absolutes.

In these areas the standards of the young deviated from conventional canons of propriety. That deviation was sanctioned by group approval and as such functioned to unite age peers. It provided the young with a much needed area of self-regulation and served as a mild form of generational differentiation. The young knew that their patterns and attitudes provided a margin of difference between them and their elders, and this gave them a vehicle for group cohesion. It is not insignificant that many of these conventions were sex-linked, for sex is probably the most self-conscious form of adolescent expression and, as Erik Erikson reminds us, the most powerful source for adolescent ego development. In the twenties, personal ego-needs took on group proportions, and thus sexuality became a fertile arena for group direction and identification. . . .

Did the young use sex and morals as a basis for conscious generational revolt? On the whole the answer would appear to be no, although their sexual attitudes and practices did distinguish them from their elders and made them appear rebellious. They welcomed the lingering naughtiness of which they were accused, but more in the spirit of play than with any serious display of anger. As eager capitalists, the young were anything but rebellious in social and political questions. They emphasized style in personal matters and severely demarcated the personal from the social sphere. In so doing they were in the advance guard of twentieth-century American culture. Their behavior signaled the growing divergence between permissible expression in the personal and cultural sphere and necessary conformity in the political and social arena, and they accelerated the process in their conduct and beliefs. This does not mean that they did not enforce conformity among themselves. They did and with vigor, because it served the peer group and its needs. But by enforcing a deviant standard, they helped to transform uniform norms into pluralistic styles and made preference and change, not tradition and morality, the guide to private behavior.

STUDY GUIDE

1. The author's principal thesis about the character of the freedom enjoyed by youth in the 1920s is contained in the first paragraph of her essay. Summarize it in one or two sentences.

2. Concerning smoking: (a) On what grounds does Fass demonstrate that smoking, although not inherently so, had sexual and moral overtones? Do you agree? If so, why; if not, why not? (b) Fass sees "a double standard of morality" operating in the 1920s regarding smoking for women. Explain. (c) How did various university officials treat the problem they saw and how did students — and spokesmen for them in the college newspapers — react? (d) What were the ultimate consequences of the practice by the end of the decade, according to Fass?

3. Concerning dancing: (a) Why were adults — including college administrators — offended by youth dancing, in view of its propriety in the past as a form of socialization and recreation? (b) What similarities and contrasts do you find between the dances of the 1920s and disco dancing of today? And, secondly, does disco dancing of today serve the same peer-group function? (c) And, lastly, how does the author account for the central role of dancing in the lives of college youth? Again: Would this be true today? If so, why; if not, why not?

4. Concerning drinking: (a) To what degree did college students drink, and was it a growing problem or a diminishing one? (b) Summarize the attitudes of students towards drink. (c) What role did fraternities play in shaping these attitudes?

5. In summary: (a) On what grounds does the author conclude (see her last paragraph) that sex and morals (e.g., dancing, smoking, and drinking) were not employed "as a basis for conscious generational revolt"? Explain. (b) How does Fass account for the proliferation of this seemingly rebellious behavior on the part of college youth?

6. In retrospect: What light does this essay shed on the youth culture of today — its dress, recreational and social activities, values, and ultimate goals?

BIBLIOGRAPHY

Surprisingly, historical research on the 1920s lags behind the work done by historians on other periods of American history. In addition to the relevant chapters on the decade in William E. Leuchtenburg, *The Perils of Prosperity,*

1914–1932 * (Chicago, 1958), an entertaining introduction to the twenties is of course Frederick Lewis Allen, *Only Yesterday* * (New York, 1931). While Allen and Leuchtenburg both contend that the cultural and social "revolution in manners and morals" took place in the 1920s, other historians place the transformation in the prewar period. For this point of view, see Henry May, *The End of American Innocence: A Study of the First Years of Our Time, 1912–1917* * (New York, 1959), and James R. McGovern, "The American Woman's Pre–World War I Freedom in Manners and Morals," *Journal of American History*, Vol. LV (1968), pp. 315–333. A series of highly scholarly pieces on various aspects of the 1920s will be found in John Braeman et al., eds., *Change and Continuity in Twentieth Century America: The 1920s* (Columbus, Ohio, 1960). A delightful and informative series of essays on this decade is contained in Isabel Leighton, ed., *The Aspirin Age: 1919–1941* * (New York, 1949).

Among the novels that provide an insight into the cultural and social aspects of the 1920s are the following: John Dos Passos, *U.S.A.* * (New York, 1938); F. Scott Fitzgerald, *The Great Gatsby* * (New York, 1925); and Sinclair Lewis, *Main Street* * (New York, 1920) and *Babbitt* * (New York, 1922).

* Asterisk indicates book is available in a paperback edition.

Rumrunners and the law.

14

ALLAN EVEREST

Heyday of the Bootlegger

The current controversy over the dangers of marijuana parallels, to a certain extent, the conflict of a half-century ago over alcohol. The similarities of the arguments, both pro and con, are striking: the damage to the moral and religious fiber of the individual; the susceptibility to immoral, if not outright criminal, activity; the deprivation the addict inflicts on his family; the implications of loss of efficiency and of productivity for the nation's economy; the deleterious effects on the consumer's health; and the ultimate argument — the impact of intemperance on our national character. Antiprohibitionists, much like those who would enact legislation permitting the smoking of marijuana, denied each of these charges, and labeled the proponents of prohibition reactionaries, exponents of a puritanical outlook that served no function in the twentieth century.

The drive to suppress the consumption of alcohol had its origins in the pre–Civil War period and rose again to prominence as a nationwide movement in the years just after the turn of the century. While the movement owed part of its momentum to an idealistic effort by progressive reformers to curb the personal and social costs of excessive drinking, many prohibitionists were also motivated by a hostility toward Italians, Poles, Russo-Polish Jews, and other recent immigrants whose lifestyles, in the eyes of a number of native Americans, were a threat to the stability of American institutions and the vitality of the nation's character. To implement the Eighteenth Amendment — to prohibit a whole nation from obtaining any beverage containing more than one half of one percent of alcohol by volume — the Volstead Act was passed.

Violations of the prohibition laws were widespread, especially in the urban areas of the North and the East. Many Americans had no qualms about buying and consuming alcoholic beverages from bootleggers who brewed these beverages domestically or from rumrunners who brought them in from abroad. Early on, it became clear to both the consumers and the suppliers of alcohol that the federal government had neither the funds nor the personnel to enforce the prohibition amendment. As the following selection by Allan S. Everest — on rumrunning in upstate New York — demonstrates, a variety of techniques emerged by which Americans were supplied with alcoholic beverages. The Wickersham Commission, an investigative body charged by Herbert Hoover in 1929 to assess the efficacy of the nation's efforts to enforce prohibition, concluded that the government had little choice but to provide the financial and human resources to enforce the law or to consider its repeal. In 1933, early in the administration of Franklin Delano Roosevelt, this latter step was taken; passage of the Twenty-first Amendment brought to an end the nation's "noble experiment."

Twenty-year-old Billy hummed a lively tune as he drove his old Dodge car south toward Chazy. If he did say so himself, he had just put on a good performance at the Canadian border. The result might have been quite different, he knew, because he was carrying ten burlap bags of beer. At the border he was stopped and questioned, as he had known he would be. Of course it helped to be recognized as the son of a prominent citizen of Plattsburgh, but he thought it also helped to project a friendly, candid personality which he had developed over the months of his new career — bootlegging.

He knew that although the border was the most crucial part of his journey, he still faced hazards on his way south. For example, Miner's Woods were just ahead. Was there a trap awaiting him there? And what about the city of Plattsburgh or Poke-o'-Moonshine? If he got through safely this time, perhaps he should vary his routine on the next trip and not appear at the same place too often. So far he had been lucky.

Men like Billy went into rumrunning for many reasons, including money and prestige. In the early years some young men had just been released from

Excerpts from *Rum Across the Border: The Prohibition Era in Northern New York*, by Allan S. Everest (Syracuse, N.Y.: Syracuse University Press, 1978), are reprinted by permission of Syracuse University Press.

the army, with no jobs in sight. A few ex-troopers and patrolmen turned to bootlegging in protest against what they conceived as unfair treatment or against society in general. But for many of the younger bootleggers the thrill of the work was more satisfying than the money. The excitement of a successful chase was enough to make them go back to Canada again and again. Bucky Ladd, whose father was the respected head of customs at Rouses Point, had a profitable brokerage business there which he neglected in favor of the more risky profits of bootlegging. Francis "Sam" Racicot, a bootlegger in Rouses Point as a young man, puts into words what he and his friends did not then: "Most of the bootleggers considered that it was an unfair law and a law which had been foisted on us, which had no validity. We knew that it wasn't being supported by the general public, that it was disliked, and that we didn't feel we were lawbreakers."

Numerically, the largest group was the petty smugglers, who had vacationed in Canada or had visited the border night spots and wanted to return home with a bottle or two. If caught at the border, they were usually relieved to get off with a small fine and the loss of the liquor. Occasionally, a man like Thomas McBeetry of Saranac Lake refused to pay the five dollar fine even when his companions did so, and too late found himself held in $1,000 bail for a session of federal court. An unexpected by-product of this traffic was the shipping of carloads of American-made pint flasks to Canada for sale to American tourists. The United Cigar Stores in Quebec became almost too busy to sell any tobacco.

In the towns along the border, teenagers comprised another category of smugglers. Elmer Caron, later sheriff of Clinton County, recalls how the boys of Churubusco used to buy a little beer at Toissant Trombly's across the border: "An officer once stopped a group of them on their return and found one bottle. The boys were considered innocent of smuggling but they were thoroughly frightened." Howard Curtis remembers that as a schoolboy in Mooers a sixteen-year-old classmate once asked him to cut school and go to the movies in Plattsburgh in his Model T. When they reached town they drove into a garage, where some cases were unloaded from the rear seat, and then they went to the show. Howard discovered that at about the age of fifteen he had unwittingly been a party to beer-running, "my only participation that I know of at this time."

The seventeen-year-old son of a member of the Board of Education in Utica came north in search of adventure and money. Another boy of the same age arrived on foot at the Sanger home on Rand Hill, recalls Ralph Sanger. Cold and wet, he had been forced to abandon his load and run into the snow-covered woods. Ralph's mother gave him breakfast while she lectured him on the foolishness of his ways, as she did others who came to her door. . . .

It was men in their twenties and thirties, however, who accounted for most of the volume of smuggled goods. One group was the self-employed who owned their own cars. Most towns had several of them, and they were often good friends who shared their fun and information with each other. Yet on the road they were usually lone wolves, traveling by themselves and seeking their own markets.

Another group included the eager beavers who could be hired to drive a load across the border. When they did so they became a part of an enterprise organized by professionals from Saratoga, Glens Falls, or New York City. The car might be furnished for them, but more often they used their own. They were paid either fifty dollars a week and expenses, ten dollars a day, a flat rate per trip, or a case of liquor. At a time when a day's pay in other work was only $1.50–2.00, bootlegging seemed a quick way to get rich. The money enabled them to dress snappily, their wardrobes invariably including a coonskin coat, and gave them some distinction among their peers.

Sometimes the contacts between professional and driver were accidental. A Plattsburgh youth once went to a dance in Rouses Point where he was propositioned to bring a load of liquor from Canada. He attempted it, got through, and subsequently made regular trips for his employer. But there were also places like the Union Hotel in Plattsburgh, which were known as meeting places of professionals and drivers, as recalled by Darwin Keysor of Plattsburgh, who clerked there during high-school. There the drivers got their instructions, and after a successful trip they were treated to a steak dinner and given a great deal of flattering attention, "and they thought they were big shots." The professional could afford to do this because he could anticipate good profits downstate while at the same time running almost no risk himself. But the driver, if caught, could expect no help, and he would almost certainly lose his car, liquor, and perhaps his freedom.

Regional hierarchies were important in the bootlegging fraternity. The "king" of bootleggers won the title by unusually daring and successful exploits. Dick Warner of Saratoga seems to have been the first, but his eventual arrest and jailing left the field open to other hopefuls. The "queen" of bootleggers was a female counterpart. For a while Dorothy Swartout of Saratoga was the unchallenged title-holder. She and Warner shared many adventures on the northern border. While the less daring might hope to be known as "baron" or "duke," none of these terms meant much in northern New York. . . .

If nothing else, the techniques developed by bootleggers were imaginative and ingenious. The petty smugglers often risked concealment of liquor on their persons. Pockets were used, but so were less obvious places. Men had belts made especially to hold bottles, and false vests with pockets large enough for a pint bottle each. Women, who were often expected to run the risks for their male partners, concealed liquor in their bloomers as well as under their corsets. A large person could more successfully disguise odd bulges than a small one, and the loose clothing styles of the day also helped.

Border residents developed some smuggling schemes in the best rural tradition. A Mooers cow made the rounds with her owner between Hemmingford, Mooers, and Champlain. "This dutiful old cow," as Howard Curtis describes her, carried a bale of hay on each side. Finally Officer John O'Hara, who seemed to have a sixth sense in detection, became suspicious of an animal that needed to be bred so often, and upon examining the hay discovered that each bale was hollow and filled with bottles of whiskey. Horses were also put to good use. Leo Filion of Champlain, who was in the business of rumrunning himself, remembers one owner who lost three horses by gunfire. He also tells of a Champlain farmer who had horses trained as bootleggers. He could load one with liquor in Canada and turn it loose, confident that it would avoid all human contact and find its way home through the woods. A great deal of local smuggling was done on foot or snowshoes or with toboggans. Filion remembers a man who could carry four cases at a time on his back. "That would be four dozen bottles and would have weighed more than one hundred pounds," he points out.

But these homely methods hardly sufficed to smuggle goods in the quantity the market demanded, so concealment in cars was tried and found amazingly successful. Sometimes nothing mechanical had to be done to the vehicle. The Mooers undertaker found his hearse perfectly suited to a sideline in smuggling. He always had all the necessary papers for crossing the border, presumably with a body in the coffin. But Officer O'Hara began to wonder about the sudden rise in the death rate, and when he opened the casket he found no body, but plenty of liquor.

Most car owners did not have the natural advantages of the hearse. Some thought that driving without lights or plates shielded them from discovery at night, even though they created hazards for other travelers when they persisted in driving fifty miles an hour. Rumrunners learned to use cars with reinforced springs to support heavy loads. They found that they could wire liquor under the car, or conceal it behind or under seats, in tool boxes, and in spare tires or trunks. They rebuilt cars with false floors of tin through which lengthened pedals and shifting levers were devised; this created a space large enough to store twenty quarts of liquor. Another ruse was the false gas tank. The tank was divided so that one part carried a little gas, but the other part could hold many quarts of liquor. Still another was a false top. Cars of the day were made with fabric tops, and between two layers of fabric a storage space four inches deep was constructed that could carry 180 pints of liquor. Such a top seems to have been the specialty of a garage in Napierville, Quebec. . . .

Bootleggers who wanted to be prepared in case of pursuit provided themselves with a means of making smoke. Some pumped oil into the exhaust. Others used a fire extinguisher filled with a chemical; the pump was bolted to the door of the car and the nozzle connected with a tube running to the exhaust chamber. One or two charges were enough to lay a dangerous smoke screen. Still others had an air-compression machine which stirred up the dust of the road. A smoke screen was illegal, dust was not, yet it was often as effective.

In the winter, whether the roads were open or not, much smuggling was done by sleigh. This traffic was quite safe because it was conducted across the fields away from the patrolled highways. Almost all farmers had flat-bottomed sleighs which they used to haul potatoes and other produce to market. But in winter they were inclined either to do a little bootlegging themselves or rent their conveyances to others. Some bootleggers also took their loads across the ice of Lake Champlain. They did not always remember to check the thickness of the ice, and in February 1924, two men and a sleighload of Canadian ale went into seven feet of water in Trombly's Bay. With help from ashore, horses and sleigh were saved, but the neighbors had to wait until spring to bring up the beer with hooks.

Sleighs were good only for slow, local traffic. Bootleggers kept their cars on the road except after heavy snows and high winds, and even then they tried to keep some of the back roads open for their own use. Diane Filion recalls doing some of this work for her friends with her new Ford; then, she says, customs officers planted two bottles of whiskey on the car and seized it: "I decided not to make a legal case of it because even if I won, my life would be intolerable afterwards."

Informal intelligence networks were organized by the bootleggers. One variety employed youngsters to watch the customs house, especially at night. When the officers left on patrol, the boys either signaled or telephoned to a loading spot across the border that the coast was clear. Youngsters were also employed to follow a patrolman by motorcycle and telephone back the direction he took. In Rouses Point the telephone operator helpfully relayed information concerning the whereabouts of enforcement officers to bootleggers who called in.

Once across the border the bootlegger had a choice of roads. He also had a choice of procedures. He might decide to make a run for it on his own. If he was part of an organization he joined a caravan, which sent scouts ahead in a pilot car to make sure the road was clear. If the pilot car was stopped no harm was done because it was "clean." If it was not challenged for ten to twenty miles, the driver telephoned back that the road was clear. The run, at least as far as Elizabethtown, was often plotted in advance, with farmers' barns or garages rented for quick concealment during a pursuit or as a rest stop while the pilot car scouted the next stretch of road. Farmers even flagged down bootleggers to warn them of danger ahead and to offer sanctuary. Normally, however, the barns were rented by the month. Patrolman Philip Auer reports that bootleggers once tried unwittingly to rent a garage from his wife. . . .

Smugglers were early drawn to the possibilities of the railroad. The small-timers, like those in automobiles, discovered many hiding places. They might tie an individual bottle to a string and hang it out of the window during customs inspection at Rouses Point. If the bottle broke the owner pulled in only a jagged bottle neck; sometimes it was only the string when local boys made off with the bottle, according to Sam Racicot. Liquor was also concealed in ventilators, light fixtures, the springs of Pullman seats, upper berths, and mattresses. Panels in staterooms and washrooms were unscrewed to provide hiding places. Trunks were constructed with false sides and bottoms where many pints could be stored. The so-called "suitcase brigade" consisted of those who simply tried to smuggle liquor in their personal luggage.

Large-scale smugglers, however, were intrigued with the possibilities of the freight car, which offered many advantages over smuggling by automobile. It could be made to carry a load fifty times that of a car. Trains were not stopped by winter weather. Furthermore, it was safer for both smuggler and receiver because false bills of lading made their identities impossible to discover even if the shipment was detected and seized. Bootleggers sometimes gained access to empty freight cars in Canada and constructed false ends three feet deep that created space for almost 200 cases of beer in each end. But just as often they shipped a full car of liquor billed as fish, lumber, hay, or lime. The car was loaded at Napierville or other railroad centers in Quebec and consigned to a receiver in New York or New Jersey. The liquor was concealed under a thin covering of the legitimate cargo named in the bill of lading, and a car could easily carry 100 to 150 barrels of beer. It was then sealed for the trip across the border. There was probably some connivance by Canadian railroad officials, but this was not necessary under the normal procedures for shipping by the carload. . . .

Except in winter, Lake Champlain offered many opportunities for transporting liquor. With a rowboat or an outboard motorboat the small-time smuggler could shuttle back and forth all night. But the professionals used high-powered craft like Chrysler, Chris-Craft, and Gray, some of them elaborate twenty to forty-foot cruisers. Billy Hicks, one of the most active of the local bootleggers, owned a forty-foot boat which he painted black and used at night. When fully loaded it carried 300–400 cases of beer and was barely out of water. A favorite loading place was in the cove just north of Fort Montgomery, but boats could safely navigate the Richelieu River all the way from St. John.

There were man-made hazards on water as well as land. The swing bridge on the railroad across the lake always had to be opened for the larger craft and for almost all boats during high water in the spring. Some rumrunners went through nevertheless, but others unloaded near Rouses Point and continued their journey by land. There were also lake patrols. If a patrol boat approached, the smugglers dropped the liquor overboard so as not to be caught with the evidence.

A capacious device for smuggling by water was the "submarine," a low-lying craft without its own power. Towed behind a large boat, it was cut loose and allowed to sink during a pursuit. With luck the bootleggers could later return and recover the sunken craft; the floating rope would show them where it lay.

A similar device made use of a small wooden box of rock salt. If a pursuit became hot the bags of liquor were dropped overboard, each attached by a long rope to a box of salt. When the salt dissolved the box returned to the surface and guided smugglers to their lost goods.

There were also natural hazards on the lake. Engine failure was always a possibility. Customs officers easily seized a thirty-foot launch abandoned off Cumberland Head lighthouse when its engine stopped. Reefs and irregular shoreline were a danger to pilots unacquainted with the lake. Their threat was made worse by sudden, violent storms that sometimes ravaged the waters. Willsboro Point was such a place, and five bootleg boats came to grief there within a period of two years. The crew usually escaped, but their load and sometimes the boat went to the bottom of the lake. . . .

The market for alcoholic beverages was almost universal, but bootleggers preferred the centers of population. The speakeasies of Rouses Point and Plattsburgh tapped into the flow, although the large markets and high prices were to be found in Glens Falls, Saratoga, Albany, and New York. Profits from smuggling depended upon the kind of liquor, the place of sale, and the number of people who had to share the proceeds. The individual operator could buy beer in Canada for $4.50 or $5.00 a case and sell it in Plattsburgh for $10.00. By carrying it to New York, he could get up to $25.00. Two trips a week were feasible in summer, one in winter if the road was open. If he took a small carload of twenty-five cases, a smuggler could make as much as $600 a run, less his expenses. When smuggling was the work of an organization, the added costs included the relays of drivers, storage charges near the border (up to $3.00 a case), and the rental of barns and storage depots along the way. These expenses were trifling considering the large volume of alcohol that a professional could keep moving.

The most popular Canadian beer in the United States was probably Molson's, closely followed by Black Horse Ale, Carling's Red Label, and Labatt's. Favorites among the whiskies were . . . Canadian Club, and White Horse Scotch. Bootleggers in Rouses Point sometimes took telephone orders for specific champagnes or whiskies for special occasions in downstate cities.

Champagne could be bought in Canada for $4–7 a bottle and might bring up to $20 in New York. Rye was available for $4, brought $7–9 in Plattsburgh and $12 in New York, for a profit of $8. Scotch provided a $12 markup. When it was available, pure alcohol was also profitable. Canadian businessmen were allowed to buy and store it for industrial purposes at ninety-eight cents a gallon. Sam Racicot found a perfume manufacturer who was willing to sell it for $2. He and Roy Ashline would "go through this little false door and pull out the five-gallon tins and load them in the car and head directly for the border and take them down to New York." There they sold it for $15 a gallon. . . .

Bootleggers wanted a fast car and one capable of carrying 25–40 cases of liquor. Cadillacs, Packards, Pierce-Arrows, and Marmons were highly regarded, although every kind was used in the trade, and beginners had to be satisfied with smaller and older cars. Bootleggers could buy cars through the usual retail outlets that other people used. They could also bid at government auctions of seized cars, but the wary decided that these cars were too well known by the patrolmen and would easily be recognized if they were put back into the smuggling business.

The major source of bootleggers' cars was, therefore, a stolen car center in Albany. Cars were cheap, no questions were asked, and since the state had not developed registration procedures, only money and a simple bill of sale containing a fictitious name changed hands. In 1922 Sam Racicot bought a 1917 Cadillac there for $200, used it for a year, and sold it, after he had wrecked it, for his purchase price. Its top speed was fifty miles an hour, and up to sixty going downhill. The speed of the early cars has been exaggerated, and even if they had been capable of eighty miles an hour, which they were not, the condition of the roads would have made such speeds impossible. The Cadillac owner found that the hill out of Elizabethtown toward Keene was so steep that he had to go up in reverse. Gasoline was cheap, but tires were expensive. A bootlegger learned to carry spares because he could not expect much more than two months of use from the tires of the day. . . .

Rumrunners had a number of advantages that lessened the hazards of their profession. The number of officers was insufficient to form more than a token patrol along the border, and bootleggers came to know the personal weaknesses of some of the officers and to exploit them. They also knew that some of them were less dedicated than others and were apt to show indulgence to petty or youthful offenders.

The terrain fitted the needs of the rumrunners. Northern New York was mostly rural, with occasional small towns between the border and Plattsburgh, twenty miles away. Numerous roads crossed the border, but only a few of them had customs stations. The many wooded areas along the highways offered refuge to bootleggers who abandoned their cars in flight; the great majority of them made good their escape, to be back in business a few days later.

Customs stations were closed at night, and the border was unguarded except for the patrols. Serious bootleggers consequently learned to make their big runs after ten or eleven o'clock, when the stations were dark. Ralph Sanger remembers seeing a caravan of as many as fourteen cars pass his home on Rand Hill. A reporter for the *Plattsburgh Republican* conducted a series of interviews along the border in 1923 and documented the extent of this traffic. He was told in Mooers that thirty cars an hour passed through the village during the night. A caravan of fourteen cars had recently passed unchallenged through Mooers, the pilot having first stopped to ask a villager whether the road was clear ahead. Residents of Champlain and Mooers said that if they got up to look every time a car roared by, they would get no sleep. At about the time of the interviews, 132 cars passed the Rouses Point customs house in one night without stopping to report. The office was then being kept open to help conscientious people obtain proper clearance in and out of Canada. Bootleggers obviously never stopped; anyway, many used roads which avoided customs completely.

During the summer months, bootleggers had another bonus at the customs stations. Students from St. Lawrence University in Canton, New York, received temporary appointments as customs officers. Young and inexperienced, they could sometimes be fooled by the tricks of the old-timers. Bootleggers assert that they were even able to walk out of a station with a suitcase full of seized liquor, unrecognized and unchallenged. The margin of safety for the bootlegger was usually the degree of assurance and naturalness he could put into his actions.

The countryside was dotted with farmers who, if unwilling to rent their barns for storage, as many of them did, sympathized with the bootleggers, gave them tips, and provided temporary shelter. Nevertheless, according to Darwin Keysor, an occasional farmer double-crossed a bootlegger by telling him that someone had stolen his load. A well-known garage in Rouses Point, located about a block from the customs house, served the bootleggers well as a transfer point. A loaded Canadian car arriving at the edge of town was made to backfire and then crawled to the garage for help. Once inside, the liquor was transferred to an American car which was casually driven away unchallenged, while the "clean" Canadian car dutifully reported to customs down the street. . . .

For relaxation bootleggers maintained camps, at least during the summer months. The one that served the Malone area was at a remote spot in the northern Adirondacks. The one for the Mooers–Champlain–Rouses Point fraternity was located at Rochester Point on Lake Champlain south of Rouses Point. Here the men enjoyed good food prepared by local women employed for housekeeping duties. Each weekend prostitutes were brought from Montreal, and nudist bathing, plenty of liquor, and other pleasures helped to ease the tensions created by the smugglers' trade. The camp also served as a depot for liquor brought by rowboat from Canada and later reshipped in power boats.

Despite the many conditions that worked in his favor, the bootlegger knew that he was only one step from a stretch in jail, although this was a part of the fascination. He was aware of the danger to his life from gunfire and high-speed driving. If captured, he could expect the penitentiary. If he was challenged but managed to escape, he faced the loss of his car and its contents. Gaston Monette recalls that the dangers he experienced were "so close they are still almost scratching my back."

The narrow, crooked dirt roads of the day often denied the smuggler the speed of which his car was capable, although this factor worked equally against troopers and patrolmen. The sheer distances involved in the liquor traffic added to its complexities. On the map Plattsburgh looked like a short run from the border, but the routes were full of pitfalls. The trip to Glens Falls was 140 miles, to Albany 195 miles, while New York City, the most profitable market, was 350 miles away. Aside from dangers from "the law," the trip was both monotonous and fatiguing. Sam Racicot and Roy Ashline wrecked their car on a trip back from New York when Sam, who was driving, fell asleep.

Car trouble brought many smugglers to grief because all disabled cars attracted attention. Rumrunners were plagued with flat tires, but broken springs and motor failures also took their toll. Gunfire caused breakdowns as well. A patrolman's shots into a gas tank, tires, or radiator usually forced a bootlegger to abandon his car, although some managed sensational escapes on flat tires or with a drained radiator. A rumrunner with a mechanical breakdown could get help by a telephone call to his buddies, but on the party lines of the day he might be overheard and reported. So some preferred to hike to the nearest garage. Billy Colerich once walked a mile for help after the breakdown of his Model T Ford containing a load of beer. On his return he took the precaution of approaching through the woods, only to see customs officers about to seize his car. He escaped and hitchhiked back to Plattsburgh. The wary ones who had breakdowns learned to conceal their loads in the woods before they went for help. William Riley of Newark, New Jersey, lacked any opportunity of getting away. In his beer-laden truck he broke through the planks of a bridge south of Mooers. Only the steel girders prevented him from plunging into the river. . . .

For the most part northern New York was spared the gang warfare that scarred the metropolitan areas during the twenties and early thirties. The so-called Yancey gang moved into the area and although tough, was willing to live and let live with the other bootleggers. When an even tougher gang from New York moved in, however, the Yancey gang opposed them, and eventually the two groups shot it out at the Meridian Hotel. Although only whispered at the time, it was presumed that two members of the new gang were killed and the rest scattered, never to return. The bodies were supposed to have been bound in chains and dumped into Lake Champlain near the railroad bridge.

If a bootlegger could stay out of jail and avoid the other pitfalls of his profession, he might make a great deal of money. Yet the consensus of opinion among the participants is that only a few held onto their money. It seems to have been "easy come, easy go" for most of them. A few substantial businessmen remain in the county who used the profits of rumrunning to start a legitimate enterprise. Farmers who rented their facilities were sometimes able to expand their farms and improve their buildings, but the majority of bootleggers seem to have dissipated their earnings on a succession of expensive cars, necessary to their trade, and on good clothes, women, and other dazzling objects so tempting to the possessor of sudden wealth. Says Keysor, "They bought the most expensive suits and they lived high, they had a good time."

STUDY GUIDE

1. After reading the selection, what impression do you get of the degree of professionalism of the bootleggers? Are there generalizations one can easily make about them as a group or were they a diverse type? If the first, how would you categorize them; if the latter, what categories would you establish in order to subdivide them?

2. What information does this essay provide regarding the competence of the government in policing the prohibition laws and amendment?

3. What appears to be the attitude toward Prohibition of the residents of these border communities? Did this hinder or help law enforcement and, if so, why?

4. Was bootlegging profitable and, if so, what factors determined the extent of the profits that could be garnered?

5. Does this essay support the recommendation of the Wickersham Commission that the federal government should either support the prohibition amendment with money and manpower or repeal it? If so, why; if not, why not?

BIBLIOGRAPHY

The literature on prohibition is abundant and interesting. Many of the comical aspects of the era are told in Henry Walsh Lee, *How Dry We Were: Prohibition Revisited* (Englewood Cliffs, N.J., 1963). Andrew Sinclair's study, *Prohibition: The Era of Excess* (Boston, 1962), published in paperback as *Era of Excess: A Social History of the Prohibition Movement,* * emphasizes the nativistic and backward-looking tendencies of the movement. A similar point of view is taken by Joseph R. Gusfield in *Symbolic Crusade: Status Politics and the American Temperance Movement* (Urbana, Ill., 1963) and by Norman Clark in *The Dry Years: Prohibition and Social Change in Washington* (Seattle, Wash., 1965). James H. Timberlake, in *Prohibition and the Progressive Movement, 1900–1920* * (Cambridge, Mass., 1963), makes a case for prohibition as a facet of Progressive reform. In "New Perspectives on the Prohibition 'Experiment' of the 1920's," *Journal of Social History* (Fall 1968), pp. 51–68, John C. Burnham disagrees with those who have labeled the prohibition movement a failure. Burnham contends, and offers a number of

Allan Everest 239

statistical studies to prove his point, that as a consequence of prohibition, the social and medical health of the nation — and particularly lower income groups — improved markedly. The preceding essay is taken from a scholarly, yet interesting, volume on bootlegging in upper New York State, *Rum across the Border* (Syracuse, 1978), by Allan S. Everest.

* Asterisk indicates book is available in a paperback edition.

V DEPRESSION AND WAR

The prosperity of the 1920s came to an abrupt end in 1929. The stock market crash in October of that year was soon followed by a breakdown of the nation's entire economy. The causes of the Great Depression can be found in the unbalanced economy — both domestic and international — of the twenties: the tendency to use profits for speculation rather than for productivity; an unregulated banking system and a lack of supervision of the stock market; declining income for the farmer; loss of jobs through automation and inadequate wages for the industrial worker; a lack of balance in international trade patterns; and a political philosophy that limited the role of government in reacting to the economic and social needs of most of the American people.

The Depression of the 1930s touched almost every facet of American life. Unemployment was the most serious problem: for almost a decade the number of unemployed Americans ranged from ten million to fifteen million. Industrial productivity declined sharply; crop prices tumbled; foreclosures on houses and farms became everyday occurrences; and the entire nation found itself in the grip of an economic paralysis to which no ready solution could be found. The first selection in this section describes the impact of the Depression on the lives of ordinary citizens; the second focuses more narrowly on its impact on the farmers of the Southwest. Both provide us with a social perspective on the 1930s that is often overlooked in history books, which tend to concentrate on the legislative aspects of Franklin Delano Roosevelt's "New Deal."

The Depression came to an end when Congress voted huge appropriations for fighting World War II — expenditures that both Congress and the nation had been reluctant to vote for peacetime needs. War brought a swift end to unemployment and to the grim texture of American economic life, and brought both prosperity to the economy and a greater sense of purpose to our national existence. Some of the social consequences of World War II for the nation as a whole are described in the last selection, taken from *Don't You Know There's a War On?* Together these three selections survey the many moods of a nation making its way — within a decade and a half — from the depths of the Great Depression to participation in a global war.

Carrying a sandwich sign in the hope of putting food on the family table, 1934.

15

CAROLINE BIRD

The Nation Confronts
the Great Depression

Karl Mannheim, one of Europe's greatest sociologists, has stressed the importance of trying to understand human behavior as a response to an experience shared by members of a particular generation. Several historical examples of an experience that served to influence the outlook of an entire generation can be cited: the bitterness and anger experienced by southern whites as a consequence of their defeat at the hands of the North in the Civil War and the humiliation of the Radical Reconstruction that followed; the disillusionment of the generation that went to war in Europe trying to fulfill Woodrow Wilson's promise to "make the world safe for democracy"; and the susceptibility of the German people to the glorious future offered them by Adolph Hitler and his Nazi regime after their defeat in World War I and their postwar social and economic agonies. The Great Depression of the 1930s was a similarly traumatic experience for millions of Americans left without jobs and, in some instances, without food or shelter. These Americans shared a common generational experience: hunger and want, an unemployed father, no money for recreation or schooling, and a constant fear of what their economic future might be.

The pervasiveness and the duration of the Great Depression is unparalleled in the history of the American people. The stock market crash of 1929 — which wiped out the hopes and the savings of all but a few — only served as the first act of a drama that was to last for more than a decade. By the early thirties, hundreds of banks were failing, tens of thousands of businesses were going bankrupt, and millions of Americans were being added to the unemployment rolls each month. Industrial production by 1933 fell to pre-World War I levels, farm prices plummeted to unprecedented lows, and foreclosures were common experiences as the farmer lost his land and the city dweller his home.

While the pursuit of material wealth has always been central to the American ethos, one may find a causal relationship between the deprivations suffered by the generation of Americans who grew up in the 1930s and their frenzied postwar pursuit of material comforts — new suburban homes, annual editions of chrome-decorated automobiles, and the numerous credit cards they carry for every occasion. The Great Depression, as this selection by Caroline Bird makes amply clear, provided an "invisible scar" — and a lasting one.

You could feel the Depression deepen, but you could not look out of the window and see it. Men who lost their jobs dropped out of sight. They were quiet, and you had to know just when and where to find them: at night, for instance, on the edge of town huddling for warmth around a bonfire, or even the municipal incinerator; at dawn, picking over the garbage dump for scraps of food or salvageable clothing.

In Oakland, California, they lived in sewer pipes the manufacturer could not sell. In Connellsville, Pennsylvania, unemployed steelworkers kept warm in the big ovens they had formerly coked. Outside Washington, D.C., one Bonus Marcher slept in a barrel filled with grass, another in a piano box, a third in a coffin set on trestles. Every big city had a "Hooverville" camp of dispossessed men living like this.

It took a knowing eye — or the eye of poverty itself — to understand or even to observe some of the action. When oranges fell off a truck, it wasn't always an accident; sometimes they were the truck driver's contribution to slum kids. A woman burning newspapers in a vacant lot might be trying to warm a baby's bottle. The ragged men standing silent as cattle, in a flatrack truck parked on a lonely public road, might be getting the bum's rush out of town. In the Southwest, freight trains were black with human bodies headed for warm weather. Railroad dicks shooed them off at stations. Deming, New Mexico, hired a special constable to keep them out of town. When the Southern Pacific police ordered the men off the train, the special constable ordered them back on again.

Everyone knew of someone engaged in a desperate struggle, although most of the agony went on behind closed doors. The stories were whispered. There was something indecent about them. A well-to-do man living on the income from rental property could not collect his rents. His mortgages were foreclosed, and his houses sold for less than the debt. To make up the difference, he sold his own home. He moved himself and his wife into a nearby basement and did odd jobs for the people upstairs in exchange for a room for some of his six children. He mowed lawns, graded yards, and did whatever common labor he could find in order to pay for groceries, until his health broke down under the unaccustomed work. The doctor told him that he needed an operation and would have to rest for a year afterward.

A 72-year-old factory worker was told that he could no longer be employed because he was too old. He went home and turned on the gas. His 56-year-old widow, who had worked as a proofreader before developing heart trouble, sat alone staring at their few sticks of furniture for three days after her husband's death. Then she too turned on the gas. The neighbors smelled it in time and saved her life.

Neither the property owner nor the widow was an uncommon case. They merely were lucky enough to be among the Hundred Neediest Cases chosen by *The New York Times* for 1932. Unlike the hardship cases of the 1960s, who are often urgently in need of psychiatric help, these people were in trouble only because they were physically sick and had no money. By the charitable standards of the rich at that time, they were regarded as the "deserving poor," as distinguished from the undeserving poor, who were thought to be unwilling to work or to save.

If the "deserving poor" had been few, charitable help might have sufficed. But there were too many, and more all the time. In December 1929, three million people were out of work. The next winter, four to five million. The winter of 1931–1932, eight million. The following year, no one knew exactly how many, but all authorities agreed that additional millions were unemployed. In 1965, unemployment is a "problem" when one in twenty is idle. In the fall of 1932, *Fortune* thought that 34 million men, women, and children — better than a fourth of the nation — were members of families that had no regular full-time breadwinner. Estimates differed, but none included farmers unable to make both ends meet, in spite of the blessing of seven-day, sunup-to-sundown employment, or factory hands who were making out on two or three days' work a week.

There were too many in want to hide. There were too many in want to blame. And even if the poor were shiftless, a Christian country would not let them starve. "Everyone is getting along somehow," people said to each other. "After all, no one has starved." But they worried even as they spoke.

A few were ashamed to eat. The Elks in Mt. Kisco, New York, and Princeton University eating clubs were among the organizations that sent leftovers from their tables to the unemployed. A reporter on *The Brooklyn Eagle* suggested a central warehouse where families could send their leftovers for distribution to the needy. John B. Nichlos, of the Oklahoma Gas Utilities Company, worked out a leftover system in detail and urged it on Hoover's Cabinet. It provided:

> Sanitary containers of five (5) gallons each should be secured in a large number so that four (4) will always be left in large kitchens where the restaurants are serving a volume business. The containers should be labeled "MEAT, BEANS, POTATOES, BREAD, AND OTHER ITEMS." Someone from the Salvation Army with a truck should pick up the loaded containers every morning and leave empty ones. The civic clubs, restaurants, the proprietors and the workers should be asked to cooperate in order to take care of all surplus food in as sanitary a way as possible. In other words, when a man finishes his meal he should not (after lighting his cigarette or cigar) leave the ashes on the food which he was unable to consume.

Many more fortunate people turned away from the unemployed, but some tried to help in the traditional neighborly way. A Brooklyn convent put sandwiches outside its door where the needy could get them without knocking. St. Louis society women distributed unsold food from restaurants. Someone put baskets in New York City railroad stations so that commuters could donate vegetables from their gardens. In New York, Bernarr Macfadden served six-cent lunches to the unemployed and claimed he was making money. In San Francisco, the hotel and restaurant workers' union arranged for unemployed chefs and waiters to serve elegant if simple meals to the unemployed.

But there was more talk than help. A great many people spent a great deal of energy urging each other to give, to share, to hire. President Hoover led a national publicity campaign to urge people to give locally and to make jobs. At the suggestion of public-relations counsel Edward L. Bernays, the first President's Emergency Committee was named "for Employment" (PECE) to accentuate the positive. In 1931 it was reorganized more realistically as the President's Organization for Unemployment Relief (POUR). Both undertook to inspire confidence by the issuing of optimistic statements; POUR chairman Walter Gifford told a Senate committee offhandedly that he did not know how many were unemployed and did not think it was the committee's job to find out.

Local groups responded by pressing campaigns of their own to "Give-A-Job" or "Share-A-Meal" until people grew deaf to them. Carl Byoir, founder of one of the country's biggest public-relations firms, declared a "War against Depression" that proposed to wipe it out in six months by getting one million employers to make one new job each.

Results of such appeals were disappointing. Corporation executives answered the pleas of PECE and POUR by saying that they had no right to spend stockholders' money hiring men they did not need. Even in New York City, where the able and well-supported Community Service Society pioneered work relief, there were enough hungry men without money to keep 82 badly managed breadlines going, and men were selling apples on every street corner. Newspapers discovered and photographed an apple seller who was formerly a near-millionaire.

The well of private charity ran dry. A Westchester woman is said to have fired all her servants in order to have money to contribute to the unemployed. "Voluntary conscription" of wages helped steelworkers weather the first round of layoffs in little Conshohocken, Pennsylvania, but the plan broke down as there were more mouths to feed and fewer pay envelopes to conscript. Local charities everywhere were overwhelmed by 1931, and the worst was yet to come.

Kentucky coal miners suffered perhaps the most. In Harlan County there were whole towns whose people had not a cent of income. They lived on dandelions and blackberries. The women washed clothes in soapweed suds. Dysentery bloated the stomachs of starving babies. Children were reported so famished they were chewing up their own hands. Miners tried to plant vegetables, but they were often so hungry that they ate them before they were ripe. On her first trip to the mountains, Eleanor Roosevelt saw a little boy trying to hide his pet rabbit. "He thinks we are not going to eat it," his sister told her, "but we are." In West Virginia, miners mobbed company stores demanding food. Mountain people, with no means to leave their homes, sometimes had to burn their last chairs and tables to keep warm. Local charity could not help in a place where everyone was destitute. . . .

A Quaker himself, Hoover went to the American Friends Service Committee. The Philadelphia Meeting developed a "concern" for the miners. Swarthmore and Haverford students ventured into the hollows, winning the confidence of suspicious miners. They systematically weighed the children, so they could feed those in greatest need first. Hoover gave them $2,500 out of his own pocket, but most of the contributions seem to have come from the Rockefellers.

"No one has starved," Hoover boasted. To prove it, he announced a decline in the death rate. It was heartening, but puzzling, too. Even the social workers could not see how the unemployed kept body and soul together, and the more they studied, the more the wonder grew. Savings, if any, went first. Then insurance was cashed. Then people borrowed from family and friends. They stopped paying rent. When evicted, they moved in with relatives. They ran up bills. It was surprising how much credit could be wangled. In 1932, about 400 families on relief in Philadelphia had managed to contract an average debt of $160, a tribute to the hearts if not the business heads of landlords and merchants. But in the end they had to eat "tight."

Every serious dieter knows how little food it takes to keep alive. One woman borrowed 50¢, bought stale bread at 3½¢ a loaf, and kept her family alive on it for 11 days. Every serious dieter knows how hunger induces total concentration on food. When eating tight, the poor thought of nothing but food, just food. They hunted food like alley cats, and in some of the same places. They haunted docks where spoiled vegetables might be thrown out and brought them home to cook up in a stew from which every member of the family would eat as little as possible, and only when very hungry. Neighbors would ask a child in for a meal or give him scraps — stale bread, bones with a bit of good meat still on them, raw potato peelings. Children would hang around grocery stores, begging a little food, running errands, or watching carts in exchange for a piece of fruit. Sometimes a member of the family would go to another part of town and beg. Anyone on the block who got hold of something big might call the neighbors in to share it. Then everyone would gorge like savages at a killing, to make up for the lean days. Enough people discovered that a five-cent candy bar can make a lunch to boom sales during the generally slow year of 1931. You get used to hunger. After the first few days it doesn't even hurt; you just get weak. When work opened up, at one point, in the Pittsburgh steel mills, men who were called back were not strong enough to do it.

Those who were still prosperous hated to think of such things and frequently succeeded in avoiding them. But professional people could not always escape. A doctor would order medicine for a charity case and then realize that there was no money to pay for it. A school doctor in Philadelphia gave a listless child a tonic to stimulate her appetite and later found that her family did not have enough to eat at home.

A reporter on *The Detroit Free Press* helped the police bring a missing boy back to a bare home on Christmas Day, 1934. He and his friends on the paper got a drugstore to open up so they could bring the boy some toys. *The Detroit Free Press* has supplied Christmas gifts for needy children every year since.

A teacher in a mountain school told a little girl who looked sick but said she was hungry to go home and eat something. "I can't," the youngster said. "It's my sister's turn to eat." In Chicago, teachers were ordered to ask what a child had had to eat before punishing him. Many of them were getting nothing but potatoes, a diet that kept their weight up, but left them listless, crotchety, and sleepy.

The police saw more than anyone else. They had to cope with the homeless men sleeping in doorways or breaking into empty buildings. They had to find help for people who fell sick in the streets or tried to commit suicide. And it was to a cop that city people went when they were at the end of their rope and did not know what else to do. In New York City, the police kept a list of the charities to which they could direct the helpless. In 1930 they took a census of needy families, and city employees started contributing one percent of their salaries to a fund for the police to use to buy food for people they found actually starving. It was the first public confession of official responsibility for plain poverty, and it came not from the top, but from the lowest-paid civil servants, who worked down where the poor people were.

Teachers worried about the children who came to school to get warm. They organized help for youngsters who needed food and clothing before they could learn. Sometimes Boards of Education diverted school funds to feed them. Often the teachers did it on their own. In 1932, New York City schoolteachers contributed $260,000 out of their salaries in one month. Chicago teachers fed 11,000 pupils out of their own pockets in 1931, although they had not themselves been paid for months. "For God's sake, help us feed these children during the summer," Chicago's superintendent of schools begged the governor in June. . . .

Men of old-fashioned principles really believed that the less said about the unemployed, the faster they would get jobs. They really believed that public relief was bad for the poor because it discouraged them from looking for work or from taking it at wages that would tempt business to start up again. According to their theory, permanent mass unemployment was impossible, because there was work at some wage for every able-bodied man, if he would only find and do it. Charity was necessary, of course, for those who were really disabled through no fault of their own, but there could never be very many of these, and they should be screened carefully and given help of a kind and in a way that would keep them from asking for it as long as possible. . . . .

The view persists. In 1961, the mayor of Newburgh, New York, cut off relief to make the unemployed find jobs. In 1965, it was thought that raising the minimum wage would hurt the poor by pricing them out of jobs.

Thirty years earlier, respectable folk worried about the idea of public relief, even though accepting the need for it. On opinion polls they agreed with the general proposition that public relief should be temporary, hard to get, and less than the lowest wage offered by any employer. In the North as well as in the South, relief stations were closed at harvesttime to force the unemployed to work at getting in the crops, for whatever wages farmers offered.

It was a scandal when a relief client drove an old jalopy up to the commissary to lug his groceries home. In some places, a client had to surrender his license plates in order to get relief, even if the old car meant a chance to earn small sums to pay for necessities not covered by relief. Phones went, too, even when they were a relief client's only lifeline to odd jobs. It was considered an outrage if a woman on relief had a smart-looking winter coat, or a ring, or a burial-insurance policy, or a piano. She was made to sell them for groceries before relief would help her. The search for hidden assets was thorough. One thrifty family in New York was denied relief "because it does not seem possible for this family to have managed without some other kind of assistance."

When a woman on relief had triplets, newspapers pointed out that for every 100 children born to self-supporting parents, relief parents produced 160. It was hard even for the social workers to see that big families were more apt to need relief. Almost everybody thought relief caused the poor to become irresponsible and to have children they could not support — if, in fact, they did not have babies deliberately in order to qualify. . . . During the Depression, if some way could have been found to prevent married couples on relief from indulging in sexual intercourse, there would have been those who would have demanded it.

People who took public relief were denied civil rights. Some state constitutions disqualified relief clients from voting, and as late as 1938 an opinion poll showed that one out of every three Republicans thought this was right. In some places, village taxpayers' organizations tried to keep the children of tax delinquents out of the local schools. People suspected of taking public relief were even turned away from churches.

During the first and worst years of the Depression, the only public relief was improvised by cities. Appropriations were deliberately low. If funds ran out every few months, so much the better. The poor would have to make another effort to find work. Every program was "temporary." In most cases, this was sheer necessity. Cities could not afford otherwise. Their tax bases were too narrow. Some of them had lost tax money when banks folded. Detroit could not collect property taxes because landlords could not collect the rent from their unemployed tenants. Bankrupt Chicago was living on tax anticipation warrants doled out by bankers. Some well-heeled citizens refused to pay their taxes at all. Cities cut their own employees, stopped buying library books, and shot zoo animals to divert money to relief. . . .

Cities had to ration relief. In 1932, family allowances in New York City fell to $2.39 a week, and only half of the families who could qualify were getting it. Things were worse elsewhere. In little Hamtramck, Michigan, welfare officials had to cut off all families with fewer than three children. In Detroit, allowances fell to 15¢ a day per person before running out entirely. Across the country, only about a fourth of the unemployed were able to get help, and fewer than that in many cities. Almost everywhere, aid was confined to food and fuel. Relief workers connived with clients to put off landlords. Medical care, clothing, shoes, chairs, beds, safety pins — everything else had to be scrounged or bought by doing without food. Those on relief were little better off than those who couldn't get it. Private help dwindled to six percent of the money spent on the unemployed.

Still, Hoover kept insisting, no one starved. In May 1932, Hoover's Secretary of the Interior, Dr. Ray Lyman Wilbur, reassured the National Conference of Social Workers meeting in Philadelphia. "We must set up the neglect of prosperity against the care of adversity," he philosophized. "With prosperity many parents unload the responsibilities for their children onto others. With adversity the home takes its normal place. The interest of thousands of keen and well-trained people throughout the whole country in seeing that our children are properly fed and cared for has given many of them better and more suitable food than in past good times."

Social workers were indignant. "Have you ever seen the uncontrolled trembling of parents who have starved themselves for weeks so that their children might not go hungry?" social worker Lillian Wald demanded. Others told how fathers and even older brothers and sisters hung around the street corners while the younger children were being fed, for fear they would be tempted to eat more than their share. The social workers knew the facts. They also knew newspaper reporters. In 1932, the public began to listen.

"Mrs. Green left her five small children alone one morning while she went to have her grocery order filled," one social worker reported. "While she was away the constable arrived and padlocked her house with the children inside. When she came back she heard the six-weeks-old baby crying. She did not dare touch the padlock for fear of being arrested, but she found a window open and climbed in and nursed the baby and then climbed out and appealed to the police to let her children out."

Eviction was so common that children in a Philadelphia day-care center made a game of it. They would pile all the doll furniture up first in one corner and then in another. "We ain't got no money for the rent, so we's moved into a new house," a tot explained to the teacher. "Then we got the constable on us, so we's movin' again." Philadelphia relief paid an evicted family's rent for one month in the new house. Then they were on their own. Public opinion favored the tenant. An eviction could bring on a neighborhood riot.

Landlords often let the rent go. Some of them needed relief as much as their tenants, and had a harder time qualifying for it. In Philadelphia a little girl whose father was on relief could not get milk at school, under a program for needy children, because her father "owned property." Investigators found some unemployed tenants sharing food orders with their landlords. In the country, where poor farmers had been accustomed to paying their taxes in work on the roads, tenants who could not pay their rent sometimes did the landlord's road work for him.

It was not true that "no one starved." People starved to death, and not only in Harlan County, Kentucky. The New York City Welfare Council counted 29 deaths from starvation in 1933. More than fifty other people were treated for starvation in hospitals. An additional 110, most of them children, died of malnutrition.

A father who had been turned away by a New York City welfare agency was afraid to apply for help after public relief had been set up. Social workers found one of his children dead; another, too weak to move, lay in bed with the mother; the rest huddled, shivering and hungry, around the desperate father.

A New York dentist and his wife died rather than accept charity. They left a note, and then took gas together. "The entire blame for this tragedy rests with the City of New York or whoever it is that allows free dental work in the hospital," the note read. "We want to get out of the way before we are forced to accept relief money. The City of New York is not to touch our bodies. We have a horror of charity burial. We have put the last of our money in the hands of a friend who will turn it over to my brother."

Health surveys were made to pound home the fact that poor people are sicker than the well-to-do. Doctors, nurses, teachers, and social workers warned that privation was ruining the nation's health. In 1933, the Children's Bureau reported that one in five American children was not getting enough of the right things to eat. Lower vitality, greater susceptibility to infections, slower recovery, stunting, more organic disease, a reversal of gains against tuberculosis — all were freely predicted. Medical care for the poor was sketchy. Doctors were hard hit financially, and they did not always live up to the Oath of Hippocrates. Frequently, the poor were afraid to call a doctor because they did not have money. New York City surgeons sometimes demanded cash in advance or delayed operations until the family could get money together.

Middle-class people put off the doctor and the dentist. "Illness frightens us," John Dos Passos writes of his Depression days at Pacific Grove, California. "You have to have money to be sick — or did then. Any dentistry also was out of the question, with the result that my teeth went badly to pieces. Without dough you couldn't have a tooth filled." Hospitals could never fill the private rooms that helped to pay for their charity cases, with the result that they had fewer patients than they do now, but sicker ones. They learned to be tough in admitting people who could not pay.

The harder the middle class looked, the more critical poverty seemed. It did not seem possible that people could stand lack of regular food, unstable homes, medical neglect. The Depression would leave its mark in the future. "If we put the children in these families under a period of malnutrition such as they are going through today, what sort of people are we going to have twenty years from now?" Karl de Schweinitz of the Philadelphia Community Council asked a Senate committee in 1932. "What will we say at that time about them?" . . .

. . . The Depression did not depress the conditions of the poor. It merely publicized them. The poor had been poor all along. It was just that nobody had looked at them. The children of Depression grew up to be bigger and healthier than their parents, who had enjoyed the advantages of a prosperous childhood. World War II recruits were more fit in every way than doughboys drafted in World War I. The death rate did not rise in the Depression. It kept going down. The health record of the Depression parallels that of rapidly industrializing societies everywhere: infectious diseases dropped, but mental illness, suicide, and the degenerative diseases of an aging population rose. . . .

. . . The poor survived because they knew how to be poor. The Milbank Foundation found more sickness among the poor than among the well off, but they also found that the newly poor were sicker more often than those who always had been poor. In the 1960s, social work provided steady jobs for people who often were close to poverty themselves. In the 1930s, charity was work for middle- and upper-class volunteers, who were charmed and awed by the techniques for survival that they discovered.

A family eating tight would stay in bed a lot. That way they would save fuel, as well as the extra food calories needed in cold weather. The experienced poor, particularly the Negroes, knew about eating the parts of the animal normally rejected. And the poor generally did not spend as much money on food as their middle-class advisers thought they should be spending.

The poor worked at keeping warm. A family with no money for the gas company would economize by cooking once a week. When it was cut off, they would cook in the furnace. They gathered scrap wood to keep the furnace going. They saved by heating only the kitchen. When fuel was low, the experienced poor would sneak into a movie house. Even if they had to spend ten cents to get in, they could sometimes keep out of the cold for two double features. When the electricity was turned off, some men found ways to steal current by tapping a neighbor's wire.

Shoes were a problem. The poor took them off when they got home, to save them. Do-it-yourself shoe-repair kits were popular with the middle class, but if you could not afford the dimestore item you could resole a pair of shoes with rubber cut from an old tire, or wear rubbers over a worn-out sole. Clothes were swapped among the family. One mother and daughter managed to get together an outfit both could wear. They took turns going to church.

The poor whose lives were laid bare by the Depression lived in the same world of poverty that Michael Harrington has recently described in *The Other America,* and Oscar Lewis in his studies of the working classes in Mexico. They lived for the present without much thought for their own past or future. They ate literally from hand to mouth. Even when they had a little money, they did not lay in stocks of food. They paid high interest rates on what they bought or borrowed, and seldom got their money's worth. Their world was small, limited to the people they saw every day, and they did not venture out of it. A trip to the relief office was a daring undertaking. They had few friends. They did not read. Without outside contacts, they could not organize or revolt or escape.

A year after his defeat by Roosevelt, Hoover — who had repeated so many times that no one was starving — went on a fishing trip with cartoonist "Ding" Darling in the Rocky Mountains. One morning a local man came into their camp, found Hoover awake, and led him to a shack where one child lay dead and seven others were in the last stages of starvation. Hoover took the children to a hospital, made a few phone calls, and raised a fund of $3,030 for them. . . .

The Depression gave the middle classes a double vision of the poor. They did not give up the notions that the poor should have saved or that they did not want to work, or that their poverty was their own fault. These were concepts hard to change. While firmly holding to these ideas, however, they saw contradictory facts before their eyes. When the Depression forced them to scrutinize the condition of the working people, they could see that wages were too low and employment too intermittent for most wageworkers to save enough money to see them through emergencies, or old age, even if banks had not failed. A favorite cartoon of the times pictured a squirrel asking an old man sitting on a park bench why he had not saved for a rainy day.

"I did," said the old man.

STUDY GUIDE

1. What would you consider to be the major socioeconomic differences (for example, in employment) between the 1930s as described by Caroline Bird and the 1970s? Are there segments of American society today experiencing the conditions described by Bird? Who? Where?

2. What services, institutions, and agencies has our nation established — during and since the Depression — to prevent the kind of suffering described by the author? Could this nation enter another depression similar to the one of the 1930s? Why or why not?

3. What impression do you get of the frame of mind of the millions of poor and the unemployed? How does the author account for the divergent responses to the Depression by various socioeconomic segments of American society?

4. Explain how each of the following institutions and groups responded to the plight of the American people during the Depression: (a) newspapers; (b) industrialists; (c) social agencies; (d) landlords; and (e) political leaders.

5. Some historians have suggested that many Americans may have accepted the sufferings of the Depression out of a feeling of guilt — an acceptance of the notion that their unemployment and their inability to provide the basic necessities for their family were consequences of their own deficiencies rather than the results of defects in the economic system of the nation. Does this idea — the passivity of the nation in the face of joblessness and hunger — seem to be borne out by this essay? Or do the American people appear to have been hostile or angry or rebellious during the Depression? If so, at whom? If not, why not?

BIBLIOGRAPHY

There is a great deal of historical literature — and journalistic material as well — on the 1930s. No serious student of the decade can afford to overlook the most concise and scholarly introduction to the decade, William E. Leuchtenburg, *Franklin D. Roosevelt and the New Deal* * (New York, 1963). More discursive — and still incomplete for the entire decade — is Arthur M. Schlesinger, Jr., *The Age of Roosevelt* * (Boston, Mass., 1957–1960). Older, yet valuable, surveys of the social problems of the American people in the 1930s will be found in Dixon Wecter, *The Age of the Great Depression, 1929–1941* * (New York, 1948) and Frederick Lewis Allen, *Since Yesterday* * (New York, 1940). The poor farmers and their lot are described in David E. Conrad, *The Forgotten Farmers* * (Urbana, Ill., 1966); the plight of the workingman is definitively treated in Irving Bernstein, *Turbulent Years: A History of the American Worker, 1933–1941* * (Boston, 1970). Also worth reading are those selections dealing with the 1930s in Isabel Leighton's edited volume, *The Aspirin Age: 1919–1941* * (New York, 1949). And, finally, a short but vivid anthology of recollections of the Depression is Don Conger, ed., *The Thirties: A Time to Remember* * (New York, 1962); Milton Meltzer, *Brother, Can You Spare a Dime?* * (New York, 1969); and Charles A. Jellison, *Tomatoes Were Cheaper: Tales from the Thirties* (Syracuse, 1977).

* Asterisk indicates book is available in a paperback edition.

A mother and her two children. For the "Okies," California held the false promise of a better life.

16

EDWARD ROBB ELLIS

The Farmer's Plight

Alterations in the economics of farming since the advent of the New Deal have greatly improved both farm income and the lifestyle of the American farmer. For many Americans, farming has become a profitable venture, and a number of the social problems that plagued many segments of rural America have, in recent decades, been either solved or contained. The New Deal inaugurated a variety of programs to assist the American farmer: price supports, commodity loans and marketing controls, a rural electrification program, soil-conservation payments, and a resettlement program. These programs, combined with the world food shortages of the 1960s and 1970s, have brought a large measure of economic security — and, in the case of the agricorporations, enormous profits — to the American farmer.

The farmer's condition during the Depression was a vastly different one, though not all of the problems that confronted American farmers in the 1930s were a consequence of the Depression itself. Throughout the twenties, erroneously and simplistically thought of as a prosperous era for all Americans, various developments on the farm were acting to produce social blight and economic bankruptcy. The high tariff enacted by the Republicans after World War I helped destroy the farmer's European market; the changing diet of the American family and immigration restriction curtailed the farmer's market at home. Low crop prices, threats of foreclosures, an inadequate credit supply, soil erosion, locusts, droughts, sharecropping, tenant farming, and migrant farming complete the dismal picture of farm conditions in the United States prior to the New Deal. Indeed, threats of revolution and the use of violence to defend home, land, and

257

livelihood were more prevalent in rural America than in the city.

The following graphic portrait of the experiences of American farmers in the 1930s generally, and the tragic plight of the plains farmers and migrant workers in particular, is in no way a journalistic exaggeration of reality. While some aspects of American farm life, especially the depressing conditions forced on migrant laborers and their families, have not improved since the 1930s, most American farmers no longer confront the economic and social hardships described in Edward Robb Ellis' essay.

Hubert H. Humphrey never forgot the days of drought and dust storms: "God, it was terrible! . . . So hot, so terribly hot. . . . The dust, it was everywhere. . . . There was a desolation, a drabness. . . . The sky and horizon — dull and bleak. . . . Hope would leave. . . . You didn't want to stay, but there was no way to leave. . . . You felt trapped. . . ."

Humphrey was born in the prairie town of Wallace, South Dakota, in 1911. When he was four, the family moved to Doland, also in South Dakota, where he grew up. Because of the plight of the farmers, the Depression hit Doland in 1927, two years before the Crash, and Humphrey's father had to sell the family home. In 1929 young Humphrey went to Minneapolis to enter the University of Minnesota. His father's drugstore business became so bad that customers were unable to pay in cash and bartered farm produce for the medicine they needed. After two years at the university the son left it to go back home and try to help his father, but the two of them could not make a go of it, so finally the elder Humphrey gave up, moved the family to Huron, South Dakota, and opened a new drugstore there. That was in 1931.

By this time a series of droughts had begun to parch far-flung areas of this country while dust storms were blowing away the top soil. And each year conditions got worse. On November 11, 1933, when Hubert Humphrey was twenty-two years old, a gigantic dust storm raged over the western plains states from the Texas Panhandle up to the Canadian border. Its effect on the 470-acre Karnstrum farm in Beadle County, South Dakota, was described by R. D. Lusk in an article in the *Saturday Evening Post:*

> By mid-morning a gale was blowing, cold and black. By noon it was blacker than night, because one can see through night and this was an opaque black.

It was a wall of dirt one's eyes could not penetrate, but it could penetrate the eyes and ears and nose. It could penetrate to the lungs until one coughed up black. If a person was outside, he tied his handkerchief around his face, but he still coughed up black; and inside the house the Karnstrums soaked sheets and towels and stuffed them around the window ledges, but these didn't help much.

They were afraid, because they had never seen anything like this before. . . .

When the wind died and the sun shone forth again, it was a different world. There were no fields, only sand drifting into mounds and eddies that swirled in what was now an autumn breeze. There was no longer a section-line road fifty feet from the front door. It was obliterated. In the farmyard, fences, machinery and trees were gone, buried. The roofs of sheds stuck out through drifts deeper than a man is tall.

The next day this black blizzard darkened the sky over Chicago, and the day after that it shrouded Albany, New York.

At a later date Hubert Humphrey said: "I learned more about economics from one South Dakota dust storm than I did in all my years in college."

In the Huron drugstore the father and son noted that as dust storms became more common, people bought more remedies for stomach ailments and constipation. Hubert understood why. Time and again his own belly churned and ached, his face paled, he felt nauseated, and then he fainted. The family doctor put him in the hospital and ran a series of tests, but after being in and out of the hospital several times, Hubert was told he had nothing physically wrong with him. The young man developed a lifelong habit of vigorously dusting everything within reach.

Sullen, disgusted, feeling trapped, Hubert went about his work mechanically, eager to get back to college, to escape a prairie turning into a desert. Seventy-two dust storms in South Dakota in one year — this was too much. One day, unable to control the ferocity building up inside himself, Hubert smashed a dozen glasses in the sink behind the drugstore counter. His father watched with sad eyes. Hubert adored his father, but even this deep love was not enough to hold him in South Dakota. The elder Humphrey, sympathizing with his brilliant son and wishing to ease his tensions, offered him half ownership in the family business. Hubert replied: "I can't stay. These dust storms — I just can't take them any more! I'm so tense I'm sick all the time. I get these pains, and I know it's because of the worry. But the depression, the dust, the drought — they're wearing me out!"

The droughts of the 1930's — worldwide in scope — were the worst in the nation's history. Their effects were felt in twenty-two states constituting almost three-fourths of the land area of the United States. Thousands of people died from heat and hundreds from dust pneumonia. The black dirt that once carpeted South Dakota blew away to become new topsoil in Indiana and Illinois. Dust storms originating in the Western states swirled all the way to the Eastern Seaboard, out into the Atlantic, and deposited grit on the decks of ships 200 miles at sea. In a single day 50,000,000 tons of topsoil blew away. Before this prolonged natural disaster ended near the end of the decade, severe damage had been done to more than one-sixth of the once-fertile earth across this country. And the havoc was worst in the plains states.

The grasslands begin in Ohio and extend westward to Illinois, where they develop into the central plains. When the first white man reached the interior, the central plains were a sea of grass, some of it higher than a tall man. Still farther west the grass did not grow so high. The Great Plains themselves start about 400 miles east of the Rocky mountains and sweep more than 1,000 miles north and south, from Canada to Mexico.

The eastern half of the country is humid while the western half is dry, this aridity increasing every few miles as one moves toward the setting sun. The winds blowing eastward over the Rockies have almost all their moisture squeezed out before they reach the Great Plains. Very little moisture from the Gulf of Mexico can reach this rain shadow of the Rockies. The semiarid West is sometimes wet, but any sporadic bounty of moisture is certain to be balanced off by a long period of almost total rainlessness. In that part of the United States weather and water are prime topics of conversation, since they are matters of life and death.

In the Mississippi Valley total precipitation is about 40 inches a year, but in the Great Plains it is a scant 8 to 20 inches. While the 1920's had been years of relatively high moisture in the grasslands, after 1930 the rains stopped coming. No longer did farmers see gully washers, as they called heavy rains. Just about the time the Depression began, so did the drought. By 1931 the Midwest needed a foot of rain.

At first the plainsmen met this developing disaster with humor, one of them drawling: "A raindrop hit a fellow over in the next county yesterday, and they had to throw three buckets of dirt on him to bring him to." The story was told about a rancher who hauled a load of gravel to his house one day and that night threw it on the roof to let his children learn the sound of rainfall.

In the grasslands there were three kinds of agriculture — the grazing of livestock, irrigation and dry farming. Dry farming is the use of methods suitable to the growth of crops in semiarid or dry climates; for example, in one-crop dry farming half the land is allowed to lie fallow each year to accumulate moisture, while furrows must be plowed farther apart than elsewhere. The drought struck at a time when the prairie already was in bad shape for a variety of reasons. The land had been overgrazed by cattle and sheep. By 1930 more than half of all state-controlled irrigation districts had failed. The soil had been eroded by wind and water. It was exhausted after generations of careless cultivation. Too much of the prairie had been plowed up to plant wheat, this sodbusting breaking the skin of soil covering the earth.

Then came the grasshoppers. First appearing in 1931, they scourged

Iowa, Nebraska and South Dakota. That year and following years they swarmed by the billions over millions of acres of grasslands with a deafening and almost metallic buzz, chewing up the dry yellow grass, the sick and wilting corn. In his book called *Humphrey: A Candid Biography,* writer Winthrop Griffith tells of a Doland, South Dakota, farmer remembering how his father reacted to the invasion of grasshoppers:

> He walked out of the house and into his field as the last 'hoppers moved away. He looked up at the sky for a minute — it was still filled with dust kicked up by the 'hoppers — then he dropped down to his knees. He stared at the ground for a long time. It was hard; there wasn't a sprout or root left in it. He starting pounding his fists against the ground real hard. His hands were tough, but blood came running out of the knuckles. Then he moaned and started screaming: "God damn you, land! . . . God damn you, earth!"
>
> I'll never forget his face — all covered with dust and a look of pain. Mom couldn't move; she just stood on the porch with her hands against her face. I was little and scared. My big brother came out. He was real good, real gentle. He took Dad over to the water pump. Dad just stood there and let my brother wash his face and hands. He didn't say anything, and got a funny smile on his face, and sort of relaxed — as though somebody else finally was taking care of things. The doc came out the next day. A couple of weeks later the sheriff came. Dad just smiled at him and let us guide him into the car. The sheriff drove him to the state hospital." . . .

People began praying for rain. A farmer said: "We went to church and knelt down. It seemed to me we were like fools there, on our knees, Sunday after Sunday, praying for rain, and no rain coming at all." In Georgia a Negro was paid $10 for offering up similar prayers. In New York State the Onondaga Indians revived their rain-prayer dance for the first time in forty years. In Russia, also afflicted by drought, Communists were displeased by the fact that some old people, still clinging to their religion, prayed for rain. . . .

It did seem that some curse lay on this and other lands. North Dakota had 399 dust storms. Mishek, North Dakota, suffered in 120-degree heat. In South Dakota men with tight grins on their faces handed out cards saying: IF AT FIRST YOU DON'T SUCCEED . . . THE HELL WITH IT! People joked about a farmer who went to a bank to ask the banker to inspect his farm so he could get a loan; the farmer happened to glance out a window and saw his farm blowing past the bank.

In 1935 this nation reaped its smallest harvest in forty years. Small lakes dried up, little streams vanished, there was a lowering of the water level of big rivers, brush fires and forest fires became more common, parched field mice crept into country schools to drink from ink bottles, fish were left gasping in dry beds of creeks, there was an increase in the sale of cowbells to put on cattle wandering far afield in search of pastures, cattle rustling broke out again, city fathers had water hauled into town, cops were told to arrest anyone using water illegally, mines and railroads suffered from the water shortage, the hunting season was shortened, in some towns the drinking water took on a milky appearance, farm prices rose as surpluses fell, and even the moist prickly-pear cactus of the Far West began dying.

The dust blotted out the sun, and streetlights burned at noon. Georgia's watermelon crop shriveled; whining windmills kept turning, but they pumped no water; people winced when they saw their sun-warped wooden churches; nights were pitch black because the stars could not pierce the dust; wells dried up; roads and barns and tractors and homes and automobiles and even telegraph poles were buried under dust. Rexford Tugwell toured the stricken areas and then reported that the soil showed through the grass everywhere, and the wheat was thin "like the stubble on an old man's chin." But the stunned farmers kept on plowing just in case a rain might come, using two horses at first and then hitching up four horses for the hard work of ripping open the hardpan left after the topsoil blew away.

A man could not roll or light a homemade cigarette in the wind that blew, blew, forever blew. Day and night one heard the soft dry clashing of parched corn in the wind. A person walking along a road would lift a thin layer of flourlike dust as high as his waist. Everyone wore a handkerchief over his nose, while some folks put goggles over their bloodshot eyes. At night they laid wet towels over their cracked lips but still felt the grit between their teeth. Housewives tried to seal up every crack in their homes with strips of gummed paper, only to watch helplessly as the choking dust filtered inside and spread in ripples on the floor. . . .

Gene Howe, the publisher of a newspaper in Amarillo, Texas, counted twenty-seven days out of thirty in April, 1935, when the dust was so thick he could not see across the street. The storm of April 15 of that year was perhaps the worst, and Woody Guthrie was in the middle of it. This experience inspired him to write the words and music of a song he called "The Great Dust Storm." A little weather-worn man with wiry hair, Guthrie later said: "This is a true song. It is about the worst dust storm in anybody's history book. I was in what is give up to be the big middle of it. Right in there north of Amarillo, Texas. I'll never forget how my wife and kinfolks looked. That was before it hit. After it got dark, you couldn't see how nobody looked. You could just reach out and get them by the hand and stand there and wonder how it would all come out. It turned wheat lands into deserts. I've seen hills change locations down there."

During one such storm a seven-year-old boy wandered away from home and was suffocated before he could be found. In South Dakota, halfway between Doland and Huron, two children left school one afternoon and were caught in a ferocious dust storm; they wandered all the rest of that afternoon and part of the night, then dropped from exhaustion and died, their bodies discovered half-buried in dust the next day. Woody Guthrie wrote another song called "Dust Can't Kill Me" — but it could.

In Kansas some rural schools were closed when board members decided things were so bad there was no use keeping them open. In Montana the drought was so devastating and the crops so poor that farmers could not afford to buy overalls for their children, so the kids had to stay at home. In Washington, D.C., a United States Senator wept as he told of the misery of his people in the Great Plains. In Texas a farmer drove his tractor around and around a field, muttering: "I just can't stand sitting 'round the house. I just got to do something, even if it's some fool thing like I'm doing now." Here and there people asked one another: "Is this dust th' end of th' world?"

Preachers quoted dour passages from the Bible: ". . . For, behold, the darkness shall cover the earth. . . . Enter into the rock, and hide thee in the dust, for fear of the Lord. . . . The earth mourneth and fadeth away. . . . The mirth of the land is gone. . . . Awake and sing, ye that dwell in the dust. . . . Behold, the Lord maketh the earth empty, and maketh it waste, and turneth it upside down, and scattereth abroad the inhabitants thereof."

And they were scattered, and they were called Okies. . . .

With the disappearance of the life-giving topsoil, with the exposed hardpan almost impervious to the plow, with water scarce and no rain to speak of, with livestock and crops dying for want of water and fodder, flat-faced farmers squatted on their hams doodling in the dust and talking in low tones about the future. The future? What future did they have in their own countrysides? Hell, a man couldn't raise enough corn to feed a baby. Call it farmin' when a feller gets only a quarter bale of cotton to a quarter section? A future, you call it, with the banks foreclosing on mortgages and sending tractors across their land? Hell, they better face up to the facts. They been tractored out and droughted out, that's what!

Over in Cochran County, Texas, they's nearly three hundred cotton farmers and their families living in sodded dugouts. Home on the range! Some of them big shots in Washington is talkin' about how they got to evacuate thousands of people from the Dust Bowl, but where's folks to go? Relocate them? Okay, but where? How about California? Why California? Well, you seen them handbills they been passin' out here lately. They need pickers in California, that's what. They say California is prosperous, and they got all them vegetables and fruits in them big valleys that need harvestin'. Great climate, good wages, plenty of work for all. From the Dust Bowl to the Peach Bowl, huh? Hey, that's purty good! Why not? I might give it a try. Yuh know, I just might, at that. . . .

From Oklahoma and Kansas, from Colorado and Texas and New Mexico, the grim men and women and children set out, by the thousands at first, by the tens of thousands, and finally by the hundreds of thousands, a drought-weary dust-worn people trekking 1,000 miles to the Golden State. Worrying about whether they would have enough money to complete this trip, they fanned out over all major highways leading to the Pacific, riding in battered old jalopies, chugging along at 35 miles an hour, their faces and arms and hands burned brown by the relentless sun, patching each tire as it blew out, anxiously counting out coins for each gallon of gas, camping at night wherever they could, met with distaste or suspicion or hostility by the people who lived along their line of march. . . .

California, now becoming a mecca for 350,000 victims of drought and dust, had gone through an agricultural revolution. In the past its chief farm products were hay and cattle. By the Thirties, by means of intensive cultivation and extensive irrigation, the state's most profitable crops had become fruits and vegetables. Agricultural production continued to mount during the Depression while farm wages fell. The long north-south valley in the center of the state had developed into the world's most fertile growing region. It really was two valleys: the Sacramento Valley lying north of the state capital and the San Joaquin Valley to the south. These lush and slender strips were trapped between the coastal mountains to the west and the foothills of the Rockies to the east.

Because of the state's wide range of topography, climate and soil, almost every species of temperate zone and subtropical fruit, vegetable and field crop could be grown. From 1909 to 1936 California's farm production rose more than 120 percent. Pears grew on the cool mountain slopes; asparagus, celery, beans, onions and rice in the black soil of the delta area; lettuce in the Salinas Valley, called the Valley of Green Gold; grapes for dry wine in the sunny foothills of Napa and Sonoma counties; and a fabulous yield of cotton in the brown silted loam of the San Joaquin Valley.

In 1925 deflation had wiped out many owners of medium-size farms, while the Depression finished off others of their kind. Now the state's agriculture was split into two extremes — stubborn men owning very small farms and grasping corporations owning very large farms. Whenever bankrupt farmers defaulted on their credits, their land was taken over by bankers and businessmen, who consolidated these tracts into gigantic and profitable units. By the middle Thirties, 2 percent of California farms controlled one-fourth of all acreage, nearly one-third of the crop value, and paid more than one-third of the bill for hired labor.

California agriculture had become modernized, mechanized, industrialized — factories in the fields, they were called. At the southern end of the San Joaquin Valley, to cite one example, a single fruit ranch of 6,000 acres shipped more than two dozen carloads of peaches, plums and grapes each day at the peak of the season and employed 2,500 men and women in orchards, vineyards and packing sheds. Every crop, every region and every specialty had its own protective association; they fixed prices paid to labor and received for their products, maintaining lobbies in the state capital and otherwise promoting the vested interests of the growers, packers and shippers. To name just a couple of these groups, there were the California Raisin Growers Association and the Fruit Growers Supply Company.

Mechanization increased with the invention of a pear-peeling machine, a hop-picking machine, a mechanical beet thinner and similar innovations. But despite these machines, the growers still had to rely on great numbers of stoop laborers. The harvesting of crops such as lettuce and cotton required men and women willing to crawl between rows of the ripening plants. Naturally, these field hands were hostile toward the inventions that had begun to menace their livelihood. One of them said: "They're fixin' to free all us fellows — free us for what? Free us like they freed the mules. They're aimin' at keeping fellows such as me right down on our knees — aimin' at making slaves of us. We've got no more chance than a one-legged man in a foot-race."

Another problem was the seasonal nature of the work. Different crops matured at different times, so the growers sought armies of pickers at harvesttime and shunned them after the crop was in. From about 1860 to 1930 most of these migrant workers were foreigners — Chinese and Japanese, Mexicans and Filipinos. Because of poor pay, racial discrimination and indifference to their welfare, some of these foreigners returned to their motherlands, some saved enough money to buy small plots of their own, and some drifted into the cities. By 1933 only about a fourth of the state's migratory laborers were Mexican. Now the growers had to find a new source of supply for stoop laborers, so they distributed leaflets throughout the Dust Bowl appealing for workers.

They hoped to attract more people than they could use because surplus labor equals low wages, but this equation backfired. California's corporate farmers were unprepared for the tidal wave of Okies that swept into their state. At first the growers had an advantage, since the hungry newcomers fought one another for jobs, but with the passage of time thousands of people were left unemployed and homeless, began to starve, turned sullen and threatening, and at last California found itself in the middle of an explosive social crisis.

Down through American history the migrant workers had been left un-organized or, at best, poorly organized. The Industrial Workers of the World had taken an interest in them, but by the thirties the IWW had lost all its influence in the fields of California. The American Federation of Labor paid almost no attention to pleas by the new harvest pickers that they be pulled together into unions and placed within the protection of the AFL. The official California spokesman for the AFL was Paul Scharrenberg, whom the New York *Times* quoted as saying: "Only fanatics are willing to live in shacks or tents and get their heads broken in the interests of migratory labor." One migrant worker said sneeringly of Scharrenberg: "He did a swell job for the bosses. He didn't organize a single local!" Another stoop laborer said: "The hay-balers organized a coupla months ago, got a charter in Stockton, but the big shots in the A.F. of L. told 'em not to take in any field workers."

The migrants, ignored by organized labor, vied with one another for jobs, took whatever meager wages they were offered and lived in unbelievable squalor. . . .

On the State Capitol Building in Sacramento there is a scroll that says: "Bring me men to match my mountains." California's ruling class members, themselves earlier migrants from other parts of the nation, did not consider the present newcomers the kind of men they wanted. They called the Okies bums, crop tramps, fruit tramps, shiftless idlers — even sexual degenerates. They growled that the migrants did not know what it felt like to plant a tree and see it grow and touch it with one's hand. Before long a "vagrant" was anybody disliked by a cop or judge. One county judge said, "California agriculture demands that we create and maintain peonage."

Laurence Hewes, director of one California region of the federal Farm Security Administration, listened in disbelief as a businessman ranted: "Go right ahead — coddle and pet these worthless people! We can't stop you. Just keep away from decent people! Do what you want! Preach socialistic claptrap like that young fool out at your camp. Make those ignorant filthy people think they're as good as the next man! Only for God's sake have the decency to keep them out of this town! If we have to, we'll find ways to protect ourselves."

A story was told about a woman and her small daughter who were strolling in a town in the San Joaquin Valley *during the harvest season.* The girl pointed to the migrant workers and asked: "Mommy, who are those people?" The mother is supposed to have replied: "Child, those are cotton pickers." Same scene *after the harvest:* "Mommy, who are those people?" Answer: "Child, those are bums!"

Eight men were given preposterously heavy sentences for trying to organize a strike of melon pickers in the Imperial Valley in 1931. The commander of an American Legion post told an observer: "The way to kill the Red Plague is to dynamite it out. That's what we did in the Imperial valley. The judge who tried the Communists was a Legionnaire. Fifty percent of the jurors were war veterans. What chance did the Communists have? That's the way we stamped it out of our county."

That same year a young man named Carlos Bulosan, born in the Philippines and brought to this country as a small boy, was *sold* for $5 to an Alaskan fish cannery owner. When he finally got back to California he tried to organize migrant workers into a union, was stripped and whipped and driven out of one town after another, lost the ribs on one side of his body and the use of one lung, but survived to become a distinguished author.

When an official of a farm association was asked what he meant by a Communist, he replied: "Why, he's the guy that wants twenty-five cents an hour when we're paying twenty." At one growers' association meeting a farmer member was accused of being "kind of communistic" because he advocated separate toilets for men and women in a local squatters' camp.

Dust Bowl refugees — the lucky ones, that is — found shelter in federal camps, state camps, houses rented by growers or squatters' camps. The federal camps run by the Farm Security Administration were the cleanest and best. Second-best were the state camps. Large farmers rented houses to workers at $4 to $8 a month; most of these houses had just one room and no running water; all 200 or 300 people occupying a group of these one-room houses had to share one toilet and one bathroom. Small farmers provided no sanitary facilities — except one or two holes dug in the ground. Lowest in the social scale were the squatters' camps. Usually these were on the bank of a river used by the inhabitants for drinking, bathing, washing their clothes and receiving their refuse. Naturally, epidemics often broke out in the squatters' camps. Carey McWilliams, a young California attorney who became head of the California Division of Immigration and Housing, said some camps were the equivalent of concentration camps.

Laurence Hewes flew to Washington to try to get more money to help the migrants. This was at a time when California Republicans were accusing Secretary Henry Wallace of scheming to influence the California vote by herding workers from Democratic states into the California camps. Wallace, who knew of Hewes' passionate interest in the welfare of the displaced Okies, asked him to attend a press conference at which Wallace would tell his side of the story to the press. Hewes was surprised when Wallace sidestepped a question and told reporters that the man from California would give them their answers. But Hewes acquitted himself well.

Late that night Hewes was told that Mrs. Franklin D. Roosevelt wanted him to have lunch in the White House the next day. He arrived at the appointed time and was ushered into a small room warmed by a blazing fire in a fireplace. Hewes had seen Eleanor Roosevelt at a distance a couple of times in the past and had not been impressed with her. Now, at close range, he was taken at once by her vitality, her charm and, above all, her sincerity. She showered him with questions about the migrants and finally said she would like to see conditions for herself. Surprised and pleased, Hewes said if she would just name the day, he would show her around himself. But there was one thing he had to know: Did Mrs. Roosevelt plan to let the press in on her inspection tour?

"Of course I want the press to be there." She smiled. "On the other hand, I don't want to make a Roman holiday out of other people's misfortunes. Why don't we make a date with the reporters at some designated place?"

Several weeks later Hewes waited at the Bakersfield airport in California to welcome the President's wife. She arrived in a small plane. With her were Melvyn Douglas, the movie actor, and his wife, Helen Gahagan Douglas, a former actress and opera singer who was now a Democratic national committeewoman for California. Hewes escorted them into a car and drove to a migrant slum at Oiltown, near Bakersfield. He stopped the automobile in a crooked, muddy, noisy alley, and Mrs. Roosevelt stepped out.

Soon she was chatting with migrant women, asking about their babies, the work their husbands did and the wages they received. Suddenly one woman pointed dramatically and cried: "My stars, ain't you Mrs. Roosevelt?"

Smile lines crinkling the corners of her eyes, the First Lady replied: "You didn't expect me, did you?"

Hewes felt that her interest in these displaced persons was absolutely genuine. When she saw a standpipe and water faucet braced against one corner of a privy, she asked in horror: "Do you get drinking water from *that?*"

"Yes'm," the woman answered, "and so do all our neighbors."

Mrs. Roosevelt was appalled: "That's perfectly dreadful! Don't you realize that water from such a place will make you sick?"

"We only rent here," the woman said, "and we can't do nothin' about it. We complained to the health people, but they only said this place was condemned and we should move out. But we can't move — leastways not while there's work."

By now a crowd surrounded Mrs. Roosevelt, and Hewes worried about extricating her, getting her back into the car and then driving away without accidentally hitting anybody. She solved this problem by telling him: "I should like to walk back the way we drove in here." Then, turning to one of the women, she smiled and said: "Perhaps you'll show me the way." The delighted migrants tagged along behind the First Lady as she left their alley. Hewes turned the car around, his famous guest climbed inside, and as he pulled away, she waved to the women.

One of them called out: "Mrs. Roosevelt, tell your husband when you see him we're sure goin' to vote for him!"

After she got back to the White House, what she told her husband was this: "Franklin, I wonder if it strikes you as it does me how remarkable it is that people can keep up their courage and struggle in the face of so many hardships?"

Squatting in the brush near Wasco, California, a former tenant farmer, the father of six children, remembered what it was like back in Cook County, Texas: "People just can't make it back there, with drought, hailstorms, windstorms, duststorms, insects. People exist here and they can't do that there. You can make it here if you sleep lots and eat little, but it's pretty tough, there are so many people. They chase them out of one camp because they say it isn't sanitary — there's no running water — so people live out here in the brush like a den o' dogs or pigs."

STUDY GUIDE

1. Hubert Humphrey, whom Edward Robb Ellis quotes in the beginning of the essay, came to be a national spokesman for liberal reform in the decades that followed the Great Depression. Can you understand why Humphrey,

as senator from Minnesota and later as vice-president of the United States, would advocate the use of government as a tool for social and economic reform?

2. Compare the problems — both environmental and man-made — of the farmers on the Great Plains to those described by Caroline Bird in her preceding essay on the impact of the Great Depression on city dwellers. What did they have in common? How did their problems differ?

3. Why did so many men and women from the Dust Bowl head for California? What did they find once they got there?

4. Many of the destitute farmers described here — the "Okies" — are today prosperous middle-class Americans living in California and in other western states. Can you offer some reasons why these Americans would be unsympathetic to the migrant workers represented by César Chavez's union and to others who are experiencing today some of the privations they experienced in the 1930s?

BIBLIOGRAPHY

A fictional account of the plight of the farmers in the Dust Bowl and their migration to California is given in John Steinbeck's widely read novel, *The Grapes of Wrath* * (New York, 1939). Two other books, by Carey McWilliams, for many decades a spokesman for the nation's oppressed, deal with migratory farm labor: *Factories in the Field: The Story of Migratory Farm Labor in California* (Boston, 1939) and *Ill Fares the Land: Migrants and Migratory Labor in the United States* (Boston, 1944). A scholarly assessment of what the New Deal meant — or failed to mean — to the poorer farmers of the nation will be found in David E. Conrad, *The Forgotten Farmers* (Urbana, Ill., 1965). The best book on the politics of the 1930s and the New Deal as a whole is William E. Leuchtenburg, *Franklin D. Roosevelt and the New Deal, 1932–1940* * (New York, 1963).

* Asterisk indicates book is available in a paperback edition.

A military wedding, 1944. Family allotments and full employment made early marriage possible for millions.

17

RICHARD R. LINGEMAN

The Home Front
during World War II

On a number of counts, World War II was an ideal war for the American people. American casualties — compared to the death and destruction brought on by the Civil War or the millions of Russians, Germans, Chinese, and Japanese killed during World War II — were relatively light. Dissent among the American people over the righteousness of the war or its justification was minimal. In addition to the exhilirating sense of national solidarity produced by the war, it brought full employment and a high level of affluence to a large proportion of the population. As the federal government pumped billions of dollars into the economy, millions of Americans were once more steadily employed — in some instances for the first time in more than a decade. Although women's hosiery and cigarettes were in short supply and it was necessary, at one point, to place price controls or rationing on consumer goods, the consequences for the American people were not enormously painful. Much of World War II was taken in good humor; the threats to the home front were few, and the attitude of the civilian population enthusiastic — and, in some respects, euphoric.

World War II marked more than a military victory over Nazi Germany and imperial Japan; the war brought profound and permanent changes in the socioeconomic policies of the American nation. World War II ended our commitment to a laissez-faire economy; the Full Employment Act and other legislation reflected the general agreement among the nation's political leaders that the federal government is responsible for maintaining the economic prosperity and the social well-being of the American people. World War II also meant a turning point in other ways: the postwar civil-rights movement for American blacks had its origins in developments that took place during the war; the war also brought millions of women out of the home into the offices and factories of the nation. Demographically, the war brought marriage to millions at a younger age, and an increase in the number of children per family.

Perhaps the most important consequence of the war in terms of the quality of postwar American life came in the field of education. Under an unprecedented piece of legislation — and a generously wise one — millions of Americans were sent to college under the GI Bill of Rights (the Serviceman's Readjustment Act); on the campuses of the nation ex-servicemen acquired the skills and the university degrees that made the United States the leader of the world in research and technology. And finally, World War II left a legacy of ominous proportions: atomic energy. How this legacy of World War II research is ultimately employed will determine the very existence of the human race.

In *Don't You Know There's A War On?*, Richard R. Lingeman has captured much of the mood of the American people during this crucial period in our history. From this book, we have selected a chapter that portrays the changes on the home front — the social consequences of an overseas war that nonetheless altered many aspects of life on this side of the Atlantic.

The end of Hard Times was a motley caravan observed on Route 66, near Albuquerque, New Mexico, a road that was both *via doloroso* and passage of hope in John Steinbeck's *Grapes of Wrath*. Now, by the same route, in early 1942 the Okies were returning home. They came in old battered sedans and wheezing trucks and Model T's, sometimes twelve in a car, with all their possessions strapped on the tops and sides — rockers, buckets, shovels, stoves, bedding and springs. A few of the migrants were fleeing what they regarded as the imminent invasion of California by the Japanese, but the attitude of most was summed up by the man who said: "We ain't war-scared or anything like that, but a lot of others were pulling up and clearing out — not all of 'em understand — and Ma and I figured that if we was going back, now was the time. And, besides, Ed Lou is pretty big now and there ought to be a job for him in the oil fields and maybe for me too."

There were still more than 3,600,000 men unemployed. So the migration had momentum to gain as hillbillies from Appalachia, po' whites and Negroes from the South, farmers from the Midwest, garment workers from New York City picked up stakes and swarmed to the centers of war production.

The factories were rising up out of the raw, graded earth. The year 1942 was a year of frantic construction — more than $12 billion worth of it financed by the federal government, most of that on military camps, factories and installation of heavy machinery.

Near the little town of Starke, Florida, Camp Blanding had been erected in six months of feverish building. The workers turned the little town upside down. "Why, people were sleeping in the streets, in the churches, in the trees," one resident recalled. The local grocer reminisced: "I had two stores and I sold groceries to the construction gangs. Two stores and I couldn't get any help. I worked 18 to 20 hours a day. My weekend profits were unbelievable, but I wouldn't want to go through it again. These fellows from the construction jobs — these carpenters and plumbers — were getting more money than they'd ever had in their lives and they had no place to spend it except in Starke. They were always hungry and they were always buying. It went for five or six months. We all got rich." . . .

To millions who had suffered the Depression years on relief, with occasional spells of odd jobs, this meant a time of opportunity, a time to pick up stakes and head to the war production centers, where there were steady jobs and good money to be had. In times of depression people tend to crawl into their holes and lick their wounds; in good times they head for the money. Estimates of the number of Americans who left their homes to seek work elsewhere — in a different county, a different state or even a different region — ranged as high as 20,000,000. Probably the true number will never be known, but the Census Bureau attempted to capture the figures as best it could, before the time was irretrievably gone. Based on a sample of 30,000 persons, the bureau took a demographic snapshot of the nation in March, 1945, and compared it with the prewar period. The Bureau estimated that by 1945, 15,300,000 persons were living in counties different from those in which they lived at Pearl Harbor; 7,700,000 of these migrants were living in a different state and 3,600,000 in a different part of the country. . . .

A major source of this migration was the farm, where, most agrarian economists agreed, there were about 2,000,000 too many people in 1940. Between Pearl Harbor and March, 1945, nearly 5,500,000 people left the farms to live and work in the city (another 1,500,000 went into the armed forces). So effectively did the war siphon off the surplus that there were severe labor shortages on the farms, and in 1943–44, farm deferments were drastically increased by Selective Service. Women, city teen-agers, Axis war prisoners, interned Japanese-Americans and even GI's were pressed into service to help out with the harvest (a time when an additional 3,000,000 laborers are needed). The grip of the agriculture depression, which had held since the early twenties, was at last broken, and farmers' profits soared to record highs. With all this farm prosperity, a reverse migration trend was also operative, for some 2,500,000 people moved from nonfarm to farm areas, presumably to take up farmwork. Still, the farm population suffered a net loss of nearly 17 percent, not counting those in the armed forces. . . .

The greatest percentage of the immigrants settled in the immediate environs of the city or cities, rather than inside the cities. This was reflected in the mushrooming growth of war worker towns and federal housing projects laid out where there were only rural fields before or, even worse, the ubiquitous "New Hoovervilles" — trailer camps, tent settlements, shanty towns, "foxhole houses" and all the other temporary conglomerations of people which sprang up over the countryside, often as satellites of the new war plants which had been erected on unused land. What this further meant was that these settlements were often located outside the service ambit of city and township governments. They were in a jurisdictional limbo, and there was no local government unit to take responsibility for them; further, many of the small towns to which they were often closest, hence most directly affected, lacked the resources with which to help them, even if they had wished to. Most of the migrants were nonvoting, nontax-paying, nonhomeowning — in effect, political pariahs.

The geographical flow of the migration was strikingly skewed. Between April, 1940, and November, 1943, thirty-five states showed a net *loss* in total civilian population. The thirteen states that gained did so in numbers varying from California's 1,020,000 to Delaware's 7,240, but the geographical pattern was clear: By far the largest gainer was the Far West — the three coast states of California, Washington and Oregon, in that order, and to a much smaller degree, Arizona, Utah and Nevada. Next to the Pacific coast states, were three South Atlantic states: Maryland, Florida and Virginia. (In a class by itself was the District of Columbia, which gained 162,469 people; the federal government was also a booming war industry.)

The people went to the Far West because the opportunity was there, and the opportunity was there because the war money went West: California alone, with 6.2 percent of the population had by 1944 received war contracts totaling $15.8 billion, or 9.7 percent of the total for the nation. More than half the wartime shipbuilding took place in the three Pacific coast states, and nearly half the airplane manufacture. Because of its location on the sea and the existence of a prewar aircraft industry, California logically helped itself to a large chunk of this production. When the war ended, an estimated 1,000,000 war workers would be out of work, but till then California was truly the Golden State. All told its population increased by almost 2,000,000 between 1940 and 1945. Per capita income rose apace, reaching $1,740 annually, the highest in the nation. Here was the real gold rush in California's colorful history.

In sum the general pattern of the great national migration seemed to be this: Deep South po' whites to the shipyards around the Gulf crescent and in the Hampton Roads–Newport News–Norfolk complex and, farther North, to the Michigan manufacturing complexes.

Southern Negro sharecroppers and tenant farmers to the shipyards and factories of the West Coast; up the East Coast and to the factories of the Middle West.

Arkies, Okies, Tennessee, Kentucky and West-by-God-Virginia hillbillies to Illinois and Indiana and Michigan or to the Southern oilfields and shipyards.

Kansas, Nebraska, Iowa, North and South Dakota plowboys to the great aircraft factories of the West Coast.

New York and other urban small-manufacturing workers to the Mid and Far West.

They came in cars, driving their rubber down to the rims and then paying exorbitant prices for used tires or retreads en route; or, more likely, they sat up or stood in the aisles for days and nights on crowded trains; or they packed their few working clothes into cardboard suitcases, made dust down the red dirt roads of the backwoods South to the crossroads store, and there waited for the bus to take them on the long trip to Pascagoula or Mobile or New Orleans. . . .

Everyone, on the move. Young wives with colicky babies, making the long journey to join their husbands at this new war job. Lone men, creased and weathered by work, and pink-cheeked young farm boys, migrating West because they heard there was plenty of work out there, sitting in the dark loneliness of the bus at night, only the glow of the orange spark of their cigarettes for company, their thoughts set free to range back and forth in time and space from regret to hope, over the vast American landscape of shadowy, empty hills and somber forests and little towns, their dark windows staring like empty-skulled eye sockets. In the next seat might be another man, he too sitting staring out at the landscape at night, he too coming from somewhere but off to somewhere else. The low voices hummed in talk of "where-are-you-going?" and "what's-it-like down there?" . . .

Men were picking up stakes and moving on. Some left signs on the doors of closed businesses, letting their customers and friends and the whole world (and maybe even God) know that they had vamoosed, flown the coop, skedaddled, made tracks, hit the road, up and went. Signs that read like the one on the door of Joe's Country Lunch in Alabama:

> Maybe you don't know there's a war on. Have gone to see what it's all about. Meanwhile good luck and best wishes until we all come home. (Signed) Joe.

Or that of Lem Ah Toy, Chinese laundryman of Seattle:

Go to war. Closed duration. Will clean shirts after clean Axis. Thank you. . . .

Signs, signs. Cocky, patriotic signs. The whole country, it seemed, was bursting out in a springtime of patriotism. . . . On bar mirrors in small dusty roadside taverns were soap-scrawled fighting slogans, like:

SLAP THE JAPS OFF THE MAP!
TO HELL WITH THE JAPS!
REMEMBER PEARL HARBOR! ! ! . . .

Young girls sitting in soda fountains adorned themselves with the unit patches of their boyfriends, sergeant's stripes or lieutenant's bars; the soda fountain they were lounging in purveyed such patriotic combinations as: Blackout Sundae, Commando Sundae (War Workers, Get Your Vitamins the Delicious Way), Flying Fortress Sundae, Morale Builder and Paratroops Sundae (Goes Down Easy). In more and more windows hung service flags: red border, surrounding a white rectangle in which were one or more blue stars. Gold ones were making their appearance too. ("THE WAR DEPARTMENT REGRETS TO INFORM YOU THAT YOUR SON. . . ." The papers printed names on casualty lists, but never gave total killed and wounded until mid-1942.) Along with the service flags in homes and places of business, small towns had erected Honor Roll signs, with lengthening lists of names and branches of service of their local boys. . . .

At last the journey would near its end, and the migrant would catch a glimpse of the city of his destination: "snowy plains where great manufacturing plants jut up among their parking lots like mesas in the desert . . . mills that smear the sky with brown smoke out of tall cylindrical chimneys. . . ."

In green, gently rolling farmland, long, low dull-red brick factories rose up where bulldozers had scraped the land bare. Walter Wiard owned a farm and orchard in an area near Ypsilanti, Michigan, known as Willow Run after a stream that meandered through it on its way to the Huron River. In early 1941, Walter Wiard's land lay next to the site the Ford people had chosen for their new bomber plant, and the Ford people came to him and offered him a nice price for the land. Then Wiard watched as the giant groundbreaking machines went to work. Later he remarked: "It took me twenty-nine years to plant, cultivate and make that fine orchard. It took those tractors and bulldozers just twenty-nine minutes to tear it all down." . . .

So the workers arrived at the towns and cities where the war plants had risen and got off their crowded buses and walked the streets looking for a job, which was easy to find, and a bed, which was not. They might have landed in LA or San Francisco or Detroit or Pascagoula or Buffalo or Mobile. . . .

San Diego, once a quiet coastal town, was inundated with a lusty gang of workers and servicemen. For a new dry dock the Navy dug a hole that seemed as deep as the Grand Canyon, and one old resident described it as "a hole that you could have dumped most of this town [into] when I first saw it 70 years ago." Another graybeard, shaking his head in wonderment, recalled, "We used to go to bed by ten, or anyway, by eleven. Now some theaters and cafes never close! I remember it was like that in the Klondike. Now when boatloads of sailors hurry ashore, and all those soldiers from Fort Rosecrans and Camp Callan swarm in on payday, this town goes crazy. In one day they eat 50,000 hot dogs! Even shoe shine boys get the jitters. Sherman's Cafe has ten bars, and a dance floor so big that 5,000 of 'em can dance at once." Ten years before, exactly 6 men worked in San Diego's one aircraft factory; now there were 50,000. Any innocent tourist who decided to sit for a moment on a park bench would find himself approached by a series of people wanting to hire him to do some kind of job. . . .

Consider the town of Beaumont, Texas, which needed an incinerator. Next door to the Pennsylvania Shipyards stood a giant garbage dump which exhaled a miasma that could be smelled miles away when the wind was right. With the nauseating smells came flies. An official of the shipyards described what the flies were like: "The flies we get from the dump in the executive offices are so thick that it is almost impossible to concentrate on our duties. Twice a day the rooms are sprayed and the dead swept out with a broom. As soon as it gets warm we have to send people around the yard to spray the men on the job, or they would be eaten up by mosquitoes and flies."

The incinerator had been approved by the Federal Works Administration, and work had been begun. Then the WPB [War Production Board] refused the town a priority on a needed bit of equipment worth about $14,000. And so work stopped, and a half-finished incinerator stood in the midst of the stench and rotting garbage, a monument to government short-sightedness, while the stink grew and the danger of typhoid increased apace. . . .

Housing was an immediate and frequently insoluble problem for the migrant war workers. The government and private builders, largely with federally insured mortgage money, built a total of $7 billion of new housing, much of it temporary — barracks, trailers, demountable homes, dormitories, and the like. The NHA [National Housing Agency] calculated that it had to provide new or existing housing for 9,000,000 migratory workers and their families. To do this, it built and it scoured up existing vacant rooms and houses with the assistance of local community groups. Existing housing took care of 600,000 workers and their families. Over and above this, private companies built something more than 1,000,000 new units and the federal government 832,000 for a total of 1,800,000 units or housing for about 5,000,000 people: housing for at best 7,000,000 out of 9,000,000 migrants was provided; the remaining 2,000,000 presumably had to scour up their own shelter.

These bare statistics do not of course reflect the flesh and blood of the housing situation — the thousands who had to live in trailers, converted garages, tents, shacks, overpriced rooms, "hot beds," even their own cars during the early part of the war; the rent gouging that went on, even though rents were regulated by the Office of Price Administration; and the difficulties people with children had, especially the wives of servicemen who followed them to their training camps.

Landlord hostility to the newcomers was endemic in this sellers' market. An ad in a Fort Worth, Texas, newspaper revealed it: "Fur. Apt., no street-walkers, home wreckers, drunks wanted; couple must present marriage certificate." On the West Coast, which had had an influx of more than 2,000,000 newcomers, it was chaotic. In San Francisco people lived in tents, basements, refrigerator lockers and automobiles. A city official reported in 1943: "Families are sleeping in garages, with mattresses right on cement floors and three, four, five to one bed." In Richmond, where the Kaiser shipyards were located, people were living under conditions that were worse than the Hoovervilles of the Depression. A trailer camp in San Pablo was crowded with people in trailers, tents and shacks; there was no sewage, and children waded about in a stagnant pond. A family of four adults and seven children lived in an 8-by-10-foot shack with two cots and one full-sized bed. A war housing project at Sausalito offered good living conditions for 4,500 people with self-government, low rentals and health insurance; but when a 90-mile-an-hour gale hit the area in January, 1943, all the tarpaper roofs of the temporary housing blew off. . . .

The philosophy underlying the governmental housing program was that "the government doesn't belong in the housing business," which meant that private housing interests were deferred to. In San Francisco, for example, which had a population increase of 200,000, local realtors had initially opposed war housing, saying there were 10,000 vacancies in the area. They were fearful of the competition, of course, but then, when the housing situation reached crisis proportions, they did a turnabout and blamed the federal government for not building enough war housing. And though they had relented on allowing government housing, they were adamant in their demands that only temporary housing, which could be torn down after the war, be built, lest property values suffer. This insistence that war workers be given only temporary or demountable housing was widespread and reflected not only the real estate man's pocketbook talking but also fear that the outsiders would stay after the war. As a result (and also because of the shortage of building materials), much government housing was jerry-built — instant slums, they might be called. . . .

One of the better federal housing projects was that erected near the Willow Run bomber plant. Because of opposition on the part of the towns-people in nearby Ypsilanti and the Ford Motor Company to a planned permanent residential area known as Bomber City . . . and material short-ages, construction of alternate, temporary units was proposed and finally got under way in 1943. The first units — a dormitory for single workers called Willow Lodge — were open for occupancy by February, 1943. There followed trailer homes and prefabricated units for families, which were completed in August, 1943. In all there was housing for about 14,000 workers — or one-third the number working at Willow Run plant at peak production.

By wartime housing standards these units were luxury housing, al-though they were not much to look at, being row upon row of gray, monotonous, flat-roofed buildings. The residents often had difficulty lo-cating their own quarters. One lady always marked her house by a bed-spring leaning against the adjoining unit. So much did she come to rely on the bedspring that she forgot the number of her own dwelling, and so one day, when inevitably, the bedspring was removed, she spent hours search-ing for her place. . . .

Most of the married workers with families overcame these minor hard-ships at Willow Run and turned it into a stable community. Still there were problems that could have been predicted among such a large and fluid population, many of them unmarried immigrants from the South. One reporter was critical of the "lack of wholesome recreational facilities and the generally drab social environment of Willow Run" which "stimu-lated private-party types of entertainment, featured by heavy drinking and promiscuous sex relations among fun-starved workers."

The center of the "promiscuous sex" was, not surprisingly, the Willow Lodge dormitory, which the FPHA [Federal Public Housing Agency] had opened to unmarried workers of both sexes. The result: "Professional gamblers and fast women quickly moved in for a clean-up." The co-ed policy was quickly dropped, however, and tenant policing, in cooperation with the FPHA, cleaned up the budding Gomorrah. . . .

Roving youngsters with nowhere to go were widespread. In Mobile, there were more than 2,000 children who didn't go to school at all, and one high school with an enrollment of 3,650 had a total of 8,217 absences during a single month. One movie theater owner joked with the local lady truant officer: "Miss Bessie, why don't you bring your teachers down here? My place is always full of children." . . .

Some towns, even without federal assistance, made an effort to set up day-care centers and nursery schools in a variety of ways, and the unions and war industries made an even greater contribution, the latter prodded by the labor shortage and the need to attract women workers, the former by a doctrine of demanding work rights. On the other hand, there was a distinct strain of prejudice against working mothers, who were regarded as selfishly materialistic; forgotten was the desperate need for them in the plants, the fact that many were servicemen's wives who needed to supplement their allotments, and the desire of others to take advantage of an opportunity to save up some money for the future. One of the leaders in the opposition to women working was the Catholic Church, which in many areas opposed nursery schools and day-care centers. . . .

Not unrelated to the shortage of day care, the overcrowded schools, the entry of youngsters into industry, and the lack of parental supervision was an increase in the incidence of crimes committed by teenagers (a term that came into wide currency during the war, along with juvenile delinquency). Juvenile arrests increased 20 percent in 1943; in some cities it was even higher — San Diego, for example, reported an increase of 55 percent among boys and 355 percent among girls. This was not a reflection of a nationwide crime wave, for crime on the whole — at least according to FBI figures — dropped during the war, with the exception of assault and rape. This was because the young men, who committed the largest percentage of crimes, were off in service. One of the heaviest areas of increase was among girls under seventeen who were arrested not only for various forms of "sex delinquency" such as prostitution, but also for violent crimes. In 1943 alone, the number of girls arrested for prostitution increased by 68 percent over the previous year.

Among the boys, it was largely theft and a striking incidence of acts of vandalism, destruction and violence. Some of these acts seemed a kind of acting-out of war fantasies — such as the thirteen-year-old "thrill saboteur" who put a stick of dynamite under a railroad track, lit the fuse and ran. The dynamite did not go off because he had attached no cap. He explained his action by saying he was attempting to close off all roads into the town and set himself up as "dictator."

With the girls, delinquency took the form of an aggressive promiscuity, and the lure was the glamor of a uniform. These "khaki-whacky" teenagers — some barely thirteen — were known as V (for Victory) girls. They hung around bus depots, train stations, drugstores or wherever soldiers and sailors on leave might congregate, flirted with the boys, and propositioned them for dates. They were amateurs for the most part, the price of their favors being a movie, a dance, a Coke or some stronger drink. (A joke of the time ran: Sailor: "I'm going to Walgreen's to meet a girl." "What's her name?" "How should I know?")

The V-girls were easily recognizable in their Sloppy Joe sweaters, hair ribbons, anklets or bobby sox and saddle shoes, trying to look older with heavily made-up faces and blood-red lipstick. In Detroit the Navy had to build a fence around its armory, located in the city, to keep out not the enemy, but the bobby-soxers. In Chicago, sailors said it was worth one's life to try to walk from the Navy Pier to State Street, where the V-girls swarmed like flies. In Mobile, the girls themselves bought contraceptives for their dates, and when one druggist refused to sell them to a group of girls, he was jeered at and called an old fuddy-duddy.

The V-girls had their similarities all over the country. Some of them followed their lovers when they were transferred to another post, but many were left stranded when the boyfriend left. These often ended up working as waitresses or as barmaids in servicemen's hangouts, passing from one uniform to another.

There had always been teen-age girls who "did it," of course; war made them more visible, more independent, more mobile. One estimate had it that the V-girls represented at most only one in 1,700 out of their age group. More conservative girls, caught up in the transitoriness of wartime meetings and the glamor of a uniform, might also "do it," but they were more discreet and less promiscuous and conducted their assignations in more privacy.

The V-girl was next door to being a prostitute, yet there was about her at least a certain refreshing lack of cold professionalism. She offered a lonely GI transitory fun and excitement, devoid of the professional's matter-of-fact indifference. She could also, of course, offer him VD, for there was a higher incidence among the amateurs than among the professionals. In 1941, Congress, worried about the mother's vote, had passed the May Act, which forbade houses of prostitution near military bases. The result was that a lot of establishments were closed down and their inmates put out to walk the streets. These and their amateur competitors were found to inflict VD at a much higher rate than the house-based girls. . . .

The guardians of morality — whose view on the subject had been expressed in a 1942 *Reader's Digest* article by Gene Tunney entitled "The Bright Shield of Continence" — of course were against any kind of sex by soldiers with women other than their wives (if that) and would be shocked at the idea of brothels near Army camps where innocent young selectees would be exposed to unholy, irresistible temptation leading to inevitable corruption. (There was a similar logic running through the efforts of temperance groups to ban the distribution of beer to combat troops or its sale at PX's.)

As for the servicemen themselves, the Army traditionally liked to say that 15 percent "won't," 15 percent "will" and the remainder occasionally would succumb to temptation if the serpent insinuated itself (these figures derived from World War I). For that wavering 70 percent, the problems of finding "nice girls" in the camp towns, whether their intent was to deflower them or take them to the Sunday night meeting of the Epworth League, were often insuperable. . . .

Still, if the number of marriages and families formed is any sort of index to the degree of adherence to the American fundamental belief in marriage, the war period could be looked upon as fostering a salubrious moral climate. Beginning in 1940, as prosperity began to take hold and the Depression receded, the marriage rate began to rise abruptly — one is tempted to say alarmingly. . . .

The rush to wed was impelled as much by prosperity as it was by the war. A justice of the peace in Yuma, Arizona, a marriage town just over the California border, explained the sudden upswing in business in 1941. Not love but "aircraft did it for us," he said. "The figures began going up as soon as those boys were given employment in those plants at San Diego and Los Angeles and were taken off W.P.A. [Works Progress Administration]." Aircraft workers had been issued 90 percent of the licenses since the summer of 1941. "You see, when they were on the dole they had girls but no money. Once off the dole and once getting good money they began sending for the girls back home — girls in the Middle Western states, a great many of them. The girls wouldn't waste any time in coming in and then on weekends — we get the great rush on weekends — they'd all come hustling over to Yuma." It was the same story in Cincinnati, where weddings involving defense workers increased 51 percent; in Baltimore, where they were up 47 percent; and in Youngstown and Akron (up 17 percent) and Detroit (up 12 percent).

Of course, at that time a wife would also qualify as a dependent and men with dependents were deferred, until Congress discouraged this by establishing an allotment system in 1942. Under it, a man's wife would receive a minimum of $50 a month, $22 of which was deducted from his pay and $28 contributed by the government. To preserve family life and also perhaps to encourage a population increase to offset anticipated manpower losses in the war, the Selective Service Act deferred fathers until 1943, when manpower needs were so pressing that so-called pre-Pearl Harbor fathers were drafted.

Whether the Selective Service Act's policy was responsible or not (and we must give the parents some credit for initiative), the birthrate did go up during the war in a preview of the postwar baby boom when returning GI's set about forming families as fast as they could. Since the 1920's the birthrate, like the marriage rate, had been declining, but in 1943, it rose to 22 per 1,000 — the highest in two decades. Most of these babies were "good-bye babies," conceived before the husband shipped out. Since the wife's allotment check would be increased upon the child's arrival, finances were no longer a major worry. In addition, there were compelling emotional reasons: The father, faced with the possibility of being killed in battle, was depositing a small guarantor to posterity, an assurance that someone would carry on his name, while the wife was given something to hold onto, a living, breathing symbol of their marriage. . . .

So they were married, this courageous young couple; perhaps they did know each other well and were in love, or perhaps they had met on a weekend pass and married in haste. Or perhaps the woman had eyed covetously the allotment check and looked forward to a life of some ease (and if he was killed, there was always the $10,000 to the widow from his life insurance). A $50-a-month allotment was of course not princely, but a GI overseas, with nothing else to spend it on, would usually send part of his regular pay home.

With the going rate only $50 per month per husband, a really ambitious girl might decide she needed four, five, six or more husbands to support her in any kind of style. Inevitably there developed the wartime racket of bigamous marriage for allotment checks. The girls who engaged in it came to be known as Allotment Annies. They posted themselves in bars around military bases and struck up acquaintances with lonely servicemen, otherwise known as shooting fish in a barrel. The men, desirous of the certainty that when they went off to battle, there would be a girl back home waiting for them, writing them V-mail letters, could often be had. So they married, the hero went off to war, and Annie stayed home and collected a lot of those pale blue-green checks from the U.S. Treasury Department.

A representative Allotment Annie was a hustling seventeen-year-old named Elvira Tayloe, who operated out of Norfolk, Virginia, and specialized in sailors shipping out from the large naval base there. Working as a hostess in a nightclub, she managed to snare six live ones and was working on her seventh when caught. This came about because a couple of sailors on liberty had met in an English pub, and as servicemen are wont, as the warm beer flowed, took out wallets and exchanged pictures of their gorgeous wives. Both were surprised, to put it mildly, when their pictures turned out to be identical, both of Elvira. A fight ensued over whose wife was being adulterous with whom. After the shore patrol had cooled them off, the boys joined forces, Elvira was traced and her career of cupidity brought to an end. . . .

Wartime marriage was hard, and the real miracle was that so many survived it. What the husband did overseas during off-duty hours is beyond our scope, but the girls back here were, largely, brave — and true. Not heroic; but they got by. Some, it is true, cracked up, or fell into dalliance with a representative of the local supply of 4-F's and joyriding war workers.

Life gave another portrait of the typical Army wife. Her husband is a lieutenant in India and her $180-a-month allotment makes her atypical right there, yet she adds some less dramatic hues to the portrait. She lives in a 3½-room apartment, rent $65 a month; she spends $45 a month on food for her herself and the baby; she doesn't go out on dates, goes to parties unescorted and doesn't have a great deal of fun ("There's always some woman who thinks you're trying to take their man away"); sometimes at night she gets the blues and cries, but her baby son cheers her up a lot; she writes her husband a letter every day; she spends her evenings listening to the radio a lot (Guy Lombardo's is her favorite orchestra); when she hears "Soon" — "their song" in 1935, when they were married — she becomes sad. . . .

Dr. Jacob Sergi Kasanin, chief psychiatrist at Mount Zion Hospital in San Francisco, went so far as to identify a neurotic syndrome characteristic of servicemen's wives in 1945. Like many men who went overseas and cracked up before they reached combat (there were estimates that as high as one-half of the combat-trained troops avoided battle by "psyching out," getting a dishonorable discharge and the like), the wives had their own form of crackup. The physical symptoms included depression, colitis, heart palpitations, diarrhea, frequent headaches. Hardest hit were the recently married who had no children. They often developed "pathological reactions" in the form of resentment against their husband or even inability to recall what he looked like. (This was true even among fairly normal wives. One such wife decided to knit a sweater for her husband. As the months of separation drew on, her idea of her tall husband grew accordingly. He sent a picture of himself in the new sweater: it reached halfway down to his knees.) These women often had followed their husbands to his embarkation point; then in symbolic identity with him, they stayed there, and some couldn't take the loneliness, away from home, and began going to the bars, meeting other servicemen in transit. (The ratio of female alcoholics — defined as those who got into trouble with the police — to male alcoholics in Chicago was one to two, compared to one in five in 1931.)

For the more mature marriages, the ones in which the couple would pick up the pieces of their life and put them back together after long separation, there were still changes to be faced. A Navy doctor took a look at himself in the mirror one day and saw that he had grown bald and fat. He wrote about this to his wife, and she wrote back, sadly, "You will find that three years have done quite a bit to me, too."

The war, then, upset the social topography as it did the physical landscape; people met new places, new situations, new jobs, new living conditions, new ways of life, new temptations, new opportunities. There were social ills aplenty, but for all their novelty, they were perhaps the familiar ones; war simply exaggerated them and made them more visible. A sociologist writing on juvenile delinquency in *Federal Probation Officer* expressed a view that most diagnosticians of society would share:

> . . . many mothers of school-age boys and girls work in normal times; families are "broken" either physically or psychologically in normal times; children are exploited in normal times; some young people have always earned good wages and spent them unwisely; families always have moved from one neighborhood or community to another; some recreational facilities of an undesirable nature can be found in most communities in normal times. . . . Actually war does not create new problems with which we are unfamiliar. It accentuates old problems and in so doing the number of boys and girls affected is increased greatly.

One can only add that, in view of the familiarity of the problems and their increased magnitude, the governmental agencies might have done more to alleviate them. But of course, to Congress, stepped-up programs of social welfare would have smacked of "New Deal social experiments," and besides — don't you know there's a war on?

The citizenry out in the provinces who thought they had problems could take a measure of malicious satisfaction, if they wanted to, over the fact that their nation's capital was perhaps the most mixed-up, down-at-the-heels war town of them all. Its traditional industry was mainly government, of course, but everybody in the provinces knew that Washington's "bit" was doing the war's desk work — paper shuffling, tabulating, enumerating, filing. What people in Washington did was concoct complicated forms and schedules, issue directives, create agencies and, when they had some spare time, which was often, sit around and lobby, trade favors, peddle influence, gossip, boondoggle and, above all, take part in colorful feuds for the delectation of newspaper readers everywhere.

An exaggeration of course, but Washington was easy to poke fun at. It was a sort of sitting lame duck for conservative writers who gleefully pointed to whopping inefficiencies, pullulating paper work, labyrinthine bureaucracies, overlapping jurisdictions and a steady stream of executive directives. (FDR issued more executive orders during his Presidency than all previous Presidents combined.) "Washington Wonderland," they called it; "A red-tape-snarled, swarming, sweating metropolis"; "an insane asylum run by the inmates"; or in the words of a taxi driver: "the greatest goddamn insane asylum of the universe."

Overcrowding was Washington's most obvious physical symptom. Since 1940, more than 280,000 government job seekers had poured into town to hold down jobs as clerks and typists in the burgeoning wartime bureaucracy. Most of them were girls; most came from small towns all across the nation. They were drawn by the lure of higher wages — a girl could make $1,600 a year as a typist — and though they reveled in their newfound affluence, they could never get over the high prices, at which they clucked and shook their heads like tourists.

They were set down into a sort of Dogpatch with monuments, plagued by an acute housing shortage, overburdened and capricious public transportation, a cost of living that gobbled up their salaries (that government typist making $1,600 was lucky if she saved $25 in a year) and temporary office buildings that were as homey to work in as a railroad station.

Washington's housing shortage became an overused comic premise in movies and plays about the city, but to the people who lived there it was not always so funny. People paid $24 or $35 or more a month for glorified cubicles or jammed into shabby boardinghouses. They jostled for bathroom access with a herd of fellow boarders and were lucky if they could get a bath once every ten days. Landladies discouraged women tenants because they were wont to do their own laundry, request kitchen privileges and entertain gentlemen callers in the parlor. "Men, on the other hand," observed one concierge, "don't wash anything but themselves and eat all their meals out."

Hotels limited guests to a three-day stay. Hospitals had reverted to something out of Dickens; it was the practice to induce childbirth, for otherwise a room might not be available at the right time. . . .

For a family — especially a family with children — it was nearly impossible to find a place. Pathetic want ads appeared in the newspapers: "Won't someone help a refined enlisted Navy man and wife, employed, no children, to obtain an unfurnished room or two with kitchen?" Houses for sale were flagrantly overpriced, and people in Georgetown bought up old, run-down houses for $3,000, renovated them and sold them for five times what they had paid. Renting a house was dearer yet: tiny Georgetown houses rented for a minimum of $250 a month, and some larger houses in other neighborhoods that were by no means mansions were going for $1,000 a month. After President Roosevelt's death, the thought quickly occurred to a lot of people at the same time that the new President would soon be moving out of his two-bedroom, $120-a-month, rent-controlled apartment. The switchboard at Mr. Truman's building was jammed with calls; the operator told each caller that the President had already promised the apartment to at least three people. . . .

Uniforms were everywhere, representing a rainbow of international military pageantry. At night American soldiers and sailors crowded into the little nightclubs, and Washington night life boomed as it never had before or since. As part of its hospitality to servicemen, Washington offered, in addition to man-starved G-girls ("Washington is the loneliest town," one of them said), the highest VD-contraction rate among servicemen of any city in the country. . . .

Like housing, office space was in short supply, even with the ugly new temporary buildings. The government resorted to pressuring businesses and private residents to move out, and the President spoke darkly of "parasites" — useless people occupying vitally needed space. About the only solution to the office shortage was for the government to move out of town. This it did, in part, setting up branch offices in Richmond, New York, Chicago, St. Louis, Cincinnati, Kansas City, Philadelphia and Baltimore. More than 35,000 government employees moved out, too. . . .

In 1942 the world's largest office building was completed across the Potomac near Arlington. Called the Pentagon, its labyrinthine corridors and offices housed 35,000 office workers. When people wondered what in the world the War Department would do with such an enormous building in peacetime, the President explained that it would be used to store government records and quartermaster supplies, which seemed to satisfy everybody.

STUDY GUIDE

1. World War II brought an end to the widespread unemployment of the Great Depression. Is there any hint in the author's narrative of a regret on the part of the nation that it took a war — and a massive one at that — to pull the country out of the Depression?

2. What impression do you get of the spirit of the nation in its newly found prosperity and employment: a sense of dedication to the war effort? gratitude to the government for a job and a weekly income? sadness that a war was going on?

3. How did the federal government respond to the *social* needs of war workers? Was housing for workers planned as well or as extensively by the government as, for example, munitions plants or airplane factories? Support your answer with evidence from the essay.

4. What similarities and what differences do you find between the behavior of teen-agers during the war and their attitudes and activities today? What is the difference, for example, between the V-girls and today's "groupies" — teen-age girls who follow rock musicians around the country and offer them sexual favors? Do you feel, on the basis of this essay, that there was more or less juvenile delinquency during World War II than there is in our contemporary society?

5. On the basis of this essay, would you conclude that marital relationships during World War II were better or worse than marriages today?

6. The title of Richard Lingeman's book is *Don't You Know There's a War On?* What is the author trying to suggest by this title?

BIBLIOGRAPHY

The volume from which this selection was taken provides an entertaining account of the American people during World War II: Richard R. Lingeman, *Don't You Know There's a War On?: The American Home Front, 1941–1945* (New York, 1970). Contemporary accounts of social developments during World War II include the following: Francis E. Merrill, *Social Problems on the Home Front* (New York, 1948); William F. Ogburn, ed., *American Society in Wartime* (Chicago, 1943); and Jack Goodman, ed., *While You Were Gone* (New York, 1946), a series of essays on American life during the war. A recent and more comprehensive and scholarly description of the war's impact on the nation is Richard Polenberg, *War and Society: The United States, 1941–1945* * (Philadelphia, 1972). Informative and interesting recent publications are Geoffrey Perret, *Days of Sadness, Years of Triumph* * (New York, 1973); William Manchester, *The Glory and the Dream: A Narrative History of America, 1932–1972* * (Boston, 1974); and Lisle A. Rose, *The Long Shadow: Reflections on the Second World War Era* (Westport, Conn., 1978).

* Asterisk indicates book is available in a paperback edition.

VI AFFLUENCE AND ITS DISCONTENTS

The material well-being of the American people in the decades since the end of World War II contrasts sharply with their poverty in the Great Depression of the 1930s. While not all Americans shared equally, or even equitably, in the postwar prosperity, tens of millions of Americans did come to enjoy a standard of living far higher than they, their parents, or their grandparents had ever achieved. Following the end of World War II, American influence abroad reached its zenith as well, reversing the isolationist posture the United States had maintained throughout most of the 1930s.

Despite the enormous increase in economic prosperity at home and military power overseas, the decades following the end of World War II were punctuated by tensions of various kinds — internal insecurities and divisions and external wars — that belied the facade of supreme confidence erected by a strong and prosperous nation. In the Truman-Eisenhower years, from 1945 to 1960, the second Red Scare and the Korean War disturbed and divided the nation. Three assassinations in the 1960s, of John F. Kennedy, Robert Kennedy, and Martin Luther King, provided further proof that social and political stability did not necessarily go hand-in-hand with material prosperity and national power. Despite Lyndon B. Johnson's announcement of the "Great Society" and Richard M. Nixon's promise "to bring the American people together," developments between the mid-sixties and mid-seventies gave little indication that either of these presidential visions would be fulfilled. On the contrary, opinion polls found Americans disillusioned with their society, particularly with their political institutions and leaders. From the mid-sixties to the mid-seventies urban violence, civil rights and antiwar demonstrations, the rise of the counter-culture, and the Watergate scandals assaulted the psyche of the American people.

The essays by Henry F. Bedford, William Manchester, and James A. Michener describe various protest movements of the era. The last essay in this volume focuses on Richard M. Nixon's presidential career, as seen through the medium of television — a medium that he employed to get into the White House and one that recorded his downfall and departure from office.

Dan Weiner

Boycotting the buses in Montgomery.

18

HENRY F. BEDFORD

The Struggle
for Civil Rights

No single issue since the end of World War II so fragmented
American society as the question of civil rights for American
blacks. From the turn of the century — when the social segregation and political disfranchisement of the Negro became complete — to World War II, it appeared that this pattern of race
relations would remain a permanent one. But it was not to be so.
As a consequence of many developments, including the bus boycott at Montgomery described in this selection, many white
Americans were moved to create a greater measure of opportunity for blacks and their integration into white society.

The first significant signs of an alteration in the racist status
quo between blacks and whites came during World War II, when
A. Philip Randolph, head of the Sleeping Car Porters Union,
threatened a march on Washington if Negroes were not granted
equal job opportunities in the rapidly expanding war economy.
Alarmed, President Franklin Delano Roosevelt issued Executive
Order 8802 establishing the Fair Employment Practices Commission (FEPC), a federal agency designed to encourage the hiring
of blacks in the nation's war industries. Other developments after
the war reinforced the militancy of American blacks and the
readiness of American whites for a change in race relations.
Shortly after the war's end, Harry S. Truman took steps to integrate the armed forces. Other developments that encouraged the
civil rights movement included the need for the United States to
compete with the Soviet Union in winning the favor of the black
and brown peoples of Asia and Africa, the model provided by

African blacks in winning their independence from the European powers, the historic decision of the Supreme Court that struck down the constitutional and legal supports for segregation in education, and the civil rights movement that grew in the black community in the United States.

Undoubtedly, the most impressive black civil rights leader of this era was Martin Luther King. In his brief, yet productive, career — he was assassinated at the age of thirty-nine in Memphis in April of 1968 — this southern-born, northern-educated Baptist minister earned the adulation of the black Americans he spoke for and the white Americans he addressed on their behalf. While there were those black nationalists at one end of the spectrum and white racists at the other who did not accept King's message of achieving integration and equality through nonviolent action, the majority of the American people recognized his stature, were in agreement with his tactics, and shared his goals.

The following selection by Henry F. Bedford is an account of one of Martin Luther King's early civil rights victories, his leadership of a successful campaign by the blacks of Montgomery, Alabama, to integrate the public transportation system of that city. In it, the basic elements of King's social philosophy and strategy — the mobilization of the black community, the stress on nonviolence, and the use of the nation's legal machinery — are clear. One can draw a line from the victory at Montgomery to the Civil Rights Acts of the 1960s, which led to the erosion of the caste system that had characterized black-white relations in the South, and in some parts of the North, since the end of Reconstruction.

Martin Luther King, Jr., did not always arise with the sun. But Monday, December 5, 1955, was a special day, and the excited young minister could not sleep. Impatiently he paced the house, waiting for the first bus of the day to reach its stop near his front porch. The vehicle was usually crowded with black domestics on their way to the kitchens and yards of the white employers of Montgomery, Alabama; it would be a good test of the boycott he and others had urged local blacks to undertake. King had prepared himself for disappointment and hoped to be cheered by partial success. But the

Excerpted and reprinted by permission of Harcourt Brace Jovanovich, Inc. from "Peaceful Souls and Tired Feet: Montgomery, 1955" in *Trouble Downtown: The Local Context of Twentieth-Century America* by Henry F. Bedford, © 1978 by Harcourt Brace Jovanovich, Inc.

first bus was empty, and the second, and the third. The exhilarated pastor undertook a wider investigation in his car.

In another part of the city, a young white reporter was conducting his own investigation. Joe Azbell, city editor of the *Montgomery Advertiser*, stood on Court Square in the dim dawn. The city's Christmas decorations caught the early sun and tinkled when they stirred. A banner proclaiming PEACE ON EARTH cast a shadow, through which an erect, middle-aged black man walked as he crossed the street. At the corner a bus stopped, and the driver opened the door. When the man did not move, the driver asked "Are you gettin' on?" "I ain't gettin' on," the black returned, "till Jim Crow gets off." Jim Crow — the personification of racial segregation — was a perpetual passenger, so the driver closed the door and drove off.

The struggle to get Jim Crow off the buses and out of American life was one of the central themes of the nation's history after the Second World War. In retrospect, the early stages of the civil rights movement may seem idealistic and naive, and the participation of Northern whites patronizing and hypocritical. The progress they celebrated seems trivial now that Americans have a somewhat better sense of the detours on their pilgrimage to equality. Yet President Harry Truman's order in 1948 ending segregation in the armed forces was no minor matter when much of the nation's male youth expected a tour of military duty. And the Supreme Court's unanimous ruling in 1954 against segregated schooling in the case of *Oliver Brown et al.* v. *Board of Education of Topeka, Kansas* was even more inclusive. . . .

Rosa Parks had had a hard day. As usual, she had fussed over fit and pinned and stitched hems at the Montgomery Fair, a department store where she worked. She had done a little shopping herself. The crowds were abnormally large with Christmas less than a month away, so Mrs. Parks hoped there would be a seat that evening on the bus that would take her home to Cleveland Avenue. She paid her fare and then stepped off to board in the rear, as local custom required. Because the rear section was full, she sat in one of the middle seats that blacks might occupy when whites did not.

The bus made slow progress around Court Square and stopped at the Empire Theater, where several white passengers boarded. In accordance with a municipal ordinance, the driver asked four blacks, including Mrs. Parks, to stand in order to seat the additional white passengers. Three blacks promptly complied. Mrs. Parks refused. "I don't really know why I wouldn't move," she said later. "There was no plot or plan at all. I was just tired from shopping. I had my sacks and all, and my feet hurt." The driver found two policemen, who charged Mrs. Parks with violation of the city's segregation ordinance and ordered her to appear in court on Monday morning, December 5. Once booked, she called E. D. Nixon, for whom she had worked as a volunteer in the local office of the NAACP. Nixon spread the word.

Jo Ann Robinson reminded Nixon that plans to boycott the bus company had been shelved some months earlier. Both agreed that Mrs. Parks, who was well known and widely respected among Montgomery's blacks, presented an ideal symbol of the injustice of segregation. Dignified and diligent, forty-two years old, with coiled, braided hair and spectacles, Mrs. Parks was no pushy adolescent. After a momentary hesitation, Martin Luther King, Jr., volunteered his church for a planning session, to which Nixon and Mrs. Robinson invited leaders of the black community. Before the group could assemble, mimeographed leaflets proposing a boycott began to appear on the street.

The chance inquiry of an illiterate maid, unable to decipher one of those leaflets, alerted the *Montgomery Advertiser* to plans for a boycott. Or rather that was the explanation Joe Azbell used to protect his source, E. D. Nixon, who wanted a report in the Sunday paper to alert blacks who might not otherwise be informed. Although Azbell knew Ralph Abernathy and had other contacts in the black community, his first story left some loose ends: he did not specify the "unidentified Negro leaders" who were organizing the protest; he knew that Rosa Parks' arrest was a critical event, but he had not interviewed her; he had no hint of the agenda for a "top secret" meeting scheduled for Monday evening at the Holt Street Baptist Church. Azbell did reach an official of Montgomery City Lines, who told him that the company and its drivers had "to obey laws just like any other citizen," as if that explained everything.

Joe Azbell thought the city unnaturally quiet as he moved about on Monday. Even the throngs that surrounded the Holt Street Baptist Church seemed subdued when he arrived that evening. Inside, however, there was no hush, from the rousing initial chorus of "Onward Christian Soldiers" to the final shouted approval of a resolution to stay off the buses until the company agreed to hire black drivers, to guarantee courteous treatment of black passengers, and to permit first-come, first-served seating, whites from the front of the bus and blacks from the rear. Between the hymn and the business, speakers arrived and departed without introduction. One of them, an intense young man, reached for history to add significance to the moment: "And the history book will write of us as a race of people who in Montgomery County, State of Alabama, Country of the United States, stood up for and fought for their rights as American citizens, as citizens of democracy."

Martin Luther King, Jr., later remembered his peroration somewhat differently, but the exact words do not matter. Both the reporter and the unidentified (and to Azbell unknown) speaker sensed that the occasion was emotionally and historically important. King wanted to link moderation and militance in his speech, to inspire action and control it. He hoped his audience would extend their day-long boycott without becoming vindictive or violent. Azbell's account suggested that King had made his point:

> The meeting was much like an old-fashioned revival with loud applause added. It proved beyond any doubt there was a discipline among Negroes

that many whites had doubted. It was almost a military discipline combined with emotion.

Montgomery's police commissioner thought the discipline came from systematic abuse by "Negro 'goon squads' " that kept nine of ten ordinary passengers off the buses. He assigned police to bus stops to prevent violence and ordered motorcycle policemen to convoy buses in the first days of the boycott. Ironically, this unusual protection may have increased participation, for some blacks apparently assumed they would be arrested for taking a bus. . . .

The dedication of Montgomery blacks was almost universal. Prominent "big Negroes" drove their big cars to take maids and handymen to work in white neighborhoods. Black owners of taxicabs charged their patrons bus fare. Hundreds of blacks insisted on walking to make their participation completely visible. J. H. Bagley, the bus company's local manager, estimated that the boycott was 90 percent effective and that "thousands" of riders had stayed off the buses. The *Advertiser* printed a photograph showing a solitary black figure in front of benches where ordinarily, the caption read, "several hundred Negroes" would be waiting. Yet most blacks somehow went where they wanted to go. Many attended the routine five-minute trial of Rosa Parks; she did not testify, was fined $10 and $4 costs, and filed a notice of appeal.

From the outset, the Montgomery Improvement Association (MIA), which represented boycotting blacks, offered to negotiate with the bus company and with the city. Jack Crenshaw, counsel for the bus line and the person who appears to have controlled the company's policy, may have misinterpreted that openness as a sign of weakness. The company held franchises from several Southern cities, and Crenshaw may have thought that any willing retreat from segregation would endanger every Southern contract. In any case, he apparently decided to do nothing without a court order. He would trade the permanent good will of Southern whites for the temporary loss of patronage by Montgomery's blacks. Until the threats and the violence ceased, Crenshaw said, the company would not even meet representatives of the MIA. (His reference to violence rested on reports by drivers of a few rocks thrown and fewer bullets fired at buses. Crenshaw assumed blacks were responsible.)

Suspecting that positions would soon become rigid, the executive director of the Alabama Council on Human Relations invited representatives of the MIA to meet with the city commissioners and officials of the company. The parley did not go well. As president of the MIA, King deplored violence, offered to report to police any offenders the organization discovered, and restated the black community's terms for ending the boycott. Crenshaw replied that the company could not permit first-come, first-served seating without a change in the city's segregation ordinance. Police Commissioner Clyde Sellers and Mayor W. A. ("Tacky") Gayle wanted no part of that hot potato and seemed to King to become "more and more intransigent" after Crenshaw had argued that point. The company would not consider hiring black drivers, but Crenshaw promised that white drivers would in the future be more courteous. Martin Luther King, Jr., among others, had heard that before. He suggested that the fruitless discussion end.

Apparently hoping a less charged atmosphere would have a better result, Mayor Gayle asked King and a few other MIA members to remain for informal conversation. Commissioner Frank A. Parks, an interior decorator at the beginning of his first term in public office, seemed ready to accept the MIA's seating proposal. "We can work it within our segregation laws," Parks said, indicating his agreement with a legal contention of the MIA. Crenshaw firmly contradicted him, and Parks soon backed down. Besides, Crenshaw went on, "If we granted the Negroes these demands, . . . they would go about boasting of a victory they had won over the white people; and this we will not stand for."

That aside helps explain the inflexible response of white supremacists to the most trivial request for changed racial practice. Any concession made under pressure would indicate both white weakness and black strength, and thereby subvert racist mythology: white men could make no concession without endangering white women. Subsequent meetings discovered no way around the impasse and both sides prepared for a siege instead of a settlement.

Indeed the company began these preparations so promptly that they were probably intended to force the MIA to a settlement. On the second day of the boycott, the local manager linked reduced revenue and reduced service. On the third day, curtailment began. Before the week was out, service to most of the city's black neighborhoods had been suspended, a step that certainly assisted advocates of the boycott. The emotional pitch in the black community drooped as the week wore on. One drenched student at Alabama State College announced that his principles would not survive one more day of rain. But when the determination of the black community faltered, there were no buses to board.

King and the MIA ran into official hostility as they improvised to provide other means of transportation. A letter from the city comptroller reminded owners of taxis that the standard fee schedule had the force of a municipal ordinance; he had heard, he continued, that some black operators were charging bus fare instead. The police chief reported "numerous complaints" about overloaded vehicles and ordered the force to be especially vigilant in checking car pools. As the weeks became months and the boycott drew national attention and support, the MIA set up regular assembly and dispatch points, raised money and purchased new station wagons, and hired full-time drivers. When somebody dumped acid on those shiny station wagons, the police were baffled.

Although transportation became readily available, some blacks continued to walk. The protest was for them a spiritual odyssey and the hardship a price they willingly paid for equality. King used the remarks of several anonymous walking blacks to illustrate for national audiences the dignified faith with which blacks met white oppression. An older woman overcame her obvious fatigue and declined a ride from one of the MIA's drivers: "I'm not walking for myself," she explained. "I'm walking for my children and grandchildren." Another woman made the same point: "My feet is tired, but my soul is at rest."

This resigned, Christian resistance to injustice was soon associated with the leadership of Martin Luther King, Jr., although his synthesis of ideology and tactic was neither original nor fully developed when the boycott commenced in December 1955. King brought no preconceived formula to events in Montgomery; indeed he did some prayerful rationalization to differentiate the MIA's boycott from unjust economic coercion of the sort advocated by White Citizens' Councils. As the boycott progressed, King gradually fused elements of Christian idealism, Gandhian nonviolence, and civil disobedience into a creed that inspired others and gave him a moral assurance that compensated for youthful inexperience, temper, and doubt.

He had some help from a gentle, sheltered, white librarian, who wrote a remarkable letter to the *Montgomery Advertiser* a week after the boycott began. "Not since the first battle of the Marne has the taxi been put to as good use as it has been this past week in Montgomery," Juliette Morgan began. Yet the city's blacks, she thought, owed more to the example of Gandhi's Salt March and to Thoreau's work on civil disobedience than to the inspiration of French troops. Montgomery's blacks faced greater obstacles than had Gandhi, for Southern whites held their prejudices more tenaciously than Great Britain had held the empire. Yet "passive resistance combined with freedom from hate" might be sufficient to the task. She dismissed as absurd the moral equation of the bus boycott with the economic coercion of the WCC; compare the speeches of white supremacists with those Joe Azbell reported from the meeting at the Holt Street Church, she urged, "and blush." . . .

The United States of America, Miss Morgan reminded Montgomery, had been "founded upon a boycott" of British tea. And now, she felt,

> history is being made in Montgomery. . . . It is hard to imagine a soul so dead, a heart so hard, a vision so blinded and provincial as not to be moved with admiration at the quiet dignity, discipline, and dedication with which the Negroes have conducted their boycott. . . . Their cause and their conduct have filled me with great sympathy, pride, humility, and envy. I envy their unity, their good humor, their fortitude, and their willingness to suffer for great Christian and democratic principles, or [for] just plain decent treatment.

"This may be a minority report," she concluded, "but a number of Montgomerians not entirely inconsequential agree with my point of view." . . .

Many whites quickly decided, as Jack Crenshaw had, that the grievance was not confined to [first-come, first-served seating]. Whatever the MIA said, many whites apparently believed the demand reached beyond equal, if separate, seats on buses to integration everywhere. Crenshaw's fear of any concession crept through the white community, as Hall later confirmed: "The whites . . . are persuaded that they cannot allow themselves to be overcome on this terrain, ill-chosen . . . though it is, lest they be routed in the schools." Hall himself had first commended the city's "admirable coolness," but he soon lost his. Perhaps he was unconscious of his military metaphor, but the mask of moderation slipped when he warned Negro leaders to "reckon with two realities."

> The white man's economic artillery is far better emplaced, and commanded by more experienced gunners.
>   Second, the white man holds all the offices of government. . . . There will be white rule as far as the eye can see. . . . Does any Negro leader doubt that the resistance to . . . Negro voting has . . . increased?

Hall held out the prospect of future suffrage (which the Fifteenth Amendment had guaranteed more than eighty years before) in response to a request for a seat on the bus. And he suggested that refusal of that unresponsive offer meant war. . . .

In spite of stiffening resolve on both sides, Mayor Gayle at last found the elusive compromise. On Sunday, January 22, he announced that the city commission, the bus company, and a group of "prominent Negro ministers . . . representing the Negroes of Montgomery" had settled the dispute, and that bus service in the black neighborhoods would resume promptly. The negotiators had agreed, Gayle went on, that the company had complete authority to hire drivers and must obey applicable regulations requiring segregation. The company promised "uniform courtesy" to all patrons, and first-come, first-served seating in the middle section of the buses; whites would fill that section from the front, where ten seats were to be reserved, and blacks from the rear. Gayle had somehow induced black representatives to accept terms Jack Crenshaw would have offered weeks before and which blacks had subsequently rejected several times. It was a spectacular triumph.

But the mayor had made it up. The MIA disavowed the unidentified "prominent Negro ministers," who protested that they had been "hoodwinked," and whose version of the conference differed from the one Gayle gave the press. King and other members of the MIA visited taverns and other Saturday-night haunts to be sure that early reports did not deceive blacks who might not be in church on Sunday. By Monday morning, Gayle's settlement looked like a called bluff.

And the mayor was angry. "We have pussyfooted around on this boycott long enough," Gayle told Joe Azbell. Apparently the city's blacks had become convinced "that they have the white people hemmed up in a corner," Gayle continued, and that they need not "give an inch until they force the white people . . . to submit to their demands — in fact to swallow all of them." The blacks were mistaken, the mayor said, for most whites did not "care whether a Negro ever rides a bus again," especially if that act endangered "the social fabric of our community." Make no mistake, Gayle repeated; the goal was nothing less than the "destruction of our social fabric." To save it, he said, he and Commissioner Parks had joined the White Citizens' Council, as Commissioner Sellers had done some weeks before. Martin Luther King, Jr., Grover Hall observed, had managed to make the WCC respectable; "the Southern Moderate," Hall continued, "is as nearly extinct as the whooping crane."

Certainly the white people of Montgomery appeared to approve Gayle's outburst and the city's new "get-tough" policy. The switchboard at city hall handled "hundreds of telephone calls praising the mayor and the commissioners." Commissioner Parks reported that "dozens" of businessmen would institute a counterboycott and fire their black employees. Commissioner Sellers instructed police to disperse groups waiting for car pools. Mayor Gayle loosed a tirade against timid whites who paid cab fare or otherwise subsidized the boycott and thereby encouraged black radicalism. "The Negroes have made their own bed," Gayle said, "and the whites should let them sleep in it."

A plague of legal difficulties beset black leaders. Pending the outcome of cases the boycott had set in motion, Rosa Parks declined to pay her $10 fine; the judge offered her jail instead. Martin Luther King, Jr., spent a few anxious hours in the Montgomery jail on a charge of speeding. Four times insurers canceled liability coverage for automobiles in the MIA's car pool. The local draft board abruptly revoked the occupational deferment of the young black attorney who had charted the MIA's course in the courts. Fred Gray was reclassified and available for immediate induction. His appeal moved like a yo-yo through the Selective Service hierarchy until officials in Washington reversed the Montgomery County board, an affront that triggered several resignations and a temporary refusal to provide any draftees from Alabama.

Of course somebody decided that legal harassment accomplished too little, too slowly. Martin Luther King, Jr., was preaching at one of the regular prayer meetings when the bomb thumped on the front porch of his house. Startled by the noise, Coretta Scott King moved toward their infant daughter, who was asleep at the rear of the residence. The bomb shattered the front window, tore a hole in the porch, and battered a column, but injured no one. By the time King reached the house, several hundred blacks had gathered in the area. The crowd's ugly mood frightened Joe Azbell, Mayor Gayle, Commissioner Sellers, and the white policemen who had rushed to the scene. "I was terrified," one officer recalled. "I owe my life to that nigger preacher, and so do all the other white people who were there."

King could not resist pointing out the logical consequences of "get-tough" public statements when Sellers and Gayle privately deplored violence. But King had swallowed his resentment by the time all three men went out on the blasted porch to try to calm the crowd. As he began, the young minister must have been speaking as much to himself as to the black faces in the darkness:

> We believe in law and order. Don't get panicky. Don't do anything panicky at all. Don't get your weapons. He who lives by the sword shall perish by the sword.... We are not advocating violence. We want to love our enemies.

He shifted to the first person singular as he regained his confidence:

> I want you to love your enemies. Be good to them.... I did not start this boycott. I was asked by you to serve as your spokesman. I want it to be known the length and breadth of this land that if I am stopped this movement will not be stopped. For what we are doing is right. What we are doing is just. And God is with us.

King's touch with the crowd was perfect. Back came a chorus of "Amens" and "God bless yous" that turned to jeers when Gayle and Sellers promised an unstinting search for the bomber and protection for King and his family. King spoke the benediction:

> Go home and don't worry. Be calm as I and my family are. We are not hurt, and remember that if anything happens to me, there will be others to take my place.

King's words did not end the sporadic violence; a few days later, a small bomb missed Nixon's house and smashed the fence in his yard. But both sides took steps to transfer the quarrel to the courts. On behalf of five black women, Fred Gray filed a suit in federal court asking that local and state regulations requiring segregated seating be declared unconstitutional. About the same time, a county grand jury, which included one black member, began weighing the prosecutor's evidence that the boycott was an illegal conspiracy against the bus company. No one could be compelled to patronize a business, Judge Eugene Carter explained to the jurors. On the other hand, "the right to conduct one's business without wrongful interference" was "a valuable property right" that merited legal protection. If the jurors found the boycott illegal, they could indict the leaders. On February 21, 1956, the second day of Brotherhood Week, the grand jury identified and indicted 115 leaders. It was, Grover Hall said later, "the dumbest act that was ever done in Montgomery." ...

Bombs and indictments indicated the "growing tension" and spreading "hate" that the grand jury noted during the third month of the boycott. Reverend Thomas Thrasher, one of the white clergymen on the Alabama Council on Human Relations, wrote of the "universal ... fear" that gripped the community:

The businessman's fear lest his business be destroyed by some false move or baseless rumor. The Negro's fear for his safety and his job. The clergy's fear that their congregations may be divided. . . . The politician's fear that he may do something disapproved by a majority of voters. And finally the whole community's fear that we may be torn asunder by a single rash act precipitating racial violence. . . .

Conciliators made no headway because both sides had handed the dispute to the courts. Conviction of the boycott's hundred-odd leaders, whites believed, would end the social pressure that kept blacks off the buses. Blacks, on the other hand, confident that their suit doomed segregated buses in Montgomery, turned the arrest of their leaders into a holiday. Sheriff's deputies brought in and booked Ralph Abernathy and others whose names headed the list. As word spread, blacks stopped at the station to find out if they were included; those omitted seemed more downcast than those indicted. Corridors filled with joking blacks, who helped the deputies with unfamiliar names and addresses. The atmosphere, Joe Azbell wrote, was "much like 'old home week.' " Martin Luther King, Jr., was out of town and could not surrender until the following day.

King was the first defendant called a month later to the drab courtroom where Judge Carter heard the case without a jury. The state had little difficulty demonstrating that there was a boycott and that King had had a good deal to do with it. Intimidation and violence, the prosecution contended, meant that the conspirators had not merely, and legally, withheld their patronage, but had violated the law. Two witnesses testified that their refusal to observe the boycott had led to harassment and harm; the state might have selected more credible witnesses, however, than an employee of the county and the maid who worked for Mayor Gayle's mother-in-law. To connect King to the violence during the boycott, the prosecutor asked Joe Azbell if King's speeches had been inflammatory. No, Azbell replied, undermining the state's case; King had consistently counseled nonviolence.

In spite of his own anticlimactic testimony, Azbell thought the prosecution had made a reasonable presentation. King's defense rested on his contention that the boycott (if there was a boycott, which his lawyers did not concede) had "just cause" within the meaning of the Alabama statute. This contention permitted King's lawyers to call witness after witness who told of degrading discourtesy and physical mistreatment at the hands of callous drivers. King's own testimony was not heroic, but convenient lapses of memory did not prevent his conviction. Judge Carter offered King a choice of a fine of $500 or 386 days at hard labor. The penalty was low, Carter said, because King had earnestly tried to keep the protest peaceful. Unmoved by the judge's compassion, King posted bond and appealed. . . .

By the spring of 1956, the boycott was no local phenomenon either. White supremacists, arguing that compromise in Montgomery would bring race-mixing elsewhere, enlisted national assistance. Those of both races who favored integration provided the financial and legal support that kept the MIA's station wagons on the streets and its lawyers in the courts. Local leaders — especially Martin Luther King, Jr. — had made out-of-town promises and had built national constituencies that had to be satisfied. The case pending in the federal courts effectively removed legal issues from local control, even if local leaders had been able to arrange a settlement. There was not much to do but wait.

Municipal officials did pull one last string. They alleged that the MIA's car pool was an unlicensed form of public transportation and went back to Judge Carter for an injunction. Martin Luther King, Jr., wondered why they had waited so long. The proceeding did not require a legal defense of segregation and would be difficult for the MIA to appeal to the federal courts. And an injunction, which King expected, might undermine the morale of the black community to the point that the boycott could not be sustained. Those polished station wagons were rolling symbols of success, a constant source of pride to blacks and of irritation for white supremacists. Even blacks who chose to walk drew inspiration and comfort from the knowledge that they could ride if they wished.

So King was apprehensive as he returned to Judge Carter's courtroom in mid-November 1956. He heard attorneys outline the city's case and then, in an entirely different mood, watched the charade play out to the injunction he had once feared. For by the time Judge Carter issued his ruling, it was irrelevant; as proceedings began in Montgomery, the Supreme Court of the United States ruled that ordinances requiring segregated seating violated the Fourteenth Amendment. The MIA could abandon the car pool and comply with Carter's injunction because Montgomery City Lines had to abandon segregation and comply with the order of the Supreme Court. The decision seemed almost providential: "God Almighty has spoken from Washington, D.C.," remarked a spectator in the Montgomery courthouse.

It took nearly a month for the official word to reach Montgomery. In the interim, a solemn march of the Ku Klux Klan roused derision rather than terror among Montgomery's newly confident blacks, and the city commissioners did nothing to prepare the community for the "tremendous impact" they warned that the decision would have. Instead they clung to their get-tough policy:

> The City Commission, and we know our people are with us in this determination, will not yield one inch, but will do all in its power to oppose the integration of the Negro race with the white race in Montgomery, and will forever stand like a rock against social equality, intermarriage, and mixing of the races under God's creation and plan.

King and the MIA used the interval to instruct blacks in courtesy that bordered on deference and in nonviolent response to provocation. On the morning of December 21, as he had done more than a year earlier, King got up to meet the first bus of the day. With Nixon, Abernathy, and a host of journalists and photographers, he waited for the vehicle to pull to the curb. "I believe you are the Reverend King, aren't you?" the driver asked. "We are glad to have you this morning." Later that day, a disgruntled rider looked around another bus and remarked emphatically, "I see this isn't going to be a white Christmas." One of the black passengers replied gently, "Yes, sir, that's right." "Suddenly, astonishingly," a reporter noted, "everyone on the bus was smiling."

There were, of course, sullen people on other buses. And there were shots, one of which hit a black passenger in the leg, and bombs, which damaged the homes and churches of several clergymen identified with the boycott, including Abernathy. A grand jury indicted seven white men for the bombings, but the two brought to trial were not convicted. Charges against the other five, and the still-pending indictments of black leaders for violating the antiboycott law, were dropped simultaneously. When legal technicalities jeopardized his appeal, King quietly paid his $500 fine. The cases were closed, the boycott concluded.

STUDY GUIDE

1. What developments in the United States, prior to the Montgomery bus boycott, laid the foundations for its success?

2. What impression do you get from Bedford's narrative of Rosa Parks's purposes — and character — when she refused to take her place in the back of the Montgomery bus? A decade or two earlier, could she have acted as she did in 1955? If you think so, on what grounds; if not, why not?

3. In assessing the role of Martin Luther King, state what impression you have of the following: (a) his influence in the black community and in the white community; (b) his organizational skills; (c) his tactics; (d) his temperament; and (e) his goals.

4. Outline the tactics employed by the city officials and others in the white leadership structure against the boycott and assess the effectiveness of each.

5. What, in your opinion, came to be the decisive element in the settlement of the boycott — and why?

6. In retrospect, can you (on the basis of material in your textbook) write a different scenario for this incident: (a) if the black community had conducted this boycott in the 1890s or in the 1920s, or (b) if the boycott had been led by Stokely Carmichael or Malcolm X, black leaders who came after Martin Luther King, Jr.

BIBLIOGRAPHY

The history of black Americans has made great strides in the last decade, and there are a fair number of books available to the student of the subject. A useful introduction to the history of black Americans is John Hope Franklin, *From Slavery to Freedom* * (New York, 1978). Concerning the civil rights movement in particular, there are a number of studies — some primary sources, written by participants in the movement, and others secondary accounts. Central to an understanding of what happened in the civil rights movement of the 1950s and 1960s are the following volumes by Martin Luther King, Jr.: *Stride Toward Freedom* * (New York, 1958) and *Why We Can't Wait* * (New York, 1964). Equally significant — and also one of the masterpieces of twentieth-century American literature — is Malcolm X's *Autobiography* * (New York, 1965). Other works include James Baldwin, *The Fire Next Time* * (New York, 1963), a prophecy of (and some say a call to) the violence that came later in that decade, and Stokely Carmichael and Charles U. Hamilton, *Black Power: The Politics of Liberation in America* * (New York, 1968). Of the secondary works, the following are useful: Anthony Lewis, et al., *Portrait of a Decade* * (New York, 1964), a narrative covering the years from 1954 to 1964; Charles E. Silberman, *Crisis in Black and White* * (New York, 1964), a perceptive survey of many aspects of the civil rights struggle in the early 1960s; and Benjamin Muse, *The American Negro Revolution: From Non-Violence to Black Power, 1963–1967* * (Bloomington, Ind., 1968); David J. Garrow, *Protest at Selma* (New Haven, Conn., 1978); and Robert H. Brisbane, *Black Activism* (Valley Forge, Pa., 1974).

* Asterisk indicates book is available in a paperback edition.

Michael Dobo/Stock Boston

The counterculture and its pleasures.

19

WILLIAM MANCHESTER

The Counterculture

The decades from the onset of the Great Depression in the early 1930s to the assassinations of John F. Kennedy and Martin Luther King, Jr., in the 1960s might well be called the Age of Consensus in the history of the American people. Despite massive unemployment and the opposition of a shrill minority to the politics of Franklin Delano Roosevelt, the Depression years were marked by overwhelming political support for the New Deal and an underlying faith of the majority of the American people in the essential soundness of the political and economic institutions of the nation. World War II further reinforced the psychic and social solidarity of the nation; in contrast to World War I, few dissented from the bipartisan foreign policy under which we fought the war, and even fewer questioned the moral or ideological justifications for the war. The years after World War II brought to a climax the spirit of consensus: at home, Americans joined hands in witch-hunts against suspected Communists in government and in the media; abroad, we waged a cold war and then a hot war against international Communism.

The consensus was reinforced by social and demographic developments within American society: in the decades after World War II, millions of Americans fled from the religious and ethnic particularism of the urban ghettoes to the homogeneity of the housing developments and the well-manicured lawns of middle-class suburbia. The American people learned about the middle-class conformity that marked their lifestyle in these years through two widely read books: William Whyte's *The Organization Man* and David Riesman's *The Lonely Crowd*. Both these authors portrayed the American as a conformist — seeking material advancement within the corporation and the emotional security of the crowd.

The era of consensus was shattered by the mid-1960s. For the rest of the decade, American society and American culture underwent fragmentation and conflict — along racial and ethnic lines, in a "generation gap," and in sharp cultural, political, and sexual divisions. The first to reject the postwar consensus were the blacks, who protested the social segregation, political disfranchisement, and economic subservience that they had endured since the end of the Civil War. The civil rights movement of the 1950s also served as the cutting edge for myriad other protest movements: the revolt of youth, the rise of the New Left, the discovery by women of the sexism in American life, the growth of organizations to improve the status of migrant workers, Chicanos, Puerto Ricans, and American Indians, and the appearance of a host of splinter groups resolved to legitimize abortion, homosexuality, and drugs. The following essay, taken from William Manchester's *The Glory and the Dream*, traces the rise of the counterculture, taking up the contributions made to that social and cultural phenomenon by the Beatles, hippies, drug advocate Timothy Leary, Twiggy, Joan Baez, and *Bob & Carol & Ted & Alice*.

In some way the great student upheavals of the 1960s were even more significant than they seemed at the time. Like the revolutionary fever that swept western Europe in 1848, they may never be fully understood. They cut across national orders and cultural barriers that had long intimidated older generations. Neither oceans nor even the Iron Curtain checked them; as Columbia exploded and Berkeley seethed, campuses erupted in England, Italy, Germany, Holland, Sweden, Spain, Belgium, Japan, Formosa, Poland, Hungary, Yugoslavia, and Czechoslovakia. Americans were preoccupied with the disorders at home, but in at least two foreign capitals, Prague and Warsaw, the damage was more extensive than anything in the United States. . . .

Nevertheless, the American role was special. The turmoil began in the United States, the world's most affluent nation and the one with the most strongly defined youth subculture. Undergraduates abroad were very conscious of events on American campuses, . . . while U.S. students were largely indifferent to the frenzies overseas. In America, moreover, it was possible to trace the powerful currents which were stirring youth. As Tocqueville noted, Americans have always taken a distinctive, almost Rousseauistic view of youth, and they have turned naturally to education as the solution to every problem, public and private.

But now youth itself had become a problem, and a major one at that. A great source of anxiety was the new political militance. A conservative educator declared that the campuses were harboring "a loose alliance of Maoists, Trotskyites, Stalinists, Cheists, anarchists, utopians, and nihilists." Spiro Agnew made several memorable remarks on the subject. In St. Louis he called student demonstrators "malcontents, radicals, incendiaries, and civil and uncivil disobedients" and said, "I would swap the whole damn zoo for a single platoon of the kind of Americans I saw in Vietnam." On another occasion he described the universities as "circus tents or psychiatric centers for over-privileged, under-disciplined, irresponsible children of well-to-do blasé permissivists."

Parents denied that they were blasé or permissive, and those who disapproved of the demonstrations said they were the work of a minority. Gallup reported that 72 percent of all students had not participated in any of them; a *Fortune* poll concluded that just 12.5 percent of undergraduates held "revolutionary" or "radically dissident" views; SDS recruited just 7 percent. But Groucho Marx spoke for millions of older Americans when he remarked, "It's no good saying that the ones you read about are a minority. They're not a minority if they're all yours and you have to wait for the car to get home to know your daughter hasn't got pregnancy or leprosy." . . .

"The fear of being labeled radical, leftist, or subversive," Harvey Swados observed of academe in the early 1960s, "seems to have all but disappeared." Many, indeed, welcomed it. The undergraduates arriving on campus were often children of the middle-class liberals who had been most outraged — and in some instances had suffered most — during the McCarthy years. Their sons and daughters were determined not to be intimidated or repressed. They joined chapters of such organizations as SDS, Joan Baez's School for Nonviolence, the W. E. B. Du Bois Clubs, and the Young Socialist Alliance. They were in dead earnest but politically inept. Before the decade ended, the tactics of their New Left would offend virtually all potential allies, including their parents — which, some thought, might have been the point.

Yet in some areas they were highly skilled. Their demonstrations were often staged for TV news cameramen with a sense of what was good theater. The picketing in support of the Mississippi Freedom Party at the 1964 Democratic national convention was one example; the October 1967 march on the Pentagon was another. It is equally true that they frequently appeared to be shocking the country for the sake of shock. In 1965 SDS repealed its ban on admitting Communists and Birchers to membership. The New Leftists proclaimed that their sacred trinity consisted of Marx, Mao, and Herbert Marcuse, and they enthusiastically embraced Marcuse's "discriminating tolerance"; *i.e.,* the suppression of points of view which the New Leftists regarded as unsound or dangerous. Their campaigns against ROTC, the draft, and napalm were logical, and walking out on commencement ceremonies was valid protest, but when they advocated dynamiting public buildings, even Marcuse demurred. Some SDS leaders all but salivated over violence. Of the Sharon Tate murders SDS's Bernardine Dohrn said: "Dig it, first they killed those pigs, then they ate dinner in the same room with them, then they even shoved a fork into a victim's stomach! Wild!"

The New Leftists' view of society was essentially conspirational. They saw it as dominated by an establishment which was itself manipulated by a "power elite" of industrialists, military leaders, and corporate giants. They talked darkly of revolution, yet a real revolution starts with strengthening the power of the state — which they were dead set against. Like all movements, theirs had a glossary of special terms: "dialogue," "creative tension," "nonnegotiable demands," and "nonviolent" among others. But their meanings were often obscure. Nonnegotiable demands could be negotiated, for example, and throwing rocks and bottles at policemen was deemed nonviolent.

The alienation of the young militants, expressing itself in disdain for conventional careers, clothing, and politics, had begun at Berkeley in 1964. The next spring, when that campus began to tremble again, President Kerr said, "The university and the Berkeley campus really couldn't face another such confrontation." In fact four more years of turmoil lay ahead. Berkeley was to be but one of many disturbed campuses. In 1965 Berkeley fallout first rocked the University of Kansas when 114 students were arrested there for staging a sit-in at the chancellor's office to protest fraternity and sorority discrimination. Then, within a few days, colleges and universities were embattled from coast to coast.

Yale undergraduates demonstrated after a popular philosophy instructor had been denied tenure. After an anti-ROTC rally at San Francisco State, five were hospitalized. At Fairfield University, a Jesuit school in Connecticut, students broke into a locked stack to put forbidden books on open shelves. Brooklyn College undergraduates booed their president off a platform. At St. John's in New York, the nation's biggest Catholic college, students demanded an end to censorship of their publications. Michigan students demonstrated against higher movie prices, and three deans resigned at Stanford over reading erotic poetry in the classroom. At Fairleigh Dickinson in New Jersey students picketed as "an expression of general student discontent." The uproar continued through 1966 and 1967, with major riots at San Jose State College, Wisconsin, Iowa, Cornell, Long Beach State College, and, once again, San Francisco State. And all this was merely a buildup for the cataclysmic year of 1968. "Yesterday's ivory tower," said the president of Hunter College, "has become today's foxhole."

For all their ardor, the militant undergraduates achieved little. Students are by definition transients; once they are graduated new students arrive, and there is no guarantee that the newcomers may not take a different line — as in fact those in this movement did. SDS, inherently unstable, split into two groups at the end of the decade: Revolutionary Youth Movement I, also known as the Weathermen, and Revolutionary Youth Movement II, which condemned the Weathermen as "adventuristic." The students had other difficulties. One of their basic premises was absurd. "The fantasy," wrote Benjamin DeMott, lay "in the notion that if you're upset about Vietnam, racism, poverty, or the general quality of life, the bridge to blow is college."

A second handicap was the students' exaggerated sense of their own power. In 1966 they confidently challenged the gubernatorial campaign of Ronald Reagan. To their amazement, he won by a margin of almost a million votes. That same day the Republicans gained fifty congressional seats. "One of the most obvious casualties of the 1966 elections," Hunter S. Thompson noted, "was the New Left's illusion of its own leverage." . . .

Hostile reactions to politicized students were not confined to California. One Midwest legislature slashed over 38 million dollars from its state university's budget and raised tuition fees. Bills intended to stifle student dissent were introduced in most other legislatures, and eight of them were passed. "Americans," Oregon's Governor Tom McCall said of the demonstrators, were "fed up to their eardrums and eyeballs." Lou Harris reported that 62 percent of students' parents believed that it was more important for colleges to maintain discipline than to encourage intellectual curiosity. "Reduced to its simplest terms," *Life* commented, "the generations disagree on the most fundamental question of all: What is education for?"

Of course, they clashed over other issues, too. The demonstrations were one of the most visible manifestations of youth's subculture in the 1960s, but there was more to their subculture than that. Throughout the decade publicists wrote of "revolutions" in, among others, communications, sex, and drugs. Youth was active in all of them and was partly formed by them, if only because it had concluded that the election returns were what Hunter Thompson called "brutal confirmation of the futility of fighting the Establishment on its own terms." The generation gap had arrived, and it was an abyss.

"Don't trust anyone over thirty!" said the banners and buttons displayed by the most arrogant, and it was cruel; so many Americans over thirty wanted to be young again, to share the fads and enthusiasms of youth. They slipped discs dancing the Watusi and the Swim and the Cottage Cheese, hopped about chasing Frisbees, endangered their lives riding motorcycles, laughed at *The Graduate* and even played with Super Balls. The Beatles having introduced long hair, the kids picked it up, and presently the middle-aged were imitating that, too. Both sexes wore wigs to make them look younger. Often the hippies set fashions for adults. "I watch what the kids are putting together for themselves," said Rudi Gernreich. "I formalize it, give it something of my own, perhaps, and that is fashion." Older Americans caught the discotheque bug and asked children where the action was; young wiseacres told them the Vincent Van Gogh-Gogh and the Long, Long Ago-go. Women went to plastic surgeons for eyelid lifts ($350), nose jobs ($500), rhytidectomies — face lifts — ($600), face peelings ($500), dermabrasions — removing acne scars — ($275), bosom implants ($165), belly lifts ($500) and thigh lifts ($650). "Being young was *right,*" *Life* observed in a special issue on the 1960s; "as everybody once wanted to be rich, now everybody wanted to be, or seem to be, young. Fashion, films, books, music, even politics leaned toward youth." . . .

At times in the 1960s it almost seemed that America was becoming a filiarchy. Adolescence, wrote the Hechingers, had "evolved into a cult, to be prolonged, enjoyed, and commercially catered to as never before." In the new suburbs, especially, the young appeared to have been reared on a philosophy of instant gratification. Agnew, Billy Graham, and Al Capp distorted the issue, but it did exist and was debatable. "Self-expression" and "child-centered" were part of the permissive jargon; in the schools the trend frequently led to a system of "elective" subjects for pupils too young to know what they were electing. The teacher was to be regarded as a pal, not a superior being. Elementary school teachers were required to work with limited vocabularies, sometimes twenty words or less repeated endlessly. (The result was summed up in the deathless line attributed to a teacher who rammed a tree with her car: "Look look look, oh oh oh, damn damn damn.") . . .

Advertisers were wary of offending youth; the nation's teen-agers were spending 25 billion dollars a year. It was ironic that student militants should take so vigorous a stand against materialism; their own generation was the most possession-conscious in history. In *The Lonely Crowd* Riesman wrote that in America "children begin their training as consumers at an increasingly young age," that "middle-class children have allowances of their own at four or five," and that the allowances "are expected to be spent, whereas in the earlier era they were often used as cudgels of thrift."

Advertisers courting them addressed teen-agers as "the Now Generation," the "New People," the "Pepsi Generation," and the "Go Anywhere, Do Anything Generation." John Brooks pointed out that they were the most conspicuous beneficiaries of Johnsonian prosperity: "American youth, like everybody else but more spectacularly, was getting rich. A combination of burgeoning national wealth and the settled national habit of indulging the young was putting unprecedented sums of cash in their hands." Keeping them solvent wasn't always easy. In 1964 the Harvard class of '39, hardly indigents, reported that providing their children with money was the chief paternal problem for 78 percent of them. Only 6 percent said that instilling moral values in them was as hard. And they weren't all that moral. For $12.50 a boy could buy a girl a "Going Steady" ring which looked just like a wedding band; certainly no motel manager could tell the difference. If they felt guilty next day, in some places they could pray for forgiveness at teen-age churches. The Emmanuel Hospital in Portland, Oregon, even had a teen-age wing. It was described by Frank J. Taylor in a *Saturday Evening Post* article, "How to Have Fun in the Hospital." Patients enjoyed "unlimited snacks, jam sessions, and wheel-chair drag races." Priggish nutritionists kept their distance; the teen-agers were allowed to "eat hot dogs and hamburgers day after day for lunch and supper." . . .

I Was a Teen-Age Frankenstein was one of the more memorable films produced for the adolescent trade. The editor of *Teen Magazine,* Charles Laufer, said that "the music market for the first time in history is completely dominated by the young set." They were the most musical generation ever, and their taste, at its best, was very good; the swing generation could hardly improve on the Beatles, Joan Baez, Bob Dylan, and forty-four-year-old B. B. King, whom the youth of the 1960s discovered after he had been ignored by his contemporaries for twenty-one years. Unfortunately the youngsters had other idols who belonged aesthetically with Andy Warhol's Brillo boxes and Campbell soup cans, among them the ruttish Presley. Presley's voice and appearance were at least his own. That wasn't true of most rock stars. To a striking degree they were all alike — short youths, running to fat, who were prepared for public consumption by strenuous dieting, nose surgery, contact lenses, and luxurious hair styles. And they couldn't sing. Most couldn't even have made themselves heard in the back of a theater. Their voices were amplified in echo chambers and then created on tape, a snippet here and a snippet there, destroying false notes. When they appeared in public, they would mouth the words while the records were being played over the loudspeakers. Wiggling their hips and snapping their fingers, their features always fixed in a sullen expression, they would desecrate good songs: "I loved, I loved, I loved yuh, once in si-ilence," or "The rain, yeah! stays mainly in the puh-lain."

"What I mean to kids," said Janis Joplin, shortly before she killed herself with whiskey and drugs, "is they can be themselves and win." John Lennon of the Beatles said, "We're more popular than Jesus now." Their listeners may have tuned such things out. They were, after all, accustomed to meaningless words — "Learn to forget," said a writer in *Crawdaddy*; it was one of the wiser apostrophes directed to that rock magazine's readers. Purdue polled two thousand teen-agers on the gravest problem facing American youth. A third of them said acne.

Policemen would have disagreed. Over the previous ten years arrests of the young had jumped 86 percent. "Teen-Agers on the Rampage," proclaimed a *Time* head after a single week which had seen violence "among high schools from California to Maine." Professor Ruth Shonle Cavan published the first sociology textbook to deal with upper- and middle-class delinquency, including what she called "alcohol-automobile-sex behavior." Felonies were almost commonplace in some neighborhoods which had once been serene. The FBI reported that Americans aged eighteen or younger accounted for almost half of all arrests for murder, rape, robbery, aggravated assault, burglary, and auto theft — and in the suburbs it was more than half. . . .

The first evidence of widespread teen-age drug parties in the paneled rumpus rooms of the affluent was turned up in 1960 by the Westchester County vice squad. After the shock had passed parents said that at least it wasn't liquor. Then police on Santa Catalina Island, the southern California resort, announced that drunkenness had become common among thirteen- and fourteen-year-old children in wealthy families, and in the future they would charge the parents $2.50 an hour to babysit teen-age drunks till parents came to take them home. Nationally the number of adolescents who drank regularly was put at between 50 and 66 percent. In Yonkers, New York, where it was 58 percent among high school juniors and seniors, 64 percent said they drove the family car while doing it. Parents in Rose Valley, a Philadelphia suburb, allowed children to bring their own bottles to parties. Their fathers did the bartending. One wondered what Clarence Day's father would have thought. . . .

In their ennui or their cups, youths of the 1960s frequently turned destructive. A brief item from Hannibal, Missouri, gave melancholy evidence of the revision of a cherished American myth. At the foot of Hannibal's Cardiff Hill stands a famous statue of Tom Sawyer and Huckleberry Finn, barefoot and carrying fishing poles; a plaque explains that this is the neighborhood where Tom and Huck "played and roamed at will." But any boys who attempted to emulate them after dark in the late 1960s would have risked arrest. Because of the rise in adolescent vandalism, loitering by the young on Cardiff Hill — and indeed anywhere in Hannibal — was forbidden after 10 P.M. . . .

Affluent youths were often the worst offenders, but disorders could break anywhere. On one Independence Day five hundred drunken youths in Arnolds Park, Iowa, hurled rocks, beer bottles, and pieces of concrete at policemen; the tumult was set off when one of them yelled at the police chief, "Hey, punk, we're going to take over this place." In Chicago a free rock concert series — arranged by municipal officials to build camaraderie with youth — had to be canceled. At the first performance the audience rose up swinging tire chains and clubs; 135 were injured, including 65 policemen. . . .

Over a fifteen-month period an incredible number of unexplained fires (120) broke out on the University of Florida campus in Gainesville. Fire marshals thought it possible that the entire campus might be razed. The crisis was resolved when residents in Hume Hall confessed they had done it. Students in the east and west wings had been competing to see which could attract the most fire trucks. What made the incident particularly striking was a circumstance which would have been unthinkable in earlier generations. Hume Hall was a girls' dormitory.

Men's rooms in genteel establishments had long displayed a sign over urinals: PLEASE ARRANGE CLOTHING BEFORE LEAVING WASHROOM. Well-brought-up boys didn't need to be reminded; they had been taught never to fasten the flies of their trousers in public. They were therefore startled when Françoise Dorleac, in the 1966 film *Where the Spies Are,* emerged from a dressing room, reached for her crotch, and casually zipped up her slacks in the presence of her costar, David Niven. It was one of those moments which served as reminders that the delicate balance between the sexes had been altered, probably forever. Women were moving into jobs which had always been considered masculine: telephone linemen, mining engineers, ditch diggers, truck drivers, Secret Service agents. More of them were sharing men's vices, too: public drunkenness, juvenile delinquency, and assault and battery. Women's Liberation leader Ti-Grace Atkinson called marriage "slavery," "legalized rape," and "unpaid labor," and disapproved of love between the sexes as "tied up with a sense of dependency." ...

The disappearance of bras among members of the movement was but one of many changes in fashion. When Mia Farrow cropped her hair girls flocked to hairdressers so they, too, could look like boys. They crowded Army-Navy stores buying pea jackets, petty officer shirts, and bell-bottom trousers. Square-toed, low, heavy shoes became popular among them, and so many coeds were using after-shave lotion as perfume that the business journal *Forbes* protested that the sexes were beginning to smell alike. In 1966 Twiggy, the Cockney model, weighed in at ninety-one pounds, and women dieted to look like her, angularity being considered antifeminine. The idea was to look tough. Shiny plastic came into vogue, and hard, metallic fabrics. Pantsuits appeared — not cute slacks but mannish, tailored slacks. The zippers or buttons were no longer on the side; they went straight down the front, like Françoise Dorleac's, and some girls reportedly made them to go all the way through and up the back, so they could stand at urinals. Barbara Tuchman protested that too many women were beginning to look like Lolitas or liontamers. A Woman's Lib leader called her an Aunt Tom.

At the very top of the movement there was some female homosexuality and bisexuality; Kate Millett said she sometimes slept with women, and Joan Baez acknowledged that she had once had a lesbian affair. There was considerable resentment in the movement over being considered "sex objects"; girls objected to being whistled at and featured in fetching ads designed to appeal to males. Most girls in the movement preferred boys, however; Gloria Steinem, a heterosexual Lib leader, said, "Men think that once women become liberated, it will mean no more sex for men. But what men don't realize is that if women are liberated, there will be more sex and better." ...

Certainly more girls were on the prowl, often roaming the streets in pairs or appearing at weekends, available, on college campuses. Bachelors dropping in for a drink at Chicago's dating bars in the Rush Street district — The Jail, The Store, The Spirit of '76 — would be propositioned by girls

who offered to "ball" them and tried to arouse them with a new gesture —
the feminine hand, slipped between the man's thighs, squeezing him there.
Over a third of the coeds at a New York university admitted to one-night
affairs with total strangers. Nationally, during the 1960s, the number of
girls reporting premarital intercourse in surveys more than doubled; in a
five-year period it rose 65 percent. European surveyors found that twice as
many boys as girls there volunteered to describe their sexual experiences;
in the United States it was the other way around. The number of coeds
reporting the petting of male genitals soared. . . . Demure women all but
vanished. Obscene language no longer shocked them; they used it themselves.
If they wanted coitus they said so. In the film *All the Loving Couples,* a
jaded wife waiting to be swapped said thickly, "When do we get laid?"

Presently she was in the throes of sexual intercourse, on camera, with
another woman's husband. The movies, once straitlaced, were exploring all
the visual possibilities of the sex act. Under the leadership of Jack Valenti,
who left the White House to become president of the Motion Picture Association of America, Hollywood adopted a rating system for films in 1968.
Those in the G category would be family movies; the others would be M
(suggested for mature audiences), R (restricted to persons sixteen or older
unless accompanied by a parent or guardian), or X (no one under sixteen
admitted under any circumstances).

In the late 1960s each season's X movies went farther than the last. Even
the movie ads in newspapers became something to put out of reach of children. *I Am Curious (Yellow)* was thought shocking when it appeared, showing nudity and coitus, but new productions rapidly made it obsolescent.
Ads for *The Minx* said it "makes Curious Yellow look pale," and it did.
Then *The Fox* depicted lesbians kissing passionately and a naked woman
masturbating in front of a full-length mirror. A beast had intercourse with
a woman in *Rosemary's Baby. Bob & Carol & Ted & Alice* was a comedy
about wife swapping. *Blow-Up* provided a glimpse of a girl's pubic hair; it
was thought daring at the time, but presently ingenious close-ups showed
the genitals in intercourse from unusual angles — some from the bottom —
and actresses masturbating actors to climax. The ultimate, or so it seemed
at the time, was *Deep Throat,* a tremendous hit about cunnilingus and fellatio. At the conclusion of it the heroine took a man down to the hilt of his
phallus, displaying a talent which the *New Yorker* compared to that of a
sword swallower. The action was photographed at a range of a few feet, and
when the man reached orgasm, so did the girl. Technicolor revealed her full
body flush. . . .

On stage a performer named Jim Morrison described his latest sexual
adventure; it had occurred five minutes before curtain time. *Oh! Calcutta!*
was billed as "elegant erotica"; its sketches ranged in theme from wife
swapping to rape. *Che!* provided a hundred minutes of faked sex acts. Those
who preferred the real thing could find it in New York's "Mini-Cine

Theater," or in San Francisco taverns where a boy and girl would strip, climb on the bar, a•ıd there engage in what was drolly called the act of love. Some spectacles shocked the most hardened observers. A reporter told of going backstage in one Manhattan show and seeing chorus girls, naked, shooting heroin into the backs of their knees while their illegitimate toddlers watched. . . .

A lot of carnal knowledge was being acquired in laboratories, observed by scientists in white coats holding stopwatches and other things. The most famous of them were Dr. William H. Masters and Virginia E. Johnson, who eventually married one another. Their findings at the Reproductive Biology Research Foundation in St. Louis were invaluable, but fastidious critics were appalled by the measuring and photographing of copulation; it smacked to them of charcoal filters and flip-top boxes. The most remarkable piece of Masters-Johnson equipment was an electrically powered plastic penis with a tiny camera inside and cold light illumination to allow observation and recording of what was happening inside the vagina. The size of this artificial phallus could be adjusted, and the woman using it could regulate the depth and speed of the thrust. . . .

All this was a great strain for the young. Previous generations had been protected from early sexual entanglements by social custom, the fear of disgrace, and the possibility of venereal disease or pregnancy — a catastrophe for the girl. Now mores had changed spectacularly; society took a tolerant view of premarital affairs. Venereal infection had vanished. (Late in the decade it would reappear as a nationwide epidemic, a consequence of the new promiscuity.) "If it feels good, I'll do it," read a pin popular among college students. Intercourse felt good, and they did it a lot, protected by the Pill, or diaphragms, and various intrauterine devices, loops and coils. . . . .

The sex-drenched state of American culture was undoubtedly responsible for much of the increase in premarital and extramarital intercourse. Sexiness was everywhere — on paperback book racks, television, in ads, magazines, popular songs, plays, musicals, and everyday conversation. Betty Friedan cited a psychological study which found that references to sex in mass media increased by over 250 percent in the 1960s. The *New York Times Book Review* noted the popularity of books about "love" affairs between animals and human beings. Complaints to the U.S. Post Office about smut doubled within six years, to 130,000 in 1965.

"Be Prepared!" proclaimed a poster showing an enormously pregnant girl, smiling broadly, in a Girl Scout uniform. The Scouts asked for damages; the court threw out the case. "Use Contraceptives: Take the Worry Out of Being Close," said a Planned Parenthood ad. The New York Hilton, Manhattan's largest hotel, was renting rooms by the hour. Frustrated persons (or couples) took out ads in the personal column of the *Saturday Review,* or in underground newspapers, soliciting new partners. Everybody knew about key parties for swapping couples; the men threw their house keys on a table and the wives picked them up at random, each then going to bed with the owner of whatever key she had.

Nicholas von Hoffman described a game, manufactured by the Diplomat Sales Company of Los Angeles, which provided "a safe, nicely structured way for two or three couples to end an evening naked, drunk, out of their minds, and lascivious as hell." Called Bumps and Grinds, it was played by the light of one candle (which was included). Players moved around a board like the one used in Monopoly, drawing "Tomcat" and "Pussycat" cards. These advised them to "Take one drink," or "Strip one article of clothing," and so on. The game was rigged for the girls to wind up nude and drunk first. Subsequent moves decided who was going to stagger to the bedroom with whom. . . .

Early developments in mid-century chemotherapy were benign. The sulfa drugs had arrived in the late 1930s. Then came penicillin (1943), streptomycin (1945), cortisone (1946), ACTH (1949), Terramycin and Aureomycin (1950), the Salk vaccine (1955), the Sabin vaccine (1960), and the tranquilizers, led by Miltown and Librium, which cut the length of the average mental hospital stay in half. All these were called "miracle drugs" when they first appeared. . . .

The first inkling that the drug revolution had a dark side came in 1962, when eight thousand European women who had been taking a new tranquilizer called Thalidomide gave birth to limbless babies. . . . If a drug could do that, anything was possible. And the amount of medication in American medicine cabinets was unprecedented. Doctors were now writing nearly two billion dollars' worth of prescriptions each year for pills which included new barbiturates and amphetamines, hypnotics, and antidepressants. In addition, an enormous black market was flourishing. Of the eight billion amphetamines, or pep pills, manufactured each year, about four billion were being sold illegally. Laymen might call the pep pills and barbiturates "soft" drugs and heroin, morphine, and cocaine "hard," but pharmacologists knew it should be the other way around; the older drugs calmed addicts, but the new ones created dangerous, unpredictable moods. Some became part of the culture, familiar enough to have popular nicknames. Among them were "bluejays" (Amytal sodium), "redbirds" (Seconal), "yellow jackets" (Nembutal), and "goofballs" (barbiturates laced with Benzedrine). . . .

LSD became a household word in 1966. Even recluses knew what was meant by tripping, freaking out, and blowing one's mind. Priests and pastors held a conference on the religious aspects of LSD. In discotheques — and also in art galleries and museums — films, slides, and flashing colored lights suggested the impact of an LSD experience. Chilling stories, some of them apocryphal, were told to scare those who were tempted to take a trip. A youth high on LSD was said to have taken a swan dive into the front of a truck moving at 70 mph. Teen-agers under its influence reportedly lay in a field staring at the sun until they were permanently blinded. That was exposed as a lie, but the Associated Press verified the case of a young man who turned himself in to police saying he had been flying on LSD for three days and asking "Did I kill my wife? Did I rape anyone?" and was then charged with the murder of his mother-in-law. . . .

But the users of LSD — they called it acid — described their trips as ecstatic. "Who needs jazz, or even beer," wrote a contributor to the *New York Times Magazine*, "when you can sit down on a public curbstone, drop a pill in your mouth, and hear fantastic music for hours at a time in your own head? A cap of good acid costs $5, and for that you can hear the Universal Symphony, with God singing solo and the Holy Ghost on drums."

The Beatles sang "Yellow Submarine," which was a euphemism for a freakout, and another song freighted with LSD meaning, "Strawberry Fields." Elementary school children dismayed their mothers by coming home chanting, to the tune of "Frère Jacques":

> Marijuana, marijuana,
> LSD, LSD,
> College kids are making it,
> high school kids are taking it,
> Why can't we? Why can't we? . . .

Fortunes were made in the 1967 "Summer of Love" from the sale of DMT, mescaline, Methedrine, LSD, and the even more popular — and safer — marijuana to the disillusioned children of the middle and upper middle class who flocked to hippy communes, leaving what they regarded as a stifling straight life to Do Their Thing. Pot, boo, maryjane, grass, or Mary Warner — the various names under which marijuana was known to them — sold in Mexico for $35 a kilogram (2.2 pounds). Smuggled into the United States, a kilo brought $150 to $200. Meted out in 34-ounce bags, it went for as much as $25 an ounce, or $850 the kilo. Joints — marijuana cigarettes — sold on the street for a dollar each. The heroin racket was even more lucrative. Undercover chemists made $700 for every kilo of morphine converted to heroin in Marseilles. Manhattan entrepreneurs paid $10,000 for it and sold it on the street in plastic bags, each containing just 5 percent heroin cut with sugar or quinine powder. In that form the original 2.2 pounds earned $20,000. And the market was expanding rapidly. The Federal Bureau of Narcotics estimated that 68,000 Americans became addicted in a single year. . . .

The great year of the hippy may be said to have begun on Easter Sunday, March 26, 1967, when ten thousand boys and girls assembled in New York Central Park's Sheep Meadow to honor love. They flew kites, tossed Frisbees, joined hands in "love circles," painted designs on each other's faces, and chanted: "Banana! Banana!" after a current hoax, that banana scrapings had psychedelic properties. On the other side of the country that Sunday fifteen thousand youths in San Francisco cheered Dr. Leary's Pied Piper spiel: "Turn on to the scene; tune in to what's happening; and drop out — of high school, college, grade school . . . follow me, the hard way."

What came next was a nightmare for tens of thousands of mothers and fathers. With the memories of their Depression childhoods still vivid, the parents of the late 1960s could not grasp that the country had become so prosperous it could afford to support tramps, or that their own children would want to be among the tramps. "The kids looked like bums, often acted like bums," the Associated Press reported, "but they were no ordinary bums. Most had spent their lives in middle-class surroundings, finishing high school, often graduating from college — the American dream." Now their photographs, forwarded by their parents and accompanied by pathetic messages pleading for news of their whereabouts, were hung on bulletin boards in police stations. The pictures weren't much help. Taken when the youngsters were straight, they bore little relation to their new lifestyle.

The police did what they could. The Salvation Army opened a coffee house in East Village called The Answer, where flower children in their early teens were urged to return home. Runaways in Haight-Ashbury were sheltered at church-sponsored Huckleberry's while mothers and fathers were contacted. A physician opened a free clinic for hippies in San Francisco. Almost immediately he was overwhelmed by pregnancies, cases of venereal disease, and hepatitis caused by dirty syringes. Virtually every hippy in Hashbury had a cold or the flu. Many had tried sleeping in Golden Gate Park, unaware that a hidden sprinkling system automatically started up at dawn.

The greatest health hazard, of course, was the drugs. The hippies had no way of knowing what they were buying; Dr. Louis Lasagna found that many were getting veterinary anesthetics or even plain urine. In that summer many were experimenting with STP, a new compound named for a gasoline additive used in the Hell's Angels motorcycles. Between 5,000 and 10,000 STP capsules were given away. The flower children, liking it, christened it "the caviar of psychedelics." Doctors discovered that it was extremely dangerous; when taken in combination with chlorpromazine, an LSD antidote, STP could prove fatal. The "speed freaks" or "meth monsters," as other hippies called them, were taking Methedrine; when high, they were capable of almost anything. Meantime, in Buffalo, Dr. Maimon M. Cohen announced that preliminary findings in an investigation of LSD and chlorpromazine indicated that mixed together the two could result in chromosome damage, spontaneous abortions, or deformed infants. . . .

Clearly something ghastly was happening to that summer. Exploiters and predators were also stalking the young. In *The Family* Ed Sanders compared the flower movement to "a valley of plump rabbits surrounded by wounded coyotes." He wrote: "One almost had to live there to understand the frenzy that engulfed the Haight-Ashbury district of San Francisco in the spring and summer of 1967. The word was out all over America to come to San Francisco for love and flowers." But more awaited them in Hashbury than that. "The Haight attracted vicious criminals who grew long hair. Bikers tried to take over the LSD market with crude sadistic tactics. Bad dope was sold by acne-faced Methedrine punks. Satanist and satanist-rapist death-freaks flooded the whirling crash pads. People began getting ripped off in the parks. There was racial trouble." In the midst of it, haunting Grateful Dead concerts in the Avalon Ballroom, was a bearded little psychotic who liked to curl up in a fetal position right on the dance floor, and whose secret ambitions were to persuade girls to perform fellatio with dogs and gouge out the eyes of a beautiful actress and smear them on walls. Later he would be well remembered in Hashbury. His name was Charles Manson.

Hippiedom would survive in one form or another, as beatism had — the bohemian strain runs wide and deep in America — but the movement as it had been known that year was doomed. All that was lacking was a final curtain. That came on the night of Saturday, October 8, 1967. A generation earlier, on June 8, 1931, the death of a New York girl bearing the singularly poetic name of Starr Faithfull had symbolized the magic and the depravity of an era then ending; John O'Hara had based *Butterfield 8* on it. Now the squalid Manhattan murder of another genteel girl ended the hippy summer of 1967. Her name was Linda Rae Fitzpatrick. She was eighteen, a blonde, the daughter of a wealthy spice and tea importer. Her home of record was her parents' mansion in Greenwich, Connecticut, but on Sunday, October 9, her naked corpse was found in a boiler room of a brownstone tenement at 169 Avenue B on the Lower East Side.

It was not a good address. Flanked by a flyblown junk shop and a dingy bar and grill, the boiler room reeked of dog excrement and rotting garbage. One naked light bulb shone down on peeling paint, decaying plaster, whitewashed bricks crawling with cockroaches, and a filthy mattress. Linda had come to this noisome trysting place with a tattooed drifter named James "Groovy" Hutchinson. As detectives and the police surgeon put the story together, she had stripped and sprawled on the mattress. At that point Linda and Groovy had discovered that they were not alone. This room was often used as an exchange point for the sale of drugs, and four speed-freaks, all of them flying, decided to share Groovy's girl with him. She refused. When Groovy tried to defend her, his face was bashed in with a brick. After Linda had been raped four times, her face was smashed, too. The bodies had been left face up; her black lace pants were found in a corner.

Three Negro men were swiftly arrested, but the public was more interested in the girl than in her victimizers. Linda had apparently led two lives. In Greenwich she had been the sheltered, well-bred child of an upper-class home. Like her parents she had been an Episcopalian; her favorite relaxation had been riding on the red-leafed bridle paths of the exclusive Round Hill Stables. The previous August, her father recalled, he had expressed his abhorrence of hippies, and her comments had been "much like mine." Her mother recalled that "Linda was never terribly boy crazy. She was very shy." Over Labor Day weekend she had told her mother that she didn't want to return to Oldfields, her expensive boarding school in Maryland. Instead she wanted to live in New York and paint. "After all," her mother said afterward, "Linda's whole life was art. She had a burning desire to be something in the art world." Her parents agreed to her plan when she told them she had a room in a respectable Greenwich Village hotel. Her roommate, she said, was a twenty-two-year-old receptionist of a good family called Paula Bush.

"*Paula* Bush?" said the desk clerk. "Sure, I remember Linda, but there wasn't no Paula Bush. It was *Paul* Bush." In East Village she had consorted with many men, her family learned, and she had used money sent from Greenwich to buy drugs for them and herself. Late in September she thought she was pregnant, and she had confided to another girl that she was worried about the effect of LSD on the baby. Saturday evening, three hours before she died, she had told a friend that she had just shot some speed and was riding high. The cruelest part of the sequel for her parents was the discovery that her East Village acquaintances were indifferent to her death. One hippy girl said that though they mourned Groovy, "The chick wasn't anything to us."

In San Francisco's Golden Gate Park that same week hippies burned a gray coffin labeled "Summer of Love." In it were orange peels, peacock feathers, charms, flags, crucifixes, and a marijuana-flavored cookie. The ceremony was called "The Death of Hip." After the mourners had watched the fire while singing "God Bless America" and "Hare Krishna," they shouted, "Hippies are dead! Now the free men will come through!" Violence had crippled the movement, and so had commercialism. Tourists were crowding craft shops in both the Haight and East Village. Hippies hungering for money were acting in *Indian Givers,* a full-length psychedelic western, in which the sheriff was being played by, of all people, Dr. Timothy Leary. Ron Thelin, proprietor of San Francisco's Psychedelic Shop, said dolefully, "The spirit is gone"; then he went out of business, and Roger Ricco, a veteran member of The Group Image, said, "It isn't the same any more. Where have all the flowers gone?"

STUDY GUIDE

1. Concerning the student rebellion: (a) Given the small percentage of students who participated in demonstrations of various kinds, how do you account for their high visibility and impact? (b) What view of the United States did the New Left posit? (c) What techniques did they employ to publicize their views? (d) What, according to Manchester, were their ultimate achievements?

2. In his discussion of the cult of youth, Manchester offers *demographic* as well as *socio-psychological* reasons for its proliferation. Identify them. And

further: The cult of youth appears to have been correlated with the middle- and upper-middle-class levels of American society. From Manchester's narrative, or from your own experience, can you offer a rationale for this correlation? Or, to rephrase the question: Why would youngsters from the more affluent segments of our society be more prone to rebel against its norms and institutions than would the less affluent?

3. What, according to Manchester, were the principal elements of the women's lib movement and, secondly, what similarities can you find between this phase of the counterculture and the rebellion of the young?

4. What evidence does Manchester provide for his statement that the United States, in the 1960s, had become a "sex-drenched ... culture"? Has there been an alteration in the attitudes and practices he describes since the publication of this essay, in 1974? If so, how?

5. Is Manchester's description of the drug culture of the 1960s an accurate portrayal of the current situation in American society? Is there more of a drug problem — or less?

6. Where did the hippie culture originate, where did it flourish, what were its principal characteristics, and what caused its demise?

7. In retrospect: There are those who maintain that, far from rejecting the basic elements of the counterculture (drugs, pornography and sexual permissiveness), the nation as a whole has incorporated — legitimized, as it were — many of its elements. Do you agree, and if so, on what grounds? Or, if you disagree, on what grounds do you do so?

BIBLIOGRAPHY

Books on the counterculture are legion, and the student has only to decide on what aspect of it he or she desires to concentrate. You might begin with Theodore Roszak, *The Making of a Counter Culture* * (New York, 1969), a sympathetic and scholarly attempt to explain this phenomenon. Equally sympathetic are Charles Reich, *The Greening of America* * (New York, 1970) and Philip Slater, *The Pursuit of Loneliness* * (Boston, 1971). Critical comments on the youth culture — a pervasive and central aspect of the counterculture — can be found in Lewis Feuer, *The Conflict of Generations: The Character and Significance of Student Movements* (New York, 1969) and John W. Aldridge, *The Country of the Young* (New York, 1970). Books on particular segments of the counterculture include the following: Carl Belz, *The Story of Rock* * (New York, 1969); Nicholas Von Hoffman, *We Are the People Our Parents Warned Us Against* * (Chicago, 1968) on the hippies; and Rosa Gustaitis, *Turning On* * (New York, 1969) on the adult experience in the counterculture. Various issues of *Playboy* magazine contain both primary and secondary accounts of aspects of the counterculture.

* Asterisk indicates book is available in a paperback edition.

Randy L. Wallick

A tragic confrontation.

20

JAMES A. MICHENER

Kent State:
What Happened on Monday

As the American people enter the 1980s, it is clear that the temper and outlook — and the foreign policy — of our nation has been determined, in large measure, by the war in Vietnam. The Vietnam war, although fought in faraway Southeast Asia, and seemingly having no impact on the day-to-day material well-being of the American people, affected our nation deeply and in many ways. There are those who look upon the Vietnam war as the first defeat suffered by our nation on the field of battle and the beginning of our decline as the defender of the non-Communist world; there are others who trace the beginnings of our economic troubles — inflation, "stagflation" (rising unemployment and price rises), and the like — to policies pursued by our government at the height of our participation in the war in Vietnam. The war generated intense opposition at home, toppled one president, and helped elect another. The shootings at Kent State University in 1970, the subject of the narrative by James A. Michener that follows, mark the culmination of the national tragedy in which all of our post–World War II presidents and major political parties played a role.

American involvement in the affairs of Vietnam began after World War II, when Harry S. Truman — contrary to the demands of Ho Chi Minh — favored a return of Vietnam to France over independence for that former French colony. Truman, and later Dwight D. Eisenhower, sent military aid to the French. While Eisenhower resisted the advice of those who urged him to send American troops or naval forces to support the French in Viet-

nam in 1954, the result of his diplomatic policies was a commitment by the United States to the security and independence of
South Vietnam, an involvement that was expanded militarily and
diplomatically, first in a covert and modest operation under the
administration of John F. Kennedy, and to its fullest extent —
more than a half-million American troops — in the administration of Lyndon B. Johnson. Although he was returned to office in
1964 on the basis of promises to refrain from escalating American
participation in the war in Southeast Asia — "We don't want our
American boys to do the fighting for Asian boys," he said —
Johnson failed to fulfill that promise; in the campaign of 1968,
promises along similar lines by Richard M. Nixon (in several addresses Nixon promised the American people that he had a "secret plan" for ending the war) proved to be equally false. Many
Americans came to feel that the graffito on one Vietnam wall
contained much truth: "This is a war of the unwilling led by the
unqualified dying for the ungrateful."

Opposition to the war in Vietnam, particularly among the
nation's youth, was widespread and violent, ranging from marches
on Washington and demonstrations at political conventions to
campus protest. Much of the opposition to the war, paradoxically, came from those very elements of American society — the
middle- and upper-class youngsters — who were exempted, by
virtue of being enrolled in the colleges and universities of our
nation, from being drafted to fight in the war. While violence
erupted on many campuses, the symbol of student protest and
the coercive reaction of government is what took place at Kent
State in 1970.

A final note: In 1974, the eight guardsmen who shot the
Kent State students were indicted but were acquitted in a criminal trial; in lawsuits filed against twenty-seven guardsmen, the
president of Kent State, and the governor of Ohio at the time of
the shootings, James A. Rhodes, all were acquitted of responsibility. In 1977, the state of Ohio, in a sense, admitted its guilt by
agreeing to an out-of-court settlement of another Kent State suit.
In addition to paying more than $600,000 to the parents of the
students who died and to the nine injured students, the state,
under Rhodes, again the governor, issued the following statement
to be read in court: "In retrospect, the tragedy of May 4, 1970,
should not have occurred. . . . We deeply regret those events, and
are profoundly saddened by the deaths of four students and
wounding of nine others. We hope that the agreement to end
this litigation will help assuage the tragic memories regarding that
sad day."

The crucial event at Kent State was, of course, the action of the National Guard on Monday, May 4. Here is what happened.

At 11:00 in the morning of a bright, sunny day, students began collecting on the commons as their 9:55–10:45 classes ended. They came casually at first, then in larger numbers when some of their 11:00–11:50 classes dismissed early because the confusion on campus made it too difficult to teach. Many students wandered by, as they always did, to check on what might be happening. Another set of classes, 12:05–12:55, would soon convene, and it was traditional for students who where involved either in leaving one class or heading for another to use the commons as their walkway. Without question, they had a right to be on the commons. But were they entitled to be there this day? A state of emergency had been declared . . . , presumably outlawing any unusual gatherings. Classes would meet, and that was about all. Yet testimony from students is overwhelming that they believed their campus to be operating as usual. On Friday a rally had been openly announced for Monday noon, and invitations to attend it had been circulated on succeeding days; in fact, announcements for this rally had been scrawled on certain blackboards and were seen by students when they reported for classes on Monday. Furthermore, those students and faculty who had left the campus Friday afternoon could not have listened to local radio stations and would have had no personal knowledge of what the situation was. Later we shall watch several professors, absent over the weekend, as they specifically instruct their students, with the most laudable intentions, to leave class and observe the campus rally. The rally may have been forbidden, but there were too many who either were not aware of this fact or did not believe it.

At 11:15 leaders of the National Guard, in discussion with school officials, became aware of this confusion and asked that the university radio station WKSU and the school intercom announce: "All outdoor demonstrations and gatherings are banned by order of the governor. The National Guard has the power of arrest." This was repeated several times but reached only a small proportion of the students, because the intercom system operated in only certain classrooms and none of the dormitories. But the rally had been forbidden; everyone knew it except the students.

At 11:30 General Canterbury, fresh from the inconclusive and even contradictory meeting with university and town officials, arrived at the burned-out ROTC building, surveyed the commons which lay before him, and concluded that the crowd was orderly and did not constitute any kind of significant threat. He could not at that moment have known that the impending dismissal of the 11:00–11:50 class would promptly crowd the commons.

At 11:45 General Canterbury, unaware that the radio broadcast canceling the rally had been heard by so few people, and not knowing about the nor-

From *Kent State: What Happened and Why*, by James A. Michener. Copyright © 1971 by Random House, Inc. and the Reader's Digest Association, Inc. Reprinted by permission of Random House, Inc.

mal movements of students going from class to class, was astonished to see so many students proceeding as if the rally were still authorized. The crowd was growing larger every minute. He saw about 600 students massing not far from his troops and became justifiably concerned. Giving a clear order, he commanded that the students be dispersed. This order was given before any rocks had been thrown.

At 11:48 someone began ringing the Victory Bell. Two students climbed onto its brick housing to issue frenzied calls to action. The bell continued clanging intermittently during the next fifteen minutes, and this coincided with the end of another class period, so that a constant press of new arrivals kept pouring onto the commons, while a much larger group watched from various walkways, driveways and porches of classroom buildings.

At 11:49 Officer Harold E. Rice, of the campus police, stood by the ruins of the ROTC building and read the riot act over a bullhorn: "Attention! This is an order. Disperse immediately. This is an order. Leave this area immediately. This is an order. Disperse." Unfortunately, he was so far away from the students that they could not hear him, and his words had no effect.

At 11:50 a National Guard jeep was driven up, with a driver at the wheel and two armed Guardsmen perched high atop the rear seat. Officer Rice climbed into the right front seat and with his bullhorn proceeded to read the riot act repeatedly as the jeep moved slowly along the edges of the crowd: "This assembly is unlawful. This crowd must disperse immediately. This is an order." (Later, certain students would claim that Rice *asked* them to break up the crowd but did not *order* them to do so, and it is possible that in one or another of the repetitions he may have used those words, but the evidence is overwhelming that he recited the version, as given, at least eight times.) The jeep was greeted with catcalls, boos, cursing and a shower of rocks; few of the latter reached the jeep and none appear to have struck any of the four passengers.

At 11:52, as the jeep made its slow progress, with Rice still shouting over the bullhorn, he spotted in the crowd someone he recognized as a leader of riots on the two preceding nights, and he wanted to arrest him. So the driver edged the jeep right into the edge of the crowd, but the young radical saw what Rice was up to and slipped away. So that all students might be properly warned, the jeep made three complete circuits.

At 11:55 the order was passed to the Guardsmen: "If you have not already done so, load and lock. Prepare for gas attack. Prepare to move out."

At 11:58 it was obvious that Rice in the jeep was accomplishing nothing, so Major Harry Jones ran out, banged on the jeep with his baton, and ordered it to return to the ROTC building.

At 11:59 General Canterbury gave the order: "Prepare to move out and disperse this mob." There is considerable variance in published reports as to the number of troops he had at his disposal. Inaccessibility of accurate records makes any estimate arbitrary; some seem much too low. It would appear that the total contingent contained 113 Guardsmen. . . .

According to the plan that General Canterbury had worked out with his commanders, the Guardsmen were to sweep the commons toward the south-east, driving all demonstrators across the crest of Blanket Hill, keeping Taylor Hall on their left, the pagoda on the right. The troops would then push the students down the far slope of the hill toward the practice football field, and the operation would be completed. Captain Snyder had suggested an additional detail: his left-flank Charlie Company would sweep left of Taylor Hall and take a holding position between it and Prentice while the center and right flank completed the main sweep on the other side of Taylor. To this General Canterbury assented, adding, "Before you step off, fire a barrage of tear gas."

It is important to visualize the number of students confronting the Guard. At 11:45 Colonel Fassinger had estimated the number of students on the commons — that is, in position to constitute a threat of some kind to the Guard — as "more than 500." In the interval this number had grown to 600 and then to something over 800. Now it might number as high as 1,100; for students were piling in from all directions as their classes ended. But a much larger crowd had assembled on the terraces of halls like Johnson and Stopher to the west, Prentice and Engleman to the east. And the largest group of all filled the open spaces directly in back of ROTC toward Administration. All of these must be considered as spectators only, and they could have numbered as many as 2,500. Included among them were townspeople, high-school children, professors and, of course, university students. As they were situated that morning they formed a gigantic amphitheater focusing upon a small stage of green.*

At 12:00 sharp, before the order to march could be given, an unidentified spokesman for the students, perhaps a faculty member, ran up to Canterbury and said, "General, you must not march against the students," to which the general replied that the students congregated illegally. "These students," he told the intercessor, "are going to have to find out what law and order is all about." Then he nodded to his commanders; the first slim gray tear-gas canisters popped out in their long parabolas toward the demonstrators, and 103 Guardsmen plus 10 officers stepped off into the history of contemporary America. The three senior officers, apparently by accident, distributed themselves among the units: Major Jones stayed with Charlie Company on the left flank; Colonel Fassinger marched with G Troop in the center; General Canterbury went with Alpha Company on the right flank.

At 12:01 Captain Snyder positioned himself on the extreme right of his men, so that when the gas stopped and his troop broke off from the other

* Eszterhas and Roberts believe the crowd to have been much larger: "By a few minutes before noon nearly fifteen hundred students had gathered around the bell. Another two thousand to three thousand students were assembled on the opposite side of the commons behind the National Guard lines. Another two thousand were on the northern edge of the commons near the tennis courts." One member of the research team, working independently, came up with almost these same estimates, but other members, reviewing each available photograph, convinced him that his figures were too high.

units for the drive to the east end of Taylor Hall, he would be anchor man on the right flank. Following his custom, he kept up a barrage of tear gas. A tear-gas canister launched by an M-79 is a most effective crowd-control device; if fired on a level trajectory (none were), it has sufficient velocity to kill a man at twenty-five yards. A sudden crosswind blew up to spread it across the field and up the Taylor Hall slope — before long the smoke would be inhaled into the Taylor Hall air-conditioning system, filling that building and affecting all those inside. Now, as Snyder's men moved ever closer to the crowd, those among the more daring demonstrators came darting forward, seizing the hot canisters and flinging them back. Most of these fell short of the approaching Guardsmen. One says *most* because certain unusually aggressive — or brave, if you prefer — young men not only grabbed the canisters but also ran good distances with them back toward the troops, throwing them from such short range that canisters sometimes landed in the ranks.

At 12:02 Snyder's men reached the point at which they would detach themselves from the center unit for the swing left. As they reached the Victory Bell a "bushy-haired young man" (Snyder's description) came darting down out of the trees on the slope and gave the bell a final swing. Then he wound up and hurled a fistful of small stones. Ron Snyder turned his back on the stones, spun around and brought his baton down across the boy's shoulders with such force as to snap off the tip of the baton. The young man then reached in his pocket and brought forth a piece of metal with four finger holes — a brass knuckle. Snyder hit him again. He dropped the piece of metal and dashed back up the hill.

At 12:03, as Charlie Company began to climb up through the trees, they could see a number of demonstrators along the brow of the hill. They fired more tear gas in that direction and kept climbing. At the top they beheld an even greater number of students gathered below them in the Prentice Hall parking lot, and here Snyder decided to form his line. He placed his men in a single row from the northeast corner of Taylor toward the nearest corner of Prentice, leaving twenty yards open at the Prentice Hall end as an escape route.

At 12:04 they were in the position they would hold for the next twenty minutes, and we shall leave them there as we follow the center unit, but before we do so, one incident should be noted. Clustered in front of Snyder's formation were a number of frantic coeds, and he began calling to them through the voice emitter in his M-17–type gas mask (all officers and noncoms were equipped with these special masks, through which voice instructions could be issued). He shouted to them, "Come on, come on! It's safe." Like a herd of frightened deer, the girls suddenly made their decision and bolted through the opening and around the side of the building. In the next few minutes Snyder estimates that he let upward of 100 students pass, all trying to escape the agony of drifting tear gas.

At 12:04, as Captain Snyder's troops were reaching their final position at the east end of Taylor, Captain Srp's center unit of eighteen soldiers was approaching the pagoda, undergoing as they marched a heavy barrage of curses and their own tear-gas canisters thrown back at them by determined students. The canisters were of little consequence to the Guardsmen, who, having anticipated this maneuver, were wearing gas masks, but this in itself posed a problem. As one Guardsman says, "It was a hot day, and this was the hottest part of the day. The gas masks were heavy, and as soon as you put yours on, you were hemmed in and sweating. Your vision was restricted to a narrow field and sometimes you couldn't even see the man next to you. It was like being tucked away in a corner . . . sweating." To the outsider, seeing a Guardsman in mask evoked a sense of the unreal, the mechanical, the monster from outer space, and this was an advantage, for it frightened the observer; but to the man inside the mask, there was a sense of remoteness, of detachment, of being alone in a crowd, and that was a disadvantage, for it cut a soldier off from his fellows and from reality.

At 12:05 the unit reached the pagoda, where it was met by a good deal more than returning gas canisters. Students began throwing rocks at them, and chunks of wood studded with nails, and jagged hunks of concrete. Where did they get such missiles? At least two witnesses swear they saw girls carrying heavy handbags from which they distributed rocks to men students, and some photographs would seem to substantiate this charge. At a nearby construction site some students had picked up fragments of concrete block. And some of the students had armed themselves with bricks. In addition, there were a few — not many — small stones and pebbles available on the campus itself, but these were inconsequential; on a normal day one could have searched this commons fairly carefully, without finding a rock large enough to throw at anyone.

Did any of the missiles hit the troops? Not many. The distances between the mass of the students and the Guards were later stepped off by expert judges, who concluded that students would have required good right arms like Mickey Mantle's to have reached the Guardsmen with even small stones. But as with the canisters, some students were bold enough to run back down the hill and throw from close range, and their stones did hit.

Worse, in a way, than the missiles were the epithets, especially when launched by coeds. A steady barrage of curses, obscenities and fatal challenges came down upon the Guard, whose gas masks did not prevent their hearing what they were being called. Girls were particularly abusive, using the foulest language and taunting the Guardsmen with being "shit-heels, motherfuckers and half-ass pigs." Others called them less explosive but equally hurtful names: "toy soldiers, murderers, weekend warriors, fascists." During the half hour that the Guardsmen were in action, this rain of abuse never let up.

In addition, a special few among the students — perhaps a dozen men and four girls — kept running at the Guardsmen, daring them to retaliate. One young man, with extremely long hair held in place by a beaded band, displayed a large black flag at the end of a pole, and with extreme bravado waved it at critical moments at the troops, almost in their faces, retreating to eight or ten yards at other times. Guardsmen behind their masks were unsure whether it was a Vietcong flag or not. Certainly it was not any with which they were familiar.

As this central detachment reached the top of Blanket Hill, they found that the mass of students had melted away before them. Never were the students very close, except for the daring ones, and people who have studied the facts and the photographs become irritated when someone asks, "Why didn't the Guard surround the students and arrest them?" The Guards were never within a hundred yards of being able to surround this ebbing and flowing mass of people, and besides, there were not nearly enough men to have done so had they desired. It was like asking a group of six people why they didn't surround a flock of pigeons who kept flying in all directions.

At 12:06, with the central unit perched atop the hill, the officers faced an awkward decision. They now stood between Taylor Hall on their left and the cement pagoda on their right, with almost the whole body of students, who a few minutes ago had been on the commons, facing them in the various open spaces that lay ahead. Also, many hundreds of additional students who could have known nothing of the preceding sweep, now arrived from their 11:00–11:50 classes, which had been held in buildings at distant parts of the campus, or were on their way to 12:05–12:55 classes in buildings nearby. For anyone to say of these students "They had no right to be on the campus" is to misunderstand the nature of a university; they had every right to be precisely where they were, but they did add to the visual confusion. If at this crucial moment the Guard had returned to their ROTC station, they would have had an absolutely clear escape route, but in all likelihood the radical students would have followed behind them, so that the situation would have wound up exactly as it started, with the Guard at ROTC and the students occupying Blanket Hill.

So an understandable decision was reached that the Guard would push on and try to clear the large area that lay ahead, an open field used for practice football, with a soccer goal at the south end and a baseball diamond at the north. What none of the Guardsmen apparently realized was that along the eastern side of this field ran a sturdy six-foot-high chain-link fence, topped by three strands of heavy barbed wire. What was worse, at the baseball end this fence took a right-angle turn to the west to form a catcher's backstop; it would be difficult to find on the campus a more perfect cul-de-sac. It was inconceivable that soldiers would march with their eyes open into such a trap, where they would be subjected to hostile students who would have large numbers of rocks at their disposal. But this is what happened.

At 12:07 the center unit, led by Colonel Fassinger and reinforced by large numbers from Captain Martin's Alpha Company on the right flank, marched down from the pagoda and smack against the steel chain-link fence. They had placed themselves in a position from which they could escape only by retreating, which, when it happened, would have to be interpreted by the watching students as a defeat for the Guard. How large was this combined unit? Photographs show at least 69 Guards against the fence, but one meticulous investigation augments that number. There were 75 Guards present, comprised as follows: two senior officers (Canterbury, Fassinger) with 53 men from Alpha Company, including three officers, plus the two casuals from Charlie Company, to which were added 18 men from G Troop, including two officers. However, Major Jones now ran across the grass to join the group. We have seen that he started with Charlie Company, which halted at the far end of Taylor Hall, so that during the first few minutes when the Guard stood penned against the fence, he had been with Captain Snyder. But quickly he discerned what was developing; elbowing his way through the crowd of students, he joined the larger contingent at the fence, where he would play a conspicuous role in what was to follow. The unit therefore consisted of 68 enlisted men led by 8 officers.

As soon as the students saw that the Guard was pinned against the fence, they began to close in from the parking lot to the north, cursing, throwing rocks, waving flags and tossing back gas canisters. The word *surrounded* has often been used to describe the Guard's condition at this moment. Nothing could be more inappropriate. To the east, across the fence, there was no one but Mike Alewitz, the socialist leader whose presence there will be explained later. To the south — that is, behind the Guardsmen on the practice field — there was no one for more than a hundred yards, as numerous photographs attest. And to the west, over the path to the pagoda which the Guard had just traversed, students had not yet re-formed. Far from being surrounded, the Guard had empty space on all sides.

At 12:10 the Guard underwent a heavy assault from the north, where students had grown bolder and were dashing in close to unload. What happened next remains obscure, but the sixteen enlisted men of G Troop, plus one other, believing their supply of tear gas to have been exhausted, knelt on one knee and assumed a firing position, aiming their rifles directly at the gadfly students who were pestering them. It appears that they must have been ordered by some officer to assume this frightening and provocative position, and if a further command had been given at this moment, students on the parking lot would have been mowed down, but no such command was uttered. (Actually, the beleagured troops had more gas. Specialist Russell Repp of A Company still carried eight canisters, a fact known by his immediate superiors, Srp and Stevenson, but not by those in command.)

The brazen young man with the black flag ran close and waved it before the silent rifles, daring the Guardsmen to fire. When they refrained, he and others were convinced that they would never shoot, that even if they did, the bullets were blanks. That much of the situation is ascertainable; what is still unknown is what took place at the core of the unit, where General Canterbury discussed this dangerous and ridiculous situation with his officers.

At 12:18 Colonel Fassinger issued the order: "Regroup back at ROTC." And the contingent began to form up for retreat, assuming the pattern of a flying wedge, point foremost and flanks trailing, with officers inside the V. (It may seem strange that a colonel should have been issuing orders to the troops when a general was present, but this was not unusual. In the navy, for example, it is customary for a five-star admiral attended by three- and two-star admirals to choose some warship as headquarters afloat; when they do so, they are technically under the command of whatever captain is in charge of the ship they occupy, and all personnel attached to that ship take their orders from the captain and not from the admirals.)

At 12:19 Fassinger radioed: "For the third time I am asking for more tear gas."

At 12:22 Fassinger gave the order to march, and his unit left the fence, where they had suffered much humiliation, some of it at their own hands, crossed the service road, and at an increasing speed, hurried back up to the pagoda. They were hot, and angry, and disgusted at having been pinned down against the fence, infuriated by the students who had challenged them, and bitterly resentful of the girls who even now trailed them up the hill, cursing and reviling them. Their gas masks prevented them from seeing just what was happening, and they were only vaguely aware of students still massed on their right flank. They had a long hot hill to climb and they were sweating. Were they in danger? On their left flank there was nobody except a few Guardsmen stationed at Johnson Hall. In the rear there was a handful of gadflies, mostly girls, who posed no threat at all. Straight ahead the commons was almost empty. At Taylor Hall the porches were crowded with students, at least half of them girls, and some teachers who were observing the scene. On the right flank, however, at a distance of seventy yards, there was a large mass of students, including many of those who had been pestering the Guard at the practice field but also many who were merely passing by between classes. The closest student seems to have been at least twenty yards away; the bulk were more than a hundred yards distant. But there was movement, and in the confusion of the march, it could be interpreted as hostile.

At 12:24, with the escape route back to ROTC completely unimpeded and with alternate ones available either to the left flank or to the rear, some Guardsmen on the trailing right flank suddenly stopped, wheeled 135 degrees to the right — that is, they turned almost completely around — faced the students who had collected on the south side of Taylor Hall, and dropped their rifles to a ready position. It so happens that three tape recorders, operated by would-be reporters from the School of Journalism, were running at this moment, and their testimony as to what happened next is incontrovertible.

There was a single shot — some people heard it as two almost simultaneous shots — then a period of silence lasting about two seconds, then a prolonged but thin fusillade, not a single angry burst, lasting about eight seconds, then another silence, and two final shots. The shooting had covered thirteen seconds, which is a very long time under such circumstances, and fifty-five M-1 bullets seem to have been discharged, plus five pistol shots and the single blast from a shotgun. Twenty-eight different Guardsmen did the firing, but this fact should be remembered: If each of the men had fired his weapon directly at the massed students, the killing would have been terrible, for a steel-jacketed M-1 bullet can carry two miles and penetrate two or four or six bodies in doing so. Fortunately, many of the men found it impossible to fire into a crowd and pointed their rifles upward — avoiding what could have been a general slaughter.

But some Guardsmen, fed up with the riotous behavior of the students and in fear of their lives, did fire directly into the crowd, and when the volley ended, thirteen bodies were scattered over the grass and the distant parking area. Four were dead, and nine were wounded more or less severely.

On the afternoon of the shooting, a governmental agency took careful measurements (which have not previously been released); here are the dry statistics. Thirteen young people shot: eleven men, two girls. All were registered at the university and all were attending classes formally. If the wounded were arranged in order of their nearness to the Guard, the closest young man was 71 feet away from the rifles, the farthest 745 feet away, or nearly two and a half football fields. The seventh body — that is, the median one — happened to be Doug Wrentmore, who was 329 feet away. The distances of the four dead at the time they were hit are as follows:

Jeffrey Glenn Miller, fifth closest	265 feet
Allison B. Krause, eighth closest	343 feet
William K. Schroeder, tenth closest	382 feet
Sandra Lee Scheuer, eleventh closest	390 feet

Of the thirteen who were struck by bullets, two were shot in the front, seven from the side, and four from the rear. Ten of the wounded were struck directly, three by ricochets. We came upon fairly strong evidence that a fourteenth student was hit in the left arm, but not seriously; he fled the area with his wound concealed, apprehensive lest he become involved with police or FBI investigations. He was more than 600 feet away when hit, and obviously not involved in the immediate action, though what he might have been doing earlier, we have no way of knowing.

Ascertaining the correct time of the firing is difficult, for whereas most of the other events can be confirmed with minute accuracy, often by three or four people, it is impossible to state precisely when the shooting occurred, even though hundreds of eyewitnesses observed it. The time indicated here is by no means a consensus, but it does represent the best-educated guess. Estimates vary from 12:12, which hardly gives the Guard time to cover the distances involved, let alone take action at any of the resting points, to 12:45, which is the solid report of one of the most careful investigating committees but which seems ridiculously late to those who participated. A highly placed Guard officer who was in position to know what was happening, who looked at his wristwatch at the moment of firing, and who was responsible for calling the information in to the command post, affirms, "The shooting took place at exactly 12:20, for I checked it as it occurred." But the official log of the action recording his report times it at 12:26. The apparent impossibility of determining a precise time is not critical; if an early time is used, it means only that the Guardsmen had conducted all their operations on the practice field in less than three minutes, which seems impossible; if a late time is used it means that they dallied there for more than half an hour, which seems contrary to evidence and common sense. The time given here was noted by a journalism student at Taylor Hall, who made no great claim for its accuracy, but it does conform to the judgment of many.

At 12:25 (or 12:46, if the extreme time is accepted) the firing ceased, thanks to the energetic efforts of Major Jones, who can be seen in photographs beating his troops over their helmets with his swagger stick, pleading with them to stop. General Canterbury can also be seen, turning in surprise from the direction in which he had been heading — down the hill to safety — which lends credence to the theory that if an order of some kind had been given to fire, he at least had not been informed of it.

At 12:29, after a lapse of at least four minutes, during which frantic officers did their best to restore order, the unit re-formed, retreated in orderly fashion to their staging area at ROTC, and surrendered their guns for registry and inspection. Jack Deegan, a Marine Corps reservist majoring in history, who had followed the unit at extremely close range all the way from the link fence, reports, "I saw one young Guard lying on the ground, tossing himself back and forth in hysteria and moaning something I couldn't hear." He may have been William Herschler, whom the FBI reported as having cried, "I just shot two teenagers." At this point a veil of silence descended over the Guard.

STUDY GUIDE

1. Begin by making an outline of the events that took place *prior* to Monday, May 4, that led to an air of confrontation on the Kent campus.

2. As you read the narrative, compile two lists: (a) the *fortuitous* events that led to the tragedy, those developments that were *unplanned* and could not be foreseen as contributing to the end result; and (b) those gestures — by both the students and the National Guard — that could and should have been perceived as potentially dangerous.

3. What do you make of Michener's statement that, on one hand, the students were never very close to the guardsmen and, on the other, that there was no possibility for the guardsmen to surround and arrest the students?

4. In reading the narrative, is it possible to say that there was a single point of no return, as it were, a point at which the Kent State tragedy became inevitable? If so, at which moment — or event — did this occur? Or do you feel that there was no single gesture or moment that can be so named? Elaborate.

5. Focusing on the climax of this tragic sequence of events, what are Michener's views on the following assertions: (a) that the students were a physical threat to the guardsmen; (b) that the students had no right to congregate on the campus; and (c) that there was no explicit order to the guardsmen to fire on the students.

6. What is your personal reaction to what took place on that day on the Kent campus? Are your sympathies with the guardsmen and their officers or with the students? Given the circumstances, should the demonstrations have been handled differently? If so, how? And what do you make of the settlement and the statement made by the State of Ohio in 1977? Would you construe that as an admission of guilt on the part of the state and its governor? If not, why not?

BIBLIOGRAPHY

The literature on the Vietnam war is massive and one might begin with two books by a firsthand observer of the country and the war: *The Two Viet-Nams: A Political and Military Analysis* (New York, 1963) and *Last Reflections on a War* (Garden City, New York, 1967) by Bernard Fall, who was killed while reporting on the war there. American participation in the Vietnam war has been criticized by Richard J. Barnet in *Roots of War* (New York, 1972) and by David Halberstam, in *The Best and the Brightest* (New York, 1973), while Guenter Lewy, though critical of American military tactics, justifies the war as both legal and necessary in *America in Vietnam* (New York, 1978). A recent publication, George C. Herring, *America's Longest War: The United States and Vietnam, 1950–1975* (New York, 1979), sees American participation in the Southeast Asia struggle as the logical extension of Harry S. Truman's policy of containment, a posture that he feels the United States must abandon for the future.

The domestic aspects of the war — the response of the American people to the war — are covered in the two studies of public opinion during the war:

Louis Harris, *The Anguish of Change* (New York, 1973) and Samuel Lubell, *The Hidden Crisis in American Politics* (New York, 1970); a study of the wars in both Korea and Vietnam by John E. Mueller, *War, Presidents, and Public Opinion* (New York, 1973); and three studies on the impact of the war on various segments of American society: Milton J. Rosenberg, Sidney Verba, and Philip E. Converse, *Vietnam and the Silent Majority: The Dove's Guide* (New York, 1970); Robert L. Beisner, "1898 and 1968: The Anti-Imperialists and the Doves," *Political Science Quarterly*, 85 (June 1970), 187–216; and Lawrence M. Baskir and William A. Strauss, *Chance and Circumstance* (New York, 1978).

The literature on the Kent State shootings, apart from James A. Michener, *Kent State: What Happened and Why* (New York, 1971), from which this selection is taken, includes I. F. Stone, *The Killings at Kent State* (New York, 1971); and Robert M. O'Neil, John P. Morris, and Raymond Mack, *No Heroes, No Villains* (San Francisco, 1972). The larger scene of generational tension and rebellion is covered in *Students in Revolt* (Boston, 1969), a collection of perceptive essays edited by Seymour Martin Lipset and Philip G. Altbach; *Young Radicals: Notes on Committed Youth* (New York, 1968) by Kenneth Keniston, who generally is in sympathy with the ideological perspective of the student rebels, and *The Confliction of Generations: The Character and Significance of Student Movements* (New York, 1969), by Lewis Feuer, who takes an opposing view.

* Asterisk indicates book is available in a paperback edition.

Richard Nixon's manipulation of the media — particularly television — played an important part in his rise — and fall.

21

ERIK BARNOUW

The Tube of Plenty

From Franklin Delano Roosevelt to Jimmy Carter, each president has sought to use the mass media, radio and television in particular, to advance his political fortunes. Roosevelt, who came to office in the midst of the Great Depression, sought to bring a measure of comfort and reassurance to the nation through his periodic "fireside chats" on radio. Television, as a political medium, was first employed with great effectiveness by General Dwight D. Eisenhower, particularly when he first ran for the presidency in 1952. Prepared by the advertising agency of Batten, Barton, Durstine, and Osborn, Eisenhower's "crusade" for the presidency was packaged for television with all the expertise the agency gave to its more obviously commercial accounts.

B.B.D. and O., as they were known in the industry, divided the script for Eisenhower's half-hour television appearances during the campaign into three acts: a) the hero's arrival; b) his speech; and c) the hero's departure. Wherever Ike spoke — in Des Moines, Iowa, or Bangor, Maine — the agency arranged for the television scenario to include the following shots: Ike making his appearance in the back of the auditorium; the unrestrained enthusiasm of the gallery; Mamie, Ike's wife, seated demurely in a box near the stage; Ike striding to platform; the crowd going wild; Ike waving to the crowd, looking at Mamie, and Mamie smiling in response; Ike holding up his hands to stop the tumultuous welcome; the crowd cheering him on and, only then, the speech, carefully tailored to end with time left for the crowd to respond — on television — with an enormous roar of approval for their candidate. Adlai E. Stevenson, Eisenhower's Democratic opponent in 1952, refused to participate in this kind of television pageantry, rejecting the notion that he should be merchandised "like breakfast food." Although Eisenhower's victories over Stevenson in 1952 and 1956 were not solely the result of his use of the media, Eisenhower and his advisors clearly understood the dictum of the Canadian philosopher, Marshall McLuhan: "the medium is the message."

Radio and, to a greater degree, television contributed to the success and failure of other political figures and causes in the 1950s and '60s. The bully-like image projected by Senator Joseph R. McCarthy in the televised Army-McCarthy hearings contributed significantly to the ultimate fall from influence and power of the Wisconsin demagogue. In 1952, Richard M. Nixon was being pressured to resign as Eisenhower's running-mate because he accepted an $18,000 slush fund from a group of California businessmen after he had been elected to Congress. Nixon kept his place on the ticket by his nationally televised "Checkers" speech (so named because of Nixon's admission that his family had accepted from a Texas admirer the gift of a tiny cocker spaniel named Checkers). In 1960, Nixon did not fare as well on television and his poor showing in the first of his four televised debates with John F. Kennedy contributed to his defeat in the presidential campaign of that year. President Kennedy's decision to permit live television coverage of his news conferences added to his growing reputation for wittiness and nimbleness of mind. Lyndon B. Johnson, who succeeded to the presidency after Kennedy's assassination in Dallas in 1963, was no less interested in the medium, but was unable to use it as effectively as had his predecessors. In the late 1960s television brought into the living rooms of millions of Americans the tragedy of war in Vietnam and urban riots and protest movements at home. It was on television that President Johnson, mindful of the failure of his actions in Southeast Asia and the divisiveness they caused, announced in 1968 that he would not seek or accept another nomination for the presidency.

In *Tube of Plenty*, Erik Barnouw, Emeritus Professor of Dramatic Art at Columbia University, traces the evolution of television in the decades after World War II and the medium's growing impact on American society. His description and analysis of television's role in the presidency of Richard Nixon is both fascinating and instructive. One can only conclude that while future presidents may employ that medium differently, neither they nor the American people will be able to ignore its importance.

There was good reason why Richard Nixon, veteran of televised unAmerican activities hearings, of the Checkers speech, the "kitchen debate," the Great Debates, countless campaign telecasts, and "the most historic phonecall," should be intent on television as an instrument of presidential power. Among all Presidents of the television age, he became its most avid practitioner — in the frequency of his appearances, and in the range of devices used to influence, cajole, and control the medium.

Throughout broadcasting history, Presidents have been given air time at their request, and under circumstances of their choosing. This has never been a legal requirement, but a practice that seemed essential to the "public interest, convenience, and necessity." All Presidents from Franklin D. Roosevelt on have been thought to misuse the privilege, exploiting it for partisan political ends; yet curtailment has seemed inconceivable.

Presidents have found many ways to use the television spotlight. The study *Presidential Television,* written in 1973 by former FCC chairman Newton N. Minow and others, summarized them succinctly:

> He may make a formal address, hold a press conference, consent to an interview, telephone an astronaut, go to a football game, receive a visiting chief of state, take a trip abroad, or play with his dog on the White House lawn. He may send his family, his cabinet members, or his political allies before the cameras. In almost every case, he, and he alone, decides. His ability to choose when and how to appear without cost before millions of viewers is completely unmatched by his political or Congressional opponents.

Unlike Lyndon Johnson, Nixon was not a compulsive viewer. But he was devoted to televised football, and liked to offer advice on tactics to favorite teams. And he often talked of political strategy in terms of "game plans."

Many of his presidential telecasts, especially in his first term, were supremely successful in solidifying his position, as indicated in Gallup polls. Coming into office with a minimal constituency, he rapidly won wider support. Though he often seemed ill at ease on camera, his awkwardness — or lack of show-business charisma — may at times have worked in his favor in his appeals to "middle America."

He had pledged an end to the Vietnam war — a "peace with honor" — and soon after his inauguration announced a plan for removing combat ground troops from Vietnam in phased withdrawals. In numerous on-camera appearances he stressed the withdrawals.

The networks, taking their cue from this, adopted a similar stress. Av Weston, executive producer of the ABC-TV evening news, telegraphed orders to his Saigon bureau to de-emphasize battle footage in favor of material on the theme *"We Are on Our Way Out of Vietnam."* A follow-up

From *Tube of Plenty: The Evolution of American Television* by Erik Barnouw. Copyright © 1975 by Erik Barnouw. Reprinted by permission of Oxford University Press, Inc.

order said: "This point should be stressed to all hands." The theme thus became a pervasive one.

Unfortunately, it misrepresented events, of which the withdrawals were only a part, the televised part. While television viewers saw constant glimpses of homebound soldiers, some were still being replaced by new draftees. A few days after his inauguration, President Nixon sent a secret American sweep into Laos, and a few weeks later began secret, sustained bombing of Cambodia, a country officially recognized as neutral. The U.S. Air Force, under presidential orders, put into effect a systematic falsification of reports to conceal these attacks from the American people. Off-shore naval forces and Thailand-based air units were meanwhile strengthened for these attacks and for intensified bombing of North Vietnam and Vietcong areas. Armament supplies to South Vietnam were increased to give it one of the largest air forces in the world. Thus while Americans believed that the President was "winding down the war" — a theme constantly dramatized via "going home" film sequences on the evening news — he was actually enlarging it in quest of a decisive military victory, the "peace with honor" he wanted to win, in place of the compromise available at Paris conference tables.

The "winding down" theme remained largely unchallenged in the mass media for several months, so that the President had won time for his game plan. But by mid-1969 it was clear that the war was building in fury, and that no "peace with honor" was in sight. Revelations by the New York *Times* concerning the secret Cambodia bombings helped to rekindle protest. That fall, huge demonstrations again converged on Washington and seemed to imperil the Nixon strategy. At this point he pre-empted a prime-time period on November 3 and, to an audience of more than 70 million, made one of his most potent and successful appeals. It was addressed to a "silent majority."

> And so tonight — to you, the great silent majority of my fellow Americans — I ask for your support. . . . For the more divided we are at home, the less likely the enemy is to negotiate at Paris. Let us be united for peace. Let us also be united against defeat. Because let us understand: North Vietnam cannot defeat or humiliate the United States. Only Americans can do that.

Nixon recognized that defeat, or the appearance of it, was more appalling to many Americans than war. His words did not end protest but stirred increased anger against protesters. He put protesters on the defensive, placing them outside the mainstream of American life. It was a telling maneuver, and again gained him time.

While viewer reaction to the speech was mainly favorable, there were diverse assessments from columnists and television commentators. The "instant analysis" on television seems to have been particularly infuriating to the President. He was determined to restore the more cooperative environment of earlier periods of the Vietnam war, when the broadcast media were almost automatic conduits for administration reports and rationales. The President now began to make extraordinarily effective use of Vice President Spiro Agnew, whose speaking style lent itself to smooth invective. In a speech prepared for him by White House speech writer Patrick J. Buchanan, Agnew mounted a powerful offensive against the television networks. The speech was made at a regional meeting of Republicans in Des Moines, but all three networks, forewarned of the contents, felt that the best defense was to carry the speech. Thus they gave it nationwide impact. Agnew began by referring to the President's speech of ten days earlier, and the ensuing words of commentators.

> The purpose of my remarks tonight is to focus your attention on this little group of men who not only enjoy a right of instant rebuttal to every Presidential address, but, more importantly, wield a free hand in selecting, presenting and interpreting the great issues of our nation. . . .
>
> The American people would rightly not tolerate this concentration of power in Government. Is it not fair and relevant to question its concentration in the hands of a tiny, enclosed fraternity of privileged men elected by no one and enjoying a monopoly sanctioned and licensed by Government? The views of the majority of this fraternity do not — and I repeat, not — represent the views of America. . . .
>
> Perhaps the place to start looking for a credibility gap is not in the offices of Government in Washington but in the studios of the networks in New York.

As Nixon had done in his Checkers speech, Agnew triumphantly turned the telecast into a referendum. Suggesting that network "bias" be protested via mail and telephone, he managed to let loose on the networks a deluge of letters and phone calls — some reasoned and sober in tone, others vituperative, scurrilous, and ugly.

A striking aspect of the Agnew attack was that it echoed liberal complaints against the monopolistic nature of the industry. Yet the target of the attack was the one small segment of television — the news segment — that was not wholly submerged in the monopoly atmosphere, and was occasionally at odds with military-industrial views. The thrust of the speech was to smother this segment. Thus it sought to establish precisely the "concentration of power" it pretended to abhor.

Agnew, returning to the attack in the following weeks, became celebrated as a phrase-maker, especially for his alliterations. Commentators were "nattering nabobs of negativism." Bob Hope, resolute Nixon and Agnew supporter, had his gag-writers devise jokes for Agnew speeches. Car stickers proclaimed: "Spiro Is Our Hero."

In several speeches, Agnew included reminders that television was "licensed" by government. Other government spokesmen echoed the theme. FCC chairman Dean Burch, a recent Nixon appointee — and former campaign manager for Barry Goldwater — found the Agnew attack "thoughtful" and urged broadcasters to heed it. White House aide Clay T. White-head, who in 1970 became presidential adviser on "telecommunications policy," added a new note. Television stations could expect more security in their licenses, he suggested — he even mentioned the possibility of *longer* licenses — if they would be more careful about news programs and docu-mentaries they accepted from the networks. He thus turned the affiliates against the networks. According to Walter Cronkite, the Nixon-Agnew-Whitehead era brought affiliate pressures on networks for a more cautious news policy. Some affiliates even superimposed disclaimers over network commentators. The networks themselves showed a sharply reduced interest in covering protest demonstrations.

The Agnew campaign received admiring tribute from the President's daughter Tricia. She said he had had "amazing" impact and helped tele-vision "reform itself." She added: "You can't underestimate the power of fear. They're afraid if they don't shape up — "

Some months later William Paley decided that CBS would drop "instant analysis" of presidential addresses.

White House efforts during these months to control television — a "TV Blitzkrieg," *Variety* called it — went beyond overt criticism. They included also varied covert harassments of newsmen regarded as enemies. Daniel Schorr of CBS, after a dispatch that displeased the White House, found that the FBI was questioning friends and acquaintances about him. Most such operations did not become public knowledge until much later.

The chilling effect of the White House maneuvers was, however, only temporary. By the winter of 1970–71, protest was again rising in pitch. It received impetus from reports of atrocities, at My Lai and elsewhere; of horrors inflicted by "lawnmower" bombing of Vietnamese towns, leaving a swath of death hundreds of feet wide; and catastrophic defoliant operations, which were said to sport a slogan adapted from television public-service spots: "Only you can prevent forests." Amid reports of such matters, "peace with honor" seemed not only remote; to many, the phrase began to have ghoulish overtones.

On television, the new surge of protest found expression on CBS — Janu-ary 1971 — in *The Selling of the Pentagon,* by Peter Davis. At once de-nounced by Vice President Agnew as "disreputable," it documented with stunning impact the cosiness between the Pentagon and its corporate con-tractors, and the vast sums expended by the Pentagon on pro-war propa-ganda. The spirit also found expression on public television.

The public-television system had made a cautious start in its new incarna-tion as a service supported in part by federal funds. Importing several superb British series, too long ignored by American television — *The For-syte Saga, Civilization, Upstairs, Downstairs* — public television was begin-ning to build an ardent following. Its schedules also included the widely applauded *Sesame Street.* But during 1970–71 it also launched the inventive, occasionally brilliant series *The Great American Dream Machine,* a composite of short items, often sardonic and even iconoclastic. White House observers seem to have been angered by its war-related items, and also outraged by *Who Invited US?*, on the interventionist tendencies of American foreign policy; and, on the series *Behind the Lines,* by a documentary about the FBI's use of *agents provocateurs* to discredit anti-war groups.

But during these months of rising opposition, President Nixon was preparing to muffle protest again with the most spectacular and successful phase of all his television operations. In the midst of the Vietnam fury he was moving for a détente with China and the Soviet Union, to be implemented and dramatized via televised journeys. It was a maneuver certain to throw the world's ideological battle lines into confusion, and to confound his opponents. Secret journeys by presidential adviser Henry Kissinger set the stage. In July 1971 the President, on a few hours' notice, requested network time — without a hint to the networks of what was in store. When he suddenly appeared on the tube — interrupting *The Dean Martin Show, NYPD,* and the movie *The Counterfeit Killer* — it was to announce to the world that he would start a series of diplomatic travels with a visit to Peking. Enormous plans for television coverage began.

The fact that Richard Nixon, a leading generalissimo in a quarter-century of cold war, had taken this initiative, added to the drama and its impact. His cold-war credentials may also have made the venture possible. The Chinese felt secure in his overtures, knowing they were not from a liberal who might — like Woodrow Wilson in another time — be repudiated by a conservative Congress. As a result, the Nixon move stirred worldwide feeling that a new era was at hand.

Early in 1972, plane-loads of television equipment and personnel were flown to Peking, and camera positions were prepared on the Great Wall and elsewhere. The events aroused expectancy comparable to the first moon landing: a *terra incognita,* a world of mystery, was opening at last.

What audiences eventually saw *was* mysterious, in a fashion characteristic of television diplomacy. They saw spectacular banquets, toasts, handshakes, and smiles, but learned almost nothing of what was said in off-camera talks, beyond a report that the two powers had agreed to "normalize" relations, and to trade. But perhaps they learned what there was to learn. For this was not a television glimpse of a diplomatic maneuver. The telecast itself was the maneuver: a symbolic moment for the eyes of the world.

The venture was planned with awesome efficiency. The President knew exactly where to stop on the Great Wall to survey the world before him. It was noted that he had arranged to land in Peking in network prime time. Later his plane arrived back in Washington in prime time; it did so by waiting for some hours on the ground in Anchorage, Alaska.

Three months later came the first visit of an American President to Moscow. Again the world saw symbolic handshakes; it learned few specifics, but witnessed harmony and enthusiasm. Major network newsmen were again on hand to add descriptive details — Walter Cronkite, John Chancellor, Howard K. Smith. There was no "instant analysis." En route home, further handshakes and pageantry and waving crowds were telecast from Warsaw.

Then Nixon climaxed the travel sequence with an unprecedented video tour-de-force. Landing at Andrews Air Force Base on June 1, he went by helicopter directly to the Capitol — the first time a President had thus descended on Congress — to report to a joint session, and via television to the nation and the world, on his "journey for peace." He was interrupted repeatedly by bursts of applause.

With this sequence of summit telecasts, Nixon had scored a reverberating political coup. Those who had deplored the cold war, and generally opposed Nixon, were neutralized, in many cases won over. The anti-war forces were thrown off balance. For many people it was now impossible not to believe that the Vietnam war would be resolved within the context of Great Power amity and good-will.

A few cold-war zealots were indignant that Nixon had befriended communist China. But he was not likely to lose their support; they had nowhere else to go.

The televised journeys set the stage for the 1972 presidential elections. Nixon returned on the eve of the nominating conventions. His renomination had long been assured. On the strength of his world exploits, overwhelming reelection now seemed likely.

But Nixon was not one to settle for a likelihood. Perhaps he was haunted by memories of past defeats — in the 1960 presidential election and the 1962 California governorship race, both of which had seemed to promise victory. This time certainty would be made more certain by any means available. A Committee for the Reelection of the President was raising the greatest of all campaign war chests, swelling it — it was later revealed — by various illegal means. And clandestine espionage and sabotage operations, already set in motion before the President's journeys, were in progress against major Democratic contenders. Documents were forged to discredit Senators Hubert Humphrey, Henry Jackson, and Edmund Muskie. A unit under ex-CIA agent E. Howard Hunt, veteran of Guatemala and the Bay of Pigs and now in service at the White House, gave special attention to Edward Kennedy and the Kennedy family, past and present. Forged material was prepared for possible use in the event of his nomination. The White House hoped Senator George McGovern would win the nomination; he had campaigned almost solely on opposition to the Vietnam war and could find himself without an issue

The covert operations, in large part conducted from the White House, proceeded with highest professional efficiency — until the night of June 17, two weeks after the President's return, when a bizarre news item erupted into headlines and television newscasts. Five intruders were arrested in the middle of the night in Democratic Party Headquarters in the Watergate apartments in Washington. Bugging equipment was confiscated; also cameras, and many $100 bills numbered in sequence, and address books which listed, among other names, "Howard Hunt, WH" — apparently, the White House.

Ronald Ziegler, Nixon press secretary, dismissed the episodes as a "third-rate burglary attempt." Two days later the President scheduled a televised press conference, telling the cameras and microphones that electronic surveillance had "no place whatever in our electoral process or in our governmental process." The FBI said it was investigating. The Republicans hinted they were having similar "security" problems. Most newscasts treated the episode with a light touch — an oddity in the news.

A speculative explanation, discussed at length on the public television series *Firing Line*, featuring the writer William F. Buckley, was that the intruders — several of whom were anti-Castro Cubans and alumni of the Bay of Pigs — were seeking evidence that the Democratic Party was getting help from Castro and had made a deal with him. This theory deflected suspicion from the Republicans to the Democrats.

No network made its own inquiry into the Watergate mystery. Among news media only the Washington *Post,* at this time, felt the episode called for intensive investigative efforts. Meanwhile the break-in was pushed from the headlines by the nominating conventions. In July television viewers watched a deeply divided Democratic Party nominate McGovern; in August they saw a festive Republican convention renominate Nixon and Agnew by acclamation.

During the following months Nixon made few campaign telecasts of a conventional sort. In news telecasts he was seen receiving foreign dignitaries; the image was that of a world leader above the conflict, busy with world issues.

In October he announced that his Vietnam strategy was bearing fruit: Henry Kissinger had reached a breakthrough in talks with North Vietnam. Kissinger, on television, said a few details needed to be resolved, but peace was "within reach." He gave no further details.

Throughout these weeks the Washington *Post* — and then the New York *Times* and others — reported new Watergate clues that seemed to reach into widening circles of criminal activity. Network news programs cautiously mentioned the astonishing allegations — along with White House denunciations of them as libelous "innuendo."

McGovern, switching in his final campaign telecasts from the war issue — which seemed to be disappearing — to the rapidly accumulating Watergate reports, called the Nixon regime "the most corrupt" in American history. Republicans dismissed the accusations as the rantings of a desperate candidate, and they seemed so to many voters.

On election day Nixon won 49 states; McGovern won only Massachusetts and the District of Columbia. With an electoral vote of 520–17, Nixon had achieved one of the greatest of landslides.

The first Watergate trials — of those arrested in connection with the break-in — began early in 1973. On January 21 sequestered Watergate jurors were permitted to watch on television the jubilant inaugural festivities, without having an inkling of the President's involvement in matters they were considering. The defendants had, at the direction of the President, received large sums for their silence. Extensive perjury was committed.

The Nixon administration had apparently weathered the Watergate episode. On January 27 an agreement "on ending the war and restoring peace in Vietnam" was signed in Paris. The President stood high in prestige throughout the world.

But during the following months further evidence accumulated, and by March began to ensnare the President. The Senate voted a Watergate inquiry, to be chaired by Senator Sam Ervin of North Carolina. It decided to open its hearings to television.

Until mid-1973 President Nixon, by exercising the prerogatives of presidential television to the full, had remained in control. Again and again he had been able to deflect criticism, stifle opposition, shift attention, set the national agenda, dramatize achievements, pillory detractors — all this supported by clandestine warfare against "enemies." But in mid-1973 presidential television was confronting something else — congressional television.

This was a phenomenon that erupted seldom but, when it did, had explosive possibilities. Congressional television rested on premises quite different from those of presidential television. Preemption of time, whether prime time or marginal time, was not a congressional privilege. Congress or its committees could only, from time to time, invite cameras and microphones into their deliberations. This might result in a 40-second newscast item — seldom more. In the case of Vietnam hearings, an *I Love Lucy* rerun had seemed to CBS a preferable offering. Occasionally, the impending drama seemed promising, as well as important.

The Watergate hearings came at a crucial moment in the history of public television. In 1972 Congress had passed a two-year authorization of $155 million for public broadcasting, but the President had vetoed it, as well as several lesser authorizations. Public broadcasting found itself living on a starvation diet. Clay Whitehead, White House spokesman on such matters, made it clear what public television should do to secure federal funds. It should stop competing for big audiences with things like *The Great American Dream Machine*. Its service should be supplementary. It should be decentralized, with the emphasis on local programs. To many this seemed a prescription for returning to the first disastrous days of "educational television" — academic lectures, panels, interviews. During 1972–73 the field was swept by layoffs and resignations. Its conservative elements meanwhile pushed for the reforms demanded by the adminstration. Then came the Watergate hearings.

Public television decided to carry them — live by day, repeated via tape at night. For months its talent bills were minimal, but the response was staggering. In the way that the Army-McCarthy hearings had given ABC-TV a blood transfusion, so the Watergate hearings gave public television a new lease on life. Some of its stations gained the highest ratings in their history. To many of their executives, it seemed ironic that the President's displeasure, and their resulting poverty, had pushed them toward this salvation.

Commercial television also decided to carry the hearings, rotating live coverage among the three networks, to minimize advertising losses. They were somewhat discomfited to find that Watergate outpulled their own top-ranking daytime serials and game-shows.

Watergate became an obsession with viewers. Some watched live hearings all day, the taped repeats at night. Chairman Sam Ervin, with his store of Bible quotations and aphorisms, became a folk hero. The long, detailed testimony of former White House counsel John Dean — extremely damaging to the President — riveted the national attention.

As witnesses recanted perjury testimony given earlier, and told their stories, the vision that emerged for viewers was of a snake-pit of duplicity and corruption guarding the Nixon presidency — espionage, sabotage, bribery, burglary, subornation of perjury. The President's involvement became increasingly apparent.

President Nixon's "approval rating" as reported by Gallup polls had stood at 68 per cent after the January ceasefire announcement; by August it had fallen to 31 per cent, the lowest presidential rating in twenty years.

By that time a startling development had shifted the focus of attention. During testimony in July a former presidential assistant, Alexander P. Butterfield, mentioned a voice-activated recording system that had been in operation in various White House offices and at Camp David since 1971, known to only a handful of people. Tapes relevant to current inquiries were at once requested — then subpoenaed — for the Ervin committee and Watergate grand jury. Nixon rejected the requests and subpoenas; then released selected tapes, one with an 18½-minute erasure; then flatly refused to surrender more, citing "presidential confidentiality" and "national security." Since much testimony in Watergate trials, past and future, could be supported or negated by the tapes, the refusal raised an obstruction-of-justice issue. The stage was set for legal struggle over this issue. In the fall of 1973 it began to wind its way through the courts.

Simultaneously new Nixon administration scandals filled newscasts: Agnew's resignation, after revelations of bribery payments started during his Maryland governorship and continuing during his vice presidency; a finding that the President himself had underpaid his taxes by $432,787.13; charges that campaign contributions from dairy interests, ITT, Howard Hughes and others had been cash payments for favorable adminstrative decisions. Such matters received detailed comment on the three networks, and on such public television series as *Bill Moyers' Journal* and *Washington Week in Review*. CBS restored "instant analysis."

During this period of mounting reverses, Nixon made several television appearances to halt the flood. All bore resemblances to the Checkers telecast: disclosures were made, and described as unprecedented concessions, offered to lay issues to rest. In all, he pictured himself as a victim of vicious attacks. In all, he merged his cause with larger concerns — America, the world, lasting peace, history. "I want these to be the best days in America's history because I love America. . . . God bless America. And God bless each and every one of you."

It had worked in the Checkers speech. The Checkers triumph may, in a sense, have lured him to disaster, making him feel he could extricate himself from almost any dilemma by appearing on the tube and refocusing the national attention. It did not work now.

The most dramatic attempt came on April 29, 1974. The House of Representatives had voted funds for an impeachment inquiry by its judiciary committee. The President was under subpoena to deliver tapes of 141 presidential conversations to the judiciary committee — and of 64 to the Watergate prosecutor. At this juncture Nixon pre-empted prime time.

He was at a desk. Behind him viewers could see enormous stacks of bound volumes. The President said he had decided to turn over to the judiciary committee — and at the same time make public — edited transcripts of White House conversations relating to Watergate. "As far the President's role with regard to Watergate is concerned, the entire story is here." He conceded that some passages would be seen as damaging, confusing; but overall, the massive material would show his innocence.

For the moment, it seemed a masterly performance. But within hours it had plunged his Gallup rating to a new low — below 30 per cent — and brought a renewal of demands for the tapes. There were many reasons.

The President had made his own selection; many of the requested conversations were not included in the transcripts. The transcripts, punctuated throughout with "expletive deleted" and "unintelligible," had been heavily edited. Some transcripts had to do with tapes already surrendered; the judiciary committee had its own transcripts of these, and found startling contrasts between them and the President's transcripts. In the editing process, the White House had omitted damaging passages, sometimes without any indication of an omission. Among omissions were such passages as a Nixon comment on the Washington *Post:* "The main thing is, the Washington *Post* is going to have a damnable, damnable thing out of this one. They have a TV station, you know."

The transcripts, aside from these shocking deficiencies, offered horrifying glimpses of the moral tone of discussions in the Oval Office — cynical, profane, amoral, scheming. Far from establishing the President's innocence, they suggested a ceaseless obsession with game plans for crushing enemies and thwarting investigation, often by illegal or dubious methods. If the selected passages were meant to exonerate the President, what would other passages reveal?

Apparently Nixon had hoped that the juiciness of some passages would satisfy public appetite and bring the matter to an end; also, that the sheer bulk of the material (1,308 pages, about 350,000 words) would keep it largely unread, or at least keep it off the air. But he was mistaken. Noncommercial radio stations — struggling, like public television, with marginal budgets — began marathon on-the-air readings of the entire transcript, lasting some forty hours. The Pacifica radio stations did likewise, assigning roles to well-known actors, and using beeps and other symbolic sounds for "unintelligible" and "expletive omitted." Television network newscasts staged similar readings of selected passages, with montages of photographs to identify the speakers. Thus the transcripts, as edited by the White House, received saturation coverage. They set the stage for a television sequel, the beginning of the impeachment process in the House judiciary committee.

The judiciary committee decided to open its final deliberations to television, but first to hear witnesses behind closed doors. As it did so, Nixon had one more television spectacular in store — one of the most extraordinary — to seize the spotlight. He had arranged a trip to the Middle East. Once more television networks performed their miracles of coordinated coverage. Once more viewers were astounded to see screaming crowds welcoming the President — in Egypt, Syria, Israel. Then one more visit to Moscow. Once again, in this sequence, he projected the image of a world leader hard at work, in spite of lesser mortals sniping at him back home.

His return in July 1974 was very different from his previous homecoming. Instead of a joint session of Congress and thunderous applause, there was the judiciary committee preparing for the final, televised part of its impeachment deliberations. And the nation was ready to watch.

Would the presence of cameras trivialize the momentous historic occasion? Some thought it would; Ronald Ziegler called the committee a "kangaroo court." But viewers got a different impression. The thirty-eight members of the committee, one after another, assessed the evidence, weighed the balance, stated conclusions — carefully, soul-searchingly, sometimes agonizingly, often in impressive language. Some were relatively new members of Congress, unknown to the nation at large. But by the end of the week they had done much, wrote Shana Alexander in *Newsweek* "to restore one's faith in this country's moral tone." Then, on three counts, they voted for impeachment by substantial majorities.

There was an immediate and startling epilogue — bringing more drama to the tube. While the committee deliberated, an 8–0 Supreme Court decision ordered the White House to release the subpoenaed material. When the tapes, delivered after the committee vote, were finally heard by members, their content seemed so damaging to the President's case — he had lied repeatedly, to the country, the press, and his own counsel — that Congressmen who had voted against impeachment appeared individually on television to announce that they were changing their votes. The decision became unanimous. Overwhelming ratification by the House became certain. Conviction by the Senate seemed equally inevitable. Senator Goldwater was quoted: "This man must go." A deputation of leading Republican statesmen visited the President to convey the gravity of his plight.

On August 8, at 9 p.m., President Nixon appeared on television to announce his resignation, effective the following day. It had become clear, he said, that he no longer had "a strong enough political base in Congress" to continue in office. There was no acknowledgement of wrongdoing.

By some perverse obsession, he wanted even the final, devastating hours of his defeat to be on the tube. On the following morning viewers watched his farewell to staff and friends. For more than an hour he rambled incoherently and irrelevantly. He spoke as though he had been visited by some catastrophe not of his making. Then a helicopter took him to Air Force One, for the flight to California. There he was briefly seen again on television, waving to airport crowds as though campaigning. Then he vanished into seclusion.

STUDY GUIDE

1. The author assumes that Americans obtain much of their news through television. Do you agree? If so, on what grounds; if not, on what grounds do you disagree?

2. How did television help Nixon talk to the nation of withdrawal from Vietnam while he was widening the war?

3. What role did Spiro Agnew play for Nixon; more specifically, how did his attacks on the media help the Nixon administration? How did the networks respond to his attacks?

4. How did television come into play during Nixon's China trip? Could Nixon have obtained the same results through newspaper coverage?

5. How did the networks respond to the Watergate break-in? How do you account for their lack of investigative resourcefulness?

6. Explain the question over the funding of public television. What is the irony of the Nixon position on public television and the subsequent role of public television in carrying the hearings of the Watergate inquiry by the Senate Committee headed by Sam Ervin? Did you watch those hearings? Were your reactions to them similar to those of most Americans, as described by Barnouw? If so, why; if not, why not?

7. How did television heighten the drama of the final chapters in the Nixon story? Did the medium help or hurt the president in the end?

8. Does television ultimately make a decided difference in the image of a president? Or to put the question another way, can television make a success of a presidential failure, or vice versa? Explore.

BIBLIOGRAPHY

The source of the above essay is Erik Barnouw, *Tube of Plenty: The Evolution of American Television* * (New York, 1975), a segment, condensed and updated, of his definitive study, *A History of Broadcasting in the United States*, 3 vols. (New York, 1966–1970). Other studies touch upon the use, and abuse, of the media by presidents and presidential candidates. Gene Wyckoff, *The Image Candidates; American Politics in the Age of Television* (New York, 1968), focuses on the medium's role in our political processes, as does *The Politics of Broadcasting* (New York, 1973), edited by Marvin Barrett. Joe McGinniss, *The Selling of the President, 1968* (New York, 1969) concentrates on a single presidential campaign — the 1968 contest between Richard M. Nixon and Hubert H. Humphrey. A concerned analysis of the manipulation of television and public opinion by the White House will be found in Newton N. Minow, John Bartlow Martin, and Lee M. Mitchell, *Presidential Television* (New York, 1973). (Newton Minow was, at one time, chairman of the Federal Communications Commission, the federal agency that regulates radio and television.) A critical analysis of newscasting, particularly the evening news programs, will be found in Edward J. Epstein, *News from Nowhere: Television and the News* (New York, 1973). There are many excellent books on the political figures of the 1960s and 1970s and their successes and failures. Theodore C. Sorensen, *Kennedy* * (New York, 1965) covers the 1960 campaign from the vantage point of an insider; Eric F. Goldman, *The Tragedy of Lyndon Johnson* * (New York, 1969) is more critical of his subject and discusses President Johnson's enormous concern with the media. The following books will provide you with a start on trying to understand the psyche and the politics of Richard M. Nixon: Garry Wills's prophetic *Nixon Agonistes* * (New York, 1970); John Osborne's three collections of pieces from the *New Republic*, titled *The Third Year of the Nixon Watch* (New York, 1972), *The Fourth Year of the Nixon Watch* (New York, 1973), and *The Fifth Year of the Nixon Watch* (New York, 1974); and Nixon's own accounts of his presidency: *Memoirs* (New York, 1978) and *The Real War* (New York, 1980).

* Asterisk indicates book is available in a paperback edition.

To the student:

We, as publishers, realize that one way to improve education is to improve textbooks. We also realize that you, the student, have a large role in the success or failure of textbooks. Although teachers choose books to be used in the classroom, if the students do not buy and use books, those books are failures.

Usually only the teacher is asked about the quality of a text; his opinion alone is considered as revisions are written or as new books are planned. Now, Little, Brown would like to ask you about this book: how you liked or disliked it; why it was successful or dull; if it taught you anything. Would you fill in this form and return it to us at: Little, Brown and Co., College Division, 34 Beacon St., Boston, Mass. 02106. It is your chance to directly affect the publication of future textbooks.

Book title:_____ School:_____

Course title:_____ Course enrollment:_____

Instructor's name: _____

1. Did you like the book?_____

2. Was it too easy?_____

   Did you read all the selections?_____

   Which did you like most?_____

   Which did you like least?_____

3. Did you like the cover?_____

   Did you like the size?_____

   Did you like the illustrations?_____

   Did you like the type size?_____

(over)

4. Were the study questions and bibliographies useful?_____

   How should they be changed?_____

   _____

5. Are the introductions useful?_____

   How might they be improved?_____

   _____

6. Do you feel the professor should continue to assign this book next year?

   _____

7. Will you keep this book for your library?_____

8. Please add any comments or suggestions on how we might improve this
   book, in either content or format.

   _____

   _____

   _____

   _____

   _____

9. May we quote you, either in promotion for this book, or in future publishing ventures?   _____yes   _____no

   _____   _____
   date   signature